Advance Praise for

Citizen-General and ...

"Lawyer, soldier, governor, businessman, historian, scientist, law school dean, university president, statesman, Jacob D. Cox helped win the war for the Union and shaped the nation in the decades after. I was particularly delighted with Gene Schmiel's account of Cox the historian. He does a superb job in unraveling the tangled literary debates and personal quarrels of the veterans who fought the war. Gene Schmiel is to be applauded for this perceptive and authoritative account of an extraordinary American."

> —Donald B. Connelly, Professor, Department of Joint, Interagency, and Multinational Operations, US Army Command and General Staff College, and author of *John M. Schofield and the Politics of Generalship*

"Jacob Cox may be the most intriguing character from the Civil War era that most Americans have never heard of. In *Citizen-General*, Eugene D. Schmiel captures his achievements and his contradictions, allowing us to see Cox as a key figure in a convulsive moment of American history."

> —Nicholas Guyatt, University of York, author of *Providence and the Invention of the United States*

"Jacob Cox was not just a significant figure in the Civil War and the writing of its history, but an important player in postwar politics as well. In *Citizen-General*, Eugene D. Schmiel provides an account of Cox's life and career, and the forces that shaped them, that is informative, impressively researched, and consistently interesting. This is a book that will appeal to anyone with an interest in the Civil War and its aftermath."

> —Ethan S. Rafuse, author of *McClellan's War: The Failure of Moderation in the Struggle for the Union* and coeditor of *The Ongoing Civil War: New Versions of Old Stories.*

"Jacob Dolson Cox played a major role in a number of different campaigns of the Civil War, including command of the 9th Corps at the Battle of Antietam. His military service—and his career as a politician—have long cried out for a full-length biographical treatment. Dr. Eugene Schmiel has rectified that oversight with his new biography of Cox. This well-researched, fair, and balanced treatment of Cox's life deserves a place on the bookshelf of anyone interested in the role played by political generals in the Civil War."

—Eric J. Wittenberg, award-winning Civil War historian

"This is a comprehensive biography of . . . a very important figure, not only in Civil War military history but also in political and religious matters. This book makes a significant contribution by relating in a thoughtful, analytical way the life and career of one of the most important Ohioans of that era. The author has clearly done his homework, and the text is not only well researched but very polished."

—Steven E. Woodworth, Professor of History, Texas Christian University, and author of several books on the Civil War, including *This Great Struggle: America's Civil War*

Citizen-General

CITIZEN-GENERAL

Jacob Dolson Cox and the Civil War Era

Eugene D. Schmiel

OHIO UNIVERSITY PRESS
ATHENS

Ohio University Press, Athens, Ohio 45701

ohioswallow.com

Printed in the United States of America
Ohio University Press books are printed on acid-free paper ⊗ ™

24 23 22 21 20 19 18 17 16 15 14   5 4 3 2 1

Library of Congress Cataloging-in-Publication Data
Schmiel, Gene.
Citizen-General : Jacob Dolson Cox and the Civil War era / Eugene D. Schmiel.
   pages cm. — (War and society in North America)
Includes bibliographical references and index.
 ISBN 978-0-8214-2082-9 (hc : alk. paper) — ISBN 978-0-8214-2083-6 (pb : alk. paper)
— ISBN 978-0-8214-4480-1 (pdf)
 1. Cox, Jacob D. (Jacob Dolson), 1828–1900. 2. Generals—United States—Biography.
3. United States—History—Civil War, 1861–1865—Biography. 4. Ohio—History—
Civil War, 1861–1865—Biography. 5. United States—History—Civil War, 1861–1865—
Campaigns. 6. Governors—Ohio—Biography. I. Title.
E467.1.C83S36 2014
355.0092—dc23
[B]

2014000859

For Bonnie Kathryn

Figure 1. Official portrait of Jacob Dolson Cox as governor of Ohio, 1866–68; Cox is pictured wearing a formal major general's uniform, symbolizing his own recognition that he was a "citizen-general" as he made the transition from a military to a civilian office. *(Courtesy of Capital Square Review and Advisory Board, Columbus, Ohio)*

Contents

Illustrations

Preface

The Civil War Dictionary might well be titled, 'What ever happened to J.D. Cox?'"[1] When I read that sentence in that book's preface, I
knew that answering the question would be the goal of this book. In sum,
the answer is that he was one of the best Northern "citizen-generals" in
the Civil War, an influential postwar political leader, and the ablest participant-
historian of the war, one whose writings have been both recognized as
authoritative and quoted by serious Civil War historians ever since.

Cox's story was similar to that of many citizens whose lives were
immeasurably changed by that bloody conflict. Analyzing how this citizen
adapted so well and in so many surprising ways to these epic events would,
I hoped, illuminate the era in manifold ways. By the same token, I wanted
the reader to understand how and why, despite his many advantages, con-
nections, and skills, Cox did not achieve the political prominence that
seemed inevitable at war's end.

The Civil War itself is the core of this book. However, a blow-by-blow,
movement-by-movement, regiment-by-regiment retelling of the battles
in which Cox participated is *not* a part of this book, since others have
done that so well already. Instead, my approach is to evaluate how one
individual, as well as his commanders and subordinates, acted under the
incredible and bloody stress of war. I also assess how and why someone
without formal military training became both an effective leader of men
and an equally capable subordinate. I have integrated into the text both the
broad historical context of each military movement and Cox's recounting
and analyses of events, contemporaneous and historiographical. Including
his thoughts at the time and his later analyses would, I hoped, help the

reader to understand how Cox's writings influenced the historiography, understanding, and memory of the war.

The book's title reflects the centrality of the war experience for this "citizen-general." I chose Cox's official portrait as governor of Ohio for the cover because it illustrates the degree to which Cox saw the war as the key transitional event in his professional life. He was elected governor while still officially in the army, and in the painting, Cox is wearing the dress uniform of a major general. In his right hand he holds his appointment papers as governor, underscoring his civil status. Next to him on a table are his commission as a general and a general's accouterments, including his scabbard, sword, binoculars, and sword belt. They remind the viewer that, like the uniform he chose to wear, while they had been put aside, they were still a part of his life. They also emphasize that he and many other citizen-generals, like the Roman general Cincinnatus, came to the defense of the nation and then returned to civilian life. The Kurz and Allison lithograph of the Battle of Antietam, in which Cox led his men over and beyond "Burnside's Bridge," appropriately completes the cover image.

While preparing this manuscript, I had the invaluable aid of a great many people. One major contributor was Cox's step-granddaughter, Miss Mary Rudd Cochran, whose letters to me and in-person recollections of Cox as an older man were invaluable. Among those who provided useful input and advice were Professors Donald Connelly and Ethan Rafuse of the U.S. Army Staff College, Kansas. Emeritus Professor Jerry Bower of the University of Wisconsin read and assessed much of the draft manuscript and provided useful suggestions. Colonel Thomas Goss, whose incisive study of political generals was a great inspiration, and Mr. Eric Wittenberg, author of many books about the war, provided helpful advice. Dr. Tom Clemens, the editor of Ezra Carman's monumental history of the Maryland campaign, provided not only counsel but also documents not otherwise available. Professor Nicholas Guyatt of York University, United Kingdom, provided considerable insight into the evolution of nineteenth-century thought about race and colonization.

Mr. Ken Grossi, the chief archivist of the Oberlin College archives, has been very helpful throughout; I also received excellent support services at the Library of Congress, the U.S. Army Historical Center in Carlisle, Pennsylvania, Western Reserve Historical Society, and the Ohio State archives in Columbus, Ohio. National Park Service experts Jim Burgess (Manassas) and John Hoptak and Ted Alexander (Antietam) were of great assistance. I should also mention the contributions of both Professor Paul Finkelman of the Albany Law School and Ms. Angela Alexander: Paul encouraged me to move ahead on the project and suggested that Angela be my "graduate assistant." Hal Jespersen provided the excellent maps that highlight Cox's career. Gillian Berchowitz of the Ohio University Press has been a wonderful guide for this entire process, and Professors Ingo Trauschweizer and David J. Ulbrich, editors of the Ohio University Press's War and Society in North America series, provided superb support, insights, and guidance.

My wife, Bonnie Kathryn, has been my constant and major inspiration throughout this task, as well as a skilled editor. Her contributions can never be truly measured.

Introduction

"The long lines of Hood's army surged up out of the hollow in which they had formed, and were seen coming forward in splendid array. The sight," Union General Jacob Dolson Cox recalled, "was one to send a thrill through the heart, and those who saw it have never forgotten its martial magnificence."[1] Seven hours later, on November 30, 1864, the Union forces commanded by Cox successfully completed repelling the final major frontal infantry attack of the Civil War at the Battle of Franklin. Cox's warrior-like appeal to his troops at the critical moment helped cut the heart out of John Bell Hood's Army of Tennessee, ensuring the western Confederate army's ultimate destruction two weeks later at the Battle of Nashville.

Fifteen years earlier, almost to the day, Cox, then a divinity student at Oberlin College, had married Helen Finney, the daughter of college president Charles Finney, a leading evangelist and abolitionist. A career as a minister and professor of theology seemed preordained. No one could have predicted that the intellectual, reserved, bookish Cox possessed the "military aptitude" to lead men successfully in war. But as for many men of that era, the seemingly inevitable was overtaken by history. The wrenching events of the Civil War era led Cox from the tranquility of divinity school through the turbulence and bloodshed of war and into the political struggles of Reconstruction, finally returning him to the serenity of scholarship and the writing of history. This book considers how the shattering changes of that era affected one citizen, and how his life and work affected the era and the memory of those tumultuous events.

Raised in a Puritan home by a mother whose lineage traced to the *Mayflower*, Cox studied at Oberlin College, one of the nation's most radical institutions because of its advocacy of abolitionism and inclusion of female and black students. After a theological dispute with Finney, Cox left his ministerial studies early in the 1850s and became a lawyer in the Western Reserve town of Warren, Ohio. There he became active in the Whig Party and was one of the founders of the Ohio Republican Party. After being elected to the Ohio Senate in 1860, he gained a reputation as a fervent antislavery Radical.

Believing that war was possible and that he should be prepared to fight for his beliefs, Cox engaged in a diligent study of the history and theory of the military arts. Appointed a brigadier general of volunteers soon after the war started, Cox the citizen-general believed he was as intellectually qualified as any West Pointer to lead men in war. The test would be whether he had what he called "a constitution of body and mind for which we can find no better name than military aptitude."[2] Despite Cox's inexperience, General George B. McClellan came to appreciate his talents and knowledge and gave him an autonomous command in the West Virginia campaign. In 1861 and 1862 Cox played a central role in taking and holding for the Union the new state of West Virginia, while earning a reputation as a quintessential subordinate commander with a firm commitment to discipline and duty.

In mid-1862 Cox transferred to the Army of the Potomac for the Maryland campaign, during which in a period of three weeks he underwent a dizzying ascent to corps command. He initiated the successful first assault at the Battle of South Mountain. As commander of the 9th Army Corps (AC), he co-led the Union's left wing at the Battle of Antietam, for which he was promoted to major general. He then stemmed a Confederate effort to retake West Virginia. After a lengthy period in military administration, in 1864 he marched with Sherman to Atlanta as second in command of the Army of the Ohio. As commander on the defensive line at the Battle of Franklin, he played a vital role in breaking the spirit of the Confederate Army of Tennessee. Cox rejoined Sherman in North Carolina in 1865 and rose again to corps command during the battles leading to the Confederate surrender, following which he was military governor of part of that state. Throughout the war, Cox fought actively in the "political-military wars," struggling for rank and place, while seeking recognition for the contributions of citizen-generals such as himself. His four years of warfare would prove to be in many ways his most successful professional experience.

When the war ended in 1865, Cox's political horizons seemed unlimited. But while five other Ohioans with war records (Ulysses Grant, Rutherford B. Hayes, James A. Garfield, Benjamin Harrison, and William McKinley) rose to national prominence and the presidency, Cox was in political exile by 1873. This successful citizen-general with a proven military aptitude did not have the kind of political aptitude needed for national leadership in the postwar era. While in war he was comfortable with dutifully taking orders, his independent spirit led him on occasion to take the initiative without orders and to recommend alternative approaches to his commanders. That same internal demand for intellectual autonomy would not be constrained in postwar peace and politics. His independent bent, academic orientation, straitlaced and aloof personality, rigid commitment to principle, and tendency to approach issues in the tutelary manner of a preacher/professor led him to take actions consciously that would truncate the possibility of his becoming a national political leader.

In 1865, during his successful campaign for governor of Ohio, Cox decided to deal publicly with the issue of the civil rights and citizenship of the freedman. While fervently antislavery, Cox was dubious about the feasibility of racial equality, fearing it might lead to race war in the South. Instead, he proposed an academic approach to resolving the problem by creating a de facto territory in the South to which, he suggested, blacks would voluntarily migrate because they would be protected by the federal government. This impractical plan divided him from the Radical Republicans as the latter's power was on the rise. Furthermore, party leaders became worried that Cox's independent streak and lack of party discipline might make him an unreliable candidate for future elections.

His second fatal political step came when he supported President Andrew Johnson's approach to Reconstruction for a lengthy period while using his influence to try to find compromise between the president and Congress on Reconstruction policy. Despite his eventual decision to disavow Johnson, Cox was seen by some as having "abandoned" the Republican Party. Caught in the middle of what he called a "family broil," Cox decided not to run for reelection for governor in 1867, even though his reelection was likely.

As Grant's secretary of the interior in 1869–70, Cox implemented one of the most far-reaching attempts to reform Indian policy and instituted the federal government's first extensive civil service reform program. Within eighteen months, however, his rigid and idealistic position against patronage

4   led to his resignation. He broke with the Republicans and became a leader of the Liberal Republican movement trying to oust Grant in 1872. The failure of that party was the final nail in Cox's national political coffin.

The biographer of one of Cox's commanders, General Ambrose Burnside, called Cox "a veritable Renaissance man"; in an era that celebrated the self-made man, Cox assumed a wide variety of careers, including military officer, school superintendent, state legislator, governor, federal cabinet member, railroad president, congressman, university president, law school dean, scientist, and historian. His most successful professional experience was as a general, and his most successful academic pursuit was as arguably the best Civil War historian of the nineteenth century. His writings remain his enduring legacy. His book on the Atlanta campaign was the definitive study for over a hundred years. His in-depth articles on the Maryland campaign for the *Battles and Leaders of the Civil War* multivolume series (and his expansion of them in his *Reminiscences*) are bases for memory about that period. His two-volume *Military Reminiscences of the Civil War* is still cited by historians as a foundation for the memory of many aspects of the war. Cox's reviews of Civil War books for *The Nation* magazine played an important role in both shaping thinking about the war and establishing the first phase of memory about it.[3]

Nevertheless, knowledge of Cox the citizen-general is limited, and he remains a relative unknown except to specialists and buffs. One reason, Cox believed, was the bad luck "of being a second in command" and frequently ignored in the writing of history. Furthermore, as a citizen-general, his contributions and those of his political colleagues were often de-emphasized or denigrated in the postwar "battle of the books." Cox believed that in time his contributions to the war effort and its chronicling would be fully recognized by history. The objective of this book is to reconsider Jacob Dolson Cox as a major actor both in the Civil War era and in the creation of its memory. In sum, it is time to give Jacob Cox his due.[4]

1

Citizen of the Western Reserve
Maturing in Peace, Girding for War

> Himself a type of the Western Reserve boy, his marble effigy is
> the emblem of the heroic qualities developed out of the New
> England character in the pioneer life of the West. It typifies the
> courage of man and of woman, which planted new homes where
> savages still roamed: the physical vigor of body and limb . . . the
> tireless industry and thrift . . . which made it possible for every
> farmer's boy to aim at the highest flights in literature, in science,
> and in statesmanship.
>
> —Cox, dedication of Garfield memorial, 1890

In the epigraph to this chapter, Cox was eulogizing his friend
President James Garfield but also, in effect, describing himself and how the
Western Reserve had molded him and an entire generation of Ohio's leaders.[1] In 1784 Connecticut laid claim to a section of land, later called the
"Western Reserve," stretching from Pennsylvania's western border 120 miles
along Lake Erie; Congress recognized this claim in 1800. The region was
sparsely populated until the building of the Ohio and Erie Canal in 1827,
which brought a new influx of settlers from New England. Inevitably, the
Connecticut-bred moral fiber—including a focus on moral rectitude, duty,
honor, religious devotion, hard work, and pride in being Anglo-Saxons—
permeated the lives of the settlers who would fill the lands along Lake Erie.[2]

Heritage

Jacob Dolson Cox, the first son of Jacob Dolson Cox I and Thedia Redelia
Kenyon, was born on October 27, 1828. His mother, a descendant of Wil-
liam Brewster, the religious leader of the *Mayflower,* met his father in Albany,
New York, where they married on May 25, 1821. Cox's father worked as a

6   builder and roofer, and in 1825 he moved the family to Montreal, Canada, where he oversaw the construction of the Church of Saint-Sulpice. After four years in Canada, the family moved to New York City along with two children born in Montreal, one of whom was Jacob Dolson Cox II.

The Puritan tradition and her *Mayflower* roots were integral to Thedia Cox's approach to raising young Dolson, as he came to be called within the family. Her strong religious sentiment and hatred of slavery were important elements in developing his character. He wrote that his mother's "teachings were in sympathy with . . . the devout earnestness of her Plymouth and Old Bay Colony blood." He noted, "Many a boyish lesson in reading I spelled out from the little tract published by the American Anti-Slavery Society." He also learned that he had to be self-effacing and modest to meet his mother's standards, and throughout his life he was dutifully disinclined to call attention to himself.[3]

Dolson hoped to go to college, but his planning was sidetracked for a time because of the hard economic times after the Panic of 1837. He then began to study law by working in a law firm, and in his spare time he studied French, Greek, and Latin. When prosperity returned, he prepared for college entrance at age seventeen. However, he almost took another track. As Cox later confessed, "We should be astonished to find how many of us went through a youthful period of half-resolve to 'go to sea.' . . . It is in the Anglo-Saxon blood." One day he met a captain in New York harbor and agreed to become a crew member, but when he returned the next day he found the ship gone. Dolson accepted it as providential and returned to his college preparations.[4]

Also providential was Dolson's attendance at lectures in New York in 1845 by Reverend Charles Grandison Finney, one of the best-known American revivalists and a faculty member at Ohio's Oberlin College, on the Western Reserve. Finney delivered a message of rigid dedication to the Almighty that was "more in the style of a prosecuting attorney than a clergyman." He emphasized eradication of social ills, with slavery as one of the most prominent. One evening Finney called out to all present to give their hearts to God, and Dolson leaped forward. Soon afterward he was baptized, and by 1846 he was determined to attend Oberlin College to train for the ministry.[5]

Oberlin and Its Impact

Founded in 1833 as the Oberlin Collegiate Institute, this school's "radical" reputation was established as it played a major role in the Underground

Railroad and the abolitionist movement because of the influence of the Lane Seminary rebels. The presence of blacks as students and the admission of the first female students further ensured its activist character. Finney's leadership enhanced and reinforced Oberlin's and religion's central role in the abolitionist movement.[6]

To travel to Oberlin, Dolson followed the traditional route: by boat on the Erie Canal, steamboat from Buffalo over Lake Erie to Cleveland, stagecoach from there to Elyria, and then another coach to Oberlin. The crowded conditions, the long time involved, and the necessity of getting out and pushing the coaches through mud and ruts every few miles usually made passengers overwhelmingly happy when their trip was over. But the sight that greeted the exhausted Cox on his arrival was startling: "The crude aspect of the town and the surroundings and a sense of utter loneliness and loss overcame" him, and he broke down and wept. Cox wrote later, "Never was there a poor scamp more homesick than I for two days after my arrival at Oberlin."[7]

Manual labor was part of the Oberlin curriculum, and Dolson's first assigned task was a typical means for orienting a new student—cleaning out a college cistern. He accepted that disagreeable task as part of the new reality, telling his parents, "[F]or the winter you may just consider me as at work in a little missionary field, and I pray God I may be enabled to do my duty." By the spring of 1847 he was ready for college entrance, and he began the college course that fall. He even had time to impress a female student who wrote home, "There is some good folks here, and some slick fellers, too, one in particular, a Mr. Cox from New York City." He earned extra money by following the Oberlin practice of teaching local children at a country school during the summer break of 1848. For Cox, a tall, lanky, and frail youth, it was another burden. He wrote to his father, "I was tired by study when I commenced. . . . I came back exhausted, and have not been strong since."[8]

His sophomore year (1848–49) went smoothly, and Dolson hoped to skip his junior year so he could enter the theological seminary early. Two factors that entered his life in 1849 made it necessary to do so—his father's financial difficulties and his relationship with Finney's daughter, Helen. Cox's father had been badly hurt by financial reverses in 1847, so Dolson knew he would need a less expensive place to live for the next session. The alternative turned out to be the Finney house, where he met and fell in love with Helen. The young couple decided to marry in late 1849 and to live in the Finney house thereafter. He hoped to enter the theological seminary in 1850.[9]

His future wife was a tall, delicate, reserved woman with a keen intellect and refined taste. Born in 1828, Helen had often traveled with her father on his revival tours. She found the strict life he demanded to be stifling—as a child Helen liked to visit friends where, her first son wrote, she "could indulge in games with children without fear of rebuke" from her stern father. While a student at Oberlin in 1846, she had married Professor William Cochran, who died less than a year later. Her son William Cochran later wrote that her discovery of her pregnancy by Cochran and her meeting of and engagement to Dolson gave her some solace. The couple married on November 29, 1849, in Oberlin, and they began their married life residing in the Finney home. Because Charles Finney and his wife had left for England earlier on an evangelical tour, Helen and Dolson were charged with taking care not only of Helen's son but also of her younger brothers and sisters.[10]

Cox's living situation having been clarified and his theological studies having begun, a career as a minister and professor of theology seemed preordained. During his time at Oberlin, however, the straitlaced Dolson had begun to exhibit an independence of mind and an enjoyment of intellectual debate, including on the esoterica of theology. While he was always dutiful, his intelligence and independent streak made him disinclined to follow the Oberlin pattern for students of never questioning professors. Furthermore, while he was adamantly antislavery, during his school days he became more conservative than his Oberlin colleagues on racial matters. He came to believe that the "best men"—those who, like him, were educated, well-mannered, and Anglo-Saxon—were the natural leaders of American society, and he appears to have thought that blacks should accept a second-class status as their natural state.

His father-in-law did not condone freethinkers, especially on theological matters. Finney used a confrontational Socratic pedagogy, and most students regarded him with "a wholesome fear." Even his grandson Jacob Dolson Cox III found him frightening, writing later, "To me as a small boy, Grandfather Finney was a terrible man. . . . [H]e would say to me, 'Dolson, are you a Christian?' I would modestly say, 'I am afraid not.' Then he would give me a long lecture on the ways of the sinner."[11]

When Finney returned to Oberlin in May 1851 from his tour, he found Dolson's independent turn of mind irritating. During one class discussion, after Cox had questioned a particular point, Finney angrily told him, "Dolson, you are not honest; you do not *want* to see the truth." Cox felt he had been deeply insulted. A professor tried to persuade Finney to withdraw the comment, to no avail. Cox presumed that if there was to be no free debate in theology, then he could not go further in its study, though he retained a strong commitment to and belief in Christianity. Given Helen's feelings about her father's strictness, she was likely supportive. Cox accepted a position as superintendent of public schools in Warren, Ohio, and in the fall of 1851 he took Helen, William Cochran, and their first child together (Helen) across Ohio to begin his first job as a family man.[12]

Professional and Family Life on the Reserve

Warren was a small farming community of three thousand in 1851 whose school system was created in 1849. Cox's administration of the schools coincided with his firm belief in a classical education. He wrote at the time, "The great object of study is to discipline the mind. Latin is of as much use as Science after one leaves school," and he decried practical education as a "humbug." Meanwhile, he continued his studious habits and development as a polymath, engaging in "German, French, and such general philosophical and theological reading" as he could "find time for."[13]

Cox renewed his legal studies in Warren, and on April 28, 1852, he was admitted to the Ohio bar. He did not begin practicing law immediately, because he was not sure he could make a living at it, but in 1853 he decided to make his "farewell to teaching." That year Cox became a junior partner in the law firm of Leggett and Cox with M. D. Leggett, his predecessor as school superintendent and a future general in the Civil War. In 1856 he accepted an offer from John Hutchins, a future congressman, to become a partner in the law firm of Hutchins, Cox, and Ratliff, where he remained until 1861.[14]

Dolson and Helen were actively involved in the upper levels of Warren society despite his introverted character, which led him to muse often that he preferred to be alone with his family and his books. He joined the Presbyterian Church and organized a public affairs discussion group, the Home Literary Union, in 1854. Among the members were local businessman Emerson Opdycke, who would fight alongside Cox on the Atlanta and Nashville campaigns; Hutchins; and William Spear, a future justice of the Ohio Supreme Court. Though characterizing his contributions modestly, stating, "Those leisure hours I do have I use in scribbling a hasty essay to read at our 'Union,'" Cox was the group's leader.[15]

Cox first met future president James A. Garfield, then a teacher in Hiram, Ohio, when the latter "came to Warren about the year 1858 to deliver a popular lecture." The families dined together and soon formed a close bond; Cox and Garfield would become good friends and political allies. Garfield, who had a boisterous and outgoing personality, understood the intellectually oriented, aloof, and reserved Cox well. He wrote about his friend, "[Cox's] mind is of the philosophic cast, [and] he is full of good strong thoughts, though I wish he had more enthusiasm. . . . I never visit him without feeling a new impulse in the way of culture. . . . His nature and mine are in singular contrast, and yet with so many points in common as to make and keep us friends."[16]

At home Cox was a dedicated family man with strong attachments to his wife and children. Helen's and Dolson's letters during the war show the strong feelings they had for one another. Cox wrote regularly to Helen from the battlefields using her nickname, Lilla. She became his most important sounding board, and his letters gave her not only an aesthetic view of the countryside but also descriptions of battles, military personalities, and political-military issues, indicating that he saw her as an intellectual equal. These letters allowed him to express emotions and vent feelings that he would never have shown to others because of his carefully controlled mien. He always signed himself, "Your affectionate husband, Dolson."

Cox was a typical husband of the era, however, as shown in the following episode. When the Cox family bought the first sewing machine in Warren, he exhibited an intellectual interest in its mechanics. He even proposed that Helen baste the seams of garments during the day and that he would do the stitching in the evenings, after work. The first night he did his work enthusiastically. By the fourth night, however, he settled down to read after dinner instead of doing his "duty." When Helen asked if he were ready to help, he responded, "Aren't they already finished?" He never again used the machine.[17]

Helen embraced the traditions of the patriarchal Victorian family, raising the children with the values of duty, obligation, respect, and guilt, should they lapse. Two examples in letters to her son William illustrate these tendencies. In one she told him, "You know Mama's duty is to point out the errors that every child must hone so that you may be the *perfect* man she hopes to see you." In another, a few days after she had visited Cox during the war, she wrote, "My dear children, how good you must be not to disgrace such a father." As for her feelings for Dolson, Helen once wrote to Lucy Garfield during the war that she had been able to visit Dolson, "which you know was enough in itself to insure complete happiness." She also had a sense of history, writing to her son Kenyon, "My ambition has always, from childhood, been for *fame,* and although my own life has been in the quiet domestic lines, the fame of my father, my husband, my son, has been dearer than life to me."[18]

The couple had four children in Warren. The first was a son, J. D. Cox III, born May 15, 1852. He later became a leader in the industrial development of Cleveland, Ohio. The second son, Kenyon, was born on October 27, 1856, and became a famous classical artist. The third son, Charles Norton, born on July 28, 1858, became a rancher in Colorado. A fourth son, William Brewster, born on January 26, 1861, died in infancy.

J. D. Cox III described the attachment the children felt for their father: "Father thought I ought to know how to swim, and he took me to a farm. I pretended to be afraid because I didn't want him to know that I'd been there many times before. . . . I stepped off and dove and came up beside him. For a moment he was awfully frightened, but when he saw me kicking out as fast as I could, he laughed and said he guessed he had had his trouble for his pains." The children's affection and respect can also be seen in the murals commemorating his parents that Kenyon Cox painted in 1914 for the Oberlin College administration building, which is named for his father. As Kenyon Cox's biographer put it, "Cox had caught his own view of his father as reserved, dignified, and important, yet thoughtful and caring. And his mother was a personal symbol of the values he attributed to idealized women. He saw her as a true helper to his father and a sustaining force for her children. But she was an independent personality."[19]

In sum, Cox's upbringing in the Puritan tradition, his commitment to the ideas and ideals of his Anglo-Saxon and *Mayflower* forebears, and his experiences at Oberlin and Warren provided the fundamental elements of his character. By the mid-1850s he had established a reputation as an introspective and detached intellectual focused on the world of ideas, but preparing for a leadership role in society. Moreover, he was always in control of himself and his emotions, and his contemporaries recounted few examples of his ever being angry, overjoyed, or even intense. Like the idealized Garfield that he had eulogized, he was a man with the "qualities developed out of the New England character in the pioneer life of the West."

The 1850s have been described as the "critical decade," during which the sectional tensions between North and South, which had previously been resolved by compromise, reached their breaking point. As one historian put it, "To 19th century Americans the West represented the future. . . . So long as the slavery controversy focused on the morality of the institution" where it was, "the two party system managed to contain the passions. But when in the 1840's after the Mexican War the controversy began to focus on the expansion of slavery into new territories, it became irrepressible." The Compromise of 1850 delayed the confrontation once again, but that solution contained the seeds of future political firestorms. After its passage, radical elements on both sides increased their influence and power.[20]

Opposition to the Compromise of 1850's Fugitive Slave Act was a significant spur to the growth of the Free Soil Party in the 1850s and its evolution into the Republican Party. The most important Ohio leader in the emergence of opposition to slavery as a core political idea was Salmon P. Chase, later one of Cox's mentors. In the 1840s as a leader of a precursor of the Free Soil Party, the Liberty Party, Chase "transformed anti-slavery, at least superficially, from a moral crusade to a legal contest." One historian wrote, "By identifying freedom as the national and natural state of Americans, Chase pushed Ohio to the forefront of American politics." His election to the Senate in 1848 via a coalition with antislavery Democrats and Whigs provided him with a firm electoral base, which would be expanded in reaction to the Compromise of 1850. The Western Reserve was among the most vociferous Ohio regions opposed to slavery and the Fugitive Slave Act. Its leaders, especially the dominant Congregationalists, "saw slavery as unequivocal sin," and they were aroused to action to oppose its expansion. Cox wrote later that such views were the "creed of the body of progressive and earnest young men who were to mold the thought and the politics of the Northern States during the critical era."[21]

Cox had told his sister in 1852 that he probably would live in Warren practicing law for the rest of his life, but the tumultuous times inevitably propelled him into the political arena on the side of those opposing the expansion of slavery. Although Cox despised the evil of slavery, however, he was not a rabid abolitionist. His viewpoint on race had continued to evolve after his Oberlin experience. At a time when only a tiny minority in the North favored a multiracial society, Cox's belief that blacks should be free but in a second-class status would have been considered relatively enlightened. His outlook mirrored that of another emerging leader, Abraham Lincoln, who stated publicly in 1857 that "separation of the races is the only perfect prevention of amalgamation." A letter to a college friend in 1855 gave an indication of Cox's views on race before the war:

> Today the colored people of this vicinity assembled to celebrate the anniversary of Jamaican independence, and . . . I was prepared for strange actions. But at the commencement I was agreeably disappointed by having a fluent and well-cogitated speech from Rankin, a young colored man who formerly studied at Oberlin . . . but when he concluded, he was followed by a young barber . . . who succeeded most completely in making a fool of himself and disgracing his people. [During his speech the local Democrats were cheering him], but he didn't know that they were doing so to show the worthlessness of his race. . . . It is really sickening to see so much mulish folly, but we must pity them and do them good in spite of themselves. As they become educated, they will have better discernment.[22]

The first public indication of Cox's political and racial views came when in 1852 he decided to join the Whig Party rather than the Free-Soilers, in great part because the former's membership was representative of Anglo-Saxon elites with moderate views on slavery. That year Cox cast his first presidential vote, for General Winfield Scott. The Whig Party declined in popularity rapidly after Scott's defeat, so Cox had little competition in moving swiftly to a leadership position in the county organization. By mid-1853 he was one of the local party's spokesmen, though he was realistic enough to know that to salvage what remained of the party, a union with the Free-Soilers was inevitable. In a series of five articles in 1853 for the Whig Party organ, Cox called for joint action by "free and liberal" men. The Free-Soilers' organ, recognizing his abilities, called him the "only progressive there, and as much out of place as an eagle in a crow's nest." That fall the Whigs nominated Cox for prosecuting attorney, but he and every other Whig candidate lost. The Whig Party organ lamented, "The Whigs have elected nothing."[23]

The Kansas-Nebraska Act of 1854, which effectively repealed the Missouri Compromise of 1820 and introduced the concept of "popular sovereignty" to the national political dynamic, reignited sectional tensions. The issue of whether those territories would be "free" or "slave" states

inevitably provided additional impetus to a political union of those opposed to slavery expansion. In Warren, the Whigs and the Free-Soilers held
a mass meeting on February 11, 1854, to denounce the bill, and the editors of the parties' organs worked out a merger plan there. After President
Franklin Pierce signed the Kansas-Nebraska Act into law, an Ohio state
convention on June 26 merged the two parties. The new party swept all
the state offices and most of the congressional districts in the fall elections.
Renamed Republican in 1855, the new party was already strong enough
to elect Chase governor in 1855 and again in 1857.

Cox was a prototypical member of the new party. As one historian
assessed, in Ohio, the Republicans "sought the middle ground of reform.
They were opposed to the extension of slavery, but did not support radical abolitionism. They were Protestant, native-born men of Anglo-Saxon
stock devoted to the cause of progress, but opposed to the power of the
Southern Whites and the Catholic church, and concerned about the rising
number of German and Slavic immigrants." They were also committed to
"free soil, free labor, free men," a combination of limited government and
laissez-faire economics that would be a core element of party dogma for
most of the century.[24]

Another element of the ideology of many moderate Republicans,
including Abraham Lincoln, was advocacy for external colonization as a
solution for the nation's racial problems, an idea that had been supported
by many in the Whig Party. As one historian has noted, this and most
other antislavery "solutions" proffered in the North were safely theoreti-
cal: "Colonization allowed white Americans to imagine the end of slavery
without accepting black citizenship within the United States." It also "enabled its proponents to postpone the hard work of imagining a multiracial
republic after slavery," while allowing "liberal whites to project the downfall of slavery without owning the social consequences of emancipation."[25]
Cox did not address this issue in the 1850s, but the realities of the war and
Reconstruction would ultimately lead him to suggest a different kind of
colonization to heal the racial divide.

In October 1854 Cox became associate editor of the joint party
organ, the *Western Reserve Chronicle and Transcript,* "to keep watch that the
Union run the paper . . . for a stern and uncompromising war with the
aggressions of slavery." He was also named to the Trumbull County central committee in early 1855, and that fall he stumped that county as the
party was swept into power. In 1856 Cox campaigned for Congressman

Joshua Giddings and presidential candidate John C. Fremont, and in 1857 and 1858 he wrote several editorials for the *Western Reserve Chronicle* on the slavery question.[26]

Six feet tall, "slender in build, with a commanding presence and a musical baritone voice," Cox was swiftly making a reputation as a "coming" man in politics during the 1850s. However, because of his unsettled financial status he resisted running for office; by 1858 he had a wife and five children to support, and his income from the law firm was sporadic. Further, he saw politics as an avocation, not a profession, and in keeping with his classical education, he thought men should strive for public office only when duty called.

An event that year that was to have a far-reaching affect on Ohio politics would convince him that it was his duty to run for office. On September 10, a U.S. marshal and a group of Kentucky slave catchers came to Oberlin to retrieve an alleged fugitive slave. When they instead captured a freedman, a group of twenty-one local men pursued the captors and freed the man. The latter group dubbed the "Oberlin Rescuers," were convicted in April 1859 of violating the fugitive slave law. Mass protest meetings were organized on the Western Reserve to denounce the court's decisions. At a public meeting in Cleveland on May 24, Cox stated that sympathizers should take only legal means to redress their grievances and urged taking control of the state and national legislatures. The gathering voted to follow this cautious approach. A few days before that meeting, John Brown, who spent his formative years on the Western Reserve, visited Oberlin seeking support for his planned raid at Harpers Ferry.[27]

Taking to heart his own words about the influence of the ballot box, in October Cox ran for and won the Republican nomination for his district's Ohio state senate seat. His colleagues at the *Western Reserve Chronicle* said he was "a finished scholar, an eloquent orator, a ready debater with a keen wit and indefatigable industry." Garfield, also a senatorial candidate, told Cox, "I promise myself great satisfaction in making your acquaintance in Columbus. I can think of no one with whom I can work better." In October, Ohio voted for large Republican majorities in the state legislature and elected William Dennison, a Columbus banker and railroad man, as governor. Cox won his district easily, 3,160 to 1,751. In a letter to a friend a few days later, he enunciated an approach to politics and life that he would follow thereafter: he said he preferred to be at home with his books and family, but when he was "engrossed in business or on the stump, the pleasure [was] immediate" and he sometimes found himself "half in doubt which [tendency] predominates."[28]

While in the senate, Cox and Garfield boarded "with Mr. [W. T.] Bascom, chairman of the Central Republican Committee" and, as was typical in that era, shared the same room and bed during legislative sessions. Cox and Garfield, along with another new Western Reserve representative, James Monroe, a professor at Oberlin (and later Cox's brother-in-law), quickly came to be known as the "radical triumvirate." Only eleven of the thirty-five senators had served before, and the Republicans had a majority of 25–10. As a result, these young and ambitious men moved up in power swiftly, especially after Dennison took them under his wing.

Garfield was a burly bear of a man, possessing, Cox wrote, a "strong physical constitution, with a vigorous, impulsive nature, full of animal spirits. He loved humor and was always jovial." To Garfield, "[Cox was] very much a man, though I could wish he were a little more demonstrative." As one biographer of Garfield noted, "Cox gave him his cool and detached point of view, always disappointing him by his lack of fervor, but stimulating him by his intellectual keenness." Cox told Garfield prophetically, "This past winter has thrown links about us which will not easily be broken, and both our lives will have a somewhat different coloring hereafter."[29]

The legislative session began early in 1860 in an unusually tense atmosphere in the aftermath of John Brown's raid at Harpers Ferry. Democratic representatives called for Brown's execution and proposed a bill to keep Ohio "invaders" from providing arms for a military expedition against another state. Cox's first political speech decried the latter bill as "truckling" to slave states, and he called on the South to protect Ohioans before Ohio protected her neighbors. Senate Democrats unsuccessfully tried other, similar measures, but they were overwhelmed by the large Republican majority, which reenacted a personal liberty law. Meanwhile, Cox began to receive positive notices in Republican organs around the state as a rising power in the party.[30]

The Secession Crisis: Practicing Brinksmanship

In March 1860, perhaps reflecting their growing realization that there could be a civil war, Dennison appointed Cox a brigadier general in the Ohio militia. At a reception during a visit home a few weeks later, Cox's friends made satirical speeches about his potential military career, jokingly calling him "The Hero of the Crossing of the Mahoning" (a local river).

Accepting their humor good-naturedly, Cox noted Southern threats to secede and said earnestly that he might in fact have to become an active general. His friends gave him some military manuals and books on strategy and training; Cox read them and other military writings and history assiduously as he prepared to be a citizen-general. Writing of the experience, Cox said, "For more than a year before the war I had myself been giving such leisure as I could command to the study of tactics and military history. . . . It was no cursory reading, but downright analytical study, map in hand, determined to find out something of the 'why' and 'how' of it."[31]

Just before the legislative session ended on March 26, Cox decided to become a candidate for state attorney general. In one of the few examples of his engaging in self-promotion, he arranged with W. T. Bascom, who was also editor of the *Ohio State Journal,* to have a recommendation printed in that paper and for Bascom to use his influence in the party's inner circles. As he waited for the results of the June convention, Cox mused openly, "Ambition is strong in a democracy . . . and it is natural that men situated as I should reflect on these matters." But he also felt astonished at his temerity at running for that high an office at the age of thirty-one. He finished fourth in the first round of balloting, and Garfield then withdrew his candidacy, but Cox's name had thereby become better known among the party's membership.[32]

Later in the year, while disappointed that Chase was not nominated for president, Cox was confident of a Republican presidential victory, rejoicing that "absolute confusion and anarchy reign in the camp of the Democracy!" After the election and the first moves toward secession, the normally unemotional Cox almost angrily took an uncompromising stance of moralistic brinksmanship toward the South. He wrote friends in late 1860 that he had begun to fear the effect of "the crazy excitement of the Southern mind" and that he was "exasperated with their bullying determination to rule or ruin." He judged that if "any trouble arises with the Hotspurs of the South, . . . [the senate would] probably remain in session until Ohio has done her whole duty." He told Helen that he was infuriated by appeasers, especially among the Republicans, because "[t]he union-saving spirit makes men crazy here and some seem inclined to throw away everything, and honor first of all."

He translated those private views into public actions that paralleled those of the "Hotspurs of the South." In the senate, he offered a resolution that the militia committee make an accounting of the state's arms to "put Ohio in a reasonable condition of preparation for any possible exigencies which may arise." He and Garfield joined a company of forty legislators who drilled on the capitol grounds and practiced using weapons. In the evenings, the two senators pored over Cox's military books, with Cox translating from the French the works of Baron Antoine-Henri Jomini, whose writings about the Napoleonic Wars were considered the guidebook for military success in that age. They also discussed their responsibilities in case of war.[33]

After returning from leave because of Helen's difficulty in giving birth to their fifth child, William Brewster, Cox made a firebrand speech on the senate floor on January 30, 1861. He said, "The great question of public policy which now divides the country is the extension of the slave system." If Congress and legislatures let "the treason and rebellion abettors" amend the Constitution, "we begin the precedent that the administration shall be determined not by the election, but by the arms of rebellious factions. We can have no compromise with armed rebels. . . . War may come with all its horrors, but to a free people there may be worse evils than war. Slavery is hideous and if we betray our trust and consent to new constitutional guarantees, we extend that terrible curse. To do so would only prolong the bitterness and strife and bequeath to the next generation a fiercer struggle."[34] But few other Republicans felt as strongly, and in the early spring the Ohio legislature, like Congress and the nation, drifted into a policy deadlock as several states seceded from the Union.

On April 10, 1861, a frustrated and anxious Cox wrote an editorial in the county Republican organ in which he said he was hoping and praying for an "announcement from Washington of some determined and statesmanlike policy. The people need a trumpet-toned call to the path of honor, of self-respect, and of patriotic duty—God grant the demoralizing delay may not continue long." Two days later the delay ended. As Cox wrote, "On Friday, the twelfth of April, 1861, the Senate was in session, trying to go on in the ordinary routine of business, but with a sense of anxiety and strain. . . . Suddenly a Senator came in from the lobby in an excited way and exclaimed 'the telegraph announces that the secessionists are bombarding Ft. Sumter.' In the Ohio Senate, the gloomy thought that civil war had begun in our own land overshadowed everything."[35]

A Citizen and a Nation: Unprepared for the Inconceivable

The Cox family, like every other one in the nation, was ill equipped for both the nature and the intensity of the war they were about to experience, as well as the stressful decisions they would have to make about duty and responsibility. Many years after the war, Helen told her granddaughter of her conflicted views at the time, especially concerning her husband's decision to go to war without seeking her input or consent. Helen said that Dolson "had no right to make that decision alone." She continued, "He left me with little children to support alone. I, not he, should have made that decision." But, her granddaughter related, Helen added proudly, "Of course I would have told him to go."

Cox made no reference in his writings about discussions with Helen about this decision. In his letters home, however, he continually expressed his appreciation for the sacrifices she and the family had to make, while underlining his commitment to duty. In one, he wrote, "I fully appreciate your noble spirit, dear Lilla, and these trying times will give you the satisfaction of knowing that your husband sees the strong, good traits of your character." In another he stated, "I long for you very much, but this is the time for endurance and we must trust in God . . . and not flinch from the stern duty." His letters often reflected day-to-day cares, which also emphasized his love for his wife. With uncharacteristic humor, he once joked, "The woolens are just the thing and suit me exactly, but the jam and the catsup got so mixed up with the stockings that it was hard to tell which was which!" For her part, Helen once told Lucy Garfield, "Was I not assured of my husband's loving appreciation of my work and self-denial, I should faint by the way."[36]

While he did not discuss his decision to go to war with Helen, Cox frequently discussed the issue and its ramifications with Garfield. They agreed that their membership in the Republican Party and their radicalism made their responsibility to engage in military service "peculiarly urgent." Garfield was a physically active man with a strong physique, and he told Cox he thought he would be able to withstand well the rigors of war. But Garfield tried to deter his friend because of Cox's frail and slender physical makeup (he was six feet tall and weighed about 145 pounds) and the needs of his family of a wife and six children. Like Cincinnatus the quintessential citizen-general, however, Cox believed duty was calling him to war. He was adamant, noting, "It is my duty to serve. I believe my family would be better off if I left behind the reputation of a man who died for his country than if I be called a coward." The irony for the two men was that "Garfield found that he had a tendency to weakness of the alimentary system, which broke him down on every campaign . . .

and led to his retiring from the army in 1863." By contrast, Cox's "health was strengthened by outdoor life and exposure, and [he] served to the end with growing physical vigor."[37] Furthermore, despite participating in dozens of battles, he was never even wounded.

———

Neither the nation nor its government was ready for the unprecedented challenges of the next four years. One historian has written aptly, "The United States has usually prepared for its wars after getting into them. Never was this more true than in the Civil War." In 1861 the contingencies of a mass, continent-wide war fought by millions of men were understandably inconceivable to government officials and institutions. Lacking any precedents or relevant experience, the Union leadership to a great extent made up the relevant policies and implementation procedures as they went along. Given the many unique and unprecedented problems of preparing for a mass war, the administration in Washington learned and relearned lessons, made deadly mistakes, embarrassed itself on occasion, and finally stumbled forward to a blood-soaked victory.[38]

In Cox's and some other historians' views, one of the most critical mistakes by the Union was the decision by the Union army's general-in-chief, Winfield Scott, who had a disdain for volunteer soldiers, to create two separate Union armies, regular and volunteer. This action, Cox could see as early as 1863, violated an essential principle: "An army on which the nation depends for its salvation in a great crisis must be a unit, and a double organization into regulars and volunteers destroys the greatest efficiency of either." Furthermore, Cox lamented the practice of creating new regiments, frequently for political reasons, rather than merging new volunteers into old ones in which the new troops could learn from the experience of their colleagues. This inevitably led to untrained and poorly led men in new regiments fighting alongside veteran regiments that were "skeletons" because their numbers had been so depleted. One historian opined that these factors offset Union advantages in materiel and manpower in the early years of the war. By contrast, the Confederate army was organized as a unit and avoided for the most part discord between regulars and volunteers.[39]

When the war began, the Union army had 1,105 officers, of whom 296 resigned to join the Confederacy or decided not to fight. None of the officers had ever commanded a force larger than 14,000 men or administered a large army. Early in the war, the administration realized that the army was going to be so large that a rapid increase in the number of officers and generals from the private sector, including Cox, was essential. Many graduates of the U.S. Military Academy (West Point) were disgruntled about having to serve with political officers. Few were as vocal as a later general-in-chief, Henry Halleck, who commented, "It seems little better than murder to give important commands to men such as [Ben] Butler, [Nathaniel] Banks, [John] McClernand, [Franz] Siegel, and [Lew] Wallace." One historian noted, "Halleck's frustration was evidence of the twin strands of a national military heritage that shaped the armies of the Civil War: an embryonic professional spirit in the fledgling American regular army officer corps and a cultural faith in 'natural aptitude' and the perceived ability of every American to master the required military skills to command as a wartime volunteer officer." Another historian wrote, "Many regular army men had an inherent mistrust of even the best citizen-soldier generals, for reasons that went beyond questions of strict professional merit."[40]

The dominance of West Point graduates did not go unchallenged. That institution was one of the few "professional schools" then existent, and in a nation that celebrated the "self-made man," it was seen by some as an unnecessary and elitist institution. Before the Civil War, West Point had been attacked by some in Congress as a "citadel of aristocracy." The fact that some 25 percent of the cadets and many West Point graduates joined the Confederate army strengthened the position of those who believed that the institution had not instilled a strong spirit of patriotism. The congressional Joint Committee on the Conduct of the War was created in late 1861 because of dismay over Union failures early in the war, and it was an active critic of West Point and its graduates. That committee was also a hotbed of the idea that formal training was not necessary for military success; many members claimed that some West Point–trained generals who were Democrats, especially George B. McClellan, did not give their full support to the war effort and did not advocate the immediate end of slavery. An 1863 congressional debate even considered abolishing West Point.[41]

Cox wrote extensively about the conflict between regulars and volunteers in his *Reminiscences*. Though he was proud of volunteers and autodidacts like himself, his balanced analysis has been a core element of the historiography of this issue ever since, and he is frequently quoted about both his experiences and his analyses. He appreciated the leadership of West Pointers like Ulysses S. Grant, William T. Sherman, and John M.

Schofield, while criticizing those who proved lacking, including not only George B. McClellan, Joseph Hooker, and John Pope but also his good friend Ambrose Burnside. As for political generals, he wrote, "It was a foregone conclusion that popular leaders of all grades must largely officer the new troops." He added, colorfully, "It was the application of the old Yankee story, 'If the Lord *will* have a church in Paxton, he must take *sech as ther'* be for deacons.'" Political generals were also essential to ensure popular support and be effective administrators of occupied areas. Ironically, Cox disliked that duty when it fell to him in West Virginia, because he preferred to be in the field. Nevertheless, his counterinsurgency policies would prove critical in providing security and stability as that new state was created.[42]

Another contrast between regulars and volunteers that Cox lamented in his memoirs as being deleterious to the war effort was the former's "marked conservatism as to military methods and arms, and an almost slavish reverence for things which were sanctioned by European authority." Noting that during the war American ingenuity came up with several military enhancements such as the repeater rifle and the Gatling gun, Cox regretted that "the regular army influence was generally against such innovations." The improvements were either not adopted or only haltingly and begrudgingly implemented, he wrote, because of "the obstinate prejudice of a worthy man who had had all flexibility drilled out of him by routine." Cox also bemoaned the rigidity as to discipline and taking orders in some regular army officers. He wrote that all too often he heard from those generals the view of one West Pointer who told him, "cynically, 'If you had been in the army as long as I have, you would be content to do the things that are ordered, without hunting up others.'" Cox the citizen-general would not be so constrained, in great part because throughout his life he exhibited an independent spirit. On several occasions, he would go beyond his orders and succeed when flexibility was called for; he also was not disinclined to offer advice to his superiors in situations in which a "regular" might not have.[43]

The Union's lack of preparedness included naïveté about strategy, especially the beliefs that the war would be ended quickly with one decisive strike and that frontal offensive attacks were the best tactical methodology. The nature of the war meant that the Union would have to take the offensive to subdue the South; in 1861 the cry of "On to Richmond" resounded throughout the North as people demanded a speedy victory.

Winfield Scott knew that these views were misguided, bemoaning in May 1861 "the impatience of our patriotic and loyal Union friends" for a quick victory he knew was unlikely. Cox acknowledged that at first he and his men held to the "cherished belief" that a single campaign would end the war, but he was soon to learn that reality was quite different.[44]

Moreover, Cox and most military thinkers of the age believed that their strategy and tactics should be based on the principles learned from the Napoleonic Wars, as encapsulated in the works of Jomini. That author emphasized that an essential objective in war was to concentrate forces for a single, decisive attack against an outmaneuvered enemy. As General W. T. Sherman put it, "According to the great Napoleon, the fundamental maxim for successful war is to 'converge a superior force on the critical point at the critical time.'"[45]

Over time, Civil War generals would learn both that a speedy triumph was not likely and that the quantitative and qualitative edge in infantry battles had moved significantly from the offensive to the defensive. Napoleonic frontal attacks would no longer succeed when men could be shot from hundreds of yards away by muskets and artillery before they ever reached an entrenched defensive line. As historian Wiley Sword observed, "War was then so deadly, owing to technological innovations following from the Industrial Revolution, that what was once routine battlefield exposure was now virtually suicidal. . . . The American Civil War was really two wars within one in the manner it was fought. During the initial years the tried-and-true tactics of prior wars, including Napoleonic 'linear' concepts, were often used . . . in strong contrast to . . . the last two years. . . . To survive was to adapt." But generals were slow to adapt, unlike the soldiers, who could see what was happening.

Cox learned that lesson too, writing, "In spite of the fact that Wellington in the Peninsular war had shown again and again that such a column, even over open country, melted away before the 'thin red line' of British soldiers armed only with the old 'Brown Bess,' . . . the *prestige* of Napoleonic tradition kept the upper hand[:] . . . so hard it is to free ourselves from the trammels of old customs and a mistaken practice!" His conclusion, which eventually both sides learned, was that "with veteran soldiers . . . arrayed against each other, one rifle in the trench was worth five in front of it." The Battle of Franklin, with Cox's defensive preparations a fundamental element of the Union victory, would be the final proof in the war on a large scale of the validity of that concept.[46]

Among those slow to learn this particular new reality of war were the members of the congressional Joint Committee on the Conduct of the War. As the Union suffered defeats in the East and the contest continued indecisively into 1863, this committee's drumbeat of criticism and insistence on offensive tactics would only increase. Committee members often criticized generals for even mentioning tactics such as flanking maneuvers or use of the defensive. The committee's criticisms had only a small effect on the war effort, but its attitudes showed that the populace was impatient and, like most military leaders and the administration, unaware of and unready for the realities of modern war.[47]

A Citizen-General Organizes His Forces

Like the nation, Cox's approach to fulfilling his military responsibilities involved the inevitable improvisation required for a citizen experiencing war for the first time, though his preparation was enhanced by his military studies. In Cox's seminal article on war preparations in the North in *Battles and Leaders of the Civil War*, he wrote that the day after the attack on Fort Sumter, the Ohio Senate passed bills to enroll volunteers and organize the state's militia. The next day Dennison called on Garfield and Cox to help him arrange for arming and equipping the militia. Garfield headed up the legislative effort, and Cox began his military preparations by becoming Dennison's military chief of staff. The legislature appropriated $450,000 for arms purchases and equipment, $500,000 to fund Lincoln's request for Ohio's quota of the total of seventy-five thousand volunteers, and $50,000 for contingent funds. Though early enthusiasm for war led some thirty thousand Ohioans to volunteer in the first few weeks, preparing and training them inevitably proved to be a significant logistical challenge. Dennison in particular would be criticized for the many errors in arranging for supplies and weaponry over the next few months.[48]

While fulfilling his duties, Cox became acquainted with Dennison's former law partner, Aaron Perry, who provided legal advice to both the governor and, later, the new Ohio commander, General George B. McClellan. Perry would become Cox's close friend, political ally, and sounding board for his thoughts about war and politics. Cox also discussed the politics of the war with Democratic leader Thomas Key, who would later join McClellan's staff. Cox wrote that Key thought, "The people have gone stark mad," but like many other Democrats, he supported the Union and the war. Cox would recall this conversation when he renewed his acquaintance with Key at the Battle of Antietam when war policy became a matter of debate within McClellan's command.[49]

On April 23, Dennison officially named Cox a brigadier general of Ohio volunteers. A few days later, he sent Cox to the Columbus railroad station to meet McClellan, to whom Dennison offered command of Ohio's forces. After accepting, McClellan joined Cox on an inspection of the state arsenal. The few rusted, damaged, and outdated pieces they found there, Cox wrote later, caused McClellan to remark, "half humorously and half sadly, '[A] fine stock of munitions on which to begin a great war.'" Cox and McClellan then set to their planning duties, preparing schedules and estimates of the needs of Ohio's ten thousand troops.[50]

The two young men struck up a solid friendship. Cox admired McClellan, writing later, "His whole appearance was quiet and modest, but when drawn out he showed no lack of confidence in himself. . . . McClellan's report on the Crimean War . . . was valuable enough to give a just reputation for comprehensive understanding of military organization, and the promise of ability to conduct the operations of an army." McClellan had expressed disdain for volunteers because of his Mexican War experiences. But he was impressed by Cox's intellect and knowledge of military practice and history, and he treated Cox thereafter somewhat as a protégé. He recognized that the dutiful Cox had sufficient self-confidence that he could be trusted both to follow orders and to act independently when appropriate. As McClellan told Cox, "I had more confidence in you than any of my Brig. Gens." By comparison, speaking of the other brigadier generals under his command early in the war, McClellan told his wife, "I have not a Brig. Genl worth his salt—[Thomas] Morris is a timid old woman—[William] Rosecrans a silly fussy goose—[Newton] Schleich knows nothing."[51]

It was perhaps not surprising, then, that McClellan would give Cox, rather than West Point graduate Rosecrans, command of both a troop training camp in Ohio and a wing of his campaign in West Virginia. McClellan first put Cox in charge of training of Camp Jackson, near Columbus, but he was only there a few days. Cox traveled on April 29, 1861, with 1,300 men, made up of half of the 3rd and 11th Ohio regiments, to take command of training at Camp Dennison. This location north of Cincinnati lacked almost everything necessary for a military facility. That reality of war presented the citizen-general with the first tasks for which none of his readings had prepared him. Cox admitted later, "Looking back at it, the wonder is that the blunders and mishaps had not been tenfold more numerous than they were."[52]

The first fortnight in camp was the hardest for him and the troops as Cox set out to make whatever accommodations he could in the rude and barren surroundings. Recently plowed fields quickly became mired in mud because of what Cox called "villainous" weather. A severe shortage of cooks meant that many meals were almost inedible. Men had to be taught every aspect of military life, from drill and tactics to how to make requisitions. One soldier later recalled, "I found out from practical experience that my ignorance of how to draw rations from the commissary cost me about twenty dollars." Volunteers contracted new diseases such as measles, and so infirmaries had to be created. Cox wrote that a local group of nuns, the Sisters of Charity, volunteered as nurses, and "their black and white robes harmonized picturesquely with the military surroundings, as they flitted about under the rough timber framing . . . carrying comfort and hope from one rude couch to another." Another incident for which Cox's reading had not prepared him involved a woman who came to the camp as a member of the 3rd regiment. Cox's aide Gustavus Bascom wrote, "It created a great deal of excitement in camp, and everyone was crazy to see her." Even after she was ejected from the camp, she "remained determined to fight."[53]

One soldier in the 11th regiment wrote of his training experience: "We reached Camp Dennison . . . to learn the art of war. . . . Instead of finding a Camp all plotted off and fully arranged, we were marched into naked wheat fields, there to build our quarters and to prepare our own rations." In building housing, he wrote, "[t]he task we found the most onerous was carrying boards and everything else nearly a fourth of a mile over the field." The first morning was dismal, "for it rained last night, and not a few of us got thoroughly soaked before morning." The next day, after describing the miserable weather to Helen, Cox philosophized, as he faced his unprecedented duties, "The responsibility of this new position weighs heavily on one sometimes." Eventually he and his troops adapted to the regimen and rigors of army life, and the camp, one wrote, was eventually transformed "into a regular village, swarming with men, busy and active as bees."[54]

Calling upon his teaching experience at Oberlin and Warren, Cox organized instruction in drill, tactics, guard duty, and discipline in temporary "schools." He also worked hard to convince the ninety-day men to extend their enlistments; James Monroe and another Oberlin professor helped persuade an Oberlin group to put their antislavery principles into action.

Cox arranged troop reviews for McClellan's visits, which the latter utilized as much, one historian wrote, "for the purpose of being known by those in the ranks as to evaluate their progress." The straitlaced Cox's firmness and demand for strict obedience slowly but surely gained the respect of his men, though rarely their affection because of his aloof mien, proverbial lack of a common touch, and aversion to tobacco and alcohol. As he wrote to Helen, "Nothing has touched me more than the universal expression of the unwillingness of my regiments to go into the field without me."[55]

Another issue with which Cox had to deal was the administration's decision to allow newly recruited military units to elect their leaders. Cox wrote that there seemed to be no better way, since it rewarded the men who raised the volunteer companies and also strengthened political support. However, he averred, "hosts of charlatans and incompetents" were put in command, resulting in the "hopeless task to attempt much in the way of drill and discipline when the officers feel that they are dependent upon the caprice of the men for their continuance in position." One incident in particular galled Cox: when Garfield did not win command of his unit, because of the "sharp maneuvers" of another officer, E. B. Tyler. During this period, Cox was concerned about his own command and continuance in duty because the U.S. Senate had delayed his confirmation. However, in mid-June Chase advised him that his three-year commission had been ratified.[56]

In his *Reminiscences,* Cox recounted several other experiences in those early days that illustrated the transitions he as an ordinary citizen and the nation were undergoing. One incident exhibited Cox's approach to nearly every situation he faced in life: staying self-assured and calm, attributes that would prove important on the battlefield. One day while Cox's men were building huts, Rosecrans, who had been assigned to assist Cox, peremptorily ordered that the floors and bunks they had added be removed because, he said, the huts were only intended to take the place of tents. The troops complained to Cox, and "soon both parties were before me: Rosecrans hot and impetuous, holding a high tone, and making use of General McClellan's name." Rosecrans "fairly bubbled with anger" at the presumption of those who questioned his authority. Cox said nothing for a while to allow tempers to cool, and then he offered a compromise; he calmly said he would refer the issue to McClellan, and those floors already built would remain, though no new ones would be built. McClellan later agreed, and Rosecrans acquiesced. Cox, who wrote of other examples of Rosecrans's loss of control under stress, including at the fateful Battle of Chickamauga in 1863, said of

Rosecrans, "He seemed to like me the better on finding that I was not carried away by the assumption of indefinite power by a staff officer."

Another event reflected the lack of a system for determining ranks, as well as Cox's wry sense of humor. He wrote, "We had visits from clerical adventurers, for the 'pay and emoluments of a captain of cavalry' which the law gave to a chaplain induced some to seek the office who were not the best representatives of their profession." One man who was soliciting appointment as a chaplain "came to me in a shamefaced sort of way before leaving camp and said, 'General, before I decide the matter, I wish you would tell me just what are the pay and emoluments of a *Captain of Calvary?!*'" Working with that young man was likely a cross Cox did not have to bear. In another incident relating to religion, Secretary of War Simon Cameron answered McClellan's query about building "places of worship" at Camp Dennison by simply replying, "The Lord's will be done."[57]

Cox's dedication to duty and to fulfilling the unique responsibilities at Camp Dennison had a salutary effect on both his morale and his physique. In his memoirs he wrote, "The depression which had weighed upon me since the news of Sumter passed away, never to return. The consciousness of having important work to do and the absorption in the work proved the best of all mental tonics." Moreover, he told Helen, "I work like a horse and find no leisure moments. . . . I am hearty and healthy and browning like a berry." He added, as a new fashion took hold, "I've foresworn shaving this week, & shall let my whole beard grow."[58]

A few weeks later, as he was preparing his men for their first military action, the neophyte citizen-general wrote an introspective and prophetic letter to Helen about his changing life and his future. He said, "Everything about my position seems to me like a dream sometimes. . . . I go along about my duties until something occurs which forces my attention to the position I am actually in, and then I have a fit of astonishment at it. When I ask myself what the future will be, I am equally perplexed, and give up all attempts to imagine." Emphasizing a theme to which he would return repeatedly, he wrote, "If I escape the chances of war, I picture to myself a quiet home again, with my books and the pleasant shade of our quiet village street, & I love the dream." At the same time, he recognized that a successful military career might result in further prominence for him in Republican politics, stating, "I know well enough that I am embarked on a public career which circumstances will determine quite differently from my dreams."[59]

2

A Citizen-General Secures (West) Virginia

> The almost wilderness character of the intervening country[,]
> ... the weary miles of steep mountain-roads becoming
> impassable in rainy weather, and the total absence of forage for
> animals were ... all ignored or greatly underestimated. It was
> easy, sitting at one's office table, to sweep the hand over a few
> inches of chart showing next to nothing of the topography,
> and to say, "We will march from here to here"; but ... one
> general after another had to find apologies for failing to
> accomplish what ought never to have been undertaken.
>
> —Cox, *Military Reminiscences*, 1900

When the war began, Virginia was the largest and arguably most influential state in the Confederacy, but occupants of its western region, which bordered Ohio, Pennsylvania, Maryland, and Kentucky, were not sympathetic to secession. When a large majority in those counties voted against secession in the state referendum, the Union recognized an opportunity to take and hold this region. The military objective would be to deter the Confederacy's forces from the borders of the North. The political objective would be to separate the region from Virginia. From these evolved another military objective: using that territory as a base for advancing into the Shenandoah Valley and the Virginia heartland and on to Tennessee. Cox wrote that federal commanders were confident at first they would be able to achieve both military objectives relatively easily.[1] His comments in the epigraph underscore that the topography and weather of West Virginia would over the long term make those tasks onerous.[2]

Another essential reason for securing this region was that the Baltimore and Ohio (B&O) Railroad, the major rail and logistical link from Washington/Baltimore to the Midwest, ran through northwestern Virginia.

30   The Confederates recognized this too, and on May 26 their forces occupied the B&O at Grafton and burned the bridges west of there. On May 27 McClellan, based in Cincinnati, sent Ohio militia over the Ohio River to link up with two Unionist Virginia regiments to retake Grafton. That same day, the self-promoting McClellan used his portable printing press to issue the first of several melodramatic public proclamations. His message to the people of western Virginia noted their opposition to secession and emphasized that his troops' objective was to lift from their shoulders "the yoke of the traitorous conspiracy." Having ordered his subordinates to "repress all attempts at negro insurrection," McClellan proclaimed that the residents' property, to include slaves, would be protected. He said he was committed to "crush any attempt at insurrection," a view that would later be the source of considerable controversy.[3]

Autonomous Command under the "Young Napoleon"

McClellan, whose combined forces numbered about three thousand, achieved early success in the campaign, as the Union men successfully compelled the outnumbered (under one thousand) Confederate forces to retreat from Grafton, first in a panic to Philippi, and then to Beverly on June 3. McClellan's report to Washington made it seem like a major triumph, and Northern newspapers colorfully trumpeted it as the "Philippi races." As McClellan traveled in mid-June by train from Cincinnati to the battlefront, he was welcomed at each stop as a conquering hero. He told his wife that the journey was "a continuous ovation" and observed, "I never went thro' such a scene in my life." Many newspapers began to call him the "Young Napoleon," a trend that he encouraged via additional proclamations, and a cult of personality began to take root. In his memoirs, Cox assessed McClellan's evolving Napoleonic complex:

> His despatches, proclamations, and correspondence are a psychological study. . . . Their turgid rhetoric and exaggerated pretense did not seem natural to him. . . . He appeared to be in a morbid condition of mental exaltation[;] . . . he seemed to be composing for stage effect. . . . The career of the great Napoleon had been the study and the absorbing admiration of young American soldiers[;] . . . it was perhaps not strange that when real war came they should copy his bulletins and even his personal bearing. It was, for the moment, the bent of the people to be pleased with McClellan's rendering of the role; they dubbed him the Young Napoleon.[4]

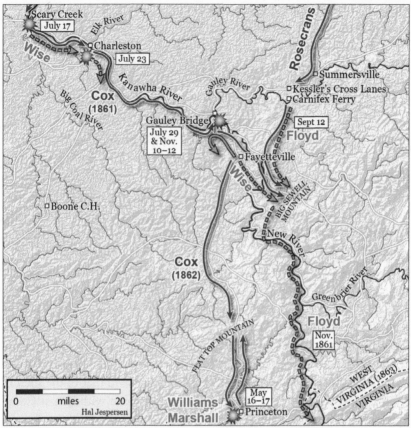

Map 1. The West Virginia campaigns, 1861, 1862. (Map by Hal Jespersen)

In late April, McClellan had proposed to Scott a comprehensive strategic plan "tending to bring the war to a speedy close," with himself in the leading role. It called for garrisoning important points along the Ohio River and using an army of 80,000 to make an offensive thrust on Richmond. Scott had dismissed the plan as unrealistic and grandiose, but McClellan decided to use one element of his proposal, an advance along the Kanawha River valley, as part of his new campaign. Cox would play a major and autonomous role in that plan.

On the Confederate side, General Robert E. Lee, commanding Virginia's forces, had responded to the Union successes in Beverly and Philippi by sending 4,500 men to block the passes from Beverly to the south. However, Lee's hopes to recruit more men from the region failed because, his local commander reported, the people were "thoroughly imbued with an ignorant and bigoted Union sentiment." Separately, Lee ordered a force under former Virginia governor Henry A. Wise to the Kanawha River valley to block what he saw as a potential Union advance there.[5]

On July 2, McClellan ordered Cox and his 2,500 men from the 1st and 2nd Kentucky and the 11th and 12th Ohio regiments and some cavalry to advance along the Kanawha route to deter Wise. While McClellan showed confidence in Cox by giving him autonomy for this campaign, he was still unsure of his untested subordinate's capabilities. He included in his order detailed explanations of the mechanics of a campaign, from how to transport wagons to where to place artillery. He also told Cox, "Remain on the defensive and endeavor to induce the rebels to remain at Charleston until I can cut off their retreat by a movement from Beverly." Expressing total confidence in himself, McClellan added that if Cox heard rumors that McClellan was hard-pressed, Cox should rapidly advance on Charleston, because the rumors would be inaccurate; "for," he assured Cox, "I shall be successful."[6]

On July 7, his appointment as brigadier general in hand, Cox and his men headed for Gallipolis, Ohio, where he was to pick up the 21st Ohio regiment and head for Point Pleasant near the mouth of the Kanawha River. Cox proudly told Helen, "My attention to my duties has been rewarded by the most independent & responsible command given to any of the Brigadiers. . . . Gen. McClellan speaks of it as the most important detachment yet made." However, Cox was not pleased that of the men in his command, only the 11th Ohio regiment had been with him at Camp Dennison. (That unit would remain under his command for nearly two years and be an important element of what later became known as the "Kanawha Division.") He told McClellan that, as a result, he would "not be disappointed if the motion is somewhat slow."[7]

Just before he left, Cox's orders were changed, and he was charged with taking the offensive, driving out Wise, and taking control of Charleston and Gauley Bridge. Cox began his movement from Point Pleasant on July 11, riding south on river steamboats. In keeping with his cautious approach, he engaged in extensive reconnaissance and placed forces at various outposts along the Ohio and Kanawha Rivers. He wrote, "It was hazardous to divide my little army into three columns on a base of a hundred miles, but it was thought wise to show some Union troops at various points on the border." Still, he told Helen with a dash of bravado similar to McClellan's, "When the rebel forces at Charleston find themselves in danger of attack by front and rear, they will run or disperse—we shall make a clean sweep in Western Va."[8]

Cox's description of his travel on the Ohio and Kanawha Rivers illustrates the innocence and overconfidence of this novice soldier: "Our first day's sail was the very romance of campaigning. . . . [T]he boats were dressed in their colors. . . . The bands played national tunes, and as we passed the houses of Union citizens, the inmates would wave their handkerchiefs to us, and were answered by cheers from the troops. . . . [T]he spice of possible danger [made] this our first day in the enemy's country key everybody to just such a pitch as apparently to double the vividness of every situation." He told Helen, "The pageant was certainly an imposing one." One of Cox's men wrote, "One would have imagined by the ovation . . . that we were heroes returning from war instead of untried soldiers with their first experience awaiting them."[9]

During the move, Cox and his men underwent what he called "our initiation into an experience of rumors." He noted that they were "always grossly exaggerated, making chimeras with which a commanding officer had to wage a more incessant warfare than with the substantial enemy." One day, he heard a rumor that Wise with four thousand men was about to attack. Cox was unconvinced, believing that "Wise's troops were, like [Cox's] own, too raw" to be a real threat. Cox's ensuing cavalry reconnaissance found only a small enemy cavalry troop. Perhaps partly as a result, he told Helen he was "confident that we shall have no general engagement with the enemy for some time to come." But he reassured her, "Of course I am cautious . . . for I do not wish to make any mistakes."[10]

Meanwhile, McClellan was moving to Cox's west, along with Rosecrans, toward a climactic battle at Rich Mountain. On the way, he sent a message to Scott that implied he understood the power of the defensive. He wrote that he would try to succeed by "maneuvering rather than fighting" and stated, "I will not throw these raw men of mine into the teeth of artillery and intrenchments if it is possible to avoid it." Instead, McClellan accepted Rosecrans's suggestion for a flank attack by one brigade. McClellan was to lead two others to exploit any successes at what would be his very first battle experience of the war. Rosecrans's regiments effectively rolled up the rebel flank on July 11, but McClellan, misinterpreting the sounds of battle, failed to launch the follow-up attack. Instead he returned to his camp, leaving Rosecrans to his own devices. As a result, most of the rebels escaped, though Rosecrans did succeed in forcing some six hundred to surrender.[11]

Although he had performed poorly and let a subordinate (as he used to put it in one of his favorite phrases) "get out of his scrape" alone,

34   McClellan took full credit for the victory. He telegraphed Scott on July 12, "Our success complete and almost bloodless." As Rosecrans's biographer put it aptly, "Subordinate Rosecrans was responsible . . . but commander McClellan wrote the Napoleonic reports and became the national hero." Northern newspapers exulted July 13 with headlines such as "Gen. McClellan, the Napoleon of the Present War." That same day McClellan exhibited another proclivity that would inhibit his conduct in the war: overstating the numbers and scope of his enemies. In a report he claimed to have driven out "10,000 troops strongly entrenched," and on July 16 he proclaimed that his men had "annihilated two armies." In part as a result, less than a week later, after the disaster at the Battle of First Manassas, McClellan was ordered to Washington to assume command. His rapid rise to power was complete.[12]

Cox's analysis in his *Battles and Leaders* article about McClellan in West Virginia is the basis of much of the historiography on these events and McClellan's personality. He wrote, "It is a curious task to compare [what really happened] with the picture of the campaign and its results which was then given to the world. . . . The Rich Mountain affair, when analyzed, shows the same characteristics which became well known later. There was the same overestimate of the enemy, the same tendency to interpret unfavorably the sights and sounds in front, the same hesitancy to throw in his whole force when he knew his subordinate was engaged." As one historian put it, "McClellan exhibited in West Virginia a nascent Napoleonic complex that manifested itself in the writing of dispatches and proclamations, though not in the handling of troops in battle."[13]

Stumbles and Triumphs

On July 14, fresh from his "triumph" at Rich Mountain, McClellan showed his confidence in Cox by telegraphing him, "Win your spurs by capturing Wise & occupying Gauley Bridge. I impatiently wait to hear from you that my expectations are justified. . . . [C]omplete the first act of our drama." McClellan told the War Department on July 15, "I am in constant expectation of hearing from General Cox that his efforts to drive the Wises out of the Kanawha valley and occupy the Gauley Bridge have been crowned with success."[14]

Cox was unable to meet McClellan's expectations at first. On July 16 Cox's men exhibited their inexperience and nervous tension when, during a night patrol, a gun accidentally went off. Cox's aide, Gustavus

Bascom, wrote, "Forthwith the companies in the immediate neighborhood blasted away into the dark in all directions," killing two and wound-
ing three of their own men. Despite this incident, Cox remained both
optimistic and naive. He wrote to Helen the same day, "There has been a
singular enchantment about this expedition up the Kanawha. The spice of
danger has added to the enjoyment." He added that the victory at Rich
Mountain would "dampen their [the Confederates'] courage." At the same
time, he complained that he had not been given sufficient cavalry or artillery and that this had slowed his advance. Knowing McClellan expected
him to be in Charleston already, Cox reported, "I have made a respectable
advance every day . . . [but] think we have gone as fast as is prudent."[15]

The tension was high on July 17 when Cox had his first combat experience at the Battle of Scary Creek, and it proved to be a dash of cold
water on his optimism and naïveté. He sent some men over Scary Creek
to push back Wise's advance forces, and at first his men caused the rebels
to retreat. But the latter returned in force and killed ten Union men and
wounded thirty-five others, leading ultimately to a standoff. Cox wrote of
his men, "As was common with new troops, they passed from confidence
to discouragement as soon as they were checked, and they retreated."
He added, "The affair was accompanied by another humiliating incident
which gave me no little chagrin." Three of Cox's officers went without
permission to "congratulate" the Union officers after the first phase but
were taken prisoner. Cox told Helen defensively that he knew the affair
"may be called a disaster by some, but it is not so. It accomplished a necessary military object, and in the encounter our troops were proven superior." He asserted that "a few days will show that the plan of operations
is a good one, & will be successfully carried out." He told Helen he would
report the facts without apology, "trusting to the future to remove the bad
impression the affair must make upon McClellan."

As Cox expected, McClellan was upset. He reported, "Cox checked on
the Kanawha. . . . Has fought something between a victory and a defeat.
. . . [I]n heaven's name give me some general officers who understand their
profession. They can't execute their orders unless I stand by them." Having
placed so much confidence in Cox, he regretfully told his wife, "Cox lost
more men in getting a detachment thrashed than I did in routing two armies
[sic]. The consequence is that I will have to take Wise myself." The irony is
that while McClellan was boasting about his military abilities, to that point
he had, one historian noted, "neither witnessed nor directed any fighting."[16]

McClellan sent Cox a stinging telegram about the affair: "I am entirely disappointed with the result of your operations. . . . You should have advanced to Gauley Bridge without a check. . . . I see that your army is demoralized." Emphasizing his high opinion of himself, while also trying to motivate Cox, McClellan told Cox to tell his men that McClellan was on the way to "accomplish what ought to have been done without [his] personal presence." He added, "In the meantime hold your own and at least save me the disgrace of a detachment of my Army being routed."[17]

While he accepted McClellan's sharp criticism, Cox felt that he had not been judged correctly. Moreover, he was dismayed that his first war experience had not been a victory. Venting his emotions in the trusted correspondence with his understanding wife, Cox complained that his lack of success was because he did not have the cavalry, artillery, or numbers of troops he had been promised. Left unsaid was that both he and his men were raw and inexperienced. But Cox acknowledged, "Military men are held responsible for success without much question being made as to the means given them to secure it." He concluded fatalistically, "Whatever blame may come, I shall do my duty as well as I know how and leave the rest with Providence as calmly as I can."[18]

Three days later, having learned that Scary Creek was not a defeat, McClellan telegraphed Cox to apprise him that he had been called to Washington. He challenged Cox again to "follow up the retreating enemy" and instructed him, "Concentrate all your troops and drive them beyond the Gauley Bridge . . . [and thus] retrieve your want of success. . . . I hope that you will by the vigor of your movements render it unnecessary for [Rosecrans] to come to your assistance. . . . It is not too late for you to justify my first impression of you."[19]

As Cox planned his next steps, he was "able to get more accurate information about Wise's forces than . . . [he] could obtain before." Much of that new intelligence came from a Union spy, Pryce Lewis, hired by Alan Pinkerton to assist McClellan's campaign. Earlier in the month, a Confederate colonel named George Patton unwittingly gave Lewis in-depth information about Wise's forces. (Patton was wounded and taken prisoner at Scary Creek, and was later paroled.) Lewis told Cox he was certain that Wise had not been reinforced and was short of food and forage. Lewis then accompanied a Union scouting party that reported the same information. In his memoirs, Lewis described Cox as pacing up and down nervously in his office as he pondered what to do, wondering whether he could trust this spy.[20]

Finally Cox decided to attack; on July 23 he struck at Wise from the east (as suggested by Pryce) in a flanking maneuver that forced the Confederates to flee in panic. The offensive continued the next day, and by nightfall Cox's men were encamped on the outskirts of Charleston. The next morning the town's mayor surrendered the city. Reflecting the instincts of a citizen-general, Cox instituted an effective counterinsurgency strategy. He composed a "Message to the People of Charleston" in which he told them that his army would act in direct contrast to the "profane and disorderly behavior of the rebel army." Cox ordered his men to "march through in soldierly order, no man leaving the ranks or shouting or making any unnecessary noise." If they did so, he assured them, "[t]he people will bless us as the restorers of safety and liberty."[21]

Cox proudly told Helen that Wise's men had "abandoned their posts and run in such haste, that our men found their supper on the table. . . . [T]oday the whole army is in full retreat, & we marched to [Charleston] in triumph." However, he was concerned that his victory had been too easy. He wondered why the Confederates did not use the terrain to their benefit, given the power of the defensive. He wrote, "I am compelled to wonder how they permit us to go through a land which in every mile has passes which a hundred men could hold against a regiment."[22] He was relieved that the Confederates had not yet learned that lesson.

When Rosecrans, who had succeeded McClellan, heard of Cox's success, he presumed that taking Charleston was all that Cox was capable of doing. He ordered Cox to stay put and defend his position, pending Rosecrans's own movement against Wise's rear. However, Rosecrans's order arrived after Cox, showing his independent streak, had decided to continue implementing his earlier orders. On July 27 he launched a quick movement toward Gauley Bridge, a key outpost forty miles south of Charleston that sits astride the confluence of the Gauley, Kanawha, and New Rivers. Again Wise's men retreated in a near panic, and Cox took possession of Gauley Bridge on July 29. He was ebullient, reporting, "Our success justified the policy of a determined advance." McClellan's and Rosecrans's plaudits improved Cox's morale and helped alleviate the sting of Scary Creek.[23]

Wise blamed his defeat on the "fact" that after Scary Creek, Cox was heavily reinforced, "with far better arms and supplies." As a result, he complained, "My situation in the Kanawha Valley was critical in the extreme." He reported that another reason for his failure (one that the teetotaling

Cox was likely amused to read about after the war) was because "Ohio has sent thousands of gallons [of whiskey] over the border, doubtless to demoralize the camp." Wise whined, "The Kanawha Valley is disaffected and traitorous. . . . [T]hey are submitting, subdued, and debased." The latter comment reflected the continuing success of Cox's counterinsurgency policy. He reported in early August that many rebel troops were deserting because, having been told they were defending their region against "outrages" from Union forces, they realized that they would be safe under Union control. Further, Cox told Helen, many former Confederate sympathizers were "cursing Wise for the barbarous course he has been taking," and local residents often brought Cox news of rebel movements.

As a result of his victories and new policy, Cox had both justified McClellan's confidence in him and helped achieve a major political-military victory for the Union. As of late July, he told Helen, "The whole of western Va. is now free from the secessionists, and we think it will soon quiet down into a permanent and willing recognition of the U.S. government." That sentiment was verified when an August convention in Wheeling enacted a statehood ordinance, which was ratified in a referendum on October 24.[24]

New Lessons for a Citizen-General

On July 26, before he had moved to Gauley Bridge, Cox "was treated to a surprise on the part of three subordinates," which he deemed "an unexpected enlargement" of his military experience. The regimental commanders came to his tent, and their spokesman, "who had the least capacity as commander of a regiment," said they would not lead their men forward unless Cox could convince them it was appropriate. Reacting with characteristic calm, Cox "dryly asked if he was quite sure he understood" what he was saying. He wrote that they probably expected an angry, curse-filled tirade typical of a "regular army" officer. The spokesman protested that "as their military experience was about as extensive" as Cox's, he ought to make no movements except in consultation with them and with their consent. Cox replied that only their ignorance could "palliate" their action, which, whether they meant it so or not, was mutinous. Cox explained that he would seek their counsel only if he felt incompetent to decide a particular matter. He said if they apologized and were earnest from that point on, he would overlook the conversation. If not, he would order their arrest. One officer apologized quickly, and all three later became Cox's "devoted followers" during the war.

Cox's introspective analysis of the incident reflected his understanding of both his own character and the context of the new realities citizen-soldiers faced, noting that "it was part of their military education as well as mine." He said that his "systematic adherence to a quiet and undemonstrative manner evidently told against [him], at first, in their opinion." He went on, "If I had been noisy and blustering" and done what seemed to be regarded as the "regulation" amount of cursing and swearing, "they probably would have given me credit for military aptitude at least." As one of Cox's aides noted, "His demeanor won their respect where mere pretension would not." Cox added in his memoirs that when his men learned "that it was as necessary to obey a quiet order as one emphasized by expletives, and especially when they had been a little under fire, there was no more trouble." He noted wryly that his understated approach led to his "chief embarrassment in discipline" coming when even his slightest "intimation of dissatisfaction caused more chagrin among the men and more evident pain than I intended or wished."[25]

A second learning experience involved Cox's initiation into the ways of the press and the use of public relations. Like McClellan, many Civil War generals effectively promoted themselves by using newspapermen to inflate successes and advance their reputations. In a day when journalism was not necessarily focused on objectivity and accuracy, reporters embellished the records of generals they favored, as well as those who treated them well or bribed them. Those who did not indulge them caused the reporters to "write them down." As one historian put it, reporters would write in the melodramatic language of the time; "Every triumph became a Glorious Victory, every retreat a Shameful Rout."[26]

Cox's first experience of these trends came when correspondents from the *New York Times* and *New York Tribune* came to Gauley Bridge in late July and asked on what terms they could accompany his forces. The self-effacing and dutiful Cox did not see this as an opportunity to engage in self-promotion. He told the reporters that they could accompany the army and would be furnished with tents and transportation. But he would require that their reports be reviewed by his staff to make sure they would not aid the enemy. The disappointed reporters suggested instead that they should be "announced as volunteer aides with military rank." Cox demurred, noting that they could be more independent if they did not feel they had to repay favors with flattery. Their reported response was, "Very well. General Cox thinks he can get along without us, and we will show him. We will write him down."

Some of the reporters' subsequent articles described Cox's army as "demoralized, drunken, and without discipline, in a state of insubordination" and the commander as "totally incompetent." One reporter wrote, "The men have no confidence whatever in their leader," although incongruously in the same article he reported that Cox had taken Charleston. At that time Cox's nomination as brigadier general could have been in trouble in the U.S. Senate because of these reports, except for McClellan's support. Cox's capture of Gauley Bridge also helped to dissipate the journalistic storm clouds.[27]

Cox did not find it easy to dismiss the criticism. He vented to Helen, "It has never occurred to me that such a mode of warfare would be attempted." He acknowledged the accuracy of the commentary that he was slow and cautious, but he emphasized that was necessary because he had "raw and undisciplined troops" and "lacked support from some regimental commanders." He admitted, "I was depressed when I first saw the malicious criticism, but now I feel that the discipline [of dealing with it] will better my character." Furthermore, "As for that 'disgusting' man in the N.Y. *Herald,* I have to say that Gen. McClellan telegraphed his congratulations to me from Washington . . . busy as he was with his new position."[28]

Securing the New State: Dealing with Death

On September 18, 1861, the *New York Times* reported, "Nowhere else in the war has the Union army so well sustained their cause as in western Virginia. . . . Considering the terrain and obstacles there, it is a great victory. . . . General Cox enjoys the unquestioned honor of winning the important valley of the Kanawha for the Union." That article reflected a new journalistic appreciation of Rosecrans's and Cox's actions in August and September as they solidified Union control of western Virginia.

Their August campaign began when Rosecrans established a chain of posts from the east to Gauley Bridge in anticipation of a renewed offensive push. Cox, newly designated commander of the "Brigade of the Kanawha," ordered his troops to ensure that Wise's retreat continued and to warn of his return. Cox was aided in this task by local residents as a result of his successful counterinsurgency policy. He wrote Helen that he had implemented "a most lenient course toward the rebels, giving leave to all to remain quiet in their homes and asking no questions as to opinions or conduct. As a result, many who might've gone to the Confederate side have laid down their arms." His treatment of Mrs. Christopher Q.

Tompkins, whose husband was a Confederate colonel, was typical. She wrote later that she thought of Cox as "an elegant, accomplished gentleman" whom "the soldiers believe is my brother-in-law, he is so attentive to protect me."[29]

Lee was displeased about Cox's military and political-military successes, admitting in a report that the Union commander was making "himself very acceptable to the inhabitants of the Kanawha valley by his considerate conduct." Another former Virginia governor who had since become a Confederate general, John B. Floyd, grudgingly agreed, noting, "Cox has certainly conciliated to a very great extent the people of all the country heretofore occupied by our troops. He furnishes bacon, coffee, flour, and sugar at very low prices, and is opening trade by the river to Cincinnati."[30]

In response to Rosecrans's and Cox's successes, Confederate President Jefferson Davis decided to send Lee himself to try to take back the region. On August 16 Cox told Helen he was concerned because "General Lee is their leader and he is an educated soldier; one of their best." Cox had reports that Floyd had united with Wise to attack him with a force numbering nearly 10,000, while Cox had only about 3,000. Fortunately for Cox, over the next few weeks Floyd and Wise would spend more time feuding with each other than cooperating. Not knowing of his good fortune, Cox requested reinforcements from Rosecrans and spread his men out to "baffle the enemy" and convince the Confederates that he had more troops than he really did. Apparently his ploy worked, and in late August Wise and Floyd's forces, in separate columns, were moving only haltingly toward Gauley.

On August 25 Cox's tactic of pushing back the enemy worked effectively when Lieutenant Colonel Joseph W. Frizell of the 11th Ohio trapped some of Wise's cavalry near Hawk's Nest, one of the region's most difficult defiles. After nearly cutting them to pieces, Frizell sent the rebel troops into such a panic that they "never again showed any enterprise in harassing our outposts; our men gained proportionally in confidence." According to the historian of the 11th regiment, however, Frizell's actions almost did not take place, because Cox had advised that there were no rebel troops in the vicinity. Just as Cox's report arrived, "the rebels opened a brisk fire on our line, but a few rods distant. With a peculiar but bitter smile on his countenance, Colonel Frizell remarked: 'No rebels in our front, hey? If my reports are not believed at Gauley, they will soon have all the evidence they want of that fact.'" After the incident, Frizell reportedly said, "The general is a mighty good fellow, but *the poorest judge of human nature* I ever saw."[31]

An incident the next day illustrated that Cox's tactics could be undermined by incompetent subordinates. At Kessler's Cross Lanes, about twenty miles east of Gauley Bridge, Colonel E. B. Tyler's regiment was routed by Floyd after Tyler failed to obey Cox's orders to watch carefully for enemy attacks. Tyler, one of the commanders who had questioned Cox's authority earlier, was, Rosecrans wrote, "surprised by Floyd while eating breakfast, and dispersed." Cox told Helen that Tyler's men "slept quite carelessly within two miles of the enemy, with picket fires burning, contrary to every military rule. . . . The rebels arranged to attack at their leisure." During the skirmish, one of Tyler's subordinates, Major John S. "Jack" Casement, restored order and led many troops to safety. This was the first of several times when that pugnacious and rough-hewn railroad man, who would oversee the construction of the Union Pacific Railroad, played an important role as Cox's subordinate. Casement was the antithesis of Cox, who described him as being "rough of speech but generous of heart, running over with fun . . . as jolly a comrade and as loyal a subordinate as the army could show." Despite their vast differences in personality, they became lifelong friends.[32]

Floyd reported that after this success, he believed he could cut off Cox's communications with Rosecrans and that if Floyd had reinforcements, "The undecided and timid portions of the people would at once side against the invaders." Cox too expected an energized Floyd to advance quickly, telling Helen, "I think the coming week must bring matters to a crisis between us and the enemy. They have been boasting that they would surround and overwhelm my little command." Instead, Floyd stayed put, entrenching at Carnifex Ferry. Floyd and Wise, their forces still separated, refused to cooperate, each insisting that the other reinforce him. Neither relented, and neither advanced. In his memoirs Cox assessed, "If Wise had been as troublesome to me as he was to Floyd, I should, indeed, have had a hot time of it. But he did me a royal service."[33]

Lee was upset both that Floyd had not advanced from Carnifex Ferry and that Wise and Floyd were not cooperating. He was even unhappier when Rosecrans and Cox used the unexpected interlude to strike a blow against the divided Confederate forces. On September 10 Cox attacked Floyd as the first part of "a joint effort with General Rosecrans" that would place Cox's troops "in a position to drive the rebels out of the valley." The attack, part of the Battle of Carnifex Ferry, was a success, and Cox wrote, "Floyd had learned that his position could be subjected to a destructive cannonade; he himself was slightly wounded, and his officers and men were discouraged. He therefore retreated across the Gauley in the night" to Big Sewell Mountain.

After Floyd's defeat, Wise sardonically commented to Lee, "Disasters have come, and disasters are coming, which you alone, I fear, can repair and prevent. As I predicted, General Floyd . . . has given way. . . . I solemnly protest that my force is not safe under his command." But Wise fared no better than Floyd; on September 12 Cox attacked him with two regiments, causing him too to retreat to Big Sewell Mountain. On September 13 the two Confederate armies were encamped near one another on that peak but were still separated. An optimistic Cox told Rosecrans, "The more I hear of them, the more thoroughly satisfied I am that Floyd's and Wise's army is badly demoralized."[34]

On September 17 Rosecrans met with his commanders to unite his forces and to coordinate strategy. At that point, Cox's autonomous responsibilities ended, with Rosecrans taking overall command. Cox told Helen that having had an independent command had been very gratifying, especially because he had justified McClellan's confidence in him. Now both McClellan and Rosecrans respected his abilities and listened to his counsel. Further, he told her, "The press too is taking a different tone." More important, he noted wryly, the Confederates hold "me in a respect quite as great as I could ask, if not as cordial."

Nevertheless, in his memoirs he wrote that after his conference with Rosecrans, he "rode back to [his] camp in the evening feeling a sense of relief at the transfer of responsibility to other shoulders." He observed, "The difference between chief responsibility in military movements and the leadership even of the largest subordinate organizations of an army is heaven-wide; and I believe that no one who has tried both will hesitate to say that the subordinate knows little or nothing of the strain upon the will and the moral faculties which the chief has to bear." Clearly he had learned from his "baptism by fire" that he had his limits.[35]

Mid-September also brought Cox one of the saddest occasions a citizen-soldier could experience: the death of a child and the inability to comfort his wife. His son William Brewster had been born on January 26, and Cox had had only one day with him. He had learned of the child's illness early in September, and he wrote to Helen, "My heart bleeds Lilla, when I think of you watching beside the little one's death-bed, or perhaps already following him to the grave alone." The child died on September 14, and Helen annotated her husband's September 10 letter with the note: "I received this letter the very day our dear little Brewster died—the 14th of Sept.—H.F.C." In his memoirs, Cox wrote, "I had to swallow my sorrows as well as I could . . . leaving my wife uncomforted in her bereavement."[36]

Cox was more emotional about the death of his son than he would be about the death of his "military sons," the men under his command. His stoic, calm manner and emotional restraint were among his greatest strengths during the stress of the battle. They were important assets for dealing with the reality of sending thousands of men into situations where many would die or be wounded. Like most military men, he learned over time to steel himself to the carnage and bloodshed around him, knowing that if he formed too close an attachment to his men, he would have difficulty sending them into battle.[37]

Securing "West Virginia" for the Union

In mid-September, the two armies spent several days engaging in feints and probes, each hoping the other would attack; but neither took the initiative, in part because of the miserable weather conditions. On September 20, on Lee's recommendation, Davis relieved Wise and ordered him to turn over all his forces to Floyd. Even then, because of heavy storms and lack of supplies, Floyd and Lee were unable to do much with their united forces. As Cox wrote colorfully to Helen, "You cannot appreciate the beauties of tent life in the driving, drenching, howling storms we have had lately. We live in a sea of mud and an atmosphere of water—cold water at that!"

Cox reported an incident during this period that demonstrated the difficulties of operating in western Virginia. One of his wagon-masters foraging for food thought he had come upon an enemy camp three miles to the rear. Cox ordered a detachment to go around the suspected enemy to drive them toward the main element so that they could be caught in between. Once the detachment got behind the "enemy," however, they discovered that they were actually facing the rear of Cox's forces! The scouts had been deceived by the tangle of rural West Virginia's wooded hills and circling roads, as well as the misty weather. Cox said, "The officers and men joined in hearty laughter over their wild-goose chase."

On October 5, Rosecrans decided that conditions were so poor that it would be best to withdraw to Gauley Bridge to regroup and shorten the supply line. Cox had hoped for a new offensive, stating, "We can whip them, and for the purpose of forcing a retreat have probably done so already," but a hesitant Rosecrans "sent imperative orders not to attack till he came up. By the time he came the opportunity for a complete victory was gone." At one point during the withdrawal, Cox observed, "[I] sat on my horse at the extreme rear of our column revolving in my mind the predicament we should be in if the rebels should have discovered our movement." Introspectively, Cox wrote that he was "very thankful that [he] was not a nervous man" and "could sit there with apparent *sang-froid*."[38]

Like Rosecrans, Lee had concluded by mid-October that there was little more that could be done before winter's onset; he left for Richmond on October 30. As he departed, he was subjected to a firestorm of criticism from the Southern press, which dubbed him "Granny Lee" and "Evacuating Lee." Floyd did not agree with Lee that the campaign was over, however; he filled the void left by Rosecrans's withdrawal and advanced toward Gauley Bridge, regaining some of the lost territory. On November 1, Cox wrote, "Taking advantage of Rosecrans's neglect to occupy Fayette Court House and Cotton Hill . . . Floyd moved northward with 5000 men and startled the Union commander by opening with cannon upon the post at Gauley Bridge." The attack was, however, more noisy than dangerous because Floyd had no means of crossing the river, and once again the two sides seemed to be in a standoff. Floyd's movements proved to be of little consequence politically either. On October 24 the referendum on statehood had received a large majority in favor.[39]

On November 2, Rosecrans decided to respond to Floyd's advance by trying to outflank and surround the Confederates. Cox's detachment crossed the Gauley River on November 10 and scaled the heights overlooking Floyd's left flank. One of Rosecrans's other brigadier generals, W. H. Benham, a West Pointer, failed to implement his part of the plan. As a result, Floyd avoided the trap, but he was forced to retreat all the way to New Bern. Cox wrote to Helen about his annoyance with Benham's incompetence, adding that he was also exasperated by that West Point graduate's relentless toadying of the press, which had given him several "fulsome puffs." The last "puff" came on November 24, when the *New York Times* reported that Floyd's retreat was attributable to Benham's efforts. Rosecrans knew better, and to Cox's satisfaction, Rosecrans had Benham arrested two days later for "unofficer-like neglect of duty." In his report Rosecrans stated, "General Cox is the only reliable man here."[40]

On November 19 Rosecrans concluded that because Floyd was no longer a threat, he would take the army, now in full control of the region, into winter quarters. Rosecrans set up his regional command at Wheeling, while Cox was put in charge of the Department of the Kanawha, with headquarters at Charleston. As Cox wrote, at that point, "West Virginia had organized as a free State within the Union, and this substantial result of the campaign crowned it with success. The line of the Alleghenies became the northern frontier of the Confederacy in Virginia, and was never again seriously broken."[41]

Winter Quarters and Military Administration

Although his political background made him an apt overseer for this occupied region, Cox quickly developed "a rooted dislike for the military administration of border districts." Having helped achieve the Union's objectives, he hoped to be rewarded with an assignment to a more active region. He was pleased in late November to be ordered to take his three longest-serving Ohio regiments and report to General Don Carlos Buell in Kentucky. He wrote, "This was exactly in accordance with my own strong desire to join a large army on one of the principal lines of operations. I therefore went joyfully to Rosecrans, supposing, of course, that he also had received orders to send me away." Rosecrans had not been advised in advance, so he blocked the order, insisting that if his forces were to be reduced, he should himself indicate which would be transferred. When ordered later to send eight regiments to Buell, Rosecrans insisted that his best commander should stay, in great part to train new volunteers. Cox told Helen that Rosecrans's decision was "very like killing with kindness."

Later, after more of his men were transferred, Cox wrote, "I am vexed and disheartened at the breaking up of my brigade. . . . The command of the District [of Kanawha] here is a humbug." He told Garfield that he was "angry that political maneuvering and petty jealousy [were] being used for promotions, division commands, etc. [while] . . . the paralysis of affairs in this department [was] extremely chafing" to him. He complained to Helen, "We are emphatically . . . hoping we may be ordered to join some great moving column instead of being kept here as a police force for Western Virginia." Not even a letter from Dennison noting that McClellan had considered assigning Cox to command of the entire Department of West Virginia improved his mood.[42]

Finally accepting that he was not going to be transferred soon, Cox focused much of his attention on training the new forces being sent to the region. He set up regimental schools and instilled the discipline of drill, as well as of picket and outpost duties. To emphasize the importance of discipline, he instituted a policy of strictly limiting furloughs, and he set an example by not taking leave, even though he was still grieving for his son. In another new experience for a citizen-general related to discipline, Cox supervised several courts-martial. One day, he told Helen, there was "a painful duty to do, in superintending the execution of a man condemned to death for desertion and mutinous conduct." He recalled that he rode slowly in front of the regiment, staring each man in the eye to emphasize the gravity of the matter. "The music of the dead-march was heard....The solemn strains, the slow funereal step of the soldiers, the closed ambulance, the statue-like stillness of the paraded troops made an impression deeper and more awful than a battle scene, because the excitement was hushed and repressed." Cox wrote that the fact that it was carried out with "perfect order and discipline" had a positive moral effect on his men.[43]

That winter introduced Cox to one of the issues that would prove to be crucial during and after the war: the status of runaway slaves and freedmen. In May 1861 General Ben Butler, a Massachusetts political general, had coined the term *contraband of war* for slaves forced to work for the Confederacy who escaped and took refuge in Union army camps. In August 1861 Congress passed the Confiscation Act, legalizing this concept. Over the next year, hundreds of slaves came to Union camps declaring themselves "contraband." Cox wrote that his interpretation of this law was based on what he understood to be Republican Party policy: there would be no interference with slavery in the states that remained loyal, but it was within the war powers of the government to abolish slavery in the rebellious states. He said that it was relatively easy to deal with "contrabands" because of their unique experiences. But he said, "[I]t was impossible to come to any agreement in regard to fugitive slaves who took refuge in our camps."

Cox tried to steer clear of the issue by ordering that slaves be kept out of the camps, but he did not order his troops to arrest and return them. He could not avoid this complicated matter entirely, however. In one incident, a wealthy pro-Secessionist, Henry Hopkins, had sent one of his slaves to assist Confederate guerrillas. The slave escaped, returned to Charleston for his wife and children, and came to Cox's camp, where he was accepted into the camp's workforce as a contraband. Hopkins and the local jailer seized the man, but the provost marshal, "knowing he was an active secessionist," arrested Hopkins. While the court process was evolving, the former slave escaped, taking his family down the river in a skiff. Unfortunately, the boat overturned and they all drowned.

In his report about this incident to Rosecrans, Cox complained bitterly that it showed not only the difficulty of dealing with "contrabands" but also the problems he was facing because of the power of the Secessionists over Unionists. He said, "The only occasions on which [Unionist officials] show any vitality is when some Secessionist's runaway negroes are to be caught. For any purpose of ordinary municipal magistracy they seem utterly incompetent." As a result, his men had to take on all the duties of municipal government, from policing to repairing roads, bridges, and wharves. That too reinforced his "rooted dislike" for military administration.[44]

As he waited for new orders, Cox also used his time to reflect on his experiences during the first months of the war. He was satisfied that he had finally earned the respect of his men, telling Garfield earlier that within his "command there had gradually grown up a very different feeling in regard to" himself. One of his colonels, future president Rutherford B. Hayes, had told his wife in September, "General Cox is a great favorite, deservedly I think, with his men." In his diary the next February, Hayes noted, "General Cox; a good talker, a sound man, excellent sense. I wish he commanded our brigade." Cox's Warren friend Emerson Opdycke told his wife in late November that he looked forward to a possible assignment as Cox's aide, saying, "I know him to be a high minded gentleman, as well as a rising General and Statesman."

On other issues, Cox told Garfield that his early problems with the press had for a time almost made him despair and "doubt whether it was possible to work down the slanders which had multiplied." Now, he thought there were no misgivings in Washington, where he said he was considered one of the best civilian brigadier generals. Still, he complained, unnamed West Point–trained generals (like Benham) were getting all the publicity, "while doing nothing."[45]

The "Pathfinder" and the "Stonewall"

During that winter and spring, the war news brightened for the Union. In the West, in addition to Buell's success in eastern Kentucky, Ulysses S. Grant's victories in February at Fort Donelson and Fort Henry boosted Northern morale. At Shiloh the two armies fought their first major battle, which paved the way for Union forces to take Corinth in late May. In late April 1862 Admiral David Farragut's fleet took control of New Orleans, leading to Union control of the Mississippi River. In the East, the "Young Napoleon," who had become general-in-chief, moved ahead on his Peninsula campaign.

Cox told Helen in late February, "I chafe at being kept here when such glorious work is being done." His mood was likely brightened on March 11 when Lincoln gave John C. Fremont command of the new "Mountain Department" of western Virginia. Cox presumed that this major political figure would be given significant responsibilities. He wrote Helen, "Most of us hail it with pleasure in the belief that it means work and that we shall not be left idle. . . . The expectation is that considerable reinforcements will be brought in the department. . . . This is what I hope."

Fremont had been given an important military position in Missouri early in the war, but he performed poorly and was fired by Lincoln in November. That decision became a cause célèbre in Republican circles, and it was a major motivating force for the creation of the Joint Committee on the Conduct of the War. Under pressure from that committee and others, Lincoln decided to reappoint Fremont to the newly created position. As part of the reorganization, Cox was given command of the 10,000 men stationed along the Kanawha and Ohio Rivers.[46]

Fremont's overall objective was to take control of eastern Tennessee, and he proposed to begin with a bold strike into the Shenandoah Valley. He then hoped to take control of the Virginia and Tennessee Railroad, which Fremont knew could bring Confederate reinforcements from Richmond and Petersburg. Once that region was secured, he would attempt to take Knoxville. Cox's role was complementary, and he once again had a degree of autonomy. Paralleling Fremont's advance, he and Colonel George Crook were to move from Gauley Bridge in separate columns down the New River valley while securing the supply line for later advances. Cox was charged with taking the Virginia and Tennessee Railroad at New Bern and destroying the railroad bridge there, after which his and Fremont's forces would be reunited for the advance to Knoxville.

Cox wrote that Fremont's plan, which was based on one Rosecrans had proposed earlier, was "an improvement upon Rosecrans's in arranging for a progressive concentration of his forces into one column." However, Cox later judged, "There was a little too much sentiment and too little practical war in the construction of the Mountain Department out of five hundred miles of mountain ranges, and the appointment of the 'Pathfinder' to command it was consistent with the romantic character of the whole." Moreover, Cox believed that the plan failed to take into sufficient account West Virginia's difficult topography, weather, and the extended supply line. Furthermore, while the Union forces had to march overland through the difficult terrain, the "[r]ailroads east of the mountains ran on routes specially well adapted to enable the enemy quickly to concentrate any needed force at Staunton, Lynchburg, Christiansburg, or Wytheville."[47]

Cox arranged his force of approximately 8,500 effectives so that two West Virginia regiments were left behind at Gauley and Charleston to guard the valley, while his eleven Ohio regiments were the vanguard of the offensive, led by Hayes's 23rd. The latter was optimistic, writing to his uncle on April 8, "It is much pleasanter carrying on the war now than the last campaign. *Now* the people, harried to death by the Rebel impressment of provisions and also of men, welcome our approach." Facing little Confederate resistance, by early May Cox had moved about fifty miles southeast to Flat Top Mountain, and in mid-May Crook took control of Lewisburg to his northeast. Meanwhile, when Fremont learned that he would be facing Thomas J. "Stonewall" Jackson in the Shenandoah Valley, Cox wrote, "Fremont limited our advance until he was ready to open his campaign in the North" to meet the threat.

Nevertheless, Cox once again showed his independent streak and decided to implement his original orders to try to destroy the railroad bridge at New Bern. On May 15 he wrote to Helen, "I shall move forward again in the hope of getting a rap at the rebels who are reported to be waiting for us in considerable force. . . . My advance was made as an experiment to see whether they had the troops which they could spare for this kind of concentration between us & the railroad." Despite significant guerrilla attacks and lack of supplies, Cox moved his headquarters to Princeton to prepare for the attack. A newly appointed commissary sergeant in Hayes's 23rd regiment, twenty-year-old future president William McKinley, did his best to find food for the troops, but with little success. Hayes's men sarcastically called their situation "Camp Starvation" or "Camp Scarce of Crackers."

Cox's gamble failed, in great part because the Confederates who had been guarding the railroad were reinforced, as Cox had feared, by troops sent from Petersburg. In his memoirs, Cox acknowledged that he should not have divided his forces at the beginning of the campaign and should have tried to take the railroad while united with Crook. On May 16 and

17 Cox's forces were hit hard near Princeton by Confederate troops, and he was soon in serious trouble as the Confederates tried to move to his rear. The situation was sufficiently alarming that he ordered a hasty retreat in the early morning on May 18. Hayes wrote in his diary that it was "a very hard day,—muddy, wet, and sultry. Ordered at 3 A.M. to abandon camp and hasten with whole force to General Cox at Princeton." Hayes, who had a pugnacious reputation, added regretfully, "What an error that General Cox didn't attack [Confederate Generals] Williams and Marshall at Princeton! Then we should have accomplished something."[48]

Cox admitted to Helen that his forces had been under a severe attack. He wrote, "[T]here was a portion of the time ... when I fully expected that was to be my last day on earth." Putting the best face on this near-disaster, he told her, "Although I have not done precisely what I intended, I have every reason to be satisfied; for we have secured a large portion of this country the rebels controlled before." Downplaying his hasty retreat, he rationalized, "The army itself and Gen. Fremont acknowledge that I have acted wisely and coolly, and have saved my troops by judicious generalship."

Following his withdrawal, Cox telegraphed Fremont that he would have to retire back to Flat Top Mountain, from which point he could still guard the region. Upon hearing from Fremont that he and his men would "be left to [them]selves till the results of the Shenandoah campaign were tested," Cox observed, "[W]e were thus thrown, necessarily, into an expectant attitude." To his east, meanwhile, Fremont continued to lose ground as he met with defeat after defeat at the hands of Jackson. By mid-June his grandiose plan was in tatters and Jackson's reputation was solidified. The only accomplishment of Fremont's campaign was Cox's extension of the line of Union control of West Virginia to Flat Top Mountain. One historian noted that as of July 9, Lee was concerned that "[f]rom every quarter the enemy [was] congregating around" the Confederate troops, in which description Lee included Cox's occupation of nearly all the western counties of Virginia.[49]

Changes in War Policy

The failure of Fremont's initiative paralleled similar negative war news for the Union during the late spring and early summer, which would lead to a change in Union policy. In the West, Union advances on the Mississippi stalled at both Vicksburg and Corinth, and the Confederates soon took the initiative there. In the East, the Peninsula campaign came to naught as

McClellan retreated from the outskirts of Richmond in late June. At the same time, the loud drumbeat of criticism of McClellan from the congressional Joint Committee on the Conduct of the War increased pressure on Lincoln to remove him.

McClellan's lack of success also dramatically increased pressure from Radicals to move away from a conciliatory policy, expand the war's goals, and use harsher methods on civilians: what historians would later call "the hard hand of war." In what would be the most important element of the new approach, on July 13 Lincoln told Secretary of State William Seward that he was committed to issuing an Emancipation Proclamation at an appropriate moment. One historian noted that "the Emancipation Proclamation would be the final step in repudiating the conciliatory policy, and the more stringent policies implemented in 1864 to demoralize the southerners and ruin their economy were designed to detach Southern civilians from their allegiance to the Confederate government."

Cox commented on this trend to Helen in early June: "Everywhere the people seem to be roused to a new determination to do everything that could be asked to sustain the administration," including freeing the slaves. Two years later, however, Cox would regret the results of the hard-line policy, telling Helen, "The evil is the legitimate outgrowth of the hue and cry raised by our Christian people of the North against protecting rebel property &c." As the "war was prolonged, discipline was construed as friendliness to the rebels," he wrote. "I get heart-sick sometimes at seeing such things, & feel as though we mocked heaven in asking a blessing on such scenes of rapine and wickedness."[50]

In other policy changes reflecting the "hard hand," Lincoln replaced McClellan with Henry Halleck as general-in-chief and, in late June, abolished the Mountain Department and named John Pope commander of the new "Army of Virginia." The latter was a collection of the forces that had been under the commands of Fremont, Nathaniel Banks, and Irwin McDowell. Cox told Helen that he had heard rumors that Pope would be his new commander, and he said he hoped this meant a return to an active campaign. When he still received no orders by late June, however, Cox told Helen he was "in great doubt—what is to become of us?" Fearing that he had been forgotten, he forlornly told her, "I wonder if they will think to enquire what has become of my division?" Even as Cox wrote that letter, Pope was in fact trying to discern Cox's whereabouts, because he had no idea where Cox was, for Fremont had taken with him all of his papers, including his message records. One subordinate commander told Pope on June 28 that Cox, "when last heard from, was on Flat Top Mountain."

Cox took the initiative on July 3, writing Pope, "In view of the report that disciplined troops are wanted at the East, I call your attention to the fact that my division is among the best seasoned and oldest troops in the field, and for discipline and drill will compare favorably with any." He wrote again on July 5, but having gotten no answer, he vented angrily to Helen that even as he sought active service, he was being criticized for inaction. He said, "The fact that malicious lying or lying puffery can make or mar a reputation to a great extent is a reason why sensible people despise the whole thing of public life." He later told her, "I venture to say that never before in the history of modern warfare was an instance known in which so important a div. of an army was ignored at headquarters."[51]

Meanwhile, on July 14, Pope, a staunch Republican who had been chosen in part because of his harsher views about the Confederacy, issued a bombastic public letter to his troops that reflected both his politics and his disdain for McClellan and his tactics. He wrote, "I am sorry to find so much in vogue amongst you certain phrases like lines of retreat. . . . Success and glory are in the advance." Pope told Cox after the war that this statement and others like it were written under the de facto dictation of Secretary of War Edwin Stanton to reinvigorate his forces and "condemn McClellan's policy of over-caution in military matters and over-tenderness toward rebel sympathizers and their property." Cox observed, "The statement was made the occasion of a bitter and lasting enmity toward Pope on the part of most of the officers and men of the Potomac army." Pope's statements and McClellan's reaction were examples of the zero-sum game "played" by generals during and after the war for credit and blame. As one observer put it, all too often in this conflict, "[t]he Generals are jealous, ambitious, and little, and want to get a step themselves, so they are willing to see [a competitor for rank and power] pulled down."[52]

A Return to "Real Soldiering"

While he was waiting for orders, Cox had used the time to train his troops. His drilling and instilling of discipline were so effective, he boasted, that "the whole command grew hardy and self-reliant with great rapidity," gaining a capacity for "sustained exertion on foot which proved afterward of great value" in the Maryland campaign. On August 5 Pope and Halleck finally discussed Cox's appeal, and on August 8 Pope ordered Cox with his whole command, nine regiments and about 11,500 troops, east through Virginia to Harrisonburg, then to Charlottesville. Cox, who had become an expert in the military geography of West Virginia, knew that the proposed routing would take at least fifteen days and that Pope might not be at Charlottesville when he arrived. Again showing his willingness to take the initiative and go beyond his orders, he suggested instead using a rail and water route over the Kanawha and Ohio Rivers and taking the B&O Railroad to Washington, which would allow his troops to make the trip in ten days. Pope agreed at first. But then, having heard of a Confederate buildup in West Virginia, he ordered Cox to stay there with a contingent of 5,000 men and to send the rest forward.[53]

Cox was exasperated. He admitted, "[W]e cannot be spared from this country, for it will be overrun if we go out of it," but he wrote huffily to Pope's staff, "I trust it will be possible for the general commanding to reconsider the determination to leave me here." Pope responded positively, and the next day Cox was ordered east with the main contingent on the route he had suggested. On August 14, with some of his men already on their way, Cox left Flat Top Mountain with his "jubilant staff," ready for, he told Helen, "active service in a large column and . . . an opportunity to do some real soldiering." On August 15 he briefed Colonel Joseph Lightburn, who was to take command of the district, and then he rode sixty miles on horseback in twenty-four hours to catch up with his forward contingent.[54]

Cox's prediction that the district would be in peril if he left would come true, in part because Confederate General Jeb Stuart's cavalry had raided Pope's supplies and found copies of Cox's orders and correspondence. A captured quartermaster told Stuart that Cox had been ordered to leave for Washington. On August 23, Lee, pleased that Cox was gone, ordered General William W. Loring to retake the Kanawha valley. Loring would advance on September 6 and soon thereafter would force Lightburn into a precipitate retreat beyond Charleston.[55]

Cox's travel went relatively smoothly, and he told Helen that he was amused when, as he sailed down the Kanawha, a band played a popular song, "Ain't you glad to get out of the wilderness." One historian called the trip "history's first instance of a movement by forced marches, steamboats, and railroad, and it remains a model for smooth planning and smart execution." As Cox noted in his memoirs, it "obtained some importance in the logistics of the war" because it was the model for the movement of two of Hooker's corps to Tennessee in 1863.[56]

Two of Cox's regiments, the 30th and 36th Ohio, under Colonels George Crook and Hugh Ewing, arrived first in Washington and were able to reach Pope's headquarters in Warrenton on August 23. Cox himself and the 11th and 12th Ohio arrived on August 24, but the troops were only sent to Alexandria because of problems with transportation. While he waited for the other troops, including Hayes's 23rd, which arrived on August 26, Cox reported to Halleck and Stanton and began preparing to advance to assist Pope. He told Helen excitedly on August 24, "The general expectation is that a great battle will be fought somewhere near Pope's position before long. I trust the Kanawha division will have the opportunity & the fortune to distinguish itself. . . . Then for home & a long reign of peace."[57]

Assessing the First Campaign

In his memoirs, Cox wrote that the most important requirement for a military leader was "military aptitude." He identified some of the necessary qualities as self-command, courage, presence of mind, decisiveness, and the ability to issue orders that were sufficiently clear to subordinates. During his first campaign, he demonstrated that he possessed many of these characteristics and, moreover, that he could fight and lead men into battle. Furthermore, he played a key role in securing and holding West Virginia for the Union, a signal achievement of which he was justifiably proud.

His "on the job training" was relatively smooth, though not entirely free of errors. Cox knew that his reserved, aloof, and austere mien was different from the gregarious and volatile manner of many professional officers. He judged that treating his men fairly, exhibiting self-control, being decisive, and paying attention to their welfare and morale would earn the respect and confidence of the corps as effectively as traditional hard-line military methods. By the time he was on his way east, he had earned the admiration and respect of his men but not their affection.

Possibly the greatest challenge Cox faced in the early days of the war was the necessity to take risks. By nature, he was cautious and conservative. He was accustomed to making decisions after a thorough consideration of relevant facts. Hasty and impulsive actions were an anathema to him; but in battle, quick analysis of situations and rapid and risky decisions can mean success or failure, and Cox showed initiative at appropriate times during this period. McClellan saw in Cox the potential for leadership and gave him unusual authority early in the war. Cox followed his orders with customary diligence, but after the muddle at Scary Creek, both McClellan and Rosecrans wondered whether he was up to the task. Unlike some army regulars, Cox had not had "all flexibility drilled out of him by routine." So, stung by his commanders' criticism and anxious to make up for the setback and his mistakes, Cox showed his self-confidence and acted on his own discretion. He charged ahead, defeated Wise, and took control of both Charleston and Gauley Bridge. A similar turn of events took place when he again had an autonomous role in Fremont's campaign. After the latter advised him to stay at Flat Top Mountain, Cox continued to try to implement his original orders. That attempt failed, and Cox had to beat a hasty retreat. But he thought the risk was worth taking.

In his memoirs, Cox wrote that he was relieved at not having autonomy after September 1861 because of the far greater responsibilities for such a role. Although yearning for action, he probably realized that, given his cautious nature and inexperience, he was not capable of a higher level of military leadership at that time. Under Fremont he again had autonomy, but on a very limited mission. A few months later, Cox would again find himself required to act autonomously, this time in one of the most important campaigns of the war. In the Maryland campaign, Cox would prove that he was prepared for that responsibility.

3 Citizen-General on the National Stage
The Maryland Campaign

> McClellan rode forward and I accompanied him. . . . The head
> of the column was in sight. . . . Pope and McDowell rode at
> the head. . . . McClellan announced that he had been ordered
> to assume command within the fortifications, and named to
> General Pope the positions the several corps would occupy.
> This done, both parties bowed, and the cavalcade moved
> on. . . . [General John P.] Hatch shouted, "Boys, McClellan is
> in command again, three cheers!" The cheers were given with
> wild delight. . . . Warm friend of McClellan as I was, I felt my
> flesh cringe at the unnecessary affront. . . . Pope lifted his hat in
> a parting salute . . . and rode quietly on.
>
> —Cox, *Military Reminiscences*, 1900

The scene described by Cox in this chapter's epigraph followed the Union
defeat at the Battle of Second Manassas and took place on September 2,
1862, a week after Cox had arrived in Washington.[1] While he had been
traveling, both the war of words between McClellan and Pope and the real
war between Pope's and Lee's forces had reached a fever pitch. Despite his
orders to assist Pope and send his troops to the latter's assistance, McClellan had moved his forces only deliberately. In his letters to his wife at the
time, he said he expected Pope to be defeated. On August 29, echoing
his treatment of Rosecrans at Rich Mountain, McClellan told Lincoln a
choice had to be made: "1st to concentrate all our available forces to open
communication with Pope, 2nd to leave Pope to get out of his scrape & at
once use all our means to make the Capital perfectly safe."[2]

McClellan's lack of support was a significant factor that led to Pope's
defeat at Second Manassas, though Pope's poor generalship was a far more

important reason. Another factor was the inadequate performance of General Fitz-John Porter, McClellan's closest friend in the army and Pope's left wing commander. On August 29, despite having been ordered to participate in the battle, Porter did not move at all. He did, however, take the time to write a snide message to Burnside: "I hope Mac is at work and that we will soon be ordered out of this. . . . [Jackson] was wandering out loose; but I expect they know what they are doing, which is more than any one here or anywhere knows." Burnside forwarded this and other similar messages from Porter to headquarters, which would prove critical later when Porter was court-martialed, convicted, and removed from the army. The relationship among McClellan, Porter, Burnside, and Cox was affected by these events and would be a critical factor in the Maryland campaign.[3]

Again with McClellan

After arriving in Washington, Cox met with Stanton, and he then began planning to advance to assist Pope with his men, the last of whom were to arrive on August 27. But Jackson's raid on Manassas that day cut the railroad connection and communications to Washington. Later that day, Cox's 11th and 12th Ohio regiments, which had arrived earlier, were sent forward without his knowledge to help protect the Bull Run railroad bridge. (That same day Cox's younger brother Theodore unexpectedly came to Washington and asked to be one of his military aides. Cox granted the request.) Anxious not to be left behind and again showing initiative, Cox told Helen, "I took the remaining two & without waiting for anything marched to Alexandria, expecting to get cars there & join the advance." While they waited for transport, two more corps, Edwin Sumner's and William Franklin's, arrived from the Peninsula campaign and were stationed forward of Cox's regiments.

While Cox waited, McClellan arrived at the railroad station; as Cox told Helen, "His view of the case was that the outcome of the enemy's movement was doubtful, that they might succeed in crushing Pope's army & in that case would make an immediate advance on Wash[ington]." McClellan stopped all forward movements and ordered Cox and the others to form defenses for Washington. General Herman Haupt, responsible for rail transport, had proposed to McClellan that Cox's and the other forces be transported to Manassas to assist Pope. But McClellan told him that would be too risky. He later told Halleck that he had contemplated sending Cox's men to Manassas to help Pope but had concluded that "a premature movement in small force [would] accomplish nothing but the destruction of the troops sent out." (He included Sumner's and Franklin's two corps, about 20,000 men, among that "small force.") Haupt wrote later that if he had not met McClellan, he would have sent the troops forward.[4]

Cox told Helen that McClellan had "received [him] with the old cordiality and confidence"; in his memoirs Cox recorded that he and McClellan began daily conversations away from either of their staffs. During these talks, he wrote, "[McClellan] put me at once upon our accustomed footing of personal friendship. . . . I found myself in a circle where he seemed to unbosom himself with freedom." McClellan needed to vent about his travails, and he saw Cox as a nonthreatening, understanding, and supportive colleague, as he had been in the early days of the war.

McClellan was depressed at losing the prestige of a clear and unquestioned leadership role; but, Cox wrote, he spoke of Pope and McDowell "without discourtesy or vilification." McClellan condemned the decision to recall him, arguing that instead he should have been reinforced. He emphasized that it was his duty to strengthen the army when it was given to someone else to command. He added explicitly, Cox said, "If Pope was the man they had faith in, then Pope should have been sent to Harrison's Landing to take command, and however bitter it would have been, I should have had no just reason to complain." Cox's partiality toward McClellan made him assume the latter's statements were accurate. He also used his influence as a loyal Republican to try to "combat the ideas in McClellan's mind that the administration meant to do him any wrong, or had any end but the restoration of National unity in view."

On August 29 McClellan ordered Cox and his four regiments to Forts Ramsay and Buffalo, where they would be part of the capital's defenses. Cox wrote that McClellan "had little expectation that Pope would escape defeat, and impressed upon [Cox] the necessity of being prepared to cover a perhaps disorderly retreat." Later, after it was clear that the Battle of Second Manassas was a Union defeat, Cox told Helen, "There's no blinking the fact that Pope has been whipped. I fear badly whipped." He said there was gossip in Washington and in the army about who was to blame for the Confederate victory. Cox noted ongoing talk that McClellan had deliberately delayed his movement north, while others were saying that McClellan should not have been pulled away from the Peninsula in the first place. Cox wrote that he did not know which of these claims was true, but at the time he was focused on finally being part of a major campaign.

60 He proudly told Helen, "The more I see of other troops, the better I like my own. They have none better here."[5]

On August 31 Cox and McClellan discussed strategy and tactics, focusing on maps of the region and their respective responsibilities should the army be driven back. On September 1 they rode together to Washington, and along the way they passed among troops who cheered McClellan. When McClellan returned for another visit on September 2, Cox noticed "at once a change in his appearance." McClellan's face was animated "as he greeted [Cox] with, 'Well, General, I am in command again!'" Cox congratulated him with "hearty earnestness," stating, "I was personally rejoiced at it. I was really attached to him." McClellan told Cox that Lincoln had put him in charge of Washington's defenses because he was the only one who could bring "organized shape out of the chaos in which everything seemed to be then." Cox was part of that effort, having been ordered on September 2, "[H]old your command ready to cover the retreat of our army." Later that day, Cox accompanied McClellan to meet Pope and McDowell as the latter withdrew to Washington as described in the epigraph at the beginning of this chapter.[6]

Cox's commentary in his memoirs about these meetings reflected his changing view of McClellan over time. Cox pictured himself as a straightforward, dutiful, dedicated subordinate with his eye solely on doing his duty. He emphasized that he took McClellan's word unquestioningly, presuming that their objectives and approach were fundamentally the same and that both were speaking from the heart. Thus, it probably should not have been surprising that after reading McClellan's autobiography, including his letters to his wife in which he commented acidly on a variety of topics and people during this period, Cox perceived that McClellan was two-faced. A clearly disillusioned Cox said of the letters and the impression they made, "Their inconsistency with his expressions and manner in conversation, or at least their great exaggeration of what he conveyed in familiar talk, has struck me very forcibly and unpleasantly."[7]

Confederate Flood Tide: Meeting the Threat

After Second Manassas, morale in the Confederacy was sky high, and in the North the images of Lee and Stonewall Jackson as unbeatable warriors began to take hold. Lee reasoned that there might not be a more propitious moment to break Union morale by taking the war to the North. He thought he knew McClellan well enough that it would be several weeks before the Union army would be reorganized. One historian concluded that Lee now believed, "The tide must be taken at the flood, and pressed on to victory." Lee began his movement into Maryland on September 4 with a force of some 55,000 men, and on September 8 he issued an address to the people of Maryland, stating that he had come to "aid [them] in throwing off this foreign yoke." This appeal fell on deaf ears in increasingly pro-Union western Maryland—a rare piece of good news for the North in early September.[8]

On the Union side, the issue of who was to command the army against Lee was up in the air in early September as Pope, McClellan, Halleck, and Stanton engaged in maneuvering and backstabbing. Pope complained loudly about McClellan's failure to support him, and he brought court-martial charges against Fitz-John Porter. Cox noted to Helen, "The general sentiment in regard to the last battles is one of supreme disgust. Misbehaviour is charged upon McDowell, & a want of capacity upon Pope." After Burnside refused to accept the job of overall commander and news arrived of Lee's having moved north on September 4, Lincoln reluctantly asked McClellan to take field command. Cox wrote that it was reasonable for him to do so because McClellan had the support of the troops and was a good organizer. However, he said, "Mr. Lincoln's sacrifice of his sense of justice to what seemed the only expedient in the terrible crisis, was sublime." The situation was further complicated when McClellan was later granted his request that Porter be permitted to join the advance despite the legal cloud over his head. Cox commented, "If the country was to be saved, confidence and power could not be bestowed by halves."[9]

McClellan had a difficult, multifaceted mission. While he had to reorganize the army and find and defeat Lee, he also had to defend Baltimore and Washington. Halleck repeatedly cautioned him about the latter objective, which hampered McClellan's flexibility. Furthermore, as Cox wrote to Helen, "The demoralization consequent upon the recent battles is such that time must be used in reorganizing," among other reasons because the Army of the Potomac had many stragglers, and some 25 percent of the Union troops were unseasoned recruits. Moreover, because of Scott's wrong-headed decisions regarding army organization, the new recruits were not "coming to regts. already well officered, & full of the proper esprit and confidence of veterans." One of Cox's new regiments, the 16th Connecticut, would prepare for real action for the first time on September 16. Finally, whereas Lincoln saw the objective of the campaign as defeating and destroying Lee's army, McClellan saw his goal as stopping the invasion, saving Baltimore and Washington, and throwing Lee "back across the Potomac [River]."[10]

McClellan's army of some 85,000 was divided into three "wings." The left was commanded by Franklin and consisted of his own 6th AC plus another division. The center was under Sumner, whom McClellan had characterized as "even a greater fool than I had supposed," and it contained the 2nd and 12th ACs. Burnside commanded the right wing, which included his 9th AC, now under Jesse Reno, and Hooker's 1st AC. Cox's troops, dubbed "the Kanawha Division," were assigned to the 9th AC, and Cox was the latter's highest-ranking officer after Reno. Cox first met Burnside on September 6, and the two quickly established a good working relationship. Cox said Burnside had a "winning smile, cordial manners, sincerity, truthfulness, honorable character, and devoted patriotism." However, eventually Cox "learned to understand the limitations of [Burnside's] powers and the points in which he fell short of being a great commander." Among those limits was his unsystematic approach to routine matters.[11]

Citizen-General to the Forefront: Lee Divides, McClellan Multiplies

Cox's Kanawha Division led the advance of the 9th AC on the march to Leesboro, and during this movement they marched in beautiful weather through rolling hills with a "park-like landscape," in sharp contrast to the rugged countryside of West Virginia and its rain and mud. Cox was "shocked at the straggling" he saw among the other forces, and he proudly stated that there were no stragglers in his division. He boasted to Helen, "[M]y command has a high reputation & we are gaining the very advantage I foresaw from the comparison with other divisions." Hayes agreed, writing, "The Grand Army of the Potomac appeared to bad advantage by the side of our troops."[12]

Cox and the other forces moved forward deliberately, six to eight miles a day on a thirty-mile-wide arc, from September 8 to September 11. Given his manifold responsibilities and his uncertainty about Lee's whereabouts, McClellan's caution was understandable. Cox wrote to Helen unsympathetically about the slow pace, "It is entirely uncertain where we are to go, or what we are to do ... & we may have a wild goose chase." But then, checking himself, he said, "As I am not now in a condition to know all that is known at Hd. Qrs., it is hardly worth while to speculate." Cox was prophetically critical of the cavalry's performance, commenting that it "did not succeed in getting far in advance of the infantry, and very little valuable information was obtained."[13]

On September 11 the pace quickened, and Cox was ordered to take the lead in the march to Frederick the next day. It was just before this part of the advance that Cox learned another valuable lesson. At New Market he was overtaken by Reno and his staff, who engaged in an informal "review" of Cox's men. The latter, Cox recalled, "had been so long in the West Virginia mountains at hard service" that they marched with solid discipline and strength. Cox "had the pleasure of hearing their [the other generals'] involuntary exclamations of admiration. . . . The easy swinging step, the graceful poise of the musket on the shoulder . . . were all noticed and praised with a heartiness which was very grateful to my ears." A general standing next to him said, "I thought you said your division was passing." When Cox replied that it was, the other general, dubious that a citizen-general could lead such a disciplined cadre, replied, "Not by a d——d sight, those are regulars." Burnside smiled and answered, "Cox is right, those are his men." As Cox's aide put it later, "[O]ur division is the corps d'elite. . . . [W]e feel as proud as peacocks."[14]

From September 12 to September 14, the Kanawha Division would be the lead element of the army's advance into Frederick and onto South Mountain. One likely reason was that McClellan's soul-searching sessions with Cox had renewed the commander's confidence in Cox's ability. On September 13 Cox wrote, "McClellan himself met me as my column moved out of town (Frederick)." The impressive show the division put on for Reno and Burnside had also demonstrated the Kanawhans' discipline and strength. Another reason may have been an incident early in the movement into Maryland that involved two of Cox's subordinate colonels, Hayes and Hugh Ewing, the latter of whom would later play an unexpected role in Cox's political-military future.

That day Hayes's men were gathering wood and straw from a farmer's fields when Reno rode into their camp and accused them of thievery, calling them, "You damned black sons of bitches!" Hayes testily told Reno that he hoped the latter would be as energetic in treating his foes as he was in treating his friends. Reno felt insulted, but Hayes assured him he had not wanted to cause any offense. After Ewing went to Cox to complain about Reno's language, Ewing wrote in his diary, "Cox did not fancy taking exception to the conduct of his commander." Ewing, who had a reputation as a hothead, went to Reno himself. Reno told him that he did not remember using profanity but apologized if he had done so. Then Reno added, "I suppose you think your troops better than those of the East. . . . I will put you in the lead in the march, and the coming battle, and we will see what your men can do." Cox's account noted that Reno only said that Hayes had referred the matter to Cox, who dismissed the incident as having no significance.[15]

On his campaign, Lee hoped to live primarily off the land, though the Union garrison and arsenal at Harpers Ferry stood in the middle of his supply line. On September 9, confident that any threat from McClellan was many days off, Lee issued his famous Special Orders no. 191, a grandiose gamble dividing his forces to attack Harpers Ferry from three directions. General James Longstreet was ordered to move the remainder of the forces to Hagerstown, leaving General D. H. Hill and 5,000 men at South Mountain as a rear guard. Meanwhile, McClellan accurately saw that the Harpers Ferry garrison's position was hopeless, and he asked Halleck to abandon it and send the troops to him before the Confederates surrounded the city. Halleck refused at first, and he and regional commander General John Wool ordered depot commander Colonel Dixon Miles to hold out as long as possible. Miles, who had been assigned to this post after having been accused of being intoxicated at First Manassas, doggedly obeyed those misguided orders.[16]

On September 9 McClellan's cavalry commander, General Alfred Pleasonton, had reported that Lee had approximately 110,000 men in Maryland. McClellan, believing that he was facing "a gigantic rebel army," told Halleck, "I am pretty well prepared for anything except overwhelming numbers." McClellan reported on September 11 that there were not less than 120,000 Confederate forces, and he asked that Porter's 5th AC be sent to him to help meet that challenge. Halleck agreed and belatedly put the Harpers Ferry troops under McClellan's command. With Porter, McClellan would have just under 100,000 men under his command; Lee would have under 50,000 effectives.[17]

Cox's analysis of McClellan's tendency to overestimate enemy numbers and the effect of these erroneous estimations on his decisions is an important source for this aspect of the war. Cox wrote that McClellan "had taught the Army of the Potomac to believe implicitly that the Confederate army was more than twice as numerous as it was in fact. . . . [I]t was natural that they should admire the generalship which had saved them from annihilation. . . . McClellan's estimates of Lee's army were absolutely destructive of all chances of success." Cox added, "[M]y predilections in favor of McClellan made me assume [at the time] that his facts were well-based." He believed that part of the problem was McClellan's "blundering spy-system"; but he pointed the finger of fault most directly at McClellan himself, stating that based on the evidence, "It is almost incredible that he should be deceived, except willingly."[18]

Frederick and South Mountain: The "Lost Order" and Lost Opportunities

One of the few examples of McClellan's getting and heeding reasonably good intelligence came on September 12. Having learned that Lee's forces were moving in separate columns, McClellan advised Washington, "I feel perfectly confident that the enemy has abandoned Frederick moving in two directions, viz. on the Hagerstown and Harper's Ferry roads." McClellan optimistically speculated to his wife, "From all I can gather secesh is skedaddling & I don't think I can catch him unless he is really moving into Penna. . . . He evidently don't want to fight me—for some reason or other."[19]

Cox was unsure of the situation in Frederick as he led the advance on September 12. This was going to be his first combat experience on the new campaign, so he approached the city carefully. One of his men wrote, "Before making the charge, General Cox rode up to our regiment and told us to keep up the reputation of the 11th Ohio volunteers." Then a young officer from the 9th AC headquarters rode up to Cox and de-manded to know why he was not moving faster, since "there's nothing there!" Cox rebuked him for his impertinence, but the officer gave one of Cox's brigade commanders, a German American colonel named Augustus Moor, the same message. Cox was astonished when Moor "dashed ahead at a gallop, with his escort and the gun." Within a few minutes, Moor ran into the Confederate rear guard, and he was captured. Cox ordered his other troops, primarily the 11th Ohio, to fix bayonets and charge, and they quickly took control of the city.

Lee had expressed concern in his Special Orders no. 191 that the peo-ple of Frederick would refuse to "open their stores" to his army. By con-trast, when Cox and his men entered the town, "the windows were filled with ladies waving their handkerchiefs and the national flag, whilst the men came to the column with fruits and refreshments." One of Cox's men wrote later that they were "treated to cakes, pies, bread, coffee, peaches." Cox noted, "[I]n fact the citizens did all they could for us." Reporting the

66   good news, McClellan said that his strategy continued to be to chase after Lee if he intended to go to Pennsylvania, but if Lee retreated back over the Potomac River, to try to cut him off.[20]

On September 13, while most of the army stayed in place, Cox again took the advance, leading his division and others of the 9th AC in reconnaissance behind Pleasonton's cavalry toward the city of Middletown. They crossed Catoctin Mountain without opposition, though Pleasonton's movements were noted by Jeb Stuart's cavalrymen and reported to Lee. That evening Cox and his men encamped outside Middletown near the base of South Mountain, and they planned to continue their reconnaissance the next day.[21]

That same day McClellan was given a copy of Lee's Special Orders no. 191. Having just received a telegram from Lincoln urging him not to let Lee get off "without being hurt," McClellan responded, "I have all the plans of the rebels, and will catch them in their own trap if my men are equal to the emergency. . . . I have the whole rebel force in front of me, but am confident, and no time shall be lost. . . . I think Lee has made a gross mistake, and that he will be seriously punished for it." To Halleck that evening McClellan wrote, "Shall lose no time," adding that he would make "forced marches" but only to rescue the Harpers Ferry garrison. Presuming that Lee had sent only small elements of his army to take Harpers Ferry, McClellan was concerned that the "main rebel army is now before us," meaning in Boonsboro, just over South Mountain. So, he concluded, "Unless Gen. Lee has changed his plans, I expect a severe general engagement tomorrow. . . . I feel confident that I have the mass of their troops to contend with & they outnumber me when united."[22]

The circumstances demanded swift action to take advantage of the divided rebel force, and intellectually McClellan agreed. That evening, he showed an old friend the "Lost Order" and proclaimed, 'Here is a paper with which if I cannot whip Bobbie Lee, I will be willing to go. . . . [I]f you people will only do two good, hard days' marching, I will put Lee in a position he will find hard to get out of. Castiglione will be nothing to it.'" The reference was to Napoleon's 1796 triumph against an Austrian general who had divided his forces. A key to Napoleon's success was that he acted swiftly.[23]

In Cox's assessment, however, "The value of time was one of the things McClellan never understood. He should have been among the first in the saddle at every step in the campaign after he was in possession of Lee's order of the 9th, and should have infused energy into every unit in his army."

Instead, other than Cox's advance, McClellan took no action to send troops forward until September 14. Cox lamented that if his men had "been ordered to be at the top of South Mountain before dark [i.e., on September 13], they could have been there. . . . When the leisurely movement of the 14th began, McClellan himself, instead of being with the advance, was in Frederick till after 2 PM. . . . Twenty-four hours, as it turned out, was the whole difference between saving and losing Harper's Ferry"; but McClellan "did not call upon his men for any extraordinary exertion."[24]

On the Confederate side, too, September 13 was an important date. Lee's ambitious schedule for taking Harpers Ferry by September 12 had stalled. Then Stuart reported Pleasonton's activity and Cox's setting up camp in Middletown, information that undercut Lee's judgment about McClellan. In response, Lee ordered Longstreet to assist Hill, who was responsible for protecting all possible approaches through South Mountain. At that point, Hill wrote later, because Lee's forces were divided, "my little force could be brushed away," but only by a swiftly moving, confident enemy.[25]

The Battle of South Mountain, a Tactical Triumph

Hill wrote later, "The battle of South Mountain was one of extraordinary illusions and delusions." He meant that McClellan was acting under the illusion of a major force in front of him and the Confederates, through skillful maneuvers, deluded the Union forces into "believing the whole mountain was swarming with rebels." On the morning of September 14, McClellan thought the main force of the enemy was still at Boonsboro and numbered at least 60,000 there. Cox wrote, "McClellan's orders and correspondence show that he did not expect a battle at South Mountain or east of it" that day. As a result, Cox saw his objective only as reconnoitering, aimed at establishing a position atop the mountain for further advances. So he first sent ahead Colonel E. P. Scammon's brigade of about 1,500 men and kept Crook's, with an equal number, behind in reserve. Hooker's 1st AC was ordered to parallel Cox's advance to the north; but having stayed put on September 13, they were twelve miles away.[26]

As Cox rode forward early in the morning, he was startled to meet Colonel Moor, who explained that he had been paroled. When Cox told him Scammon was doing a reconnaissance on the mountain, Moor exclaimed, "My God! Be careful!" Then, he stopped and said, "But I am paroled!" and turned away. Cox could only conclude that a large

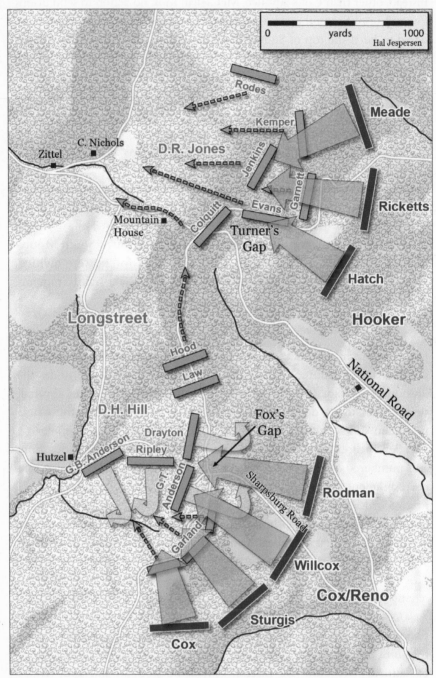

Map 2. The Battle of South Mountain, September 14, 1862. (Map by Hal Jespersen)

Confederate force was atop the mountain. He did not ask for new orders before moving. Instead, showing confidence in himself and his men and sure of McClellan's confidence, he took the initiative. He ordered his men to advance, called Crook's brigade forward, and sent a messenger to ask Reno for reinforcements. Unfortunately, as one historian noted, McClellan "had not shared the finding of the Lost Order with his senior generals and his orders for the day carried no particular urgency, and Burnside and Jesse Reno . . . had not hurried the rest of the corps forward." Nor did Reno move swiftly to send the reinforcements. That mistake was compounded when the first group of reinforcements misunderstood its orders, delaying its arrival.[27]

Presuming accurately that the bulk of the rebel force was covering Turner's Gap on the National Road, Cox decided to do a turning movement via Fox's Gap to the south. He and his men found that while South Mountain was just a large hill compared to the craggy mountains they had experienced in West Virginia, it was rough-hewn and replete with trees, brush, and boulders. Further, the Confederates would have the advantage of being on the defensive. On the way to the top, Cox's men met heavy resistance from a Confederate force under General Samuel Garland. After several minutes of exchanging fire, as Cox dramatically told Helen, "[t]he ridge was carried by two bona fide charges with the bayonet—no paper charges, but the cold steel was in steady line as our men rushed forward, & the rebels broke when the bayonets were within three yds. of them. . . . [T]he Ohio boys were the victors." Cox's aide Bascom said, "Twas maddening, and we were not men, but demons incarnate." Over the next three hours, Cox advanced to the top of the mountain, though he received significant resistance in the wooded terrain, which made visibility difficult. During this engagement, Hayes was seriously wounded.[28]

At about noon, after four hours of intense fighting, Cox decided "it was time to rest." Though he had made significant progress, his men were tired and the rebels seemingly held a strong position, keeping up their artillery fire. Cox also hoped reinforcements would arrive soon, and Confederate prisoners had told him Longstreet was en route. Further, his "line was pretty thin," and if the mountain-savvy Kanawha Division found this fighting difficult, it clearly was. Cox wrote that at that moment "[t]he two Kanawha brigades had certainly won a glorious victory [and] . . . it would be folly to imperil it." In fact, the victory would come later, after several more hours of fighting.[29]

Cox did not write about another likely reason for his inaction: the illusion of the number of Confederate forces. Like everyone else, he had relied on McClellan's assessment of the size of the rebel army, and Moor's "warning" reinforced that impression. Lacking confidence and fearing failure, he decided not to take a risk, instead taking the success he had and resting on his laurels. Not for the first time, McClellan's chimeras were a barrier to Union success; but Cox's uncertainty also played a role.

Hill alleged that after Cox wiped out Garland's forces and scattered the others, "there was nothing to oppose him." Hill wrote that he had created an imaginary force consisting of "a line of dismounted staff-officers, couriers, teamsters, and cooks . . . behind the guns to give the appearance of battery supports." As a result, "under the strange illusion that there was a large Confederate force on the mountain, the Federals withdrew to their first position in the morning to await the arrival of the other three divisions of Reno's corps." Cox disputed Hill's version, noting that the rebel "brigades were all on the mountain summit within easy support of each other." He added that for the first hours of fighting, Hill had 5,000 men to his 3,000 and that Stuart's cavalry was in the area. Cox wrote, "With less than half the numerical strength which was opposed to it, therefore, the Kanawha division had carried the summit . . . and had held the crests they had gained."[30]

Not until about 2 p.m. did the first reinforcements arrive, even as Hooker's 1st AC was deploying to the north and Longstreet was arriving to deter Hooker. Finally reinforced, Cox and his men pushed ahead after 3 p.m., but they met considerable resistance. At 4 p.m., Cox wrote, "The order came to advance the whole line, so as to complete the dislodgement of the enemy from the remaining summit." To the east and north, the four men who would command the Army of the Potomac were in action. With McClellan observing, Burnside had ordered Hooker and his subordinate George Meade to parallel Cox's advance and try to outflank the Confederates. Hooker and Cox made slow but significant advances through the afternoon as the rebels begrudgingly but inevitably gave way. Around sunset Reno rode up to urge the men forward; he congratulated Ewing on achieving his boast about the Kanawha men. Moments later, Reno was shot and killed, and his death made Cox de facto commander of the 9th AC. Burnside ordered an assault late in the day in the center through Turner's Gap, but it was easily repulsed.

After dark, the worn and outnumbered Confederates retreated on all fronts as a result of the Union's significant tactical success. However, because of mistakes by McClellan, Burnside, and Reno, South Mountain was not the "stunning operational victory" McClellan had hoped for; and "the opportunity to divide Lee and crush him in detail" slipped away. Nevertheless, historian David Hartwig noted, "Thanks to Jacob Cox's early initiative and aggressive generalship, McClellan had nearly won Fox's Gap and Turner's Gap cheaply and early in the day."

In his report, dated November 17, at a time when he was intriguing to replace Burnside as commander of the Army of the Potomac, Hooker claimed that South Mountain's "principal glory will be awarded to the First Corps." He reported that Cox's men had retreated. A clearly irritated and angry Cox wrote in his memoirs that Hooker's report reflected the latter's "characteristic efforts to grasp all the glory of the battle at the expense of truth and of honorable dealings with his commander and his comrades. . . . Nothing is more justly odious in military conduct than embodying slanders against other commands in an official report." Hooker's comments may also have reflected the fact that, as Cox told Helen, "there is much jealousy of western troops in the army of the Potomac. . . . [O]ur men are a good deal indignant that fuller credit is not given to the Kanawha division for the South Mountain battle. It had not only the advance, but had practically won the battle before the supports came up."[31]

Both McClellan and Lee judged that South Mountain had been a Union victory, and for a short period, both believed it was a significant one. Lee concluded that it was so great a setback that, begrudgingly, he decided to abandon his grand venture to the north. When he later heard from Jackson that he could take Harpers Ferry on September 15, Lee reversed himself. For his part, McClellan spent the morning of September 15 sending the news to Washington of the "glorious victory." He reported that Hooker had allegedly learned that "the enemy [was] making for Shepherdstown in a perfect panic," presumably on the way back to Virginia. He assured Halleck, "I am hurrying everything forward to endeavor to press their retreat to the utmost" and asserted that "the *morale* of our men is now restored." For the moment, McClellan thought he had achieved everything he could have wanted: a defeat of "Bobbie Lee," a Confederate retreat back to Virginia, and minimal fighting and loss of life. On September 16 Lincoln wrote McClellan, "God bless you, and all with you; destroy the rebel army if possible."[32]

Cox was overjoyed, telling Helen on September 16, "We were completely victorious, the enemy retiring hastily leaving us in possession of the field." Intensely proud of his men and their achievements, he said, "All the tedious work in western Virginia has not been wholly lost. I have made some good soldiers. The div. has done credit to itself, & given me some reputation, & and all in a few weeks, almost a few days active work after taking position in the old Army of the Potomac. . . . They say we are covered with glory. . . . Gen. McClellan & Gen. Burnside both specially congratulated me on the success. Gen McC came to me yesterday in the field, in the presence of a number of his staff & chief officers . . . and said we had done magnificently." He added, "The rebels are retreating & we are following up."[33]

Command Confusion: Porter as a "Hostile Influence"

On September 15 and 16, despite the Union victory, the only military activity of consequence was by a Confederate army that had suffered a significant defeat at South Mountain. The Confederate forces under Jackson and Lafayette McLaws took Harpers Ferry on the morning of September 15; Lee and Longstreet hurried their battered forces toward Sharpsburg, where they set up a defensive line between Antietam Creek and the Potomac River. Their ranks were enhanced by the arrival of Jackson's troops on September 16, and McLaws marched overnight from Maryland Heights to Antietam from midnight to 7 a.m. on September 17. A. P. Hill was ordered to secure Harpers Ferry and then to make his way to Sharpsburg as soon as he could on September 17.

On the Union side, on the morning of September 15, for the first of two times on this campaign, McClellan's forces were within sight of retreating Confederates and did little. McClellan may have thought there was no need for hurry, because of the reports that Lee was retreating into Virginia, which achieved the key objective as McClellan saw it. He did order each of his commanders to move rapidly forward. The ultimate impacts, however, were a slow advance and considerable repositioning, in part because that morning McClellan had ordered a major restructuring of his "wing" configuration and its command elements, and effecting the new arrangements took time.[34]

The "wing" structure had been made at Lincoln's direction, but McClellan was not happy with it, since it constrained his flexibility. He had not formally announced that arrangement to his forces until September 14. Then, less than twenty-four hours later, after the battle of South Mountain, he issued the new order. Hooker's 1st AC was removed from

Burnside's authority and put directly under McClellan, so Burnside's wing would consist only of the 9th AC.[35] Ironically, Burnside's dividing his command by ordering Hooker to the north at South Mountain may have planted in McClellan's mind the idea of having the two corps operate separately. Cox believed that another factor leading to this change was that the wily Hooker had been intriguing for greater independence. Cox wrote that "Burnside spent several hours with his chief on Monday morning [September 15], and was disturbed and grieved" about this change. His two corps had just won a solid victory at South Mountain, so he could only be startled that McClellan was significantly reducing his authority. But McClellan was unyielding.

While there can be debate about the wisdom of McClellan's decision, Cox was adamant in his memoirs that on the morning of September 15, "[i]t was perfectly easy to advance from South Mountain upon Sharpsburg, keeping Sumner's and Burnside's commands intact. The intermingling of them was unnecessary at the beginning, and was mischievous during the battle of Antietam." Moreover, while he had pointed the finger at Hooker for encouraging McClellan to make the change, Cox emphasized also that "the history of the whole year makes it plain that the reasons were personal" for McClellan's decision.

What he meant was that the arrival of Fitz-John Porter and his 5th AC on September 14 set in motion "circumstances which point to Porter as the hostile influence which becomes so manifest at McClellan's headquarters" against Burnside. In his memoirs Cox wrote, "[T]hat Porter should be unfriendly to Burnside was not strange, for it had by this time become known" that Porter's caustic messages about Pope in late August were seen as proof of Porter's "hostile and insubordinate spirit in that campaign." Burnside had passed on Porter's comments, which would be used as evidence in his court-martial, and "Porter, not unnaturally held him responsible for part of his peril."

Cox painted a picture of Fitz-John Porter as an éminence grise wreaking revenge on Burnside independently and by influencing McClellan, though with the knowledge that McClellan was thinking along the same lines. That is, he wrote that McClellan's decision to diminish Burnside's authority resulted also because "it needed a more magnanimous nature than McClellan's proved to be to bear the obligation of Burnside's personal friendship in securing for him again the field command of the army." While Cox did not allege that this was a conspiracy, he did, in lawyer-like fashion, compile circumstantial evidence that could lead to that conclusion. Cox's writing about this issue in his memoirs would create a fundamental and controversial element of Civil War memory.[36]

For Cox the most important impact of the command change was that Burnside had direct authority over only the 9th AC. Furthermore, Hooker's 1st AC would be stationed on the extreme right of the Union forces, while the 9th AC was to be on the extreme left, several miles away. To Burnside, this meant that by military practice as a wing commander, he could not limit himself to commanding only the 9th AC, since doing so would diminish his authority and prestige. In response, he began to ponder creating for his forces a revised and distinctive command structure, one in which Cox would have vastly increased responsibility.

As the advance in the center and right lumbered forward, Franklin's forces on the left at Crampton's Gap took a decidedly dilatory approach. He later noted that his "corps remained stationary without orders from McClellan until the evening of the 16th, when [he] was ordered to march the next morning to join the army and to send [General Darius] Couch's division to occupy Maryland Heights." In his report McClellan said he ordered Franklin to "protect our left and rear until the night of the 16th." In that regard, McClellan made no provision for protecting the left flank after September 16 other than via Couch's march. The fact that the latter could not protect the left against attacks farther to the west (that is, from the other side of the Potomac River) does not seem to have been something McClellan considered. Furthermore, McClellan never explained what Couch was supposed to do after his "occupation," Harpers Ferry having already fallen. Couch would march to and stay at Maryland Heights until late on September 17.[37]

Cox's judgment of Porter's role in harming both the Union cause and Burnside was based not only on the change in command structure but also on his interpretation of his own movements and orders after the Battle of South Mountain. On the morning of September 15, Cox's men, who had borne the brunt of the fighting and needed rest and rations, were ordered to stay in place, bury their dead, and send their wounded and prisoners to Middletown. McClellan apparently did not know that Cox was staying put. He had ordered Burnside to move all of his forces ahead cautiously toward Porterstown and Sharpsburg but not to take any wagons except for ammunition and ambulances, implying that Burnside should move more rapidly than usual. He ordered some divisions of Porter's 5th AC to follow Cox's.

When Porter arrived at Fox's Gap at about noon on September 15, he found Cox's men blocking his movement. He was irritated, and he ordered his troops to pass by. When Cox finally received orders to march at noon, he found in turn that "the way was blocked by Porter's corps, which was moving to the front by the same road." Cox wrote defensively, "It is possible that [Burnside's] preoccupation of mind [because of the decisions McClellan had made that morning] made him neglect the prompt issue of orders for moving the 9th AC, though I know nothing definite as to this." He added that Burnside had taken responsibility for allowing Cox's men to eat before marching ahead, and McClellan wrote in his memoirs that he had received an explanation from Burnside along those lines. Burnside's lack of prompt action could also have reflected his unsystematic style. No matter the reason, Porter's pique was understandable, though Cox did not admit this.[38]

Cox wrote, "General Porter reported at McClellan's headquarters that the movement of his troops was obstructed by Burnside's, and got at his own special push by them." Porter also took the unusual step of having McClellan's staff write him a formal message stating, "General McClellan desires me to say that Burnside's corps has not yet marched. Should the march of [General George] Sykes's division be obstructed by Burnside's troops, direct General Sykes to push by them, and to put his division in front." This reprimand, issued at 12:30 that day, is followed immediately in the Official Records by an unusual document, an "endorsement" by Porter, stating, "Burnside's corps was not moving three hours after the hour designated for him, the day after South Mountain, and obstructed my movements. I, therefore, asked for this order, and moved by Burnside's corps. F.J.P." Cox caustically commented in his memoirs, "The written order Porter preserved, and put upon it an endorsement adding to what it contains an accusation."

Cox wrote that there were always delays in such large movements and that McClellan had chastised other officers for not moving rapidly enough, but he had not made a record of those cautions. Cox, who had a firm understanding of military law and procedure, emphasized that normal practice would have been for a commander to wait for an explanation from a subordinate before putting such a reprimand on the record. Issuing it on the spot would, he averred, "to military men . . . be almost conclusive proof of a settled hostility to him. . . . [T]he ordinary reply to it would have been a demand for a court of inquiry." He believed, therefore, that these

76   two documents were among the strongest pieces of evidence of Porter's malice, especially because Burnside would not have known of the "endorsement." He wrote, "[T]he significant thing in this one was the pains taken to 'make a record' of it against Burnside," especially the addition of Porter's "endorsement."[39]

Setting the Stage for Antietam

The afternoon of September 15 saw the Union forces assembled between Boonsboro and Keedysville, a few miles from Sharpsburg. There, the cavalry reported, Lee had not retreated but rather was forming a defensive line on Antietam Creek. Probably banking on McClellan moving deliberately, Lee had only about 15,000 men on the line that afternoon and was vulnerable to an overwhelming defeat. McClellan faced him with some 60,000 men, with another 15,000 under Franklin a few miles away. Lee did his best to persuade an already-wary McClellan that he had a larger force, ordering his artillery and sharpshooters to keep up a sporadic but irritating fire.

In the late afternoon, McClellan set up his headquarters in Keedysville, from which he could see, about two miles away, parts of the Confederate line. Cox and Burnside arrived soon afterward, and they saw McClellan "surrounded by a group of his principal officers, most of whom," Cox wrote, "I had never seen before. I rode up with General Burnside, dismounted, and was very cordially greeted by General McClellan. He and Burnside were evidently on terms of intimate friendship and familiarity. [McClellan] introduced me to the officers I had not known before, referring pleasantly to my service with him in Ohio and West Virginia, putting me on an easy footing with them in a very agreeable and genial way."

The group began studying the topography and discussing troop placement but quickly became a target for the Confederates as shells began to fall nearby. McClellan ordered every general but Porter to leave for their own safety while the two of them continued the reconnaissance. It apparently never occurred to McClellan that, as one historian put it, "ordering his two former wing commanders off the ridge while he kept Porter with him struck others as improper, as well as a deliberate slight to the officers he shooed off. Surely it did nothing to enhance the army's unity of command." Lincoln had warned McClellan about complaints from senior officers that he consulted only with Porter or Franklin, and this decision could be seen as yet another insult to Burnside.[40] Nevertheless, the fact that McClellan and Burnside appeared to Cox to be on friendly terms would seem to indicate that McClellan either was not aware of the day's reprimands or did not think they were of major consequence.

As he left the gathering, Cox was pulled aside by his former colleague in the Ohio Senate, Colonel Thomas Key, McClellan's legal and political adviser, who was, according to Cox, "regarded by many as McClellan's evil genius." Key "plunged eagerly into the history of his own opinions since we had discussed the causes of the war in the legislature." Key said he had modified his views about slavery and was now satisfied that the war must end in abolition "if doing so would help our cause." Cox added that the evolution of McClellan's views on slavery and emancipation matched Key's, reflecting the latter's considerable influence.[41]

On the morning of September 16, McClellan wrote to Halleck that he had refrained from attacking on September 15 because by the time the "troops had arrived in force, it was too late in the day." His hope that Lee had retreated not having been fulfilled, he added, "This morning a heavy fog has prevented our doing more than to ascertain that some of the enemy are still there. Do not yet know in what force. Will attack as soon as the situation of the enemy is developed." Once the fog cleared, having promised fast action, McClellan wasted time by doing his own staff work, as he on occasion had done in West Virginia and on the Peninsula. He methodically rode the lines, reconnoitered the potential battlefield, assessed his forces, and gave orders about deployments. Cox wrote that while McClellan's meticulous preparations were ongoing, "Lee was straining every nerve to concentrate his forces and to correct what would have proven a fatal blunder in scattering them, had his opponent acted with vigor."

In his memoirs Cox pointed to an event on September 16 related to the positioning of the 9th AC as additional evidence of Porter's malice against Burnside. After McClellan's reconnoitering, he issued orders to Burnside to change the 9th AC's positions on the line. Cox wrote that headquarters staff officers were sent "to guide each division to its new camp. The selected positions were marked by McClellan's engineers, who then took members of Burnside's staff to identify the locations, and these in turn conducted our divisions." The engineers also told Burnside and Cox that they had found the best fords over Antietam Creek. Cox commented in his memoirs that this micromanagement was typical of McClellan's command. But reflecting his confidence in his own abilities to act independently, Cox wrote that McClellan's approach was disruptive because dependence "upon the general staff for this is to take away the vigor and spontaneity of the subordinate and make him perform his duty in a mechanical way. He should be told what is known of the enemy and his movements . . . and should then have freedom of judgment as to details." But having been implicitly told that he and Burnside were not capable of autonomous action, their response was to carry out their orders and nothing more.[42]

As they were implementing those repositioning orders in the early afternoon, Burnside and Cox were told by one of McClellan's staff that the commander wanted them to halt and wait for further orders. Consequently, not all the original movements had been made by dusk. That evening, McClellan's staff issued another sharp reprimand to Burnside. It rebuked him for not implementing the repositioning orders on September 16, and it repeated the reprimand for delaying his movement from South Mountain on September 15. The document demanded "explanations of these failures." This order, which would not be delivered until early September 17, was unsigned, probably because McClellan was too busy at the time or perhaps because he never saw it or even knew of its existence. More important, Cox noted, since McClellan had specifically told Burnside to wait for further orders, it was illogical for him to criticize Burnside for doing exactly that. Cox concluded, "It is simply incredible that McClellan dictated the letters which went from his headquarters"; in Cox's view, the order could only have been released by the chief of staff if someone in "decisive authority" in McClellan's absence was authorized to speak on his behalf. Cox implied strongly that Porter was the only one with that status.[43]

On the afternoon of September 16, Burnside formally advised Cox of McClellan's changes in the overall command structure and his own decisions as to how that would affect the chain of command in his wing. Cox noted, "Burnside's manner . . . implied that he thought it was done at Hooker's solicitation and through his desire, openly evinced, to be independent in command." Burnside said he would remain wing commander but Cox would continue as 9th AC commander and therefore have de facto command of all of Burnside's troops. Cox objected, noting that he was a comparative stranger to most of the 9th AC and that the latter looked to Burnside as their legitimate commander. He added that his division staff was too small for corps duty and that Reno's staff had left to take their commander's body home. Burnside said Cox could use his wing staff for this purpose, adding that he would help Cox until the campaign was over. Cox had no choice but to accept this peculiar and inefficient arrangement, and he was conflicted about it. On the one hand, he "had no ground for complaint" because he was being given significant authority, and this was another feather in his cap and that of the Kanawha Division. On the other hand, "the position of second in command is always an awkward and anomalous one, and such [he] felt it."[44]

Anticipating a major battle, Burnside described for Cox how they would manage their orders. He said that when he received orders for battle from McClellan, instead of taking action himself, he would immediately hand the orders to Cox to ensure that the chain of command was clear. As Cox told Helen, this peculiar and unique arrangement meant that "it is in fact, nobody but me that [Burnside] is commanding, & through me, the corps." As it turned out, Cox not only became de facto commander of the 9th AC but also co-commander of the left wing of the Union army at the Battle of Antietam.[45]

Confused Planning

McClellan had been reluctant to share his thinking about his military plans, even with Lincoln, Halleck, and Stanton. Thus, it probably was not surprising that, to the detriment of the Union effort, he did not discuss his planning for operations at Antietam with, or seek input from, his subordinates. His suspicions about potential enemies or rivals likely made him leery of meeting with them together. Further, he had not advised them of the discovery of Lee's order, which might have energized them. The most important result of McClellan's decision was that while on the morning of September 17, Burnside, Hooker, Sumner, and Franklin each thought they understood what they individually were supposed to do during the upcoming battle, they had little comprehension of the overall plan or their interrelationship. Because the command structure had just been altered, the commanders' inevitable uncertainty about authority was an additional barrier to Union success. Cox wrote that on the day of the battle, Burnside had no written instructions and was only of the "opinion" that "the part [of] the Ninth Corps was ... to create a diversion ... to prevent the enemy from stripping his right to reinforce his left."[46]

Only McClellan knew his overall plan for Antietam, and even when he explained it in his reports, he put forth two different versions, neither of which was implemented as envisioned, and the second of which was designed to distort history to his benefit. In his preliminary report, he said, "The design was to make the main attack upon the enemy's left—at least to create a diversion in favor of the main attack, with the hope of something more, by assailing the enemy's right,—and as soon as one or both of the flank movements were fully successful, to attack their centre with any reserve I might then have in hand." Hooker and perhaps Sumner would first make a major move, and Burnside and Cox would act as a diversion, presumably by moving simultaneously with the right wing. In this version, the center was almost an afterthought. In his report a year later, McClellan altered the historical record with a new version of the plan that was somewhat closer to reality. He noted that on the left, Burnside and Cox were to move "as soon as matters looked favorably" on the right. He added, "Whenever either of these flank movements should be successful," he would "advance our centre with all the forces then disposable."[47] This made the center a key to success, though only if there were sufficient reserves there.

In neither plan did McClellan address the issue of guarding his flanks. Even though he was the author of the army's cavalry manual, which states that a fundamental objective for cavalry is to guard an army's flanks, McClellan did not so order his cavalry. Nor did he give his left wing commanders, Cox and Burnside, any orders or authority to carry out that function. Thus, the responsibility for the failure to protect the left flank fell completely to the commanding officer. Cox wrote later, "A regiment of horse, watching that flank and scouring the country as we swung forward, would have developed Hill's presence and enabled the commanding general either to stop our movement or to take the available means to support it. The cavalry was put to no such use. It occupied the centre of the whole line."[48]

Meanwhile, Lee remained confident. He was not sure whether McClellan would attack en masse or use flank attacks, but McClellan's caution and ponderous movements gave Lee sufficient time to form his defenses to make the best use of his weak hand. He judged that the topography of the area, the dearth of fords over Antietam Creek, and the presence of only one narrow bridge over the creek on the Union left would make it difficult for the Union left to advance quickly. He was therefore able to achieve his objective by stationing only a few thousand men on his right wing. The most important element of those forces was a small but capable group of about five hundred sharpshooters under Robert Toombs, whose responsibility was to cover the bridge. The commanding position the sharpshooters held high above the bridge buttressed their ability to hold off the Union, despite their small numbers.[49]

One of the reasons why the Union won only a limited victory at Antietam was the uncoordinated sequence in which McClellan decided to fight. On the right, Hooker's 1st AC acted alone at first. He began his assault on the Confederate left at dawn on the seventeenth and engaged in intense and bloody fighting in the infamous "cornfield." An hour or so later, General Joseph Mansfield, who had assumed command of his 12th AC only two days earlier, led his men into the attack to reinforce Hooker. Within minutes, Mansfield was killed, and his advance stalled. Sumner and his 2nd AC on the center-right were not ordered to join the attack until 7:20 a.m., and Cox noted that "by the time he could reach the field, Hooker had fought his battle and been repulsed." Cox bemoaned that if Hooker, Mansfield, and Sumner had been ordered to attack together, "Lee's left must have inevitably been crushed. . . . It is this failure to carry out any intelligible plan which the historian must regard as the unpardonable military fault on the National side."[50]

By 10 a.m., all was relatively quiet on the Union right flank as the two sides seemed to accept a bloody standoff. Sumner was for a time in a state of shock because of the intensity of the fighting and the losses suffered by John Sedgwick's division. Sumner's men later almost breached the Confederate center at "Bloody Lane" between 1 and 2 p.m., but then they stopped, exhausted, not knowing that the rebel line might have been broken with one more attack. Instead, they followed McClellan's order to stand fast. Cox wrote that by about 2 p.m. on the right and in the center, "The aggressive energy of both sides seemed exhausted. . . . There was no fighting later but that on the extreme left, where Burnside's Ninth corps was engaged."

Cox and Burnside's forces waited until late morning for orders to attack. They did receive an order at 7 a.m. to position their men near the bridge and the fords that McClellan's engineers had designated. Having launched that mission, Cox and Burnside rode to a knoll from which they were able to observe the fighting on the right. Cox described "lines of troops advancing . . . and engaging the enemy between us and the East Wood." He went on, "From our position we looked, as it were, down between the opposing lines as if they had been sides of a street. . . . [W]e were tortured with anxiety as we speculated whether our men would charge or retreat."[51]

As Burnside and Cox waited, it appears (though the record is unclear) that the unsigned reprimand of the day before from McClellan's staff arrived at Burnside's headquarters. More than likely, Burnside thought this was his order to advance. Instead, he was startled to read a message from headquarters stating, in part, "I am instructed to call upon you for an explanation of these failures on your part to comply with the orders given you. . . . [T]he commanding general cannot lightly regard such marked departure from the tenor of his instructions." It was an inconceivable moment. In the fever pitch of a major battle, as he was anxiously awaiting orders to launch his attack, the commander of the left wing was distracted by a reprimand that he could only believe meant his commander had lost confidence in him. The situation was worsened when, Cox wrote, an aggrieved Burnside took his attention away from the ongoing battle to write an immediate response. Burnside explained the delay on September 16 but made no comment about the delay on September 15. He said he regretted the "severe rebuke" but affirmed that his cooperation would be "hearty" in following all orders.[52]

At about 9 a.m., Cox wrote, "[o]ne of McClellan's staff rode up with an order to Burnside" to begin his attack to create "a diversion in favor of our hard-pressed right." The order promised that as soon as Burnside's men crossed the bridge, they would "be supported, and, if necessary, on [their] own line of attack." McClellan's messenger later wrote that he had been ordered not only to deliver the instructions but also, in another example of McClellan's lack of confidence, to stay in place until Burnside achieved his objective of crossing the Antietam and was on his way to Sharpsburg. After receiving the order, Burnside began to implement his new chain of command. He immediately turned to Cox, "saying we were ordered to make our attack," and handed him the message.[53]

The issue of when McClellan sent the attack order (in his preliminary report he said it was sent before 10, but he claimed in his autobiography and second report that it was at 8 a.m.) would become a critical element of a political-military conflict in which McClellan and his supporters tried to shift blame for the lackluster Union performance at Antietam to Burnside and, by extension, to Cox. In the Official Records, this document is listed as being sent at "9:10 A.M.," and several minutes would have passed before it could have been delivered. In his report Cox said he got the order at 9, though in his memoirs he went into detail as to why, based on developments he viewed elsewhere on the battlefield at the time, he and Burnside got the order at about 10. He also emphasized that if McClellan had in fact sent an order at 8 a.m., Lee could have been routed.[54]

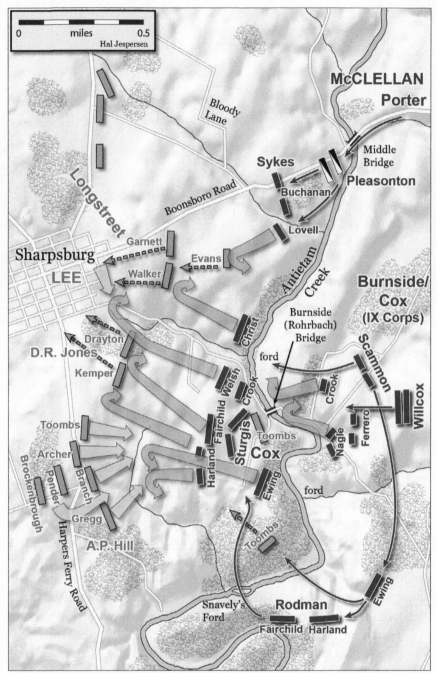

Map 3. The Battle of Antietam, September 17, 1862. (Map by Hal Jespersen)

Figure 2. Kurz and Allison lithograph, *Battle of Antietam,* ca. 1884–93. This stylized portrait of the battle is designed to portray a key moment in the battle, in this case, possibly, Jacob Cox leading the Union troops in the second phase of the battle after they have successfully traversed "Burnside's Bridge," which is in the background. (Library of Congress collection)

Taking the Bridge, Leading the Fight

Burnside's and Cox's preparations for their attack had been neither speedy nor particularly efficient. At 7 a.m., Cox arranged his men according to McClellan's orders. But, probably still chafing at McClellan's staff's insisting that their orders be followed without change and seeing no reason to doubt the advice of McClellan's engineers, neither Burnside nor Cox ordered their men to ascertain the accuracy of the information about the fords. Having been rebuked several times, Burnside apparently felt that initiative was not welcome. Cox, caught in the middle and unsure of what freedom of action he had, focused solely on the task ahead.

The debate over the taking of "Burnside's Bridge" has raged since the day it took place. The bridge itself was only about twelve feet wide, and the Confederate forces on the heights were in a commanding position beyond it, able to shoot attacking forces beneath them with a withering fire.

Moreover, when and if anyone got over the bridge or the creek nearby, he was then facing a steep incline of earth about forty feet high that could not be climbed directly. Cox wrote, "Under such circumstances I do not hesitate to affirm that the Confederate position was virtually impregnable to direct attack over the bridge." While Antietam Creek could be waded at various points, its sides were slippery on both banks and perpendicular to the water; and the Confederates were spread three hundred to four hundred yards on either side of the bridge, making "waders" susceptible to a similar fate. Cox wrote that McClellan "said in his original report, that the task of carrying the bridge was a difficult one."[55]

Given these difficulties, Burnside determined that getting across a ford downstream was to be the primary approach, while others in the 9th AC would attempt to cross the bridge. However, the plan went awry on several fronts. First, Isaac Rodman, the division commander responsible for crossing the creek to the south, discovered that the ford McClellan's engineers had pinpointed was unusable. He found another ford but did not get across until around 1 p.m. The second problem came when Cox ordered the 11th Connecticut to provide cover for an attempt to storm the bridge directly, but the attack was quickly forced back under withering fire. Third, Crook, who was ordered to move on the bridge from the north, took several hours to advance. He later alleged that he had not been briefed about the conditions he would face, although that appears to have been an attempt to cover over his own mistakes. When he finally did advance, he averred, "I had to get a good many men killed in acquiring the information which should have been supplied to me by division headquarters. . . . Such imbecility and incompetency was simply criminal." Crook eventually reached the creek three hundred yards north of the bridge. He was able to get across using a ford he discovered near there at the same time that the bridge was finally taken, around 1 p.m.[56]

McClellan, having seen his attacks at the right and center stalled, nervously sent several messages to Burnside to take the bridge as soon as possible. Burnside and Cox responded with renewed attacks and, not surprisingly, irritation. Burnside told McClellan's staff member Colonel D. B. Sackett, "McClellan appears to think I am not trying my best to carry this bridge, you are the third or fourth one who has been to me this morning with similar orders." Sackett later wrote that at about 1 p.m. Colonel Key rode up to Burnside again to urge him to move quickly and "to take the bridge at the point of a bayonet, if necessary, and not stop for loss of life,

86   as sacrifices must be made in favor of success." Allegedly Key carried with him orders to replace Burnside if he did not move forward immediately.[57]

McClellan had been observing the battle from headquarters throughout the day in the company of Fitz-John Porter. McClellan's aide Colonel David Strother wrote that early in the day, "McClellan was in high spirits. 'It is the most beautiful field I ever saw,' he exclaimed, 'and the grandest battle. If we whip them today, it will wipe out Bull Run forever!' I answered, *fortuna favet fortibus* [fortune favors the bold]." Porter and McClellan sat together, "Porter continually using the glass and reporting observations, McClellan smoking and sending orders. . . . Presently news came that Hooker was wounded, that Mansfield was killed, and that Burnside's progress was unsatisfactory. He took the bridge and said that he could hold it. A message was sent to him that if he could do no more, his command would be transferred to some other work."[58]

The bridge was taken after Cox decided to order a direct attack, sending forward two regiments from Samuel D. Sturgis's division, one from each side of the bridge, accompanied by a heavy artillery barrage. Repulsed at first, the men then sensed a reduction in fire because the rebels were low on ammunition. With one final surge, Cox's men poured across at about 1 p.m., and the two regiments charged across the bridge and up the road in column with fixed bayonets. "Toombs's brigade fled through the woods and over the top of the hill," where they set up a defensive line a half mile away. Rodman and Crook crossed the creek at about the same time.[59]

Events between 1 and 2 p.m. that day were critical for the Union on two fronts. In the center, the rebels had retreated from Bloody Lane, but McClellan had ordered a stand-down. His protégé Franklin, reversing his normally passive approach, concluded accurately that the Confederate center was poorly defended. He appealed to McClellan to make the effort to drive through the Confederate center, and at first McClellan agreed. However, Sumner, possibly still suffering from shock, disagreed, stating that if Franklin attacked and was overwhelmed by the rebels' (imagined) reserves, no one would be able to stop a return assault. McClellan rode to the battlefield for the first time to settle the matter. Fearing defeat more than he thirsted for victory, McClellan wrongly concluded that Sumner, whom he thought to be a fool, had the better of the argument than Franklin, his trusted subordinate. An assault at the time, just after Cox's breakthrough, could have shattered the Confederate army. Instead, McClellan ordered a complete halt in the center by 2 p.m., and that part of the field would remain dormant. Two hours later, several officers would come to the same conclusion as Franklin about the weakness of another section of the Confederate center.[60]

McClellan reported to Halleck at 1:20 p.m., "We are in the midst of the most terrible battle of the war, perhaps of history. . . . I have great odds against me. . . . Burnside is now attacking their right & and I hold my small reserve consisting of Porter's [5th AC] ready to attack the center as soon as the flank movements are developed." The flank movement on the left was slow to develop, however. After crossing the bridge and achieving a foothold on the other side of Antietam Creek, Cox had not charged ahead immediately. Instead, he wrote, "Our first task was to prepare to hold the height we had gained against the return assault from the enemy which we expected." Once again McClellan's chimera of countless rebel reserves led to a halt in Union activity. Exhaustion of his troops and diminished supplies of ammunition also caused Cox to delay.

He ordered forward wagons with the ammunition and more artillery, accompanied by another division of infantry, but it took nearly two hours to get everything arranged, including to pass the men and materiel over the narrow bridge. By 3 p.m., Cox had set up an attacking line of almost three divisions and about 7,500 men facing Toombs and approximately 2,500 more rebel forces just outside the city of Sharpsburg, about a mile away. Rodman's division, backed by a Kanawha Division brigade led by Hugh Ewing, was on the left and was ordered to do a flanking movement. As they began to move forward at 3 p.m. with Cox in direct command, a confident Burnside was counting on the promised reinforcements, which McClellan had just assured Halleck would be forthcoming.[61]

As Cox's forces surged forward, accompanied by artillery fire, they were met by salvos from the defending forces and Lee's superb artillery, but nothing more because Lee had not reinforced his line. A few minutes earlier, A. P. Hill had ridden up and told Lee that his division of some 3,000 men would arrive soon, and Lee gambled both that they would be sufficient to meet the Union offensive and that the rest of the battlefield would continue dormant. Both Hill and Couch heard the fighting at Antietam all day, but neither took the initiative to come north to participate. At 6:30 that morning, Lee ordered Hill to leave Harpers Ferry and come directly and quickly to the battlefield. Couch, unlike Hill, got no new orders until late on September 17, and he continued to "occupy" Maryland Heights all day.

From 3 to 4 p.m., Cox's men and the Confederate defenders engaged in intense fighting. On the right of the Union left's line, Crook's men and others neared Cemetery Hill, and the rebel lines began to give way. To the left, however, there was confusion in Rodman's forces, which included several new brigades, one of which, the 16th Connecticut, had loaded its weapons for the first time the day before. Nevertheless, the preponderance of the Union numbers allowed them to make significant advances, and by around 4 p.m., Union skirmishers were roaming the streets of Sharpsburg. The rebel forces were in desperate straits.

At about 3:45 p.m., Hill's men crossed the Potomac River at Boteler's Ford, which the Union forces had not kept under surveillance. Their advance units were sighted by Union signalmen, but their warning to Burnside did not reach him because he had crossed over the bridge and joined Cox to encourage the advance. Hugh Ewing wrote later that he had sent his cavalry to watch the flank, and they "reported a division coming on us from Harper's Ferry. . . . Notice was immediately sent to Cox, but he had orders to double up the enemy's flank and [Ewing] made a change for that purpose." Ewing would blame Cox for leaving his men at the mercy of A. P. Hill, whose "new troops took [Ewing] in flank." Cox made no reference to this warning in any of his writings, nor is there any corroborating evidence. Ewing did not note this incident in his official report, nor did he mention sending the cavalry detachment to watch for potential flanking movements. Cox told Helen that at that moment "the intense occupation of my mind necessarily withdrew my attention in part from the danger."[62]

The attack by Hill a little after 4 p.m. was, in Cox's perspective at the time, the expected assault from Lee's reserves, and it was decisive. As he said in his report, "The enemy were manifestly in much greater force than ours, and massed their troops heavily on the extreme left." Hill's success was enhanced because his men's advance had been shielded by a large cornfield, and when they were sighted by the Union forces, the latter were deceived for a time because some of Hill's men were wearing blue uniforms stolen from the Harpers Ferry garrison. They also were using weapons and riding horses that they would not have had except for Halleck's and Wool's misguided orders not to withdraw forces from Harpers Ferry.[63]

When Hill's men hit the Union left, the first soldiers they attacked were from the new brigades, who fought well but were forced to retreat. Ewing's brigade helped stem the tide, but there was considerable confusion all along the line, exacerbated by Rodman's death from a rebel bullet.

By 4:30, realizing that he had to effect a turning movement to meet the
onslaught, Cox suspended his advance, though he hoped that the promised reinforcements from McClellan would allow him to renew the attack.
His disappointed men, on the verge of victory, engaged in fierce fighting
with Hill's men as the latter attempted to force the Union men back to
the bridge. Cox told Helen that throughout the afternoon, he "reckoned
very little on [his] chances of coming out whole in life and limb." Despite
McClellan's promise, Cox was not reinforced. But he was able to stem the
Confederate advance a half mile above the bridge. He established a firm
line there that he held until sunset, when both sides ceased firing.

Although Cox and his men hoped to renew the fight on September
18, and Burnside pleaded futilely with McClellan for the reinforcements
for that purpose, they would get no further orders to attack. Cox would
hold his position for two days, and the rebel army retreated over the Potomac River on September 19.[64]

Another General Left to "Get Out of His Scrape" Alone

At about 4 p.m. on September 17, McClellan and Porter had ridden forward toward the center to be closer to the action. While he was there,
McClellan had several opportunities to fulfill his promise to reinforce and
assist Burnside and Cox in ways that could have led to the destruction of
Lee's army. The reasons McClellan rejected these options have been the
subject of speculation and controversy ever since.

The first opportunity came when at about 4 p.m. Thomas Anderson, a colonel in Porter's 5th AC, reportedly told his division commander,
George Sykes, that he had solid information that the Confederate center
was poorly manned. He said, "The advance of a single brigade would have
cut Lee's army in two." After the war, Sykes told Anderson that he had
taken this proposal directly to McClellan and Porter. While McClellan was
inclined to order an attack, Porter said, "Remember General: I command
the last reserve of the Army of the Republic." McClellan took his advice
and did not attack. Porter denied that the incident ever took place.[65]

Cavalry commander Pleasonton saw the same weakness in the rebel
center, writing in his report that at 4 p.m. he saw that the "field was open
to Sharpsburg Ridge." He was confident that an offensive there would
work, presenting McClellan with another opportunity. At that time, Mc-
Clellan had in place in the center not only much of Porter's corps but
also some 4,000 of Pleasonton's cavalrymen. One historian asserted that

90 McClellan had kept the cavalry there because he had envisioned their making a Napoleonic coup de grace charge at a critical moment. On September 16 McClellan had ordered Pleasonton to be "ready, at a moment's notice, should it be required to make pursuit of the enemy." At noon on September 17, McClellan had even asked him, "Can you do any good by a cavalry charge?"

Such a charge would have been suicidal by that stage in the war if it were made against a strong and prepared defensive line. By 4 p.m. that day, however, the Confederate center was thinly manned and weakened, and a cavalry charge in conjunction with an infantry and artillery attack could have won the day. Pleasonton reported that he asked McClellan for help to make such an advance, but the response from his staff was "he has no infantry to spare" and to consult with Porter. Pleasonton was then informed, "This request was not entertained by General Porter." In his report, Porter claimed that he told Pleasonton he could not do anything because he had only 4,000 infantry in reserve and had to protect the center.[66]

Finally, sometime between 4 and 5 p.m., McClellan and Porter were met by a courier from Burnside requesting the reinforcements he had been promised. On this third opportunity for action, McClellan thought for a moment and, perhaps looking at the negatively inclined Porter, replied, "Tell General Burnside this is the battle of the war. He must hold his ground till dark at any cost. I will send him Miller's battery. I can do nothing more. I have no infantry. . . . Tell him if he cannot hold his ground, then the bridge, to the last man!—always the bridge! If the bridge is lost, all is lost." With what one historian called "this histrionic note," McClellan lost his last opportunity to win the day.[67]

Always a quick study, only a few days after the battle Cox had already assessed that it was McClellan's wrong-headed decisions that had undermined his chances to sweep Lee from the field. He told Helen, "The only criticism I feel like making on the conduct of the battle is that we were not supported on the left by part at least of Fitz-John Porter's corps which was near us & was not brought into the engagement. With its aid . . . we would have driven his two wings back on the Potomac by different lines & probably in a panic rout." Instead, "The enemy massed his troops on our left flank, completely out flanking us." He concluded, "Not to seize the moment to throw his fresh reserves into the scale seems to have been McClellan's error, & the result is that we shall have to follow up the enemy and fight him again."[68]

In sum, Burnside and Cox did not get their promised reinforcements; McClellan's reserves and his cavalry merely observed; and McClellan once again let a commander "get out of his scrape" alone.

Plots and a Pyrrhic Victory

McClellan wrote to Halleck on September 18 that "the battle will probably be renewed today." But no attack was made, and McClellan decided to rest on what he thought were significant laurels. As he wrote to his wife, "Those in whose judgment I rely tell me that I fought the battle splendidly and that it was a masterpiece of art." He did not say who made that sycophantic judgment, though Porter is a likely candidate. By contrast, in his diary Strother more accurately described the reality of September 18: "The enemy is . . . clearly in no condition to open the battle. . . . I expressed my conviction that the enemy was beaten. . . . [T]he enemy will undoubtedly escape, and we have spent the day gathering up a few thousand worthless muskets and a few hundred lousy prisoners." Strother assessed that McClellan had been diverted by "weak-kneed counselors— respectable book soldiers—who . . . concentrated all their wits in finding something to scare at." His later writings make clear that he considered Porter a leader among those counselors.[69]

On September 19, after he was sure that Lee had retreated, McClellan told Halleck, "We may safely claim a complete victory," adding later, "The enemy is driven back into Virginia. Maryland and Penna. are now safe." He saw the Battle of Antietam as a great triumph that had achieved the primary objective, as he saw it, of pushing the rebel army back into Virginia. According to one historian, McClellan always hoped that after a short conflict, peace could be restored among brothers—and not enemies. The objective now, he firmly believed, was to make sure that Radical influence on Lincoln not lead to abolition becoming a war objective. He feared doing so would ensure strengthened opposition by a Confederacy that might otherwise be ready to negotiate peace. With what he saw as a great victory behind him, McClellan hoped that his influence would be sufficient to persuade Lincoln both to oppose the Radicals and to remove the men he believed were undercutting him in Washington, Halleck and Stanton, from office.[70]

In the months previous, the possibility that emancipation might become a war objective, as well as discontent within McClellan's inner circle with the treatment of their leader, had driven some of McClellan's advisors to advocate even stronger action to reverse Radical power in Washington. Some sympathetic Democrats and McClellan military staff members had even suggested taking the army to Washington to seize power, with McClellan as the head of a military dictatorship. McClellan's memoirs include a letter to his wife in 1861 admitting that he had been often approached about a "dictatorship" on that basis. McClellan likely never considered any such action, but he did not act forthrightly to disclaim such intentions or to discourage such speculation in his camp.[71]

Meanwhile, after the Battle of Antietam, Cox and McClellan had repeated their practice of having wide-ranging conversations about political and military issues. As Cox told Helen, McClellan "is accordingly cordial, & puts me at once in the old familiar footing, urging me to come to his hd. qts. frequently & as an intimate friend without ceremony." One of the issues they discussed was slavery. Cox wrote, "The total impression left upon me by the general's conversation was that he agreed that the war ought to end in abolition of slavery; but he feared the effects of haste." At the same time, "It was plainly evident that [McClellan] was subjected to a good deal of pressure by opponents of the administration and . . . overcrowded by more radical men around him into steps which as yet were imprudent and extreme."

Cox experienced an example of the latter a few days after the Battle of Antietam. At a church service he was approached by a civilian who "spoke of the politicians in Washington as wickedly trying to sacrifice the general, and added . . . 'But you military men have that matter in your own hands.' . . . This roused me, and I turned upon him with a sharp 'What do you mean, sir!'" Cox noted, "Though there was more or less of current talk about disloyal influences at work, I had been skeptical as to the fact, and to be brought face to face with that sort of thing was a surprise." The man was John Garrett, president of the Baltimore and Ohio Railroad. After being berated by Cox, Garrett left hurriedly and went across the room to speak to Porter, having apparently mistaken Cox for that other general. This incident could only have reinforced Cox's negative view of Porter.[72]

While McClellan thought his power and influence were at a peak, he had in fact achieved a political-military Pyrrhic victory at Antietam because Lincoln saw the results of that battle as sufficient justification to issue the preliminary Emancipation Proclamation, which he did on September 22. McClellan was displeased and unsure how to react. He sought a wide variety of advice, including from his military staff at a dinner a few days later with Cox, Burnside, and John Cochrane, a "War Democrat" from New York. McClellan told the group that some politicians and some of his staff officers had urged him to openly oppose the proclamation and that he was seeking the views of the army's leadership, especially those who supported the administration.

These generals unanimously told him that any statement against the proclamation would be a "fatal error" and any criticism of civil policy would properly be seen as a "usurpation." McClellan intimated that he agreed but "said that people had assured him that the army was so devoted to him that they would as one man enforce any decision he should make." Cox (who noted, "McClellan perfectly knew my own position as an outspoken Republican") responded "with some emphasis," indicating that the incident with Garrett was fresh in his mind. He said that those who urged McClellan to speak out were his worst enemies. The citizen-general underscored that the army was made up of men who were more citizens than soldiers. He declared, "Not a corporal's guard would stand by his side if he were to depart from the strict subordination of the military to the civil authority."

McClellan responded that he "heartily believed" this was true and wondered whether he should make a statement to show that he did not support the "would-be revolutionists." The group recommended a public declaration to his men emphasizing that the army should not "meddle with the functions of the civil government." McClellan's statement, issued on October 7, was drafted by Key. Although it was carefully hedged and implicitly critical of Lincoln's policies, Cox "regarded it as an honest effort on [McClellan's] part to break through the toils which intriguers had spread for him." Unfortunately for McClellan, one part of the statement, in which he said that "the remedy for political errors, if any are committed, is to be found only in the action of the people at the polls," was distorted by his enemies as an attack on Lincoln and his policies. Cox regretted that "what seemed to [Cox] one of his most laudable actions should have been one of the most misrepresented and misunderstood."

Cox concluded this discussion in his memoirs by noting, "It would seem that treasonable notions were rife about him to an extent that was never suspected unless he was made the dupe of pretenders who saw some profit in what might be regarded as a gross form of adulation." As a result, "we are obliged . . . to accept as one of the strange elements of this situation a constant stream of treasonable suggestions," though "McClellan cannot be held responsible for it." Nevertheless, and given Cox's moralistic and purist approach to such matters, it should not be surprising that he believed McClellan should "be condemned for the weakness which made such approaches to him possible," because "there is no proof that he rebuked it as he should have done."[73]

Return to West Virginia: Promotion

The military situation after September 19, 1862, featured two battered armies whose leaders decided they were not prepared for major battles in the foreseeable future. The general in the weaker position, Lee, at first wanted to attack again but ultimately decided against it. The general in the stronger position, McClellan, wanted to rest and wait for reinforcements as he reorganized his army, which was less than three weeks old. That was a logical conclusion but not one the authorities in Washington accepted, believing that McClellan was returning to his delaying tactics.[74]

When, despite prodding from Halleck and Lincoln, McClellan had not moved by the end of September, Lincoln visited him and his troops at Antietam. On October 1, 1862, Cox showed the president where his men had fought, and Lincoln proved to be both an excellent observer and a deft politician. Cox told Helen that Lincoln said "he was very glad to see me & that Secy Chase had often said to him, 'you ought to know my friend Gen. Cox,' showing both that the Prest. felt cordially & that Mr. Chase has been a warm friend." Cox learned later that Lincoln wrote McClellan about his next military steps, showing "a marked ability and great military analysis and comprehension," while urging the reluctant commander to renew the campaign.[75]

Cox was unaware of the war of words between Lincoln and McClellan, but in early October he was extremely optimistic about his own military advancement. His five weeks in the Army of the Potomac had been a success, and he seemed firmly ensconced as 9th AC commander. Both Burnside and McClellan praised his efforts and recommended his promotion to major general, with the assurance that the permanent command of the corps would be added. Cox's patron Salmon P. Chase noted in his diary on September 27, "McClellan and Burnside would recommend Cox for Major General, an object . . . which I would most gladly promote."[76]

On October 5, however, Cox was "taken all aback by an order to go back to Western Va. & try to retake the Kanawha Valley which our men recently ran out of." He was displeased that he would have to return to the "humbug" of duty in West Virginia because, he complained to Helen, "the labor of the year past [had] been abandoned without a struggle" by the men he had left behind. He did acknowledge, however, that it was complimentary that his return was at the express wish of the governors of West Virginia, Indiana, and Ohio. Furthermore, he was pleased that he would be able to return with his Kanawha Division and not to have to command the "beaten troops." McClellan and Burnside both promised that once he had righted the situation in West Virginia, they would bring him back to the Army of the Potomac; and, as he told Helen, "as this was coupled with a strong request to the War Department that my promotion should be made immediate, I acquiesced with reasonably good grace." He added, introspectively, "All these tokens of respect & regard are pleasant after the rather trying period of probation I had, & I am thankful for them." At the same time, he admitted, "I sometimes am sad when I think of the increased expectations of me, & feel my own deficiencies keenly."[77]

Cox's unexpected orders were also unwelcome to McClellan, who asked Halleck on October 6, "Is it still intended that Cox should march at once?" He added that if Cox did leave, he would need more troops before any new advance. The next day Halleck told him that Cox would have to leave immediately and reinforcements were on the way. But in any case, Halleck stressed, "The country is becoming very impatient at the want of activity in your army, and we must push it on." McClellan did not move; and a frustrated Lincoln lost patience and decided to replace him. To minimize the political damage, Lincoln waited until after the fall elections; on November 5 he ordered McClellan to be replaced by Burnside. In the same document, he ordered that Porter be replaced by Hooker.[78]

An Unforeseen Attack in the Political-Military Wars

During this period, in a series of events about which Cox apparently never learned, the politically well-connected Hugh Ewing dealt Cox a major blow in the political-military wars. Ewing's father, Thomas, had been a senator from Ohio and a cabinet officer in three administrations, and he had adopted W. T. Sherman, who in turn had married one of Thomas Ewing's daughters. Hugh Ewing had shown throughout his life that he lacked self-control, and his father acknowledged that he had a hasty temper, took offense easily, and was "inclined to brood over real or imagined wrongs."

Hugh Ewing also had had drinking problems since his days at West Point, from which he failed to graduate because of academic deficiencies in his senior year.[79]

A drunken Hugh Ewing's anger at Cox first manifested itself the day after the Battle of Antietam. George Crook wrote, "Our division was reassembled [Sept 18.] near a small country house occupied by some officers. Col. Hugh Ewing became full of 'jig water' and ventilated himself on Gen. Cox, abusing him for being a coward and imbecile, and declaring he would never obey an order of his again, etc." Over the next few days, Ewing wrote angry letters to his father complaining about Cox's alleged unwillingness to give him proper credit or recommend his promotion. He described Cox as "a Yankee abolitionist, soft, facile, a smooth talker & fine writer . . . a military charlatan . . . [who] does not possess or deserve the confidence of a man in this corps which he commands." He added that the troops under Cox in West Virginia "always held him in contempt; and his blundering at Antietam has earned him that of the entire corps." Ewing alleged that McClellan had recommended Cox for a major generalship only because "he had toadied McClellan assiduously."[80]

Threatening resignation, Hugh Ewing asked his father to help get him a new assignment. But his father calmly told him, "You must not resign. . . . [I]t is not at all probable you will be ordered with him, but if you are . . . do not let the disgust of temporary annoyance blight your prospects." Ewing agreed but decided to write to Stanton about the controversy, which would have a significant impact later. Ewing would make several requests for a transfer, but when they were not granted, he served in West Virginia with Cox until early January, when his brigade was sent to join Grant. Before leaving, he boosted the morale of the troops via his favorite vice. One of his captains wrote that on Christmas Day, "Col. Ewing's wife treated the regiment to a barrel of whiskey," and as a result, "quite a number of the boys were intoxicated" from drinking Hugh's "Old Rye."[81]

Crook's and Ewing's complaints about Cox's failures at Antietam ring true to some extent, though Crook's were somewhat self-serving. Ewing's plaint that Cox ignored his critical pleas about a threat to his left does not take into account that Cox's attention at that point was focused on charging ahead in what appeared to be a chance to sweep the rebels from the field. No one else corroborated Ewing's story. Further, it is illogical for someone as dutiful, methodical, and cautious as Cox to have ignored such an important warning. Moreover, Cox did not get any intimation of displeasure in the days after the battle from Ewing, who noted in his journal that Cox had visited him and his men, adding, "Cox gracious." Rather, Cox firmly believed that all his men, including Ewing, appreciated his leadership. Two men, including one in Hugh Ewing's brigade, upon hearing that Cox would be leaving for West Virginia, wrote in their diaries, "It is the universal desire of our boys to be with him," and "We did not like to see him go."[82]

Assessing the New Man on the National Military Scene

Cox's performance during the Maryland campaign was among the best in a field of generals on the Union side, none of whom performed with excellence. At the end of the campaign, his future seemed bright. He was perhaps the most effective citizen-general among the Union forces, having been given the greatest responsibility of any of that group. In only three weeks, Cox had risen from division commander to corps commander to de facto wing commander, reflecting his superiors' growing confidence in his ability. Having unexpectedly been placed in the lead of McClellan's army's movement against Lee, he proved his mettle at both Frederick and South Mountain. At the latter, his initiative was a key to success, and his achievements exceeded those of two future commanders of the Army of the Potomac: Hooker and Meade. But his delay because of the chimera of vastly larger rebel forces and poor support from Reno diminished his chances for a major victory.

At Antietam, Cox performed well despite complications arising from the personal rivalries of the leadership and his own inexperience. He found himself in an awkward position in the midst of McClellan's and Burnside's direct and indirect quarrels over authority and responsibilities. For Cox the situation into which Burnside had placed him was perplexing. He was confident enough in his ability, but he knew Burnside was looking over his shoulder. McClellan's intense scrutiny of Burnside's every action increased the stress. Though Cox and Burnside were on good terms, they had known one another for only ten days, not long enough to establish a firm relationship of trust.

A year earlier, Cox had been relieved to have the autonomous responsibility for 5,000 troops in the outback of West Virginia lifted from his shoulders. At Antietam, he found himself in de facto command of 15,000 men in the most important battle of the campaign. Like everyone else at Antietam, Cox made mistakes, though he came within minutes of sweeping Lee from the field at Antietam. The fact that he did as well as he did in unexpected circumstances is a tribute to his steadfastness and dedication to duty. In this critical period, he provided further proof of his "military aptitude"; as a result, many Union military commanders knew just how effective a general he could be. But, unknown to Cox, Hugh Ewing had cast a significant shadow over his reputation.

4 Citizen/Political General
Political Wars outside the Mainstream

> Cox was here last night. He has been made a Major General
> and ordered to West Virginia. I rejoice at his good fortune,
> which has justly come to him after so long a time. I did what I
> could for his promotion. It is a step toward the vindication of
> merit versus West Point.
>
> —James Garfield, letter to Lucy Garfield, 1862

James Garfield's enthusiasm for Cox's good fortune, evident in
the epigraph to this chapter, was matched by Cox's at the time, but both
men were soon to be disappointed.[1] Cox's trip to Washington to get his
new orders would unexpectedly begin a period of nearly fourteen months
of relative inactivity, disappointment, and frustration during which he was
primarily engaged in military administration and had his promotion nullified.

His trip began on a positive note. Halleck told him on October 6
that the governors of both Pennsylvania and Ohio had been alarmed at
Confederate successes since he had left West Virginia and that he was the
best man to meet the challenge. Cox got everything he had asked for as
part of this change. He would be promoted immediately and become
commander of the territorial district of West Virginia, and the Kanawha
Division would again be under his command. Cox met with Stanton, who
handed him the appointment as major general. Cox noted, "Mr. Stanton's
manner was so different from the brusque one commonly attributed to
him that I have nothing but pleasant remembrances of my relations to him,
both then and later." Lincoln was not available to meet with him.[2]

Retaking West Virginia

Cox was ordered to Cincinnati, from which he would launch his new offensive. On the way, he stopped at Wheeling and Columbus to discuss the

military situation with the state governors. On October 11 he reported to General Horatio G. Wright, commander of the Department of the Ohio, and briefed him on the plan to retake the Kanawha valley and reassert Union control. General Robert Milroy, who had served under Cox earlier, had already been ordered to advance from Clarksburg toward Beverly in the east, while two other groups were sent directly down the Kanawha River valley. Crook, still in Sharpsburg, was to join them later along with the remainder of the Kanawha Division.[3]

Cox confidently told Helen, "If I am successful in the campaign, as I expect to be, I may get a little rest. . . . [T]he report now is that the rebels are retreating at the mere rumor of my preparations here and at Clarksburg to follow them." Meanwhile, on October 15 Lee had told Loring, the Confederate commander there, "I do not think the enemy is able to send strong reinforcements into Western Virginia. . . . Major General Cox, with four brigades, has been detached . . . but no more." But Lee misjudged both Cox and Loring. He apparently did not realize that Loring had not been able to secure his control of the Kanawha valley north of Charleston and in fact was preparing to retreat, as Cox had asserted. Later that same day Loring was officially replaced by General John Echols, who was ordered to "march his forces back into the Kanawha Valley." But Cox pushed the disorganized Confederates back swiftly; and on October 28 Echols reported that he had had to make "a forced march of 31 miles" to escape the oncoming Union forces. Cox took Charleston for a second time on October 29. Having justified the administration's trust in him, Cox boasted to Helen, "The rebels made a show of standing a battle until we were within five miles of them, & then decamped pell-mell out of the valley." A few days later, his troops marched into Gauley Bridge, and the valley was once again secured. For a third time Cox had foiled Lee's plans, and by the end of October, Cox's and other Union successes in the West at Corinth and Iuka had slowed the Confederate flood tide.[4]

In mid-November, Cox set up winter quarters at Marietta, Ohio, from which he was in such firm control that, he wrote in his memoirs, "There was no military movement during the winter of sufficient importance to be told at length." That calm and the problems the army was experiencing elsewhere prompted Halleck to ask Wright repeatedly in late 1862 to release some of Cox's forces for duty elsewhere. Cox was opposed, telling Helen, "As I felt sure this would result in a fresh raid into the Kanawha, I have opposed further changes here." He was also determined to maintain popular morale as the statehood issue moved ahead. Cox won the argument, and the fact that both Halleck and Wright deferred to him reflected their respect for his regional knowledge. Halleck tried again on January 3, 1863, but Wright responded, "[Cox's] personal knowledge of the country makes his opinion the more important." Cox finally relented later in January, and Crook's forces, including a brigade led by Hugh Ewing, were transferred to Tennessee. Cox stayed behind, his role in securing the state still considered essential.[5]

Early in his tenure in this new assignment, Cox had been content to wait at least a while for a new and more active command, believing that he was well and favorably known in Washington and in the army. By mid-January, however, with McClellan and Burnside both having been removed as commander of the Army of the Potomac, his hopes for returning to that force were dashed. His unhappiness was exacerbated when, even before he took Charleston, critics of his earlier counterinsurgency approach began writing in the papers that his return meant reinstitution of a policy they deemed to be insufficiently harsh. Cox told Helen, "I find my command will be made in many respects unpleasant by the jealousies and envies of petty men & a small clique have already commenced exercising their literary proclivities by newspaper correspondence questioning my loyalty! Or at least intimating that I have been in the habit of favoring rebels. . . . The gnats must buzz and bite in their small way, & were it not for them we might lose our humility."[6]

Intellectualizing While out of the Mainstream

Once he had reestablished control in the region, Cox used his free time to intellectualize about relevant issues, including racial matters, war objectives, national politics, and military organization and strategy. His writings from the period would provide a foundation for his future political positions and historical writing, while demonstrating that at times he enjoyed reflection purely for its academic value, irrespective of practicality. On November 17, 1862, Cox wrote the first of many letters to Aaron Perry, who would become his political-military sounding board. He told Perry that he feared that the Democratic triumphs that year in congressional races, in part because of opposition to the Emancipation Proclamation, might bring the ascendancy of the "peace-at-any-price" party and an inglorious end to the war. To add insult to injury, he complained, he and his veteran, proven men were being wasted in West Virginia watching "the gaps in the Alleghenies while the Army of the Potomac is weakened." A few weeks later, depressed by Burnside's defeat at Fredericksburg, Cox floated by Perry the first element of his thinking about the issue of the postwar freedmen. He put forth the purely academic idea of letting the South have its independence and then persuading Canada to form a new country with the Northern states. This would, he wrote, "rid us of the negro problem" and avoid the difficult Reconstruction the South would have to undergo.[7]

In a third letter to Perry in February 1863, Cox again sounded like a Radical Republican state legislator, emphasizing, "We must destroy the slave power and the administration must end all dreams of reconciliation." One way to do so would be to "get rid of the traitors at home and unite with true Anglo-Saxon stubbornness." Another way would be to enhance the Union's military effort with black troops. Cox noted that he had read Jomini's studies of the French wars in Santo Domingo and Guadeloupe and had concluded that "blacks would make good troops . . . and military drill and discipline may be the best preparation for freedom and self-dependence." That freedom, he conjectured, should be accompanied by internal colonization of the freedmen, an idea to which he would return later as his political career was relaunched. He advocated that blacks who served honorably in the army be given a homestead in "a military colony on the southwestern frontier which can absorb the surplus black population and solve the emancipation problem with a system of colonization." Because that area would be under the control of the military, "blacks would be well protected and would flock there" to develop to their maximum ability free from white repression.[8]

Cox also wrote to Chase in April on the topic of black soldiers. Blacks had been permitted to join the armed forces by the middle of 1862, but not until 1863 were large numbers of black soldiers organized into "colored units" and ordered into battle. Cox told Chase that though "it is in vain to expect philanthropic conduct and refined sympathies from a considerable part of the army," arming blacks would be a significant help to the war effort. He asserted, "No reasonable man will question the fact that the Negroes will make good soldiers," but, he emphasized, they should be kept in peripheral roles, since white soldiers would not accept anything else. Echoing his letters to Perry, Cox said that in the military blacks would develop "the habits of discipline and obedience . . . which would be guarantees for their good conduct in civil life after the war."[9]

Cox also took the time to ruminate about military education, organization, and the roles of the professional and volunteer soldier. Garfield's comment that Cox's promotion was "a step toward the vindication of merit versus West Point" reflected the ongoing conflict between West Pointers and citizen-generals. In an era when there were few professional schools, intellectuals like Cox were firm believers in the abilities of educated men to become effective military leaders. While he respected some West Pointers with whom he had served, including McClellan, Rosecrans, and Burnside, he had negative opinions about the quality of some others in the regular army, including those at lower levels. His successful military experience had led him to question both the necessity for and the value of training at West Point. A letter Cox wrote in mid-1862 to his brother Charles illustrated the depth of his feelings. Charles had asked for help to get an appointment to West Point. Cox declined, in part because by the time Charles would have graduated, the war would be over. Moreover, he wrote acidly, "I know of no position so little adapted to develop a young man as a subordinate in the army. . . . [R]egular army officers have had their intellects belittled and their intellectual growth stunted by such a life." They "cannot study and must follow the fashion of smoking, drinking, and gambling," leading to the "monstrous littleness of the life. . . . [Y]ou will be thankful at 30 that you did not bury yourself in the torpid semi-death of an army life" in peacetime.[10]

Given these sentiments, Cox was pleased when in late November 1862 Stanton created a military board to review the articles of war and army organization and invited commentary from military leaders. Cox saw this as an opportunity to share his ideas and to gain recognition and status for volunteer soldiers. Unlike a regular officer who might have felt constrained not to criticize too strongly his career organization, Cox was very much inclined to do so. In tutelary letters to Chase and the board, headed by E. A. Hitchcock, he once again took on the mantle of preacher/professor, explaining his views on the problems and offering solutions.[11]

Cox wrote first to Chase in the hope that the latter's prominence would give his ideas greater impact on the military establishment. He knew that Jomini thought war was more of a science than an art, but he disagreed, telling Chase, "There ought to be no differences of opinion among intelligent people on the proposition that war is an art. Like every other art it demands careful study of its principles and rules from those who would practice it successfully against skilled opponents." Given that premise, Cox concluded that any intelligent man could become a skilled military leader, whether he was a professional or a citizen-general. Furthermore, by emphasizing that war was an art, Cox believed both that the ability to exert military leadership was innate and that the greatest military commanders were born, not made via formal professional training.

In this letter, Cox discussed the growing political-military divide between regular army and citizen-generals, which was an inevitable by-product of Scott's misguided decision to create two parallel armies. He acknowledged, unhappily, that the system was being kept in force because of "feelings of possessiveness by the heads of the army," all West Pointers. Keeping the two armies separate, he stressed, had made relations between regulars and volunteers "anomalous and hurtful" and was a significant drag on the war effort. Regular army personnel refused to acknowledge the equality of the volunteers; in response, the latter saw "the regulars as a would-be aristocracy and deride[d] them as martinets." He added that regulars saw volunteers as a "mushroom organization which would soon pass away." But, he claimed, two years of war had shown that volunteers were just as necessary and capable as regulars. He pointed to the experience of his Kanawha Division in the Maryland campaign as evidence that volunteers could be superior to regulars.

His solution, based on his reading and experience, was that the Union had to follow the example propounded by Napoleon of creating a united citizens' army. He asked the following rhetorical questions: If the "regular army organization is so narrow it can't be expanded in time of emergency, what use is it? If a volunteer organization is fit to decide the *great* wars of the nation, is it not ridiculous to keep an expensive organization of regulars for the petty contests with Indians or for an ornamental appendage to the State in peace?" The obvious answer, he wrote, was to create a "system flexible enough to provide for the increase of the army to any size required, without losing any of the advantage of character or efficiency which, in any respect, pertained to it as a regular army." The unspoken corollary, which he would state firmly in his memoirs, was that in a unified army, citizen-generals should have access to every command position.[12]

His letter to the military board echoed those themes, but he added a discussion of the importance of discipline, which he said had been deficient for various reasons. One was the disparity of officer selection methods. Some were appointed solely because they had gathered a group of volunteers. Once they had gained a position, however, they were "never examined for military knowledge or soldierly characteristics." Furthermore, the practice of creating new regiments wholly of raw recruits and not merging new volunteers into old regiments had led to unskilled and untrained regiments fighting in parallel with veteran regiments, as had happened at Antietam. Cox concluded by asking for "a thorough reexamination of the question of whether success is probable for an army with a double organization, raw regiments, and all the worst elements triumphant." In the end, nothing came of Cox's input, because the commission did not produce a report and Chase eventually lost influence with Lincoln. However, Cox would use these letters as the basis of his expanded thoughts on these issues in his memoirs.[13]

Losing a Battle in the Political-Military Wars

In March 1863, still without a new assignment, Cox suffered what he called "the one severe disappointment of [his] military career" when he was informed that his promotion to major general had not been confirmed by the Senate. Earlier in the year, Lincoln had reached a compromise with Congress to limit the number of generals, and he had had to remove six men from the major general list, including Cox. Among the others removed were his current commander, Horatio Wright, and a future commander, John M. Schofield. Cox's commission as major general expired and his rank reverted to brigadier general on March 4, 1863. Cox told Chase that he was mortified, astonished, and disheartened by this turn of events. He wrote in his memoirs that he was particularly unhappy because "the commands which [he] had exercised and the responsibilities intrusted to [him] had been greater than those of the large majority of the appointees." He acknowledged, "In such a scramble it was only a question as to who had or had not powerful friends on the spot" who would voluntarily champion his cause.

Cox understood most of the reasons for this development. Throughout his life, he had a natural tendency toward modesty and reticence, and so was not a skilled self-promoter. While he asked friends like Garfield, Dennison, and Chase to lobby for him, he did not follow up assiduously. Nor did he seek favors from reporters to "write him up" for his achievements. Most important, he had no "powerful friends on the spot." He hardly knew either of Ohio's senators, Ben Wade and John Sherman, and he had supported Dennison's candidacy against the latter. Garfield was still in the army and would not take office as a congressman until later in

March. Chase was now in Lincoln's bad graces. McClellan and Burnside were no longer influential. So Cox was out of both luck and friends.[14]

Cox apparently never knew that another reason he lost this rank involved Hugh Ewing and the Battle of Antietam. Stanton apparently accepted Ewing's version of events as laid out in his vituperative letter. Stanton reportedly said that "he would not have made Cox a Maj. Gen. if he had received it sooner." Moreover, Thomas Ewing was in Washington in early March, and he lobbied the committee on military appointments to make sure they knew of the family's opposition to Cox's promotion. He reported to Hugh, "I do not find him among the nominees—perhaps he has been estopped." He had. Some months later, when Garfield tried to lobby for Cox, the ever-volatile Stanton brushed him off, still convinced that Cox did not deserve promotion. What had happened to him resembled what Cox tellingly once described as Stanton's reaction in another soldier's situation, namely, "Mr. Stanton, in his characteristic way, condemned him first and tried him afterward."[15]

A disheartened Cox told Helen, "I feel that I have been shabbily used, & am determined to find out fully & in what proportions I am indebted for it." He wrote that everyone was complimentary of his military ability, so he focused on the divisions between regular and civilian generals as the cause of his demotion. He told her he was "convinced that two adverse influences [were] at work. One was the jealousy of some officers appointed like myself from civil life, and the other the determination of Halleck to put every active command into the hands of the regulars when it is possible to do so." He assured her that despite his disappointment, he remained "confident that justice [would] soon be done." He continued, "I am taking matters very quietly, biding my time."[16]

United Again with Burnside: The 23rd AC

In his memoirs, Cox wrote that after his demotion, "It took a little time and some philosophy to overcome" the inevitable depression. His spirits were uplifted when in late March Stanton sent him a message to "report in person, without delay, for orders" in Baltimore. When he got there on April 3, however, he was disappointed to learn that he was only being ordered to aid Ohio's governor, David Tod, in organizing new draftees. He was assured once again that he was under consideration by Stanton for a more active campaign. In his memoirs, Cox conjectured that his letter to the military commission had led to this new appointment. While unhappy that his new orders did not involve active duty, Cox was pleasantly surprised to learn that he would be working again under Burnside, who had just been appointed commander of the Department of the Ohio, encompassing Ohio, Kentucky, and Tennessee.[17]

Cox arrived in Columbus on April 9 and met with Tod and Burnside. Despite the latter's disastrous defeat at Fredericksburg and problems with his subordinates, Lincoln had wanted to retain Burnside's services. The president intended that Burnside would eventually organize a force, later designated the 23rd AC, to regain control of eastern Tennessee. That corps would include the new recruits Cox was to organize in Ohio, and it would ultimately be Cox's "home" corps for the final years of the war.

Burnside decided to place Cox in command of the military district of Ohio, headquartered in Cincinnati. Though Cox made no reference to it, he would spend much of his remaining military and postwar life in a city named after the quintessential "citizen-general," Cincinnatus. Because Burnside's regional headquarters were also there, the two men soon were working closely together again with overlapping responsibilities, as they had at the Battle of Antietam. Cox soon discovered that the unsystematic Burnside could at times be inattentive to his administrative responsibilities. As a result, Cox "often found occasion to supply the formal links in the official chain, so that business would move on according to 'regulations.'" In other words, Cox often did Burnside's paperwork for him! Cox also used this time to get to know the leaders of the Cincinnati press, including Murat Halstead of the *Cincinnati Commercial,* who would play an influential role in Cox's postwar political career.[18]

In their military administrative positions, Burnside and Cox were responsible for what Cox told Helen were "a thousand quasi-military and quasi-civil questions . . . which will be full of knotty points." While his experience in administering parts of West Virginia and his political and legal background were excellent preparation for those duties, Cox had developed a strong distaste for military administration because he was being kept from the actual fighting. Further, because there were many Confederate sympathizers in Cincinnati, Cox unhappily told Helen that he now had to "act as a sort of chief-of-police in a great state like Ohio."

His job was made more difficult because of another of Burnside's quirks, impetuosity. Cox wrote, "Burnside was so convinced of the widespread and multiform activity of the disloyal element that he tried to subdue it by the publication of his famous General Order No. 38" on April 13,

1863." This measure threatened the punishment by death or banishment of persons who "commit acts for the benefit of the enemies," including "declaring sympathy for the enemy." Cox defended Burnside's decision as consistent with Lincoln's policy, but he admitted that "Burnside was apt to act impulsively, and his impulse was to follow the bent of his ardent patriotism." Cox thought that before acting, Burnside should have consulted Washington and also sought advice from Cox, whose background would have helped provide a useful perspective.[19]

Early in May, Copperhead leader Clement Vallandigham tested the legality of the order by publicly calling for an end to the war and asserting that Burnside's action denied him freedom of speech. Burnside again reacted impulsively and, without consulting Cox or Washington, ordered Vallandigham arrested. Vallandigham was tried by a military tribunal at which Aaron Perry led the prosecution team. He was convicted and sentenced to imprisonment for the duration of the war. Stanton applauded Burnside, assuring him, "You may count on the firm support of the President." In fact, Lincoln was upset, and to minimize the political damage, he banished Vallandigham to the South. Stanton, as he often did, switched positions on the issue, criticizing Burnside in a letter of quasi-reprimand. Cox told Helen that Stanton's "conduct therefore takes the form of a tactical retreat before a theatrical popular storm."[20]

In late June, Cox and Burnside faced an unusual military threat from Confederate General John H. Morgan and his small group of some three hundred cavalry "raiders," who moved from Kentucky through southern Ohio in early July. With no army troops available to meet this small threat, Cox had to rely on militia, whom he feared were not up to the job. Further, there was considerable concern among the populace, which was now experiencing war for the first time. The forces Cox put together proved adequate. He called up regiments from West Virginia to assist the militia, and Morgan and his men were captured by July 26. Morgan's raid was a failure, and ironically for the Confederates, it likely reduced even further Ohio's support for Vallandigham, the Democratic Party candidate, in the gubernatorial election in October.[21]

In early August, Burnside got his long-awaited orders to take eastern Tennessee for the Union, leaving Cox with responsibility for the political-military duties of the district. Cox's only substantive political activity that autumn came after the Democrats nominated Vallandigham, then in exile in Canada, for governor. Cox announced publicly that if Vallandigham tried to return to Ohio to campaign, he would be arrested and sent to a military prison. Vallandigham remained in exile and was soundly beaten in the October election. The only military event of consequence came on November 9 when Cox was advised of a possible attempt from Canada to free Confederate officers housed in a military prison in Sandusky Bay in Lake Erie. Cox quickly had the island's defenses reinforced, and no attack took place. He remained for a few days to supervise the refortification of the prison.[22]

Return to "the Chivalry of Fair Field Warfare"

The months between July and December 1863 were among the most crucial for the Union war effort, and Cox read about Gettysburg, Vicksburg, and subsequent events with envy as the war seemed to be passing him by. In his memoirs, he wrote, "My aversion for the anomalous position of a military commandant out of the actual field of war had not been lessened." Unaware of Stanton's antipathy, he stated, "I had been told that the Secretary of War awaited only an opening which would permit him to assign me to duty with the advanced grade which had been given me after Antietam." He also told Helen that he hoped that Garfield, who had just taken his congressional seat, would be able to lobby on his behalf. Having been disappointed so many times, however, he mused unhappily, "Everything I hear of the mode of doing business at Wash. satisfies me that 'out of sight is out of mind' there, & that once being drifted aside, nothing but accident will move me into the current again."[23]

While Cox was in Sandusky, Burnside, who had successfully fended off Longstreet's attempts to take Knoxville, fulfilled his promise and arranged for Cox to become commander of the 23rd AC. On December 2 Cox was ordered to report to the "general commanding" at Knoxville. Cox hurried to Cincinnati, but when he got there, he learned that Burnside had been replaced by General John G. Foster. Fearing that if he delayed, his orders might be changed, Cox took the initiative and hurriedly left with his staff for Tennessee on December 9. After an arduous journey through terrain he found even more difficult than that of West Virginia, Cox reported for duty on December 18. That day he learned that, as he had feared, Foster had issued orders for him to administer the District of Kentucky. Cox wrote to Helen, "[I will] protest with all my power, as I do not mean to be out of field service if I can help it. . . . I am in a very vexatious suspense." Impressed by Cox's determination, Foster reassigned him to command the

23rd AC. But Cox knew that because he was only a brigadier general, he could be superseded later.[24]

There was very little fighting in the region over the next few weeks as Foster and Longstreet maneuvered against one another, to little effect, in the poor conditions of the Tennessee winter. Cox told Helen, "The nature of the country is such that neither party inclines to take the offensive." He added that the wretched environment his men had to bear while in winter quarters was worse than that he had experienced in West Virginia. Their morale needed constant bolstering, and part of Cox's role as commander was "going through the regimental camps and giving such encouragement and cheer" as he could. The men bore up well, and Cox told Helen, "The spirit of the troops is magnificent. It would hardly be believed, but yet it is true, that these brave fellows lying here on the frozen ground, without shoes, clad in tattered rags, & fed on half rations are re-enlisting for a new term of three years by whole regiments." The general staff was better off than the enlisted men. Cox's staff scoured the countryside in late December, and on Christmas Day Cox hosted them and Opdycke, who was stationed nearby as part of George Thomas's Army of the Cumberland, to a festive dinner. Opdycke recalled that they ate "oyster soup, roast turkey, roast chicken, roast mutton . . . coffee with coffee sugar in it, and a pudding . . . but no liquors of any kind!"[25]

In February 1864 Foster, who was in ill health, advised Cox that he would be replaced by John M. Schofield, who had been promised a leadership position by Grant because of his service in Missouri. Cox knew that he inevitably would be replaced by a senior deputy, and he told Helen that he would apply to Grant for a division command under Thomas. Schofield and his new deputy, George Stoneman, arrived in Knoxville on February 9, leaving Cox without orders. Cox wrote Helen an introspective letter about his situation, noting, "I see that the bitterness of disappointment at my being relieved of the command of the corps has been chiefly on your side. About this time last year, I went through the experience of learning that intrigue, pretense, & self puffing are surer roads to promotion than modest performance of duty. . . . [I]t marked the transition from the buoyant confidence of early manhood to the soberer (though I think not cynical) view of human ambitions & so-called successes, which belongs to the more mature years & steady middle age of man."[26]

Fortunately for Cox, he and Schofield quickly established a solid and mutually beneficial relationship. Both men were reserved and scholarly, and

Schofield soon learned, as McClellan had before, that Cox was not only an intellectual with a command of the theory of war but also someone with a well-deserved reputation as an effective leader of men. Further, he came to see, as Cox's other commanders had, that Cox was a quintessential subordinate. As Cox wrote to Helen, "The fact that Gen S. is unpopular [because of his Democratic politics and the opposition to him by some Radicals] has no influence with me. He is the military commander here, & I, like the rest of his subordinates, am bound to give him the best assistance in my power." Also, lacking extensive battlefield experience, Schofield discovered both that the experienced Cox could be an important adviser on tactics and strategy and that Cox was not disinclined to offer useful advice. As Cox wrote to Helen, "My influence upon affairs is undoubtedly greater than it would be as a division commander; indeed more weight is given to my opinion than I could ask." Cox's aide noted, "Schofield has learned what kind of a man [Cox] is, and he can have just about anything he wants that Schofield can give." A politically aware Democrat, Schofield may also have recognized that Cox had an important political future.[27]

Assessing Schofield in his memoirs, Cox wrote that he "had a reputation for scientific tastes, and had, after his graduation at West Point, been instructor in astronomy there." Cox went on, "The obstruction, thus far, to his confirmation in his higher grade so far resembled my own experience as to be a ground of sympathy between us. . . . I may also say that his hearty recognition of my own service and experience inspired me with sincere friendship. I look back to my service as his subordinate with unmixed satisfaction." That satisfaction began when Schofield offered him the job as chief of staff in early March. Lacking a better alternative while he waited for new orders, Cox accepted, telling Perry, "I won't let personal pride determine a refusal of it." However, he still held out hope for an active field command.[28]

His aspirations would be fulfilled in late March as a result of Grant's creating the Union's first coordinated, multiple-pronged attack plan, one with the goal of destroying the rebel armies, not conquering specific cities. William T. Sherman was to lead the western armies against Joseph Johnston, and Schofield was to be commander of the Army of the Ohio (which consisted primarily of the 23rd AC), one of the three "wings" of Sherman's new force. Preparing for the campaign, Schofield offered Cox the position as permanent chief of staff; but when he declined, Schofield named him commander of his 3rd Division, which contained many of Cox's former associates and officers. Because of seniority, Cox was second in command of the 23rd AC, and when Schofield went to Knoxville on business in early April, Cox proudly told Helen, "I am in command in the field" of the Army of the Ohio. His long period of inactive duty was finally over, and he was "very anxious to get . . . into a field where armies will meet with something like the chivalry of fair field warfare."[29]

———

Cox's reversals in the political-military wars of 1862–64 reflected the fact that no political general could ever hope to "win" those conflicts without numerous friends in high places and a strong measure of self-promotion. West Pointers' professional links to their peers in the military cadre in the two-part Union army were always going to lead to major commands and the majority of promotions. Few of them would accept that a nonprofessional could rise to a position of command legitimately. Furthermore, the use of the term *political general*, rather than *citizen-general*, underscored the popular belief that these men were not, like Cincinnatus, disinterested patriots but rather political animals looking to use military achievements for postwar advancement.

Cox did not fit the professional military's stereotyped image of the political general, in part because he had performed well but also because he had not had a prominent prewar political career. Nevertheless, he suffered by being considered part of the group. Now fate had placed him under a commander who had had almost no major active duty experience. Schofield was impressed by Cox's experience and knowledge and saw Cox as both a useful subordinate and a capable adviser. As the Atlanta campaign was about to begin, Cox, who had been "forgotten" at headquarters, had the opportunity and the necessity to prove himself all over again. For his part, Schofield had the opportunity and the necessity to prove himself for the first time. That in turn made their relationship that much stronger as the success of each reinforced the reputation of the other.

Plate 1. Formal photographic portrait of Jacob D. Cox as major general, 1862. (Oberlin College Archives)

Plate 2. Portrait of Jacob D. Cox as major general, 1862. (Library of Congress collection)

Plate 3. Formal photographic portrait of Major General Jacob D. Cox, 1865, dressed in formal mourning for President Abraham Lincoln. (Oberlin College Archives)

Plate 4. Formal photographic portrait of Jacob D. Cox as secretary of the interior, 1869–70. (Library of Congress collection)

Plate 5. Formal photographic portrait of Jacob D. Cox as a member of Congress, representing the Toledo, Ohio, district, 1877–78. (Library of Congress collection)

Plate 6. Formal photographic portrait of Jacob D. Cox as president of the
University of Cincinnati, 1885–89. (Oberlin College Archives)

Plate 7. Cox-Cochran family photograph, on the porch of the Cox family home, Cincinnati, Ohio, 1889. (*From left:*) Mary Rudd Cochran, Jacob D. Cox, two (unidentified) Cochran children, Helen Finney Cox (Mrs. Cox), and Charlotte Hope Cox (the Coxes' youngest daughter). (Oberlin College Archives)

Plate 8. Formal photographic portrait of Helen Finney Cox, 1899. (Oberlin College Archives)

5

Division and Army Commander
The Atlanta Campaign

> The campaign as a whole will remain a most instructive
> example of the methods of warfare which may be said to be
> the natural outcome of modern improvements in weapons, and
> in the means of transportation and communication. . . . Each
> of the opposing armies . . . had found that with veteran soldiers
> now arrayed against each other, one rifle in the trench was
> worth five in front of it.
>
> —Cox, *Atlanta,* 1882

Cox's book about the Atlanta campaign was the definitive
study for over one hundred years and a foundation of historical memory.
In it, Cox noted that as part of his strategic plan, Grant ordered Sherman
"to move against Johnston's army, to break it up, and to get into the interior of the enemy's country as far as you can, inflicting all the damage you
can against their war resources." The Union forces Sherman had available
to implement the campaign consisted of three "armies" totaling about
100,000 men. Schofield's Army of the Ohio, comprising the 23rd AC and
a few cavalry, was by far the smallest, with about 13,500 men. The Army of
the Tennessee, Sherman's former command, was led by James M. McPherson and numbered approximately 25,000. The Army of the Cumberland
under Thomas numbered over 60,000.[1]

The "Indirect Approach": The Campaign Opens

In his order, Grant told Sherman, "I leave you free to execute in your
own way." In contrast to Grant's bloody methodology against Lee, Sherman chose a strategic approach involving maximum maneuver and min-
imum loss. The eminent military analyst Basil Liddell Hart would later

praise Sherman's method, calling it the "indirect approach." Cox wrote that "Sherman's calculation . . . was that the Army of the Cumberland in his centre was always strong enough to hold Johnston at bay until one of the wings could attack his flank or rear. This simple plan controlled the whole campaign." While Thomas dominated the center of the line, Cox wrote, "the lighter organizations of the Tennessee and the Ohio were thrown from flank to flank in zigzag movements from one strategic position to another." One result was that Cox's men would not be heavily engaged in fighting during the campaign. Rather, their contribution proved to be their maneuverability as they tried to outflank the enemy and force a retreat.[2]

In his memoirs, Cox included incisive appraisals of the two most important men in the Atlanta campaign, Sherman and Thomas, as well as of Grant. Cox saw the decisive and committed Sherman as an ideal commander. "He knew when it was time for debate to stop . . . and to bend every energy to decisive action. . . . [O]f all the men I had met, he was the one to whose leadership in war I would commit my own life and the lives of my men with most complete confidence." As for Thomas, "His reputation for cool intrepidity and stubborn tenacity could not be excelled. . . . No sobriquet conferred by an admiring soldiery was more characteristic than the 'Rock of Chickamauga.'"

As for Grant, Cox initially found him unimpressive in person. For someone like Cox, who reveled in discussion and debate, Grant's taciturn mien and lack of the "faculty of drawing other people out and putting himself in easy accord with them" would be a disappointment. To his dismay, Cox would find that Grant as president acted the same way. At the same time, Cox recognized Grant's abilities as a commander. He noted, "If we supplement it [this judgment] by a reading of the daily and hourly dispatches in which the clear practical judgment, the unswerving faith in final success, the unbending will, the restless energy and industry, the power to master numberless details, and a consciousness of capacity to command, all plainly stand forth as traits of Grant's character."[3]

Opposing Sherman was a Confederate force of about 60,000 situated near Dalton, Georgia, under General Joseph Johnston, who was later reinforced by some 15,000 under General Leonidas Polk. Johnston was urged by Davis, with whom he had a difficult relationship, to take the offensive against Sherman. Johnston had agreed, but only if "the relative forces of the opposing armies should justify . . . such a measure." Otherwise, he decided, he would maneuver to be on the defensive. Cox wrote later that

Johnston's approach was appropriate, given the disparity in forces and the situation he faced. He stated, "The days for brilliant detached campaigns . . . were over. Lee, as well as Johnston, settled down to patient defensive operations behind carefully constructed earthworks, watching for a slip in the strategy of the Federal commanders which might give hope of success to aggressive return blows by their smaller forces." Johnston planned to continue this approach until he could win a defensive-oriented battle, cut Sherman's supply line, or weaken Sherman sufficiently that he would give up on the campaign.[4]

As the campaign began in early May, Sherman moved slowly forward, seeking to get a "feel" for the enemy and assess his capabilities. As Cox colorfully put it, Sherman had to find "out by experiment how the nut was to be cracked." Schofield and Cox had crossed the Georgia line and advanced to Red Clay on May 5, and Cox told Helen, "We are all glad at the prospect of having a part in a campaign on a large scale. Soldiers always are." Opdycke, serving in the 4th AC of Thomas's army, told his wife that Cox looked tanned and healthy and was in good spirits.[5]

On May 9 Cox's division was on the extreme left in the advance to the outskirts of Dalton. That day he experienced firsthand the results of the strategic decisions by both commanders. Cox told Helen that his movements were "rather maneuvers for position than fighting." He first clashed with Confederate forces under John Bell Hood, whose men had set up strong entrenchments. Making a "demonstration," Cox forced the enemy's advance troops to move back to the main trenches, but Hood made no effort to attack in return. As Cox advanced further, the Confederates retreated, "making occasional stands" when the Union attacked, "usually by outflanking their strong positions & forcing them to fight at a disadvantage. When after an engagement more or less severe, they again retreat. Each army throws up breastworks & artillery parapets as it moves, & the process is a slow one."[6]

On May 14 and 15 the first major battle of the campaign was fought at Resaca. During it, Sherman first exhibited his overall plan on a large scale, hoping to bring Johnston out of his defenses or force a retreat. Cox told Helen that he had engaged in significant "pitched battle" and had been "victorious, gaining position after position . . . and finally taking the key of his last stronghold." Cox wrote, "[M]y division had the honor of the advance on the 14th, the hardest day, & we are proud of the honors awarded us for our work." During the fighting, Johnston had become aware that

McPherson's forces were moving around his left. Realizing that this meant that Sherman could "put himself upon the railway near Calhoun," Johnston retreated on the evening of May 15 to "Cassville and prepared for further battles."[7]

As Sherman's army advanced in mid-May, Schofield came to appreciate Cox and his talents even more after his other two division commanders proved to be unfit. On May 10, Schofield asked Sherman to remove 1st Division commander General Alvin Hovey, a political general from Indiana. Schofield said he had determined within a week of the campaign's launch that Hovey was "utterly inefficient and worthless as a division commander," and Schofield attributed his lack of ability to "some sort of mental disease." Sherman responded that he could not remove Hovey, because the latter had been given his assignment as a promise to Grant. For the moment Hovey remained, despite Schofield's official view: "I dare not trust him in the handling of troops."[8]

The 2nd Division commander, Henry Judah, a West Point graduate, was removed on May 18 because of his misconduct at the Battle of Resaca, and he was replaced by General Milo Hascall. At Resaca Schofield had ordered Judah to coordinate his movements with Cox, but instead Judah rushed his men forward without waiting for reconnaissance or support. His impetuosity required Cox and forces from the 4th AC to come to his aid. Not surprisingly, Cox told Helen that after the Battle of Resaca, Schofield, having seen his other two division commanders prove incompetent, "grasped [Cox's] hand warmly and said with evident feeling, 'You have done nobly today, General, & I am glad to see you safe.'" Cox continued, "Gen S. is so proverbially reticent & uncommunicative that I regard this as of much meaning.'"[9]

The Army of the Ohio's command situation would be complicated again when on June 8 Hovey tendered his resignation and asked to leave the campaign. His unstated objective was to go to Washington to lobby for a promotion. Sherman recommended accepting the resignation, which, Cox wrote, "spread the official censure of General Sherman . . . upon the records of the War Department, . . . that department having made a tender of resignation in the presence of the enemy a cause for summary dismissal of inferior officers." Then, in an "addition by subtraction" move, Sherman authorized Schofield to disband Hovey's division and divide the three thousand men in it between Hascall and Cox. By mid-June, the Army of the Ohio consisted of two large divisions, each of which finally had solid leadership.[10]

As the armies moved south in mid-May, Sherman sent his forces forward in four separate columns, but because of the unknowns of the territory, there was inevitable confusion. The delays and division of forces presented Johnston with what he had hoped for: an opportunity to attack one of Sherman's wings while it was isolated. Johnston publicly announced on May 19 his plan to take the offensive at Cassville, which was "heard with exultation" by his men. Johnston ordered Hood to initiate the attack, but Confederate scouts reported Union cavalry approaching to their rear. Cox's and other batteries then opened fire on the rebel line, and Hood and Polk advised withdrawal. Johnston reluctantly agreed and retreated on May 20. In his memoirs, Cox said that Johnston's decision weakened the morale of the Confederate troops because "hardly anything is more destructive of the confidence of an army than vacillation. The order to fight had been published, and even a defeat might be less mischievous than the sudden retreat in the night without joining the battle which had been so formally announced. Either the order had been an error or the retreat was one. Every soldier in the army knew this, and the *morale* of the whole was necessarily affected by it."[11] This incident also heightened Davis's frustration with Johnston's Fabian tactics.

After Cassville, Sherman decided on a major advance, ordering the army to stock up supplies for a twenty-day disconnection from the railway supply line. Schofield's army was "held back a day's march to cover the rear as well as the left flank and the supply train." The armies next clashed on May 25 at Dallas and New Hope Church. Sherman wrote that his men called the area "Hell's Hole" because the two armies fought over ever-extending lines of trenches and barriers. As each army moved to defend itself, Cox wrote, "Every advanced line on both sides intrenched itself as soon as a position was assumed." Cox noted that foreign observers were amazed at the men's initiative in digging their trenches without orders. To Cox, however, it was not surprising: the indirect approach on this campaign had led to a near-institutionalization of procedures to move to the defensive.[12]

The armies fought extended battles all along the line until June 4; Cox wrote Helen, "[T]he campaign is so anomalous that we can hardly tell when one battle ends and another begins." That day Sherman began to maneuver his entire army around Cox's division, moving Cox from the extreme left to the extreme right. In response, Johnston set up a new defensive line just north of Kennesaw Mountain. Cox wrote that Sherman hoped to have a decisive engagement by mid-June. In keeping with his campaign plan,

Sherman told Halleck on June 5, "I expect the enemy to fight us at Kennesaw Mountain, . . . but I will not run head on his fortifications."[13]

Kennesaw: Changes of Command

In early June, Sherman advanced slowly as torrential rains, Cox told Helen, "played pranks with us . . . with terrific thunder and lightning . . . miring the spongy ground and spoiling the roads and fords." On June 22 the battle of Kolb's Farm led to a further stalemate and extension of the trench lines. Cox wrote, "It began to look like dead-lock, and that of all things was what Sherman could not endure." By June 24 Johnston had put his troops into what Cox described to Helen as "nearly a horseshoe form . . . at Kennesaw Mountain." From there, the rebels were "unassailable by direct assault . . . and able to look down on and view every movement of ours[:] . . . an advantage in itself worth half an army."

That same day Cox told Helen that while his luck at never having been wounded continued, he had had several narrow escapes. He wrote,

> I did not tell you that I was stunned by the explosion of a shell at Resaca, because it was not true. . . . I was simply deafened for a few seconds. It was a providential escape. . . . [T]he bystanders thought we were all killed, & it was for a time so reported. If I told you all the narrow escapes you would be kept uneasy all the time, & it is much better that you should only reflect upon the fact that so far I am unhurt, & the escapes will do to talk about at home, when the war is over, & I can fight my battles over again by the fireside.[14]

In Cox's interpretation, Sherman was frustrated by facing a lengthy stalemate in late June, and so, as Cox observed, "It was with reluctance that Sherman was brought to the determination to make a front assault" at the Battle of Kennesaw Mountain on June 27. Cox described the battle and his role in it to Helen with a clear sense of relief that he had not been involved in what he feared would be a fruitless effort, given the power of the defensive. He wrote, "Two attacks and attempts to carry the enemy's line by assault were made, in front of Thomas's and McPherson's Corps, both of which failed to break the line. . . . The orders had at first assigned that my command should assist in the assault nearer the center, but Gen. Sherman finally concluded that I could do more good by the flank movement and changed the order accordingly, for which I was not sorry."

As Cox moved to Johnston's west on his flanking movement, one historian wrote, "Cox put together an effective plan [that] . . . worked beautifully, in part because Cox was up early and . . . pushed his subordinates relentlessly." Cox discovered and took control of an unguarded ridge that threatened the rebel position. Schofield told Cox, "I don't think the importance of the position you have gained can be overestimated," because it outflanked Johnston and, along with additional federal flanking movements, soon forced the rebels to retreat again. That same historian added, "Meticulous planning and brisk execution, along with a surprisingly lax defensive attitude by [General William H.] Jackson, had accounted for a Federal success." Cox told Helen proudly, "Gen. Sherman himself said I accomplished the only valuable result of the whole day's fighting." Johnston withdrew on July 2, admitting that because of Cox's and other maneuvers, "[t]he Federals intrenched line had brought it nearer to Atlanta than was our left and had made our position otherwise very dangerous."[15]

On July 5 Johnston formed a new defensive line ten miles north of Atlanta. Sherman then ordered a reconnaissance along the Chattahoochee River to find an opportunity to flank Johnston and force him to retreat into Atlanta. Cox took an initiative and carried out a key maneuver to achieve that objective. At that point he was at the extreme left of the army, so far away from the center that Johnston may not have expected a movement there. Cox and his men moved stealthily to and over the river on the evening of July 8. Cox told Helen, "Every precaution was taken to keep the enemy ignorant of our approach . . . and we were completely successful." Cox's men "congratulated each other on being the first div. over the Chattahoochee. . . . Gen Schofield said the movement was the prettiest thing he ever saw done," and it was accomplished without a single casualty. Cox had such firm control that he "went for [his] first swim in three years" in the river. Johnston's right flank was now exposed, and he was forced to move his entire army over the river and to select a new defensive line. Cox wrote that a new Union offensive was then ordered to "find and drive back the enemy upon Atlanta," and by July 20, Schofield and McPherson were a few miles east of the city.[16]

On July 17, as the Union advance toward Atlanta continued, Davis replaced Johnston with Hood, noting that Johnston had "failed to arrest the advance of the enemy . . . and express[ed] no confidence" that he could "defeat or repel" the Federals. Sherman asked his commanders, some of whom knew Hood, for their appraisal of the new rebel leader. Schofield,

Hood's classmate at West Point, said he was "bold even to rashness and courageous in the extreme." O. O. Howard made the most incisive and cutting analysis, writing his wife, "He is a stupid fellow but a hard fighter—does some very unexpected things." Presuming that Hood would discard Johnston's effective defensive-oriented tactics and go on the offensive, Sherman told his commanders, "This was just what we wanted, viz. to fight in open ground, on anything like equal terms instead of being forced to run up against prepared intrenchments."[17]

In Cox's judgment, "The change of commanders undoubtedly precipitated the ruin of the Confederate cause. . . . We regarded the removal of Johnston as equivalent to a victory for us. . . . The action of the Confederate government was a confession that Sherman's methods had brought about the very result he aimed at." Further, the rebel army's morale suffered because of the change. The troops knew it meant that they would be taking the offensive, which they felt would be unsustainable. Several offensives thus far in the campaign had been led by Hood, and all had been bloody failures. Moreover, Hood was a relative newcomer to the Army of the Tennessee, and his men were unsure of both his abilities and his concern for their welfare.[18]

During his first few days in command, Hood fulfilled the predictions of the Union generals. His first offensive effort, the Battle of Peachtree Creek, on July 20 was a standoff, though his losses were considerable. Hood attacked again in the Battle of Bald Hill/Atlanta on July 22, which Cox called "a great battle along five miles of front and rear," as Hood tried to swing around and destroy McPherson's army. Hood's attack was thwarted, but McPherson was killed, and he was replaced on the field by his deputy, John "Black Jack" Logan, a political general from Illinois.[19]

On July 25, after these two significant defeats, Hood further verified the judgment of the Union commanders by issuing a fateful "general field order." It said, in part, "SOLDIERS: Experience has proved to you that safety in time of battle consists in getting into close quarters with your enemy. Guns and colors are the only unerring indications of victory." In a knock at Johnston, he said that if the army continued to be flanked out of position, "[o]ur cause is in great peril." This trumpet call to return to Napoleonic-style frontal charges was an important indicator that while Hood was a valiant warrior well suited to subordinate command, overall command and comprehension of the realities and broader aspects of military administration and strategy were beyond his ability.[20]

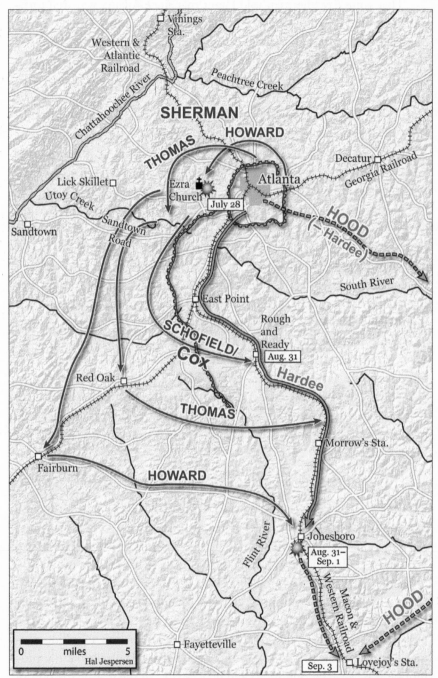

Map 4. The taking of Atlanta, August 31–September 1, 1864. (Map by Hal Jespersen)

That same day Sherman told Grant that since Atlanta was well fortified, he would try to force Hood to abandon it by cutting Hood's supply line via the Macon and Western Railroad to the south. Sherman ordered yet another zigzag movement that left Cox "on the extreme left flank again," which, Cox wrote, "necessitat[ed] a change of all [his] lines, a ticklish thing to do in the presence of an enterprising and desperate enemy." Hood acknowledged that "the holding of Atlanta . . . depended upon [his] ability to hold intact the [rail]road to Macon," and in response he launched a new offensive at the Battle of Ezra Church. Cox wrote that this attempt failed for several reasons, one being that "Hood had suffered so severely in the battles of Peachtree Creek and on the east of Atlanta that his troops were losing their stomach for assaulting intrenchments." But having just issued his "general field order," Hood felt compelled to plunge ahead. In response, Cox wrote, "The [Union] breastworks grew as if by magic . . . and again the gray columns were beaten back." Some Confederate troops, recognizing the futility of their situation, "stolidly refused to continue the assaults." Cox wrote that despite officers waving swords to encourage them, "[t]hey remained motionless and silent, refusing to budge."

While Hood wrote that the battle was a standoff, in fact he had failed again. Cox wrote, "Johnston could hardly have dreamed of quicker or more complete vindication of his generalship." On the other hand, Union morale had received a considerable boost, as Sherman reported that he was so close to Atlanta that the men could see the city's parapets. A state of siege began in August as the Confederates set up batteries to keep the Union forces at bay.[21]

Heightened Political-Military Wars

The last weeks of July and first weeks of August saw three events with significant political-military repercussions for both the Union army and the reputation of political generals. The first was the news that Hovey had been promoted to major general. Cox told Helen, "This is a wanton insult to the whole army in the field. . . . [W]e hear that this skulker is made a Major Gen. & no recognition is given to the other general officers in the Corps." Undoubtedly reflecting on the fact that he had had his promotion pulled out from under him, he told her angrily that it was a "galling mismanagement of the army." A fuming Sherman told Halleck that the promotion was "an act of injustice," and he went on, "If the rear be the post of honor, then we had all better change front on Washington." Sherman was amazed to receive on July 26 a telegram about these issues from Lincoln, who tried to calm the storm, noting that he looked forward to Sherman's recommendations for other promotions. Sherman responded that promotions like Hovey's were a scandal and that ambitious officers (like Cox) would approach Sherman "and point them out as evidences" that their commander was "wrong in encouraging them to a silent, patient discharge of duty." Cox was pleased not only to hear of Sherman's indignation but also to read Lincoln's letter, which Sherman distributed to all commands.[22]

The second event, which had major repercussions for years, was Sherman's decision not to recommend that Logan replace McPherson as commander of the Army of the Tennessee. "Black Jack" Logan was a proven, fierce fighter who was popular among his men. Sherman nevertheless noted in his memoirs that politicians "were mistrusted by regular officers like Generals Schofield, Thomas and myself." He said Thomas, with whom Logan had had some serious disputes earlier in the war, "remonstrated warmly against my recommending General Logan." Sherman admitted that Logan "had some reason to believe that we intended to monopolize the higher honors of the war for regular officers." But he said he looked on Logan as a volunteer who "looked to personal fame and glory as auxiliary and secondary to political ambition, and not as professional soldiers." Sherman instead appointed O. O. Howard, former commander of the 4th AC, to the job. An angry Logan told his wife, "West Point must have all under Sherman, who is an infernal *brute*." Nevertheless, he accepted the decision and continued to do his duty.[23]

When commenting in his writings about this critical decision for political generals, Cox's close friendship with and admiration for Sherman would lead him to "pull his punches." In his book *Atlanta,* he rationalized, "It is possible that in [Sherman's] ultimate choice a predilection in favor of officers bred in the so-called regular army might have had some little influence, but Sherman repudiate[d] any purpose but that of securing the best organization." Cox made no reference there to Sherman's statement that political generals were more interested in political ambition than "personal fame and glory" through successes on the battlefield. Perhaps he reasoned that Sherman did not include Cox among the "politicians mistrusted" by him, Thomas, and Schofield, because Cox was not a self-promoter and because, unlike Logan, Cox had not been a prominent politician before the war. Cox did mildly criticize Sherman's decision in his 1875 review of the latter's memoirs in the *Nation,* stating that "Sherman was wrong in failing to give civilian generals top commands because they are activated by political ambition." However, the review was unsigned, so even then Cox did not go on the record.[24]

The third event came on August 4 when Sherman issued orders that "Major General Schofield with his own command and General [John] Palmer's corps [14th AC, part of Thomas's army] will move directly on the [Macon railroad] and not stop until he has absolute control of that railroad." The mission did not succeed, and Cox told Helen that certain aspects of the reasons for the failure had "disgusted [him] exceedingly." As the troops moved toward the railroad, Palmer, a political general from Illinois, announced that he and his men would not follow orders from Schofield, whom he outranked. He asked to be relieved. That, Cox wrote, "was the beginning of cross-purposes, misunderstandings, half obediences, protests, &c lasting through two days" about "a paltry quibble about rank [which] could cost the army perhaps two thousand lives." By August 7, Cox's and Hascall's divisions were within a few miles of the railroad, but the delay and their lack of support from Palmer allowed the rebels to block the "ground [the Union] might have taken almost without a shot."[25]

A "Cursing Cox" and the Fall of Atlanta: "Reunion" with McClellan

On August 7 Cox told Helen, "It is said the opposition to Hood's policy of hurling [his men] against our works has become so strong that he has had to give it up." On August 2 Hood wrote to Davis that he would try an alternative approach: using his cavalry under Joseph Wheeler to try to cut Sherman's supply line and force Sherman "to fight . . . in position or retreat." Endorsing that plan on August 5, Davis ironically noted, "The loss consequent upon attacking him in his intrenchments requires you to avoid that if practicable." Implicitly having recognized the power of the defensive, Davis added that Hood's objective should be "to compel the enemy to attack you in position or retreat," which was exactly the approach Johnston had taken. Hood later claimed that while his cavalry made significant strides toward cutting Sherman's supply line during August, he did not have enough men to do the job. Hood did not come to that conclusion until late in August; he thought at one point that the effort had been successful. A related miscalculation would lead to the fall of Atlanta.[26]

On the Union side, Cox wrote, "Sherman was now convinced that he could expect no permanent results from cutting the enemy's communications [and supply line] unless it were done in force." Sherman ordered a comprehensive flanking maneuver, entrenching the 20th AC to the north of the city and swinging the rest of his army toward its south. Cox's division was to be the "pivot of the movement," and by August 27 "most of the army was between Atlanta and Sandtown." In his diary on August 26 Cox noted, "The enemy is excited and watches to see what this means, but does not interfere."[27]

Sherman had not intended this effort as a subterfuge, but it became one when Hood concluded that Sherman might be retreating via the Sandtown road because the effort to cut the Union supply line had succeeded. Hood's chief of staff wrote in his journal on August 26, "The prevailing impression is that the Federals are falling back across the Chattahoochee River." Hood's communiqués of August 25 and 26 included a report that his cavalry had captured a thousand head of cattle and that Sherman seemed to have "disappeared." At the same time, Hood warned all of his commanders to be alert to the possibility of subterfuge or another turning movement.

An incident on August 27 in which Cox was allegedly involved was, by some accounts, critical to convincing Hood that Sherman had indeed retreated. According to W. J. Hardee, one of Hood's key subordinates (but with whom Hood had difficult relations), who related the story to Cox after the war, a female spy told him that she had been within Schofield's lines on August 18 and had asked for food. She said she had met personally with Cox, who refused her request. According to both Hardee and Hood's chief of staff, who also reported the incident, Cox had told her that he had been "living on short rations for seven days" and further complained, "[N]ow that your people have torn up our railroad and stolen our beef cattle, we must live a damn sight shorter."

Cox wrote in his memoirs that he did not remember the incident, blushingly adding, "[A] laugh was raised at my expense as Hardee in telling the story repeated some profane camp expletives as having added emphasis to the refusal. . . . Schofield merrily rallied me on a change of habits of speech when not with my usual associates, and refused to credit my protestation." Hardee said he had taken the woman to Hood to tell him her story and in response "Hood exclaimed, 'There, Hardee! It proves that it is just as I told you. Wheeler has broken Sherman's communications; he is short of provisions and is retreating north by the Sandtown road.' . . . To this conviction he stubbornly adhered for forty-eight hours longer."[28]

On August 30 Schofield's army was moving again toward the Macon railroad, and Union forces "fully expected a blow from Hood." But, Cox wrote, Hood "had contented himself with a brisk cavalry reconnaissance," perhaps because he "was strangely misconceiving the situation." Instead, Hood sent a large force south to Jonesboro to meet a threat there. On August 31 Cox, meeting minimal resistance, moved rapidly toward the railroad at the city of Rough and Ready. At 4 p.m., Schofield reported that he had "Cox's division in position fortifying and breaking track" and, later in the day, that Cox had pushed ahead for two miles and "encountered no enemy." A train coming south from Atlanta stopped when it heard the combat at Rough and Ready, and on its return "carried the news to Atlanta that Sherman's infantry was moving northward, . . . [which] carried consternation with it. Hood himself seems to have been bewildered." As one of Cox's men put it colorfully, "What was their surprise and amazement when they found the Yanks had a death grip on their cornmeal." As Hardee snidely wrote in his report, "The fate of Atlanta was sealed from the moment when General Hood allowed an enemy superior in numbers to pass unmolested around his flank and plant himself firmly upon his only line of railroad."[29]

Cox had now taken the critical step leading to the fall of Atlanta, and Schofield wrote Cox later in the day that "General Sherman expresses the highest gratification at what [you] have done today." Sherman had now achieved the major objective of cutting the Confederate supply line, and, Hood later admitted, "The Federal army's control of the Macon road . . . necessitated the evacuation of Atlanta." He defensively wrote to Davis later, "We should have saved Atlanta had the officers and men of the army done what was expected of them." He did not include himself among that group, but it was his failures that led to the fall of this pivotal city.[30]

Cox's success at Rough and Ready was the final occasion when he and George McClellan would interact during the Civil War, though at a great political-military distance. The two generals had begun the war together, shaking their heads in dismay at the miserable equipment in the Ohio armory. They had fought together in West Virginia and Maryland, and they had been confidantes before and during the Maryland campaign. After Antietam, Cox the politician had focused on his military career, while McClellan the military man had become a politician.

McClellan would receive the Democratic nomination for president on August 31, and his chances for victory seemed excellent. Democratic optimism reflected the fact that in the previous months Northern morale had deteriorated because of the stalemates in both East and West. Taking advantage of this war weariness, the likely party platform, authored primarily by Vallandigham, would condemn the war and all related military activities, including those which McClellan had led. The military situation was sufficiently dire that Lincoln wrote a memorandum in August that presumed McClellan would win. Lincoln wrote that the cabinet would have to save the Union before the inauguration because McClellan "will have secured his election on such ground that he cannot possibly save it afterwards."[31]

Cox's taking of the Macon railroad on the same day as McClellan's nomination was a key blow to McClellan's candidacy because it led to the abandonment of Atlanta. Northern morale escalated when Atlanta fell, and optimism about an early end to the war and the chances of a Lincoln victory increased. It was hardly a confluence of events either man could have predicted. But given the other peculiarities of this war for Cox, the divinity student turned warrior, it was perhaps the final irony of a unique political-military relationship.

The Commanders Ponder Their Next Steps

As the rebel army abandoned Atlanta, Sherman had an opportunity to destroy the divided Confederate forces, half of which were at Jonesboro, and half of which were retreating from Atlanta to the east. Instead, satisfied with the capture of the city, Sherman decided to let Hood go. He told Howard that because Atlanta had fallen, he did "not wish to waste lives by an assault." Perhaps forgetting that the objective of his campaign was to destroy the opposing army, Sherman told his commanders on September 4, "The army having accomplished its undertaking in the complete reduction and occupation of Atlanta," it would take a month's rest until a new campaign was launched. Cox agreed with that approach, telling Helen, "Having compelled them to evacuate Atlanta, Sherman had no desire to invest them in their new position, & our own supplies running short, we came back as at first intended." He added proudly, "This closing movement . . . has been a very brilliant one, & has closed the campaign with a *coup d'éclat* which will place Sherman very high in the list of successful commanders of great armies."

Both Sherman and Hood ultimately realized that Sherman should have continued the campaign. Hood wrote later, "I have often thought it strange [that] Sherman should have occupied himself with attacking Hardee's intrenched position, instead of falling upon our main body on the march round to his rear." Sherman admitted to Halleck on September 4, "I ought to have reaped larger fruits of victory," but he blamed the slowness of his commanders instead of his own decision making. He later acknowledged, "I had not accomplished all, for Hood's army, the 'chief objective,' had escaped. Then began the real trouble."[32]

Both commanders began early September pondering what to do next. Sherman told Grant he had several ideas, including moving toward Hood and taking the cities of Augusta and Macon. He admitted, "I do not think we can afford to operate farther, dependent on the railroad." While he considered his options, Sherman implemented policies that brought the hard hand of war to Atlanta. He told Halleck on September 9 that he would order the evacuation of all noncombatants from the city, stating, "I want a pure Gibraltar." He also wanted to stop the practice of using his troops for garrison duty to guard civilians instead of having them available for war. He notified Hood of his intentions, and in a series of vituperative letters the two accused one another of a variety of war crimes. Trying to boost morale, the Confederate authorities publicized Sherman's order as evidence of Northern barbarity. Sherman told Halleck he was not concerned: "The more he arouses the indignation of the Southern masses, the bigger will be the pill of bitterness they have to swallow."[33]

Hood, faced with the problems both of deciding on his next steps and of how to keep his job, invited Davis to Georgia in late September to discuss strategy and to argue his case for keeping command. Hood told Davis that the best approach now was "to assume the offensive, cut the enemy's communications, select a position on or near the Alabama line in proximity to the Blue Mountain Railroad, and there give him battle." The plan was optimistic, but Hood averred that it "offered the sole chance to avert disaster." Encouraged by Hood's commitment and the new plan, Davis decided not to accept Lee's advice to replace Hood as army commander.[34]

During the visit to Hood's troops, Davis made a series of bellicose public speeches in a desperate attempt to boost morale. He told a cheering audience in Macon that Johnston had been a failure, Hood was going to reverse the fortunes of war, and Sherman could not hold his supply line much longer and would soon have to retreat. When that happened, Davis said, it would be more disastrous than Napoleon's retreat from Moscow, and it would be followed by a Confederate advance all the way to Ohio.

On September 25 Davis spoke to the troops at Palmetto and was received with a sullen silence and occasional shouts of "Give us Johnston!" and "Give us our old commander!" Hood admitted in his memoirs that he regretted that he had been the cause of the discourteous reception. He did not mention the discontent among his men at being sent to their deaths repeatedly against fortified and entrenched positions. In a separate speech to the Tennesseans in the army, Davis promised them, as they advanced into their home state, "If, in their future campaigns, they met an entrenched enemy, their lives should not be uselessly sacrificed and . . . they would be ordered only to charge 'temporary breastworks.'" That promise would be broken when Hood decided to launch the war's final mass frontal infantry attack at Franklin, Tennessee.[35]

Promotion: Role Reversals

As the commanders pondered, Cox gained additional responsibility and honors. On September 12 Schofield formally recommended, and Sherman endorsed, Cox's promotion to major general, noting, "He is the senior brigadier general of volunteers in active service. . . . I have no hesitation in saying that I have never seen a more able and efficient division commander." Three days later Schofield decided to take advantage of the hiatus in the campaign to travel north on departmental and personal business. This step gave Cox interim command of the Army of the Ohio for more than a month, during which time Sherman would launch the next campaign.

Hood began his campaign by moving north on September 29; his army crossed the Chattahoochee River southwest of Atlanta the next day. This forced Sherman into a reactive rather than a proactive stance. Cox assessed, "It was now the important question to Sherman to decide what his adversary would do, for he did not mean to be led off upon a wild-goose chase if he could avoid it." As he began planning his reaction, on September 30 Sherman telegraphed Schofield, "I was surprised when I heard you had gone to Illinois. . . . You should be with your army here or in Tennessee."

On October 1 Sherman ordered Thomas and most of the 4th AC to Nashville to thwart a possible Hood offensive in that direction. He then explained his planning to his other commanders, Cox and Howard: "If Hood swings over to the Alabama road and then tries to get into Tennessee, I may throw back to Chattanooga all of Major-General Thomas' men as far down as Kingston, and draw forward all else[,] . . . [then] destroy Atlanta and make for Savannah or Charleston. If Hood aims at our road this side of Kingston, and in no matter threatens Tennessee, I will

138   have to turn on him." Sherman told Cox to be ready to move quickly. Cox, proudly signing himself "Brigadier General, Commanding Army of the Ohio," responded, "We shall be the 'minute men' in the contingency you mention."[36]

During the next three weeks, the Union and Confederate armies, in effect, reversed the Atlanta campaign. Instead of the Union pushing the Confederates farther and farther south, Hood "pulled" Sherman farther and farther north as he tried to destroy the railroad while also looking, he claimed, for a situation to give battle. There was more feinting than fighting during this period, in great part because Hood knew he did not have the capacity to deal with even these reduced Union forces. Cox's army had a minimal role in the campaign, primarily holding and repairing the railroad as Hood moved north. Sherman chased Hood to Gaylesville, Alabama, but stopped there on October 19, convinced that "to pursue Hood is folly, for he can twist and turn like a fox and wear out the army in pursuit." Hood, desperate for supplies, retreated west through Alabama to Florence in early November. Sherman wrote later, "Hood remained at Florence, preparing to invade Tennessee and Kentucky, or to follow me [on the march to the sea]. We were prepared for either alternative."[37]

Cox described this short campaign in his memoirs as "a good example of what soldiers regard as pleasant work." He meant that there had been "magnificent weather," accompanied by "constant activity, with no severe fighting. . . . [I]t had been like a hunt for big game on a grand scale." He also wrote about another new experience for a citizen-general during this period. He noted that the men needed diversions, and a popular one was acquiring a pet, usually a dog. Cox acquired his own pet, a small "gold and green lizard," which he had tamed. He wrote, "The little thing seemed to become fond of me, running about on my papers, climbing my arm." Wherever Cox rode, the lizard sat on his hat rim "like a most gorgeous aigrette." Cox joked that his men called the beast "an attaché of the staff." One day when Cox was consulting with a colleague from another corps, however, one of the latter's staff, seeing the lizard on Cox's shoulder, knocked it off and killed it, thinking he had saved Cox's life. When Cox's staff told the man he had "killed the general's pet," he "slunk away, the picture of shame and remorse." Cox concluded, "Pets were sacred by the law of the camp, and he felt and looked as if he were a murderer."[38]

When Schofield had not returned by mid-October, Sherman told Cox he "thought . . . he should separate the Twenty-third Corps from the

Department of the Ohio and take it with him" for the march to the sea, with Cox as its commander. Cox likely believed (and probably hoped) that Sherman assumed Schofield would prefer to remain in the higher-ranking position of department commander rather than leave it for the field. Cox told Helen on October 17 that he doubted Schofield would "remain with us even if he comes down." Cox told Sherman that he was anxious to participate, and he was clearly pleased by the confidence Sherman showed in him.[39]

Schofield finally returned on October 21, and that day, during a meeting with Sherman and Schofield, Cox told Helen he was pleased to hear Sherman tell Schofield, "Your command has been handled in your absence to my complete satisfaction. Indeed it has been beautifully handled." Sherman briefed Schofield and Cox about his plans for Thomas and for the march to the sea and said he planned to include the 23rd AC in the latter. When Schofield objected, Sherman apparently interpreted that at first as an effort by Schofield to return to the Department of Ohio, leaving Cox in command. Sherman had shown during the Atlanta campaign that while he appreciated Schofield's diligence, he thought, as he told Halleck, "Schofield is also slow and leaves too much to others." Among the "others," Cox was *primus inter pares*. Sherman had also seen over a period of five weeks that Cox could be a capable corps commander in Schofield's stead, and he saw Cox as a suitable, dutiful replacement.

Schofield and Cox spent some time discussing the pros and cons of the two possible missions. Schofield assured Cox that compared to Sherman's march, the campaign against Hood would be far more active and important and that "another veteran corps, though a small one, might make all the difference between defeat and victory." Cox wrote Helen, "[T]ill the war is ended I want to be with the biggest and most active moving column in the West," and that attitude helped convince him that Schofield was right. Schofield told Sherman both that he wanted to keep active command and that the 23rd AC should stay behind to help stem Hood's advance. Sherman agreed. For his part, Cox appreciated being treated as an equal, stating in his memoirs, "I still look back with pleasure to this incident as proof of the hearty comradeship between Sherman and his subordinates, which continued to be shown toward me by both him and Schofield to the end."[40]

As October ended, Sherman was finalizing his plans to split his forces into two parts. One would march east through Georgia, laying waste to the South while facing no real opposition. The other would engage in the last major campaign of the western war. On October 30 Sherman issued orders putting Schofield under Thomas's authority, and on November 1 Sherman told Thomas, "You must unite all your men into one army and abandon all minor points if you expect to defeat Hood." Thomas telegraphed Halleck, "With Schofield and [4th AC Commander David S.] Stanley I feel confident I can drive Hood back," though he expressed concern that he had not yet heard when his promised reinforcements, A. J. Smith's division from Missouri, would be joining him. On November 2 Grant agreed to Sherman's plan, on the condition that "with the force . . . left with Thomas, he must be able to take care of Hood, and destroy him." Sherman reassured Grant that "Thomas will have ample time and sufficient troops to hold him until re-enforcements reach him from Missouri and recruits."[41] In the end, however, Sherman's intense focus on his march to the sea may have blinded him to the problems Thomas would have, and his gambol to the sea made the campaign in Tennessee a high-risk gamble.

Assessing the Division and Army Commander

The Atlanta campaign gave Cox the opportunity to reestablish his military reputation. Forgotten by Washington for over a year in the drudgery of garrison and administrative duties, he was desperate for another chance to prove himself. To do so, he had had to convince an entirely new group of commanders—Foster, Sherman, Schofield, and Grant—that he was capable of the new responsibilities. Having failed at self-promotion, he had to prove his military worth by exhibiting again the skills he had demonstrated during the early days of the war. Although he played only a minor role in the Atlanta campaign, he took advantage of every opportunity he had to prove his capabilities. He did so well that he was once again endorsed for promotion to major general and Sherman wanted him to be the commander of the 23rd AC for Sherman's march to the sea.

One reason for Cox's success was establishing a close relationship with Schofield, who was building a military reputation for himself for the first time. Schofield was perceptive enough to open himself to Cox's counsel based on the latter's extensive experience. He also apparently discerned that Cox would be a more effective subordinate if his acumen and intellect were recognized and his ideas given the chance to be implemented. This discernment included praising Cox for his achievements: overcoming Johnston's advantage at Kennesaw Mountain; stealthily outflanking

Johnston by crossing the Chattahoochee unnoticed; and seizing the Macon railroad. Schofield also learned how incompetent subordinates like Hovey and Judah could harm his effectiveness, whereas capable ones like Cox were essential to making his own reputation.

Cox also proved himself to Sherman, especially during the five-week period when he was acting commander of the Army of the Ohio. Sherman's distaste for politics and politicians was well-known, but he apparently never saw Cox as a typical politician. Sherman's readiness to appoint Cox as the 23rd AC's commander for the march to the sea was his highest compliment, given the centrality of that effort in Sherman's thinking at the time. The fact that Sherman would suggest to Cox toward the end of the war that he stay in the regular army with the rank of brigadier general underlined further Sherman's judgment that during the Atlanta campaign, Cox had reestablished his reputation as one of the Union's better generals, civilian or professional.

6 Citizen-Warrior
The Franklin-Nashville Campaign and War's End

> Gen. Cox remained mounted [to see and to be seen] . . . while
> the confusion was greatest, and during the break, he was in
> the midst, displaying heroic bravery, with hopeful look and
> sword poised above. The men saw his conspicuous figure, [and]
> rallied around him. . . . If ever an example of personal bravery
> turned a tide of battle, surely at this point Gen. Cox's quiet but
> superb magnetism impelled every man who caught his eye to
> redoubled effort in wresting victory from defeat.
>
> —Levi Scofield, *The Retreat from Pulaski to Nashville, Tenn.*, 1909

The events leading to this chapter's epigraph's extraordinary description of Cox as an emotionally charged warrior at the Battle of Franklin began during Sherman's preparations for his next campaigns.[1] On November 12, as Sherman prepared to leave Atlanta, Thomas telegraphed him, "If he [Hood] does not follow you, I will then thoroughly organize my troops, and believe I shall have men enough to ruin him unless he gets out of the way very rapidly." Cox wrote, "The task before Thomas was to conduct a cautious and purposely dilatory campaign till his reinforcements should be well in hand, and then, resuming the aggressive, to drive Hood southward and follow him wherever he should go."

Thomas's plan called for Schofield's 23rd and Stanley's 4th AC to play the primary role in stemming Hood's advance northward from Alabama. They were to be augmented eventually by the 16th AC under General A. J. Smith as well as the men in the garrisons and posts then in Tennessee. Thomas had decided on November 4 that Schofield would be in charge of the united force, stating his view that "Schofield is much the more reliable commander of the two." Separately, Grant commented that for Stanley, "a corps is a very high command . . . [and] authority had better be given Schofield to remove the latter when, in his judgment, the good of the service requires it."[2]

Cox was unaware of Sherman's orders or Thomas's planning as he moved northward from Atlanta to join Schofield, arriving on November 7 in Chattanooga. Along the way, he happily told Helen that Opdycke would be participating in the campaign as part of the 4th AC. The next day, he noted in his memoirs, "was the Presidential election-day, and . . . the officers and men voted at the halts of the train when they could get to the voting place." He told Helen that he was "seeing the end of the war manifestly approaching." On November 9 Cox reached Nashville, where he, Thomas, Stanley, and Schofield began to implement the next phase of the campaign.[3]

Setting the Stage

Hood's plan for his next campaign was to work together with Nathan Bedford Forrest to take Nashville and then move into Kentucky, if possible. Cox assessed that Hood's best, and perhaps only feasible, tactic was to "risk everything on the quickest and strongest advance against Thomas" while the latter's forces were still divided. Fortunately for the Union, Hood took several weeks to launch his campaign. In his memoirs, Hood blamed supply problems, heavy rains, and high water on the Tennessee River, as well as Forrest's delay in joining him. Cox conjectured that Hood also delayed until he knew exactly what Sherman was going to do. "Sherman's march southward had a most perplexing effect, raising portentous problems as to its result upon the Confederacy. . . . Torn by doubts, [Hood] found excuses for postponing action." Finally, on November 17 Hood was ordered to advance north "at the earliest practicable moment, striking him [the Union forces] while dispersed." On November 20 Hood ordered Forrest and his cavalry to try to break Federal communications, and the next day he ordered his infantry to advance north.[4]

Thomas estimated that Hood had about 55,000–60,000 effectives for this campaign, including Forrest's cavalry. Thomas reported on November 20 that he had some 65,000 men "present for duty" under his regional command and that Schofield's forces, which would face the Confederate advance, were "numbering less than half those under Hood." In fact, Schofield commanded less than 25,000, the bulk of which were Stanley's 4th AC (some 12,500) and Schofield's 23rd AC (estimated at 9,500).[5]

Schofield's forces included some 1,500 cavalry, but they were far less capable than the Confederate horsemen. Perhaps in part to compensate for the disparity, Thomas repeatedly reassured Schofield that when Smith and his approximately 15,000-man corps arrived, he would be sent immediately forward to help. But Smith would not reach Nashville until November 30, the day of the Battle of Franklin.[6]

Sherman wrote Cox later that he and Grant "expected that Thomas would concentrate before Hood at Florence not only the two Corps . . . but all that he could draw from Chattanooga, Murfreesboro, Decatur, Nashville &c so as to fight Hood near the Tennessee River." Thomas did not concentrate his forces. Unsure whether Hood's objective in moving north would be Nashville or the railroad toward Chattanooga, he decided on a reactive rather than a proactive strategy. Cox wrote that instead of reinforcing Schofield, Thomas decided to station almost 20,000 men "in small packages (to use Napoleon's phrase) along the Chattanooga route." Those men would do almost no fighting during the campaign.

Cox was critical of Thomas's plans in his books, attributing them to, among other things, overconfidence, a vain hope that Smith's troops would arrive in time, and a concern that Hood's real objective was the railroad and not Nashville. Cox theorized that, as Sherman and Grant had envisioned, "it can hardly be disputed that the true military course would have been to concentrate at Pulaski a force superior to Hood's, and give him battle if he dared to advance north from Florence." Instead, "The delay in concentration was fraught with the very gravest perils to the portion of the army under Schofield . . . who took the gravest risks. . . . [T]he slightest mistake on his part might have proved disastrous."[7]

A Mirror Image of the Atlanta Campaign

On November 3 Thomas had positioned Stanley and his 4th AC at Pulaski, a village about thirty-five miles northeast of Florence, Alabama, and sixty-five miles south of Nashville. Schofield assumed command of the total force on November 13, the day when Cox's division arrived. Soon thereafter, Schofield got his first inkling of the limitations of Thomas's planning when Stanley advised him that placing such a small force at Pulaski left them susceptible to a flanking movement to the west, directly from Florence to Columbia. When Schofield reported to Thomas on November 20 that Hood and Forrest were finally on the move, he emphasized, "[T]his is not the best position for the main body of our troops, at least so long as we are inferior in strength to the enemy." Thomas authorized Schofield to use his discretion to meet any threat, while assuring him that Smith's forces were on the way.[8]

The next ten days would play out as a mirror image of the Atlanta campaign, with the "indirect method" the dominant tactic. While on that venture Sherman was on the offensive, using flanking maneuvers against the Confederates, in this campaign Hood was on the offensive, using flanking maneuvers to try to get around or behind Schofield. The latter, like Johnston, tried to retard the enemy's advance, while looking for an advantage or a position where he could use the power of the defensive to ward off the threat or retreat. Then, just as happened to Sherman, Hood became frustrated by Schofield's success and decided that a frontal attack, à la Kennesaw Mountain, was his wisest choice, at Franklin. The result was similar.[9]

Fortuitously for the Union, on November 20, the day Hood's advance forces under Forrest were on their way north toward Columbia, "[t]he rain changed to snow, driving in flurries and squalls all day." This began several days of bad weather, hampering the Confederates' offensive movement. On the evening of November 23, Schofield "received word that the Union cavalry were unable to resist the determined advance of Forrest, and before daybreak of November 24 [Schofield] put his little army in rapid motion for Columbia." Schofield chose his most reliable man to meet Hood's first thrust, ordering to Columbia Cox and one of Stanley's divisions led by George Wagner, one of whose brigade commanders was Opdycke.[10]

Cox's timely arrival allowed him to deter the Confederate advance. Cox told Helen that he arrived "just in time to interpose between our retreating cavalry who were in precipitate retreat, & the rebel Gen. Forrest, who was following them up sharply." Cox added, "We were not a moment too soon." While not a major event, Cox's intervention illustrated the importance of speed both to make and to deflect flanking movements. Furthermore, warding off Forrest, who had become the kind of mythical figure Jackson had been earlier in the war, would have some symbolic value. Hood characterized the episode as a "narrow escape" for the Union, which through "forced marches day and night" by Cox prevented its forces from being cut off.

Cox commented to Helen, "[W]e do not believe Hood will keep the bulk of his army here, but are looking for further flanking movements with a view to force us back to Nashville. We however are looking for reinforcements which will enable us to turn the tables upon him." On

146   the afternoon of November 24, Thomas sent several messages that implied he finally realized the threat was greater than he had thought and the forces to meet it were insufficient. In one, Thomas advised Schofield to do what he had already done: cut off the rebel advance toward Columbia. In another, he promised additional reinforcements, but he sent only an additional one thousand cavalrymen. That group would join the forces of the newly arrived cavalry commander, Major General James H. Wilson, a twenty-seven-year-old "boy wonder" who would perform poorly for much of this campaign.[11]

Schofield determined on November 25 that he had to withdraw farther to meet potential flank attacks. He gave Cox the critical role as the army's rear guard to ensure that the other forces' movement would be unmolested, stressing his reliance on Cox by stating, "I shall want the benefit of your information in selecting a position for the army." The bulk of Schofield's troops crossed the Duck River south of Columbia on the evening of November 27 and moved north. After all the men had crossed, Schofield ordered the pontoon bridges they had utilized destroyed so Hood could not use them.[12]

Schofield faced a difficult position on November 27 and 28 that would worsen because of unexpected breakdowns in communications. First, Schofield's civilian cipher clerk abruptly abandoned his post, leaving Schofield and Thomas unable to communicate in code. For those days, communications were carried out by couriers, and some of those messages never got through or were captured by the Confederates. Second, looking ahead to a potential withdrawal to Nashville, Schofield inquired of Thomas, because a bridge over the Harpeth River in Franklin had been destroyed, "[W]ould it not be well to replace it by a pontoon bridge?" Thomas responded, "You can send some of the pontoons you used at Columbia to Franklin to lay a bridge there." Schofield repeated his request for pontoons over the Harpeth on November 29 but did not state in either message that he had destroyed the other pontoons. Thomas did not act on the second request until it was too late. Schofield's biographer wrote, "The delay to repair and improve the bridge triggered the ensuing battle at Franklin and would fan discord and suspicion between Thomas and Schofield."[13]

Hood and "the Immortal Jackson"; Spring Hill

On November 28 Hood decided to try to outflank Schofield three miles to the east of Columbia using half his infantry and Forrest's cavalry. He wrote, "The situation presented an occasion for one of those interesting and beautiful moves upon the chess-board of war" as had been done by "the immortal Jackson" at Chancellorsville. Hood planned to keep Cox's rear guard busy in Columbia with half the army and most of his artillery and then circumvent Schofield at or near Spring Hill to the north. Not trusting his subordinates and sure that the situation was ripe for success, Hood "resolved to go in person" to lead the effort.[14]

Hood knew that achieving his grandiose vision would require that he confuse Schofield as to his true intentions, and for a time he succeeded in this attempt. Schofield had seemed confident on November 28 that he could watch all of the potential crossings of the river for possible flanking maneuvers. He reported to Thomas that he trusted Wilson would be able to protect his flank while observing and checking Forrest and Hood to his east. Meanwhile, Thomas told him in a message sent at 3 a.m. on November 29 to fall back to Franklin and leave a force at Spring Hill to fend off Hood's potential advance. In the same message, he once again noted that Smith had yet to arrive. Schofield never received that message, but Hood did, his men having intercepted the courier on November 29.

November 28 and 29 were testing days for Schofield. Not knowing that he had been ordered to move north, he continued to hold fast, awaiting both orders from Thomas and news from Wilson. But during this period Wilson was firmly convinced that Forrest and the leading edge of Hood's infantry were focused on attacking the railroad to the east of Nashville. He moved his forces in that direction and lost contact with Schofield's main force. Wilson even reported on the afternoon of November 29 that the "enemy has disappeared." Cox concluded, "Mischiefs are to follow the forgetfulness of the principle that . . . it is the primary duty of the cavalry to keep in touch with the main body of the army." The "mischief" in this case was that Hood's hope that Schofield would be confused was coming true.[15]

Early on November 29 Forrest crossed the river to Schofield's east, and the rebel infantry began marching toward Spring Hill, to Schofield's north. Schofield told Wilson at 8:15 a.m. to try to hold the enemy in check, which was impossible because Wilson was out of position. At about 8 a.m., Hood's artillery began a "vigorous cannonade" against Cox and his rear guard in Columbia in an attempt to convince Schofield that his main force was still there. By the early afternoon Hood's tactics seemed to be working, and Cox told Schofield he was not sure how long he could hold out, because he was susceptible to strong artillery fire and a surge.[16]

Faced with several choices of action in this difficult situation, Schofield decided to gamble by attempting them all. He ordered Stanley and about 6,000 men to Spring Hill, advising him that Schofield would "try to hold the enemy until dark and then draw back." He then issued a general order to all forces to "retire to Franklin" and again asked Thomas to "please have pontoons put down at Franklin at once." Cox told Helen that his role in this complicated scenario was to "hold in check one corps of the rebels which remained in Columbia and prevent them from putting a bridge over the river during the day of our movement." He added, "This gave me warm work, as I had a lively skirmish all day & sharp combat a little before night. The rebels were repulsed in my front, & between dark and midnight I drew off and rejoined the remainder of the army." Thanks to Cox's efforts, S. D. Lee's corps and much of Hood's artillery would not cross the Duck River into Columbia until 2 a.m. on November 30 and would play no significant role in the battle that day.[17]

On the morning of November 29, Forrest advanced directly toward Spring Hill, arriving at about noon. Stanley arrived at almost the same time, and he checked Forrest's advance. Stanley then arranged Wagner's three brigades in a strong defensive line to prepare for the infantry attack that he knew would be coming. Hood's infantry's advance had been delayed because of bad roads and questionable intelligence, so the infantry did not arrive near Spring Hill until midafternoon. Meanwhile, Schofield had sent a large force to assist Stanley, and this apparently concerned Hood enough that he sent Alexander Stewart's corps west instead of aiding Benjamin Cheatham's corps in the main attack at Spring Hill. At 4 p.m., the Confederate forces at Spring Hill numbered about 15,000, facing Stanley's 6,000. The Confederate attack began at that hour, but was uncoordinated, sporadic, and inefficient. Stanley took advantage of the power of the defensive to ward off several offensive thrusts, and by 5:30, with darkness setting in, both sides ceased firing.[18]

Hood, Cheatham, and Stewart, meeting at about 6 p.m., agreed that Stewart should be sent north to try to take the pike to Nashville and thereby get behind Schofield, but he got lost on the way in the darkness. Stewart rode back to Hood for new orders. Hood, who had been asleep, was awakened. Stewart wrote later that Hood told him, in essence, "It was not material" and instructed him "to let the men rest" and then "to move before daylight in the morning, taking the advance to Franklin." Hood apparently believed that a still-confused Schofield had continued to keep most of his men in Columbia, so that only a small force was holding Spring Hill. Having had only a short time to fight that afternoon before sunset, Hood was confident that he could overwhelm the Union forces in the morning. So he went back to sleep. Most of his men soon did, too.[19]

At about 7 p.m. on November 29, Schofield learned of both Stanley's success and the considerable Confederate forces nearby. He wrote, "Cheatham's corps lay in front of Stanley, his camp-fires within half a mile of our road, seeming much nearer in the darkness." Meanwhile, after Cox arrived at Spring Hill at 11 p.m., Schofield told him that his division should lead the advance to Franklin, twelve miles to the north, where he should begin to set up defenses. Wagner was ordered to be the army's rear guard, and Opdycke's brigade was designated as the southernmost segment fending off Hood as the remainder of the army marched north.[20]

During the night of November 29–30, the entire Union army engaged in forced, silent marches along the pike, careful not to attract the attention of the Confederates just hundreds of meters away outside Spring Hill, most of them asleep. Cox's men were the first to arrive in Franklin and Opdycke's were the last, having left Spring Hill at 6 a.m. and not arriving until 11 a.m. Hood wrote that during that night he was told the enemy was marching along the road and that he ordered Cheatham to intercept them. But, he wrote later, "Nothing was done. . . . I could not succeed in arousing the troops to action when one good division would have sufficed to do the work." Cox was dismissive of this comment, writing in his copy of Hood's memoirs, "When I came along with my division near midnight, I had to brush back their sentinels off the road in order to pass and could hardly believe my own eyes that it was the enemy's camp in the fires so near. But I was moving 'left in front" and ready to halt and fight." One of Cox's men, Levi Scofield, described the march as even more harrowing, noting that "the proximity of the two armies was such [that] it seems incredible there were not frequent clashes during the night, or even a general attack to break our line on the night march." But in one of the mysteries of the war, there were no attacks. Cox wrote Helen, "By a long night's march of twenty miles . . . we reached Franklin next morning Nov. 30, just before day break & went into position to cover the rest of the army's movement."[21]

Franklin and the Unexpected

As his army was entering Franklin, Schofield's primary objective was to continue the movement over the Harpeth River to Nashville, where he hoped at last to rejoin Thomas and welcome Smith's division. He hoped he had enough time to complete the withdrawal before Hood would be able to challenge him. Stanley was ordered to cross the Harpeth River and direct operations there after the wagons and men crossed. But first, Cox wrote, Schofield "was especially anxious to know whether the pontoons had arrived which he had requested." After they met in the city, Schofield told Cox that he would check the river crossing.[22]

Cox and his staff then went to the first house they saw, belonging to the Carter family, which was situated on the Columbia Pike. They commandeered part of the house as a headquarters. Cox wrote, "Loosening sword belts and pistol holsters, we threw ourselves upon the floor to get a few minutes of greatly needed sleep. I had fallen into a doze when General Schofield returned." At that moment, the stress and strain of that tumultuous week, combined with fatigue, as well as his reliance on Cox, all coalesced for Schofield.

Cox wrote, "In all my intimate acquaintance with him, I never saw him so manifestly disturbed by the situation as he was in the glimmering dawn of that morning. Pale and jaded from the long strain of the forty-eight hours just past, he spoke with a deep earnestness of feeling he rarely showed. 'General,' he said, 'the pontoons are not here, the county bridge is gone, and the ford is hardly passable. You must take command of the Twenty-third AC, and put it in position here to hold Hood back at all hazards till we can get our trains over. . . . [E]verything depends upon it.'" Schofield, better qualified because of his West Point engineering training, decided to take personal command of the task of preparing a new way to get the army over the Harpeth River. He placed Cox in temporary command of the 23rd AC and orally ordered him to become what Cox called "commandant on the line" to prepare the army's defenses. Schofield and Cox both presumed that if there were to be a Confederate attack on November 30, it would be on their flanks. But, knowing of Hood's unpredictability and offensive orientation, Schofield gave Cox total discretion to set up a defensive line to protect the wagons and men as they moved through the city, but also to meet a potential frontal infantry attack.

The only formal commands Schofield would issue for the Battle of Franklin were to order four pieces of artillery and Nathan Kimball's division of the 4th AC to report to Cox "for position on the line." As a result, Cox told Helen, four of the five divisions under Schofield were "under my command, the remaining div. crossing the river & taking up a position on the North side." Wagner's division of the 4th AC, including Opdycke's brigade, which was fending off Hood as the rear guard, would also report to him. Ultimately, Cox would have approximately 13,000 men under his command that day on the defensive line, facing a Confederate force of about 20,000.[23]

On November 30 the cumulative effect of Hood's shortcomings as an army commander, including what one historian called his tendencies toward "poor preparation, lack of attention to logistics, and poor reconnaissance," reached a climax. That morning, when the sleeping Confederates awoke in Spring Hill, they were startled to discover that the Union forces had marched stealthily past them overnight. In response to this missed opportunity, according to Hood, his troops exhibited "a determination to retrieve, if possible, the fearful blunder of the previous afternoon and night." Hood himself was "wrathy as a rattlesnake," and he characteristically blamed his subordinates rather than himself. He was also angry that "the Army . . . was still, seemingly, unwilling to accept battle unless under the protection of breastworks," and he wrote, "In my inmost heart I questioned whether or not I would ever succeed in eradicating this evil."[24]

Later that morning, as his men marched after the Union army, Hood's anger and anxiety grew, his warrior spirit unleavened by a commander's ability to take a broader, unemotional view of the situation. He reached the outskirts of Franklin at about 1 p.m. After surveying the Union line some two miles ahead by binoculars from a nearby hill, Hood announced, "We will make the fight." Having failed at Spring Hill to defeat Schofield in the manner of the "immortal Jackson" at Chancellorsville, Hood decided to try to defeat him at Franklin in the manner of Robert E. Lee on the third day at Gettysburg. He decided to launch a frontal infantry attack, which he hoped would succeed in eradicating the "evil" of his men seeking the protection of breastworks.

His commanders were stunned, and they tried to change his mind. They knew the power of the defensive. They could see in the distance that the Union forces were preparing entrenchments and would be able to observe the rebel advance for more than a mile over relatively open country. They knew that Lee's corps and most of Hood's artillery, still in Columbia, were unavailable. They did not know, because Hood failed to do any reconnaissance, that, as one of his generals reported later, "the works to the left . . . were not strong, and with a vigorous assault should have been carried." At Gettysburg, Longstreet had been unable to convince Lee of the futility of Pickett's charge, advocating instead a flank attack. At Franklin, Forrest was unable to convince Hood of the futility of his planned frontal attack, though Hood did authorize him to engage in a flank attack. With those decisions made, arrangement of the infantry for the attack began around 1:30, but the plans were not finalized until a short time before sunset, as at Spring Hill.[25]

The Union Prepares

Schofield experimented successfully during the morning with alternative means to transport his men and wagons; as the day progressed, some 4th AC troops and much of the wagon train slowly passed over newly created bridges. In the early afternoon, Schofield learned that Smith's troops had arrived in Nashville but still could not come to his aid. Instead, Thomas said he hoped Schofield could hold Hood off for three more days. An exasperated Schofield responded that he could only hold Hood off for one day at the most. He added that "a worse position than this for an inferior force could hardly be found." He told Thomas that he expected a flank attack and that Hood seemed "prepared to cross the river above or below." He added, "I have no doubt Forrest will be in my rear tomorrow." So at the very moment that Hood was finalizing preparations for the frontal attack, Schofield made no reference to that possibility.[26]

All morning Cox had focused on his immediate task of protecting the retreating troops and wagons from what he presumed might be harassment and feints. Knowing Hood's propensity for taking the offensive, however, Cox perceived that if the rebels did attack, the "situation and the general topography of the region made it probable that Hood . . . would push his right flank forward on the shortest line to our communications with the north bank of the Harpeth." Cox gambled successfully that Hood would not realize that "the only weak place was our extreme right," for an attack there "would have changed the character of the battle."[27]

Utilizing the topography as well as minor fortifications left over from previous battles, Cox took advantage of the discretion Schofield had given him to creatively innovate a strong defensive position. He arranged his main line in an irregular horseshoe formation, with the two extremes touching on the Harpeth River east and west of the city. From there, his men would have excellent sightlines because "very few battlefields of the war were so free from obstruction to the view." He placed the 23rd AC in its entirety from the river to the right center of the line, just over the

Columbia Pike. He realized late in the morning that he needed more men to complete the formation, and so he ordered Kimball's 4th AC forces to link from the end of the 23rd AC's line to the river to the west. In a necessary compromise, however, "the full width of the road was left open, for it was all needed to enable the doubled lines of wagons and artillery to pass, and a retrenchment crossing the road a few rods in [the] rear was built to command the opening and its approach." As a result, Cox's strong defensive line had the peculiarity of being wide open in the center. To compensate, he created the second line (the "retrenchment"), and he posted artillery and some regiments in reserve nearby.

Despite their exhaustion, Cox's men, utilizing their extensive experience from the Atlanta campaign, set to the task of creating a strong defensive bulwark. They dug deep ditches both in front of and behind their breastworks. To form the latter, they used whatever materials they could find, tearing down buildings for wood and cutting nearby locust trees to form an abatis. A local bush, the Osage orange, was cut and spread in front of much of the line, because even though "it was too small in size" to be much of a barrier, "it was tough and very thorny, and proved to be a useful obstruction, troublesome to meddle with under fire." Because Kimball's forces did not arrive until late morning, their "barricades were of a slighter kind."

Confederate General Stephen D. Lee was complimentary in his report of Cox's work, noting, "The position he held was, for infantry defense, one of the best I have ever seen." By contrast, Hood was dismissive, stating that the Union was only able to construct "slight" breastworks formed "by felling some small locust saplings," adding that there were none at all on the right. Hood did not comment why, if the defenses were so slight, his effort failed or why, if the Union right was so weak, he did not attack there in force.[28]

Schofield took several additional steps to stem the Confederate tide. Having established a command center at Fort Granger, north of the city, he ordered Thomas J. Wood's division of the 4th AC to back up Wilson's cavalry, which guarded the Union left against a flank attack over the Harpeth River. Schofield also set up artillery on the eastern side of the river and at Fort Granger. Schofield ordered Wagner's division of the 4th AC to remain in front of the main line as a kind of trip-wire. Cox's report noted that Wagner's orders "were to hold the enemy back until they developed a heavy force manifestly superior to his own, and then slowly retire within [Cox's] lines to fend off any attack." Wagner's men were stationed about five hundred yards in front of the main line in the midafternoon.

By 3 p.m., Cox was reasonably confident that his defensive line would be able to counter anything Hood could throw at him. At that point, "[t]he trains were nearly all over the river, and Schofield had issued orders that the troops should also pass over at six o'clock if the enemy should not attack before sunset" (about 4:35 p.m.). One historian wrote, "Schofield hadn't even bothered to personally inspect these fortifications, so certain was he that the enemy would not attack." A more important reason was that with the fate of his entire army and his own career in the balance, Schofield was certain that as always Cox would have effectively fulfilled his duties, so there was no need to inspect the fortifications. That confidence, added to Wilson's successful fending off a flank attack by Forrest a few minutes after 3 p.m., created a situation, according to Schofield's biographer, wherein "[b]y 3:30 . . . Schofield was feeling quite secure."[29]

The Union Fumbles

In normal circumstances, Hood's plan would have had little chance of success, because of Cox's careful planning and strong entrenchments. Hood's odds improved because of impetuous acts by Opdycke and Wagner, both of whom disobeyed their orders. As the rear guard, Wagner and his men had been exposed to Confederate skirmishing all day, with Opdycke's 1st Brigade often in the lead position. At midday, Wagner ordered Opdycke once again to join the rest of the division in a defensive line. Opdycke, who could be impetuous and hotheaded, was tired of seeing his men denied the opportunity to rest. He refused to obey the order and instead marched his men toward the main defensive line. Wagner rode up to him and demanded that he stop, but Opdycke proved obstinate. Wagner supposedly then told him, "Fight wherever and whenever you think best." When Opdycke reached the main line, the two friends from Warren greeted one another. Cox, who did not know about Opdycke's dispute with Wagner, ordered him to act as a reserve in the center, behind the second line he had created.

At about 3 p.m., Wagner rode up to the main line and met there with Cox. During this conference, Cox wrote, Wagner remarked on the extent of the defensive preparations that had been made "to meet any serious attack." Cox reemphasized to Wagner that he would need to retire to the main line if attacked. Having seen Wagner fight effectively during this campaign, Cox presumed that Wagner would do his duty and obey this order. As Cox rode off to tend to his other responsibilities, Wagner remained on the main defensive line and did not return to his forces in front of the Union line.[30]

Soon thereafter, according to Cox's aide, his brother Theodore, one of Wagner's men rode up to Wagner and reported that the enemy was

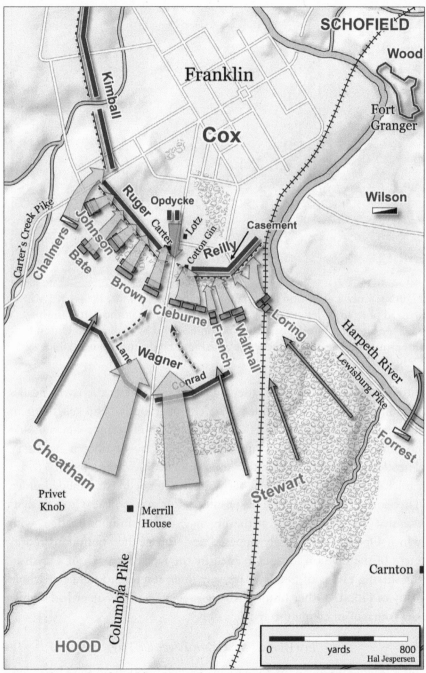

Map 5. The Battle of Franklin, November 30, 1864. (Map by Hal Jespersen)

Figure 3. Kurz and Allison lithograph, *Battle of Franklin,* ca. 1884–93. This stylized portrait is designed to portray a key moment in the battle, in this case, possibly, to represent Jacob Cox (on horseback) leading the Union troops in repelling the Confederate attack on the defensive line. (Library of Congress collection).

moving forward in line of battle and could overwhelm the two brigades in front. "Go back," responded Wagner impetuously, "and tell them to fight,—fight like hell!" Wagner even ordered that reluctant soldiers should be forced back to the forward defensive line by bayonet if necessary. Theodore Cox told Wagner that those instructions were contrary to his earlier orders from his brother, but Wagner reiterated his misguided order. Theodore Cox went to find his brother, but it was too late. Cox's analysis was that "Wagner, chafing at the urgency, akin to insubordination, with which Opdycke had wisely opposed any stop in the continuous retire-ment of the division . . . and excited by the rapid approach of a crisis in the stirring events of the day, gave way to an impulse to fight the whole army of Hood." Other historians have suggested that Wagner had "whis-key courage" in taking this reckless step.[31]

Two Warriors from Warren Save the Day

After leaving Wagner, Cox rode to an elevated position on the Union left, where he saw that "it was evident that Hood was deploying." But he still thought it possible Hood was "encamping in line of battle just beyond the range of projectiles, as he had done at Columbia before beginning his flanking movement." Cox knew that if Hood was going to attack his line, it had to be soon, since daylight was fading. Cox was dismayed to see Wagner's men trying to dig trenches and set up their own breastworks.[32]

Then, at about 4 p.m., Cox wrote, "The long lines of Hood's army surged up out of the hollow in which they had formed, and were seen coming forward in splendid array. The sight was one to send a thrill through the heart, and those who saw it have never forgotten its martial magnificence." The assault of some twenty thousand men, nearly twice the size of Pickett's charge, was the focus of everyone's attention at that critical moment. Cox told Helen, "The enemy came on in magnificent style, in three lines of battle. . . . [I]t was the grandest fight I have seen since Antietam."[33]

To Cox's dismay, and "to the amazement of the thousands who were watching, instead of retreating as ordered, Wagner's infantry opened fire. There was a rattling fusillade for a few moments; [Patrick] Cleburne and [John C.] Brown were checked for an instant." Viewing the scene, an astonished Schofield felt his "heart sink." Inevitably, "the enemy drove in the two advance brigades who were . . . in fault only in fighting too long, as it made their retreat to our breastworks so hurried as to cause some confusion . . . the central point of attack being the turnpike which ran between the divisions of the 23rd AC." The Columbia Pike was wide open, and the panicked Union men and their Confederate attackers rushed toward it. Cox said, "It looked very squally for a while" because "officers and men had been conscious that with the centre broken, nothing but superhuman exertions could keep one wing, at least, of the little army from being driven into the river." On the other side of the line, Hood saw the panicked retreat and, thinking his men were attacking the Union's "first line," believed that he was about to reap a great success.[34]

As Wagner's men ran in disorganized panic through the opening, the Confederate forces right behind them could only have been encouraged as they saw the wide gap in the main defensive line. Their seeming lucky streak continued as the Union line dared not fire for fear of hitting Wagner's men. Furthermore, some of the new recruits on the line were "confused by the crowd trampling over them, and hearing Wagner's officers calling upon their men to rally at the rear, were carried away by the surging mass" and retreated. The critical moment had arrived, and the balance between victory and defeat teetered at first toward the rebels.[35]

Within seconds, there began what Cox called "superhuman exertions" by the Union forces to meet the challenge. It is a matter of dispute who or which group reacted first to the crisis, in great part because in the twilight and the chaotic maelstrom, most men on both sides were acting on instinct, not specific orders. Cox ordered Opdycke forward, though he later acknowledged that Opdycke may not have received that command. Opdycke stated later that he acted on his own in the disorder of the moment. Driving his horse like a man possessed, Opdycke led his men into the maelstrom, further inspiring his and the other Union forces, many of whom had already moved to meet the threat. Stanley also came to help, crossing the Harpeth and riding onto the field to encourage his 4th AC and the reserves forward, but he was wounded after only a few minutes and left the field.

Cox too engaged in "superhuman exertions" in perhaps the most important example in his military career of innovation and creativity in a moment of intense duress. When the rebels hit the main line, the tired and worn Cox may have been thinking that all of his careful planning and everything he had been fighting for was on the verge of destruction. In reaction, in those chaotic moments, his calm, controlled, and reserved mien fell away. In that terrifying atmosphere, sensing disaster, Cox the warrior emerged for the first and only time during the war. With fear and bloodlust mixed in his heart, he rode first behind Opdycke's men and then to several other points behind the lines, back and forth, waving his hat and sword and screaming at his men to push the rebels back. As one of Cox's men later wrote, "General Cox appeared . . . at this critical moment at the point of danger. . . . [H]e plunged into the wavering troops. . . . No finer picture could be painted of a commander in battle, rallying the breaking line" as the men plunged into desperate hand-to-hand combat.[36]

Even though his emotions were so vividly coming forth, Cox's characteristic sangfroid and residual calm were also displayed during these tense moments. He wrote that he had tried "to time [his] ride" to "reach the centre before Wagner's men." But on the way, his horse, spooked by the noise and smoke, "commenced rearing and plunging violently." Cox calmly dismounted and soothed the animal by holding his head and rubbing his nose and ears. He then remounted and "went on [his] way" into the maelstrom to encourage his men.[37]

Characteristically modest, Cox described his actions to Helen a few days later:

> I exerted myself, as did most of the brigade and regimental
> commanders to rally the broken regiments, & as Opdycke's men
> came up, the whole went back with a rush driving the rebs over
> the parapet again. . . . [T]he battle was fought out under my orders.
> . . . Opdycke's charge saved the day for though all the rest of the
> line stood firm, if the enemy had succeeded in penetrating there
> we could not have held the place. . . . I fully expected to be hit,
> but as before Providence willed it otherwise & I was unscathed,
> though not even at South Mountain was I under hotter fire.

Opdycke told his wife, "I saw Genl. Cox during the battle with his hat off, rallying the stragglers, under a terrific fire." Describing his own performance, he added, "Every one here says, 'Col. Opdycke saved the day,'" the acceptance of which phrase would become his lifelong obsession.[38]

In one of the ironies of this battle, Wagner's impetuosity led, Cox wrote, "to the mistake, on Hood's part, of supposing that his first advantage at the centre was much greater than in fact it was. This resulted in greater destruction to the Confederate troops, by repeated assaults after all real chance of success was gone." Cox wrote in his report, "Prisoners captured continually expressed the utmost surprise, declaring they had supposed and had been informed that our lines were occupied by their troops." Cox wrote to Helen, "Again and again they came on but were foiled every time." The Union center bent but did not break; and by about 5 p.m. the Confederate thrust had been stemmed and a reconfigured line had been organized.[39]

The fighting elsewhere along the defensive front was a classic example of why frontal infantry assaults by that stage of the war were doomed to failure unless the attackers far outnumbered the defenders or if the latter made a mistake, as at the Battle of Chickamauga. Cox wrote that once the new defensive line had been secured, the Union troops "stood steadily without flinching, and repulsed the enemy, inflicting terrible loss upon him, and suffering little loss in return. . . . [A]s darkness came on[,] . . . the two breastworks were lines of continuous flame, as the men fired at the flash of each other's guns" and the rebels were met with "the terrible withering fire from . . . the brigades and the batteries." The Confederate assaults "were obstinately repeated until night-fall" and were met by a continuous "sheet of fire." Commanding a key part of the line was Colonel Jack Casement, who typically was among the most active defenders that day.[40]

The fighting continued intensely until after 9 p.m. as the rebels fruitlessly hurled themselves forward. The darkness was a further benefit for the defenders as the attackers tried to organize one attack after another in a murky atmosphere punctuated by thick smoke on this windless day. Perhaps still convinced that "safety would be found in close quarters with the enemy," Hood continued to order assaults. His dutiful men found neither safety nor glory but only death and carnage in those close quarters as they continued to get mowed down. Cox wrote that after about 10 p.m., the fighting seemed to die down. This was the time "when the enemy definitely accepted defeat, and sought only to reform his lines. . . . [Soon] we became satisfied that no further attack would be made, and the enemy concluded in like manner that we were determined to hold our position through the night." At that point, Cox assessed, "[n]o intelligent officer on either side was ignorant of the fact that the heart of the Confederate army was broken, and the character of the fighting was, from that day, in marked contrast with what it had been before."[41]

The "Ghastly Spectacle"

The situation was so well in hand that even before 7 p.m., Cox confidently advised Schofield's staff, "We who were upon the line knew that the impetus of Hood's assault was broken, and that we could hold our position." Schofield telegraphed Thomas at 7:10 p.m. that the enemy "was repulsed at all points, with very heavy loss, probably 5,000 or 6,000 men. Our loss is probably not one-tenth that number." He added that he would implement Thomas's orders to continue the withdrawal over the Harpeth River. Thomas congratulated Schofield on the "glorious news," adding that [James B.] Steedman, with 5,000 men, and A. J. Smith, with 15,000, would reinforce him at Brentwood to the north.

Schofield's withdrawal orders were drafted at 7:15, but Cox, with the fighting still going on and his warrior spirit still strong, was disappointed by that decision. Additionally, he may have recalled that at Antietam the advantage was lost through inaction. Relying on the trust Schofield had in him and his commander's willingness to listen to suggestions, Cox decided to try to convince Schofield to stay and fight. "Fearing that General Schofield did not know the full confidence I had in our ability to hold our lines," Cox sent his brother Theodore to Schofield to say "strongly" that there was no need to withdraw and that Cox would be "personally answerable for holding the position." In response, Schofield stressed his complete confidence in Cox and congratulated him on his "glorious victory." But he stressed, "However much [Cox's] suggestions weigh with me, my orders from General Thomas are to fall back to Nashville." Schofield said in his memoirs that with the reinforcements at last available, his mission had been accomplished. Around midnight, Cox told Helen, "We were withdrawn as originally intended." Upon arriving at Brentwood, north of the city on December 1, Cox took his men into bivouac.[42]

Like Cox, Hood hoped that the Union forces would stay in Franklin, and he issued orders for renewed battle on December 1. The Confederate warrior leader refused to face the reality of his battered and severely weakened army. He even issued a proclamation congratulating "the army on the success achieved yesterday over our enemy by their heroic and determined courage." He reported to headquarters that his men had done well at Franklin and that they were ready to continue the campaign and succeed. He was trying to keep his dream alive, but by then it was only a sad and bloody nightmare.[43]

Most Confederate soldiers took a different view than Hood's of the "success." Private Sam Watkins wrote, "I shrink from butchery. . . . My flesh trembles, and creeps and crawls when I think of it today. It was the finishing stroke to the independence of the Southern Confederacy." Major J.W.A. Wright of the 36th Alabama wrote that as the men marched toward Franklin on the morning of December 1, they beheld "one of the most ghastly spectacles . . . that [they] had witnessed in more than two years of active service," and he concluded, "Our dead lay thicker . . . than we have ever seen them on any battlefield." Wright added that as the men observed the stout defensive wall Cox had created, "[t]he exclamation was frequently heard, 'Here are your temporary breastworks!'" This alluded to the promise made by Davis that the troops would be ordered to charge only "temporary breastworks." Wright wrote, "Our men felt—and with some reason—that here the promise had been disregarded. . . . They held General Hood responsible; from that day their confidence in him diminished."[44]

Hood never accurately reported the extent of his losses, in part to hide his failures. The final numbers from official Union reports are revealing. Of Hood's approximately 20,000 troops engaged that day, almost one-third were casualties, with about 1,800 dead, 4,000 wounded, and 700 taken prisoner. Six general officers were killed, and more were wounded. By contrast, the Union infantry of about 13,000 on the line that day had some 2,300 casualties, mostly from Wagner's forces. Only 189 were officially listed as dead and some 1,000 missing. Those numbers were proof positive of the power of the defensive in the Civil War.[45]

Nevertheless, Hood plunged on, and on December 2 he took up a position about two miles from Nashville, where he ordered "strong detached works to be built to cover our flanks." In his memoirs Hood wrote of his final pipe dream at that point: "The only remaining chance of success in the campaign, at this juncture, was to . . . await Thomas's attack which, if handsomely repulsed, might afford us an opportunity to follow up our advantage on the spot, and enter the city on the heels of the enemy." Missing the irony of following a path that he had described as "evil," Hood settled into a defensive posture. On the other side of the line, Cox told Helen in early December, "Hood may be fool enough to attack us here. . . . We hope he will as he will have a smaller army left for future operations." He wrote in his first book about the campaign, "Hood's situation was a very difficult one, and to go forward or to go back was almost equally unpromising. He followed his natural bent, therefore, which always favored the appearance, at least, of aggression."[46]

Post-Franklin Political-Military Wars

As the armies waited for the inevitable next battle in early December, behind the scenes the political-military stage was extremely active as actors in the campaign vied for credit and recognition. One of those conflicts involved Opdycke and Cox, in great part because the former wanted the lion's share of the credit for "saving the day" at the Battle of Franklin. That claim and its relationship to a parallel conflict between Thomas and Schofield over credit and blame would be a major focus of several historiographical imbroglios in the zero-sum game of refighting the war. His differences with Opdycke would also play a role in spurring Cox to launch his career as a historian.

In his private letters, official reports, and books, Cox was consistent: he gave due credit for the success at the Battle of Franklin to all of the major actors (sometimes even more than they deserved) and often softened his criticism of those, like Wagner, who deserved blame. Regarding Opdycke, he told Helen the same thing that he put in his reports, that Opdycke made a gallant charge and played a key role in driving the enemy back and restoring the line, but that there were many others, including himself, whose contributions were essential at that critical moment. As he would tell Opdycke many times in later letters, to limit the credit to him alone would diminish the contributions of everyone else, a concept that Opdycke never would accept.[47]

Opdycke's obsession with being recognized as the only one who "saved the day" first manifested itself when he complained to his wife early in December that Stanley had returned home to Cincinnati and claimed credit for ordering Opdycke to restore the line. In early December, after so many years of an almost-reverential view of Cox, Opdycke began exhibiting a lifelong fixation on the idea that Cox did not give him sufficient credit. He complained to his wife that Cox never said in an official document the exact words, "Opdycke's charge saved the day." Opdycke told her, "I was much hurt that Genl. Cox should fail to state the whole truth in his 'Official Notice' of me. I had thought him _true_ to _truth_." Despite these injured feelings, Opdycke still thought well of Cox, telling his wife in late January 1865, "I sincerely wish Gen. Cox had command of the 23rd Corps for I candidly believe Gen Schofield to be incapable."[48]

A related issue that arose during this period came on December 2 when Wagner wrote his official report in an attempt to retrieve his career. He did not mention telling his men not to retreat, nor did he note that he was not with his troops when they were routed. He did make a strong recommendation for Opdycke's promotion, but only after Cox suggested he do so to try to limit the damage to himself. In his book _Battle of Franklin,_ Cox wrote that because at the time he did not know exactly what had happened and he had not yet personally interviewed Wagner's subordinates, he was disinclined to criticize Wagner strongly in the preliminary reports, which Thomas had asked him and Schofield to write by December 2. Wagner met that day with Cox to try to save his career. Acting in a generous spirit that later would cause him some problems, especially with Wagner's men, Cox agreed that, pending an investigation, his first report "provisionally and preliminarily" would note that Wagner's men retreated "leisurely" and not in a panic. He gave Wagner an unofficial letter noting his understanding that "an excess of bravery" had caused the problems in the center. Cox promised that he too would recommend Opdycke's promotion.[49]

Wagner's attempt to save his career failed. On December 3 he was demoted, and on December 9 Thomas granted his request to be relieved from duty. Cox wrote later that his investigation found that Wagner's subordinates' charges against him were valid, which was reflected in his final report, written a month later. Cox also noted in the latter that Opdycke's action in disobeying Wagner proved to be both the right thing to do and critical to the Union's success.[50]

In an unrelated political-military episode during this period, Cox experienced another setback in the political-military wars when Darius Couch became his superior in the 23rd AC. The Union had instituted a new military policy, which Cox had supported, to force generals who were supernumeraries to go back to active duty or resign. Couch, who had been in Pennsylvania leading militia, was ordered on December 5 to report to Stanley for duty in the 4th AC. Stanley had left the army to recuperate, so Couch became by rank commander of the 4th AC. Thomas's officers in the 4th AC complained, and on December 7 he revoked the order and "convinced" Schofield to take Couch as a division commander in the 23rd AC. That decision did not enhance the already-difficult relations between Thomas and Schofield, and Cox was intensely displeased. In his memoirs, he wrote, "I had been senior of the division commanders . . . and actually in command of the corps in the absence of its regular chief." Now Couch was in that status. Cox did admit that "Couch's position was by no means a desirable one for him; for he could not be ignorant of the sentiment of the army." In the end neither man let their resentment harm their working relationship.[51]

Political-military wars at a higher level resulted from the delay in completing the destruction of Hood's army. Early in December, Thomas was at last following Sherman's orders to concentrate his forces, and he now had an army of over 50,000 men, far outnumbering Hood's approximately 20,000. Despite his clear and significant advantages, however, Thomas did not act for almost two weeks, primarily because of extremely bad weather. Grant, Sherman, and Stanton all had believed that Thomas was too slow and deliberate when executing his orders, and this delay only confirmed that judgment. As early as December 2 Grant showed his concern about Thomas's dilatory tactics, telling him, "After the repulse of Hood at Franklin . . . we should have taken the offensive against the enemy where he was. . . . Should you get him to retreating, give him no peace." Stanton snidely wrote the same day to Grant that "this looks like the McClellan and Rosecrans strategy of do nothing and let the rebels raid the country." He added later, "Thomas seems unwilling to attack because it is hazardous, as if all war was anything but hazardous. If he waits for Wilson to get ready, Gabriel will be blowing his last horn." When Thomas did not move by mid-December, Grant decided to replace him. At first he chose Schofield, then Logan, but both orders were ultimately put aside. By December 14 Grant had become so frustrated at

Thomas's inaction that he decided to take command in Thomas's place himself, with Schofield in charge in the interim.[52]

This dispute echoed the hard feelings that Schofield and Thomas exhibited toward one another during this period. Schofield was angry that he had not been well supported by Thomas, who he thought had not appreciated the difficulties he had faced in being outmanned by Hood, had not provided the requested pontoon bridge, and had not reinforced him. For his part, Thomas was unhappy that Schofield had not held off Hood for three more days, as requested. Added to these rifts, suspicions among Thomas's men that Schofield was scheming to replace Thomas by undermining him with Grant would lead to an intense political-military controversy after the war.[53]

Finishing Hood's Career: Major General Again

Thomas finally launched his attack, the Battle of Nashville, on December 15, and Grant reversed his decision to replace him. The day before, Hood had sent Forrest on a mission to Murfreesboro and did not realize until too late, as Cox judged, "his mistake . . . to allow Forrest to become so far detached." Cox played only a small role in the first day's fighting, during which Hood was pushed back several miles. On December 16 a concerted Union attack on the Confederate left at Shy's Hill led by a division of Smith's corps broke the rebel line and its spirit. One of Cox's divisions played a supportive role in the rout. Cox wrote that at about 4:30 "the whole Confederate left was crushed in like an egg-shell." He told Helen, "The rebels were evidently dispirited & easily panic stricken. My command was engaged on the final charge which broke the enemy's line. . . . We look upon this engagement as finishing Hood's career for the present." A crestfallen Hood wrote, "I beheld for the first and only time a Confederate army abandon the field in confusion. . . . I soon discovered that all hope to rally the troops was in vain." A Confederate private described the scene: "The army was panic-stricken. The woods everywhere were full of running soldiers."[54]

Hood's retreat from Nashville to Alabama was the reverse of his movement north. The fearsome force that had confidently marched toward Franklin became a tattered throng scattering southward as the Union army nipped at its heels. The progress of the Union forces on the chase was inevitably slow because Forrest destroyed the bridges along the way and the weather was atrocious. Cox told Helen that "the two or three days &

nights after the battle were among the most uncomfortable" he had "ever experienced." One night the rain and mud were so overwhelming that he had to sleep standing up. During the chase Cox would become very ill, and he was bedridden for much of the rest of December.[55]

The remnants of Hood's army crossed the Tennessee River on December 28, and by that point, one soldier commented, "The once proud Army of Tennessee had degenerated to a mob." Thomas logically decided to close the campaign, and he ordered the 23rd AC to Dalton for winter quarters. For Cox that meant he could apply for a furlough, and on January 2 he wrote to Helen, "Last night my trunk was packed for home, & my leave of absence for thirty days was snug in my pocket." Before he could depart, however, all leave was cancelled, because Grant, Halleck, and Stanton all thought Thomas was back to his inactive tendencies. Halleck ordered that he continue the pointless pursuit. Cox wrote unhappily to Helen, "If the administration would apply a little of the 'go ahead' to [Grant and] the Army on the James, we would appreciate it better. Here we know for an absolute certainty that the army is stuck in the mud, but the administration would not believe General Thomas." He complained, "I am getting ragged & barefoot. My boots are worn out, my coat is worn out, my waistcoats are worn out, my hat is worn out. . . . If I ever get near civilization again, I shall be obliged to hide in bed somewhere till I can get some clothes made." After several more days of chasing the Confederate remnants, Grant finally agreed to end the campaign, and Thomas was ordered to Nashville.[56]

With the western war effectively over, many of Thomas's forces would be transferred to more active sectors. For Cox the most important of those transfers was a by-product of Schofield's bad relations with Thomas. Schofield wanted both to be more active and to avoid further service under Thomas. He lobbied for an assignment to the East, suggesting that his forces join Grant or Sherman. On January 8, 1865, Grant told Halleck to order Thomas to send Schofield east to Annapolis if he was convinced that Hood was no longer a real threat. Cox learned of the new orders on January 15, noting in his diary the "expectation that we shall go to Sherman, in Georgia." The same day he learned that his long-awaited second promotion to major general had been confirmed, dated December 7, 1864, the date of Schofield's report on the Battle of Franklin.

With his two stars again achieved and the chance to reunite with Sherman in the offing, Cox was pleased in mid-January when Schofield authorized his furlough. He spent a week in Warren, his first trip home in two years. His eldest son described the happy scene when Cox arrived: "I opened the door to see a very tall man with big bushy beard in a soldier's uniform. He stepped in and asked if Mrs. Cox was home, and I flew off to the nursery to tell mother that there was a big soldier in the front room. . . . Imagine the surprise of her children when the big soldier soon came back into the nursery and routed us all out of bed. It proved to be father home on a furlough."[57]

Endings and Beginnings

During the first six months of 1865, the final days of Cox's active military service paralleled the relaunching of his political career. On January 25 Halleck ordered Schofield to gather his forces at Alexandria, Virginia, for transport to Wilmington and Beaufort, North Carolina. Their objective was to capture Wilmington, the last major port under Confederate control. Thereafter, to prepare the way for Sherman's movement north into North Carolina, Cox's forces were to take Goldsboro, where the two armies would be united. Schofield was to command the Department of North Carolina with two provisional corps, one of which Cox would ultimately command.[58]

On his way to his new assignment, Cox spent a few days in Washington, where he met with Garfield and Chase, who had become chief justice of the Supreme Court, and Dennison, who was postmaster-general. These consultations with the leaders of Ohio politics focused on Cox's postwar political ambitions, and these men likely encouraged Cox to think seriously about becoming a candidate for governor at the state Union Party convention in June. Over the next several weeks, as Cox considered becoming a candidate, the movement for his nomination, headed by Aaron Perry in his position as a member of the party's central committee, would gather momentum. As early as May 13, Perry could confidently write to him, "The prospect now is that we shall make you Governor of Ohio."

One evening during his stay in Washington Cox gained insight into coarser elements of national politics. As he noted, he had the opportunity of "observing . . . the spirit which animated political circles at the capital," an atmosphere he would find disturbing because it was so different from the idealistic, issue-oriented brand of politics he and Garfield had practiced before the war. After this incident, he realized for perhaps the first time how the growing professionalization of politics was affecting men

168   like Garfield. He wrote, "Garfield arranged a little dinner at which, besides himself, I met General [Robert] Schenck and Henry Winter Davis, all of them playing leading roles in the House of Representatives." During the gathering, Cox was shocked that Davis, a War Democrat, "let loose in a witty and scathing denunciation of Lincoln and all his works. The current epithets among the President's opponents, of which 'baboon' was one of the mildest, were flung at him with a venom that, to me, was half shocking and half comical." Cox was especially taken aback when "Garfield treated the outburst as a sort of extravaganza, and . . . rallied his friend with good-humored persiflage and prodded him to fresh explosions by shafts of wit." Cox was obviously startled at both the rough nature of political "discourse" and also how much his old friend had evolved into the kind of "practical" politician who had chosen politics as his career and went along with the current tide. It proved to be a valuable lesson as Cox planned his own political advancement.[59]

Another important event for his political career took place on January 31, as Cox sat in the House of Representatives' gallery while Congress debated the Thirteenth Amendment. He wrote to Helen that the bill "finally passed amid the most tremendous excitement." Cox was likely one of those applauding the loudest, as were the blacks who were allowed to sit in a separate section of the gallery for the first time in 1864. Later, he wrote, "Breakfasting with Chief-Justice Chase, I met also Henry Ward Beecher, and the great historical event was, of course, the central subject of conversation. The forecast by such men of the effect upon the country and upon the world made a blending of solid wisdom with brilliant eloquence not to be forgotten." The abolition of slavery, one of Cox's lifetime goals, was about to be accomplished. The question of the status of freedmen was now even more front and center in national politics, as were the related issues of how to "reconstruct" the defeated states and what to do about their white citizens.[60]

In early February, Cox and some 1,800 of his men sailed south for North Carolina. He joked to Helen, "[M]any of our Western men are seeing the ocean for the first time, and expect enjoyment in full of the delights of sea-sickness." For Cox, who would enjoy sailing on the ocean as a postwar recreation, the outdoor exposure proved just as healthful as his other war experiences. He told Helen, "The air was bracing, the rain had ceased, and the swell rolled magnificently. I thoroughly enjoyed it." He said he was now "feeling as rigorous as a young lion." After landing on the coast, Cox reassembled his 3rd Division, which was augmented with new

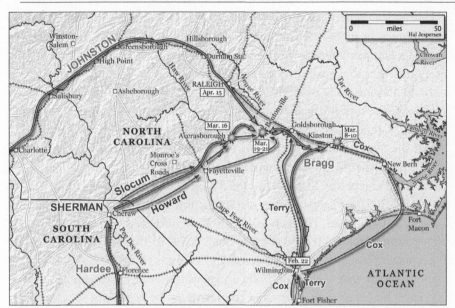

Map 6. The North Carolina campaign, February–April, 1865. (Map by Hal Jespersen)

forces. On February 9 he began his movement toward Wilmington, supported by naval bombardments. On February 13 he was ordered to cross the Cape Fear River and to approach from behind Fort Anderson, which controlled the passage up the river. Cox and his men, led by Jack Casement, drove the rebels out of the fort on February 19.

Cox pushed the Confederates over Town Creek to the environs of Wilmington the next day, but on February 21 Schofield ordered him to stop his advance and send help to General Alfred Terry's forces nearby. In response, for the final time in the war, Cox took the initiative instead of just following his orders. Taking advantage of the trust Schofield had in him, Cox told Schofield that he should continue his attack because the city might be about to capitulate. Showing what Cox described as a "liberality of judgment, Schofield warmly approved his subordinate's exercise of discretion." Braxton Bragg ordered a retreat from Wilmington on February 22, and Cox's men occupied the city.[61]

The taking of Wilmington and Sherman's capture of Columbia, South Carolina, a day before were major blows to the dying Confederacy. Cox wrote that the Confederate abandonment on February 17 of Charleston, "the original cradle of secession, seemed a portent to the people of the South, and well-nigh destroyed all hope." Another portent took place on

February 22 when Lee appointed Johnston to be commander of the Army of Tennessee in North Carolina. He told Johnston that while "nothing can be sent from here to your assistance," he hoped to hold off Grant long enough that their two armies might unite and attack either Sherman or Grant. Johnston was pessimistic, responding, "It is too late to expect me to concentrate troops capable of driving back Sherman. The remnant of the Army of Tennessee is much divided. So are other troops." Later, he added that the forces available were "too weak to cope with Sherman," though they might be able to stop Sherman's progress.[62]

On February 25 Schofield ordered Cox to take command of the "District of Beaufort" and oversee reconstruction of the railroad from New Bern to Goldsboro. The same day Schofield informed him, as Cox happily wrote Helen, "[H]e has made application to the War Dept. for my permanent assignment to the command of the 23rd AC." Cox noted in his memoirs that Couch dutifully accepted the decision to appoint Cox despite his lower rank. Cox went to New Bern by boat with some of his forces, and on March 2 he began his march to the interior with his command. He told Helen that "the troops here are odds & ends, & will not be as efficient as our own Corps." One of the more efficient was Casement, who utilized his experience in railroad work to good effect in reconstructing the railroad line.

Having had no hard fighting for several weeks and having seen little Confederate resistance, both Cox and his men may have become somewhat overconfident. In what would be Cox's last serious conflict, the Battle of Kinston, Bragg successfully attacked Cox's advance forces on March 7. Cox quickly formed a defensive line that checked the rebel advance for two more days. Couch's support force was late in arriving to help, but Cox wrote proudly to Helen that when the men of Couch's 3rd Division were told of Cox's difficulties, "The cry went up from the men, 'If General Cox wants us, he can have us,' and they dashed into the stream in solid column, forcing the pace till they reached the field." The Battle of Kinston again proved the power of the defensive. As Cox wrote, "The character of the engagement was the oft-repeated one of a destructive repulse from a stoutly held intrenchment." Late on March 10 Bragg withdrew. Cox told Helen, for the final time in the war, his "usual personal good luck" held and he "was unhurt," though several aides saw their horses killed within several paces of him.[63]

On March 14 Cox occupied Kinston, and as he told Helen, the next day he received another acknowledgment of the respect of his men when the 16th Kentucky regiment "surprised [him] by sending [him] a very fine roan mare, a splendid animal of good Ken. Blood." On March 22 he took Goldsboro, and the armies were reunited. That same day Schofield reminded Grant of his recommendation to issue formal orders to make Cox commander of the 23rd AC, and that decision was officially announced on March 27. Sherman had told his subordinates in late March that he would renew the campaign on April 10, but he had to first discuss future policy with Grant and Lincoln. During that trip, Sherman had Lincoln sign the papers for Cox's promotion.[64]

Lee abandoned Richmond on April 3, and when Cox began to move his corps to Raleigh on April 12, he received from Sherman a message that Lee had surrendered. One of Cox's men described the scene: "General Cox opened it in the usual businesslike manner. . . . I noticed his face suddenly brighten, and in great animation he turned and directed the escort and staff to be drawn up in line. . . . With head uncovered he read a brief dispatch stating that General Lee, with his entire army, had surrendered to Grant at Appomattox. . . . It meant home, and wife, and children, and happy meetings, throughout the land." Cox wrote in his diary that day, "The army nearly went crazy with joy . . . [and] we hope the last battle of the war has been fought."[65]

Soon after, Sherman and Johnston began negotiating the latter's surrender terms. Lincoln's assassination on April 14 prompted Sherman on April 17 to order Cox and the other commanders to strengthen their garrisons to prevent retaliation by their men. They succeeded, and Johnston's final agreement to surrender on April 26 effectively ended the war for Cox and his men. But his joy about the end of conflict was tempered by developments that would have an important effect on his postwar political career. Having heard that Vice President Andrew Johnson had been drunk at Lincoln's inauguration, Cox wrote prophetically in his diary as he began his transition from citizen-general to citizen-statesman, "What adds to our grief is that Mr. Johnson's disgrace of himself at the inauguration gives no little room for satisfaction in thinking of him as the President."[66]

Military Government and Reconstruction

Cox's final military responsibility in the South had a significant affect on his evolving views about race and Reconstruction. When the war ended in April 1865, Cox was named military commander of western North Carolina, based in Greensboro, serving under Schofield, who was overall commander in North Carolina. After arriving on May 1 in Raleigh, Schofield and Cox met with Johnston to discuss parole regulations and procedures to keep the rebel troops in order. Setting up his men to guard against the mischief and thievery the Confederate troops had been perpetrating until he arrived, Cox then began paroling the latter. In a few days he had finished that task, and for all practical purposes Cox's contact with the enemy army ceased. The remainder of Cox's tour of duty in North Carolina was taken up in mundane military occupation duties as Schofield, Sherman, and Grant all tried to get firm decisions on Reconstruction policies from a stunned postassassination federal government. Cox would leave North Carolina in early July, having been assigned on June 30 to be commander of the District of Ohio.[67]

In administering this region of North Carolina during May and June, Cox used the model of his counterinsurgency approach in West Virginia to implement a measured and moderate policy. He had not a trace of bitterness toward the Southerners, believing that an early return to normality would be in the best interest of the country. He spent much of his time meeting with North Carolinians and observing the reality of the defeated South. In his memoirs, he wrote that the most surprising thing he learned was that most of the people of North Carolina had become supporters of the Confederacy either out of state loyalty or from fear of retaliation. Although they feared that they would have their liberties taken away by an avenging Northern army, they were pleasantly surprised to find this to be untrue. That in turn made it easier for many to accept that slavery was dead.

Cox wrote later, "Very few of the whites were in favor of emancipation on principle, but they all admitted that the fate of the 'system' had been the real issue at stake, and that the surrender meant universal freedom. But the colored people were ignorant, and had cherished strange illusions as to the change which was to come to them." Blacks were under the impression, Cox wrote, that freedom meant that they no longer had to work, and many believed that they were going to be given the property of their former owners. Cox did his best to dispel the notion that wealth and idleness were to follow emancipation, making several public addresses during which he advised both blacks and whites to accept the new realities.[68]

At the same time, he used his power to admonish whites "to deal with the freedman with perfect sincerity as free laborers." He subtly yet firmly pushed whites to open facilities to blacks. In one example, he authorized a letter to a Greensboro pastor that noted that blacks were afraid that they would no longer be allowed to use a church building. Because, as Cox's aide wrote, "the general commanding presumes that you will readily agree that the cultivation of religious sentiments among all classes" was important "at this time of civil and military turmoil," Cox "desires that the portion of your church heretofore placed at the services of the colored people be still continued."

Cox wrote approvingly in his memoirs that eventually blacks and whites in his district, under strict Union army oversight, reestablished something resembling a functioning economic system and began planting crops for the new season. In taking this action, he said, "[t]he natural authority of known character and wisdom asserted itself," meaning that whites reassumed authority and blacks accepted it. "Everybody soon went to work to make a living, and the burning problems of political and social importance were postponed." But while Cox could see that his benevolent yet strict military rule was a success, his philosophical adherence to laissez-faire principles would result in his being opposed to further extension of martial law. In his memoirs he wrote a melancholy yet naïve note about Reconstruction that showed that even then he would not admit that the calm after the war was a product of military rule. He wrote, "Why it was that the mellowness of spirit which seemed then so prevalent could not have ripened without interruption or check into a quicker and more complete fraternization belongs to another field of inquiry."[69]

Assessing the Citizen Soldier

For four years Jacob Cox practiced a profession for which he was seemingly poorly suited but in which he achieved the most significant successes of his long and varied professional life. The introverted and intellectual divinity student evolved into a highly respected military leader with a well-developed "military aptitude." Rising to the level of major general and corps commander, he functioned well in his methodical, predictable, controlled, and efficient way and gained the respect of his men and his superiors. He knew, perhaps intuitively, that he lacked the ability or instinct to be an overall commander. He did, however, prove to be a quintessential subordinate commander, always dutiful and never ambitious to supersede his superiors. Because the characteristics of military life meshed neatly with Cox's personality, he was comfortable in this systematic organization in which discipline and order were essential to success and the chain of command clearly defined position. In addition, on several occasions he proved capable of instinctively knowing when to go beyond his orders or when to act without orders, and he was respected for being able to provide useful advice on strategy and tactics.

The Battle of Franklin and the Maryland campaign were the pinnacles of Cox's military career. While South Mountain and Antietam were his "baptism of fire" on a major stage, by the time of the Atlanta campaign, he had been forgotten by the Washington leadership. In effect, during the Atlanta-Franklin campaign he had to reintroduce himself to Washington. He did so to almost universal acclaim. On December 19, 1864, Schofield recommended, and Thomas endorsed, Cox's promotion, emphasizing that he had merited it "scores of times" and that Cox's loss would be "irreparable to [Schofield's] command."[70] Cox's achievements during the Franklin-Nashville campaign were a by-product of his role as Schofield's right-hand man and principal adviser. Schofield had nearly unlimited confidence in Cox: he had called on his most trusted subordinate to stem Hood's first advance on Columbia, to hold off S. D. Lee at that city, and to set up the crucial defensive line and repel Hood at Franklin, all with little input from headquarters. These were among the finest examples of Cox's ability to rise to the occasion with the kind of approach needed at that critical moment. Whether or not Opdycke alone "saved the day" at the Battle of Franklin, Cox and the men who served under him saved the army there.

The "pale and jaded" Schofield who gave Cox the responsibility for the defensive line at Franklin would have been a beaten man, and his army might have been devastated, if someone less reliable had prepared and commanded the line. At that intense moment, Cox was seeing everything he had been fighting for and everything he stood for about to be destroyed, and the exhausted former divinity student felt his reserved demeanor crack. He called up from within himself a warrior spirit infused with a bloodlust intensely focused on destroying the enemy. He inspired his men to herculean efforts, while retaining enough self-control to ensure effective management of their efforts. After five hours of carnage, the warrior spirit was still strong within him, and he appealed to Schofield to continue the battle the next day. That spirit would dissipate, however, and the calm, stoic, and determined leader would reemerge for the remaining six months of the war, his reputation reestablished.

Most historians as well as his peers judged Cox to be one of the best of the North's civilian-generals, but that outcome was not obvious at first. Cox's advancement was slow but steady, with some flashes of excellence and some setbacks and mistakes. By the end of the war, Sherman knew Cox was an able and trusted soldier, and he offered Cox the opportunity to become a brigadier general in the regular army. Cox turned him down both because he wanted to return home to the orderly life he had known before the war and because he saw nothing inviting about "the torpid semi-death of an army life in the time of peace." Several months later Sherman would again exhibit his respect for Cox the military man when he recommended that Cox become the army's civilian commander, secretary of war.[71]

Perhaps the best example of Cox's personal understanding of the role of his military career in his life came in a letter he wrote to Schofield after the war: "So far as my personal enjoyment of life is concerned, I have never been more content or happier than during our field campaigning."[72]

7

From Citizen-General to State and National Political Leader

> Because there could be no real unity of people between the
> Southern whites and Southern blacks, it seems manifest to me
> that there could be no political unity, but rather a strife for
> the mastery, in which the one or the other would go to the
> wall.... I see no hope whatever that the weaker race would not
> be reduced to hopeless subjection, or utterly destroyed.
>
> —Cox, "Oberlin Letter," 1865

As Ohio became a major focus of postwar national politics,
its leaders, especially those who had played critical roles in the war, inevitably emerged as powerful political figures. Every president during
the remaining years of the nineteenth century save one had both roots
in Ohio and a military background. One historian commented, "Of the
Ohioans whose military reputations furthered their political careers,
Major General Jacob Dolson Cox was in many respects the ablest." He
was young and ambitious, had a sterling war record, and was recognized
as a leading antislavery Republican. He had high-level political and
military contacts in Washington and Ohio as well as a reputation for integrity and honesty. Yet while Cox's fellow Ohioans Grant, Hayes, Garfield, Harrison, and McKinley all rose to the presidency, by 1873 Cox
was in political exile. His experience in the Civil War demonstrated that
he had a well-developed military aptitude, but Cox's postwar forays into
state and national politics would prove that his political aptitude was
lacking.[1] His views on race and Reconstruction noted in the chapter
epigraph and how he made his views known would be important elements of that process.[2]

In March 1865, as the war neared its end, Ohio soldiers requested that the Ohio Union Party's Central Committee admit representation from Ohio soldiers in the field to the state gubernatorial nominating convention. Soldiers had been allowed to vote while in the field, but now they wanted to have some influence on the nomination process. On April 10 the Central Committee announced that it would give each Ohio regiment, battalion, and battery the right to select delegates. For many Ohio troops, their choice for governor was an easy one—Jacob D. Cox, especially since he had the support of Chase, Dennison, Garfield, and other party leaders. As noted previously, Perry was confident by mid-May that Cox would be nominated and would win easily; the path to victory was cleared by late May after all potential opponents declined to run.

Cox had been ruminating about his candidacy since his January visit to Washington, and it was in the back of his mind as he fought his last battles. While he was confident of a victory, he was ambivalent about running. His professional advancement as a lawyer had been interrupted by the war; he had a wife and six children to support; and his military salary had been barely enough to get by. Cox believed that participating in public life was an important duty not to be shirked. But he was dismayed about the incertitude of winning and holding office and the inevitable compromises that might have to be made. He would later point out to friends that he did not want to be one of those who, like Garfield, made politics a profession instead of an avocation. In his view, such men became so entrenched within the political system that they could no longer return to their "normal" careers. Moreover, reflecting on the changing nature of national politics in 1865, Cox was disturbed that unlike the ideology-driven politics he had experienced before the war, "The strife is in some respects a dirty one." At the same time, he believed "it still seems possible to go through [politics] undefiled, and the importance of the era in which we are, no one can question." Furthermore, he told Garfield, "The circle of acquaintances I could get as Governor would be valuable" for a future law practice. Eventually he resolved his doubts, and with duty calling again, he agreed to be a candidate. Cox was still relatively unknown outside military circles, however: in June, a Republican paper referred to him as "Joseph" D. Cox.[3]

As he pondered about running for governor, Cox continued the process of intellectualizing about race and Reconstruction that he had begun in 1862 in his correspondence with Perry and Chase. Several events during this period would affect his thinking and have an indirect role in his political future. Johnson's accession to the presidency was the most crucial factor because of its impact on national policy. Sherman's decision early in 1865 to use the government's war powers to extend favored status to blacks would also have an important philosophical impact for Cox.

On December 30, 1864, Halleck had told Sherman that Lincoln was coming under intense political pressure because of Sherman's policy of discouraging blacks from accompanying his men on the march to the sea because he had no means to care for or feed them. A frustrated Sherman said the charges against him were typical examples of "poison influences" from politicians at a time when he was doing far more than they were to end slavery by trying to win the war. Stanton, the most important critic of Sherman's policy toward blacks, visited Sherman in Savannah in early January and interviewed black leaders to seek their views about Reconstruction. Asked whether they would rather live with whites or separately, most of the black leaders answered that separation was preferable because of white prejudice. They said the right to buy and own land would be the best way to prove themselves as freedmen.

In response, Sherman took direct action; as one historian wrote, "The conservative general prepared the most radical field order of the war," Special Field Order no. 15, dated January 16, 1865. The order stated that the islands from Charleston south, the "abandoned rice fields along the rivers for thirty miles back from the sea, and the country bordering the St. John's River, Fla. [near Jacksonville] are reserved and set apart for the settlement of" freed blacks. No white person except soldiers would be permitted to reside there. Each head of a black family could be granted forty acres of land, to which he would be given a "possessory title" under the protection of the military "until Congress shall regulate their title." By early 1865, through this action and the creation of the Freedmen's Bureau, the federal government had used its war powers to establish a policy of military protection of freed slaves living in specially designated regions and owning land taken from whites.[4] Those concepts and their inherent recognition of expanded federal powers would be among the implicit philosophical underpinnings of Cox's later proposal to resolve the question of the future of the freedmen.

Another episode, one that unwittingly exposed Cox's evolving views on these issues, was the decision by Cox's mentor Chase to advocate full black suffrage, a position he hoped would advance his own candidacy for president in 1868. On May 7, 1865, Chase wrote to both Sherman and Schofield about how military occupation might be managed to achieve full black suffrage. He told Schofield that he believed that he and President Johnson had agreed on a feasible Reconstruction policy. That approach would entail returning the Southern states to the Union by ensuring loyalist governments and reinstating an earlier North Carolina constitution that "recognized all free men as voters." Once the Thirteenth Amendment came into force, Chase asserted, all freedmen would be legal voters. Chase believed this power would be sufficient to guarantee that blacks would be able to secure economic and social rights. Chase knew that his protégé Cox was the favorite to become governor of Ohio and potentially a major national political figure. Presuming that Cox would support his presidential candidacy, Chase told Schofield, "Permit me to say that you may find conference with General Cox on this class of subjects useful. I have known him well as a civilian, and have the highest opinion of his ability and judgment."[5]

Schofield's response was noncommittal, though he did note, "I agree with you fully in your estimate of General Cox. I have had frequent and full conference with him during the last year on all subjects of public interest." Two days later Schofield revealed to Grant his true feelings. He said that Chase's policies "would lead to disastrous results" because he called for the illegal replacement of the current state constitution. Furthermore, the proposals would give voting rights to blacks, who, Schofield believed, were unfit "as a class, for any such responsibility." He acknowledged that the federal government had the legal authority to impose Chase's ideas through military rule if the Southern states were judged to have lost their status as states. But he added, "I understand President Johnson repudiates this doctrine."[6]

While Chase undoubtedly expected that Cox would agree with him, he was mistaken. Cox's prewar Radical Republican beliefs applied only to the issues of slavery and the Union. With the "peculiar institution" abolished and the Union restored, the more conservative, libertarian-oriented, patrician, ethnically proud Cox emerged. His intellectual bases emanated not only from the antislavery Oberlin experience but also from Whiggery, the political and economic laissez-faire orientation of the Republican Party, and Anglo-Saxon pride. Cox's extensive reading of history and authors such as Alexis de Tocqueville and Charles Darwin were also key influences in his thinking. In addition, Cox was knowledgeable about the prewar discussions about black colonization, and he had read articles by journalist Daniel Goodloe, who as early as 1861 had advocated "internal colonization" through a new black state. Cox also knew about federal support for both the Port Royal Experiment and Sherman's designation of part of the coastal South for the exclusive use of blacks, both of which were examples of de facto federally supported internal colonization. Finally, he likely understood intellectually, as one historian put it, that before the war colonization had "enabled its proponents to postpone the hard work of imagining a multiracial republic after slavery," while allowing "liberal whites to project the downfall of slavery without owning the social consequences of emancipation."[7]

It is also important to remember that Cox was firmly convinced of the evil of slavery but not of the capabilities of blacks. Before the war he believed, as did most other Whigs and Republicans, that in a free society, blacks would be second-class citizens but little more. His wartime experience reinforced those views. In his memoirs, he occasionally mentioned the services of his black aides who did his cooking and washing. But he only once mentioned the name of one of them and he never seemed to have ever thought about them other than as faceless servants without personalities. This was matched during his tenure as military governor, when he wrote his almost blasé analysis that after the war blacks and whites in North Carolina were moving toward implementing the sharecropping system, in which blacks would inevitably be subservient, as well as his assumption that blacks were content with that new social order.

With the end of the war, the issue of what to do about the freedman could no longer be postponed, and Cox the intellectual wanted to help find a solution. Cox had begun to ruminate about Reconstruction and related issues during the war, but his thinking was necessarily abstract because he had no experience in and limited knowledge of life in the South. To Aaron Perry he had proposed the idea of making blacks with military experience the base of "a military colony on the Southwest frontier which could absorb the surplus black population and solve the emancipation problem with a system of colonization." He reasoned that because the area would be "military in nature and well-protected," blacks from North and South would flock there and create a voluntary separation of the races. Reflecting his belief in laissez-faire economics, Cox theorized that in such a scheme, because the blacks remaining in the South would be fewer in number, their labor would be more valuable and they would be more highly paid.[8]

Cox's living in North Carolina after the war's end was his first real contact with Southerners. That experience further solidified his previously abstract views about race and Reconstruction. He wrote in his diary on May 12 that "a general amnesty is best for the country and will tend most effectively to a rapid and lasting pacification. . . . The great cause of the war being removed and the institutions of the Country having been made homogenous, there is no danger that anything can disturb the Government again, and it can therefore afford to be magnanimous."[9] His use of the term *homogenous* in this context is critical to understanding both Cox and his views on Reconstruction. As he had hinted in correspondence during the war, this former Radical came to see his Southern brethren—having removed disunion and slavery, the reasons for his prewar hostility—as once again part of the dominant Anglo-Saxon brethren. This vision of a homogenous nation helped Cox foresee the potential for cooperation across the former battle lines in dealing with Reconstruction.

On May 25, 1865, in a letter to Perry, Cox put forth some preliminary ideas about resolving Reconstruction. In an overly optimistic and unrealistic assessment based on the relative tranquility in western North Carolina, which he was enforcing by military rule, he predicted that if the South were taken back into the Union while its people were in a humble mood, Reconstruction would not be difficult. He advocated that the "better" men (Cox's term for the well-educated leaders of society) be allowed to guide each state back into the Union, since they would not only control the white community but also would have a sense of noblesse oblige toward blacks. He warned that the only thing to fear was delay. He believed military rule had to be ended quickly, because civil law "can be set aside for only the strongest reasons . . . as in the case of Vallandigham." The irony was that he had experienced how effective his own military governance had been in enforcing the new order, but his philosophical repugnance for that approach overcame any inclination to consider it as part of a longer-term solution.

In this letter, Cox echoed Schofield in stating that it required "a hardier faith in pure democracy than [Cox had] to believe it safe to transfer millions of uneducated slaves to full responsibility as electors and law makers in one bound." Further, he doubted whether "a republic can exist without homogeneity of race in its citizens," and he feared that a racially mixed society could lead to a war between the races for political dominance. He understood the problems and pressures blacks in the South faced but said that "most show a commendable degree of sense," by which he meant they were accepting their second-class status.

He told Perry that he had hoped the issue of black suffrage in the South could be delayed. More immediately, he knew there could be a strong push for a black suffrage plank in the Ohio party platform, and he wondered whether holding these views might be problematic for his gaining the nomination. He firmly believed that Ohio's soldiers would abandon the Republican Party if there were a push for suffrage in the platform. Cox told Perry that if a platform were adopted that conflicted with his views, Perry should withdraw his name as a candidate. He concluded, "Our party must stand or fall on the motto, 'Principles, Not Men.'"[10]

On May 29 President Andrew Johnson issued proclamations to create new state governments and allow most Southerners to regain their rights, including to their property, by taking oaths of allegiance. This critical decision meant that the executive branch was not going to "regularize" by civil action steps taken under the war powers, including Sherman's decree giving land to blacks. Having told Perry on May 25 that he did not want to run on a platform advocating black suffrage, Cox was not surprised to hear from Perry on June 4 that the uproar over Johnson's actions meant that suffrage might be a major focus of debate at the state convention. Assured that Perry would block a suffrage plank, Cox wrote that while he did not support blanket suffrage for blacks, he did favor giving them the vote in Ohio because "they are in a different category from the plantation negroes."[11]

When the party gubernatorial convention met on June 21, the 143 soldier delegates were almost solidly for Cox and against black suffrage, as he had predicted. Cox was nominated unanimously, and the plank on suffrage only called on the party to keep in view the principles of the Declaration of Independence. On June 30 Cox's responsibilities as military governor ended when he was named commander of the District of Ohio, based in Columbus. He now had the explicit responsibility of mustering out Ohio's troops and the implicit one of campaigning for governor. Soon after, Cox would receive a critically important endorsement from Sherman, who had been rumored as opposing him. In a July 13 speech, the notoriously antipolitician Sherman, having offered Cox the chance to become a brigadier general in the regular army, said, "The newspapers had no right to say I didn't favor his election. I've always spoken in the highest terms of his ability and high qualities for office. I just wonder why he wants this instead of a [military] commission—I would not do so."[12]

On his way to Columbus, Cox stopped in Washington to visit Dennison, Chase, Garfield, and other Washington acquaintances to discuss his campaign strategy and to get a further sense of postwar and postassassination national politics. Garfield and Dennison recounted Johnson's plan to complete Reconstruction by the end of the year while following what he interpreted as the policy that Lincoln had intended. They told Cox that opposition to Johnson was growing within the party, especially because the new Southern state governments showed little sign of accommodation to the changed political order. At the same time, the Radical Republicans were frustrated by their inability to block Johnson's policies, because Congress would not be in session until December, as was the practice of the time.

Both Practical Politician and Ideologue: A Unique Proposal

As of early July, Cox had shown considerable practical political acumen in winning the gubernatorial nomination, avoiding a commitment on the suffrage issue, and proving that he had accurately judged the nature of the soldier vote. His practical and his ideological sides would soon clash, however, because of the intensity of the public policy debate over race. That conflict reflected the fact that at this point Cox supported Johnson's approach for both ideological and political reasons. He thought its implementation would keep the party united and help his electoral chances, while ensuring long-term Republican political dominance through an early return to civilian government in the South. He believed that once the new governments were in place, an alliance of homogeneity of institutions and peoples led by the "best men" in the South and moderate Republicans in the North would evolve. That would, he thought, effectively prevent the Democrats from gaining power in either North or South. The unaddressed factor in Cox's vision was the role of freedmen. If blacks were not to be given equal rights as citizens but were to remain in the South, what would be their position in society? Cox's answer during his campaign would be a key to his political future.

When he arrived in Columbus in early July, he learned of rampant speculation about his racial views. Most papers presumed that he was still a Radical. One Democratic paper wrote that he was "a nonentity from nowhere, a foppish incompetent, whose military career was based on the fact that he went to Oberlin, studied with negroes, ate with negroes, and in all probability, slept with them." A Radical Republican paper wrote, "Cox is at this moment an ardent advocate of free suffrage."[13] Cox had told the Republican leaders in Washington that he planned to address these issues in depth during the campaign; but he was still ruminating about them in July and so did not want to make his positions formally known until the campaign began, in August.

Cox's concept of politics reflected his academically oriented nature. His ideal political world was one in which there would be a free exchange of ideas debated and assessed in an open, respectful manner that stimulated the mind and intellect. He remembered this idealized atmosphere in the creation of the Republican Party, when the issues and differences were clear-cut and the Republican Party's positions were high-minded and philosophical. In the postwar era, he believed that all views on Reconstruction and the future of the freedmen should be propounded publicly, not sublimated or hidden from the voters. Cox always enjoyed intellectual debate, and so now, like the minister and professor he originally intended to become, he was determined to put forth his independently-arrived-at ideas in a tutelary fashion. He would try to teach and mold the electorate, regardless of the political consequences.

In pondering the best approach to race and Reconstruction, Cox aspired to find an intellectual and policy middle ground between the evils of slavery and a Reconstruction policy enforcing racial equality. He sought an approach that he believed could win votes for the Union/Republican Party from an electorate that did not support equal rights for blacks. He also wanted to avoid another extreme choice, as he saw it, between external colonization and a multiracial society. In addition, he took into account that by early 1865 the federal government had by its war powers established a policy of military protection of freed slaves living in specially designated regions and owning land taken from whites.

His ruminations were almost complete when, in early July, he asked Dennison to be a sounding board for his plan. Cox wrote, "Reconstruction is so important that I must contribute my ideas to the common stock and try to mold public sentiment. . . . Discussion won't imperil the party, which is too strong, and it is of more importance that the question be settled than if I get a heavy majority." In that statement, Cox's transition from practical politician to impractical ideologue began as he gave greater weight to his independence of thought than to party discipline.

Cox told Dennison that after giving the matter great thought, he had come up with a solution to the racial issue that involved a paternalistic and

compassionate program of social change: "Segregate the races and guarantee the weaker, in a separate corporate existence, the right and opportunity of full political activity and progress under the protection and with
the assistance of an organization" in a region akin to a territory. Because
he believed foreign colonization made no sense, he advocated instead a
type of internal colonization. The federal government could, he wrote,
carve out by eminent domain a significant segment of land along the coast
of Georgia, Florida, and the Carolinas, where, he noted, the majority of
Southern blacks already lived. Underscoring his commitment to laissez-
faire thought, he emphasized that this process would be entirely voluntary,
with no element of coercion. Blacks would be encouraged and enticed,
but not coerced, to go there. Their incentive would be the clear benefit of
living in the only place where, protected by the federal government and
assisted by the Freedman's Bureau, they would have political rights and
power. They would also have economic and educational advantages and
could develop free from repression. Cox thought that whites who lived in
the region should not be coerced to leave, but he presumed they would do
so voluntarily. He emphasized that the plan was "prompted by a real and
earnest philanthropy and a free admission of all the rights of man" while
being consistent with Johnsonian Reconstruction. As he told his brother
a few days later, his plan would "settle sectionalism by making the South
homogeneous with us."[14]

Not surprisingly, Dennison disagreed with this plan, and he advised
Cox not to propound it publicly, because it could create divisions within
the party. He thought Cox should simply declare his support for Johnson's
policies and otherwise keep silent, as a practical politician would. Dennison believed that Congress should act to help blacks only if the Southern
state governments did not fulfill their responsibilities. Cox responded that
he had carefully considered Dennison's "suggestion of the danger of . . .
being thought reactionary" but that he was convinced of the rightness
of his ideas and the necessity to make them known publicly. He added,
"I have never been more certain of any future thing" than that political
disaster would result if the Radicals succeeded in implementing their plan
of Reconstruction: either the party would split or the Democrats would
win Congress, because the populace opposed black suffrage.[15]

Cox expanded on these themes in a letter to Garfield on July 21. He
stressed that his plan was a better political alternative than the Radicals'
push for black suffrage in both North and South. He said, "I am much

186   burdened by the feeling [that] we are in great danger of making a ship-
wreck of the Union organization. . . . Separation with Johnson will lead
to defeat and destruction. The South will refuse Negro suffrage and will
appeal to the nation because our states are unlike on this issue." Then,
he feared, the Democrats would win in the North and by uniting with
the South ensure an even worse scenario than what the Radicals wanted:
black suffrage would never be implemented. Garfield seemed to agree,
noting, "I confess to a strong feeling of repugnance when I think of the
negro being made our political equal. . . . I would be glad if they could be
colonized, sent to heaven, or got rid of in any decent way."[16]

On July 22 Cox sought the views of college classmate and Oberlin
professor John M. Ellis, and in this letter he added additional thoughts to his
thesis. He said that if Congress refused to readmit the Southern states because of the issue of black suffrage, then the nation, including a majority of
soldiers, would vote into office congressmen who would do so without such
conditions. At that point, power would be transferred to the Democrats and
"blacks will be at the mercy of their former masters." He predicted that if
blacks had the vote, they would not stop there in their political development.
They would form their own party, which whites would then gerrymander
out of existence. The result would be a race war that the blacks could not
win. The only solution Cox saw was internal colonization. He admitted,
"It is not a perfect plan and if men were more benevolent it would be better.
. . . Would to God I could see the matter otherwise."

A few days later, two officials from Oberlin, probably having been
advised by Ellis of Cox's evolving views, wrote to ask him for his position
on black suffrage. Cox, believing that his thoughts were sufficiently ma-
tured, responded with his famous "Oberlin Letter," an expanded version
of his missives to Dennison and Ellis, which he intended to make public
later. Presenting his thesis on an elevated, intellectual level in an attempt to
avoid being seen as a "negrophobe," Cox put forth what he saw as a high-
minded treatise, based on historical evidence, biology, and anthropology.[17]

He began the letter by emphasizing his credentials as a long-time opponent of slavery, a founder of the Republican Party, and a soldier. He acknowledged that blacks were facing a dangerous situation in the South and
needed support, but he argued that the intense racial animosity resulting
from the war had made peaceful racial intermingling "an absolute impos-
sibility." Giving blacks the franchise, he said, would not solve the problem,
but rather worsen it by alienating the soldier vote and ultimately giving

the Democrats and Southerners a political majority. The only way to avoid that would be full support of Johnson's policies, because they would keep the Republican Party strong and the Copperheads out of power.

Cox cited the historical difficulties of amalgamation even of peoples who were racially and ethnically close. He pointed out that despite their ethnic similarities, groups like Normans and Saxons in England and the various tribes of France had not united for many centuries. He emphasized his belief that "the only basis of permanent nationality is to be found in complete homogeneity of people, of manners, and of laws." For the United States that meant "the Yankee race," descendants of the peoples from western Ireland to eastern Germany. Given these realities as he saw them, Cox asked the fundamental question: "What encouragement have we that success will attend a forced political fusion of bitterly hostile races from the antipodes of the human family?" Forcing conflicted races together would, he predicted, result in a direct and immediate struggle for supremacy. Prophetically, he said that in that scenario, he could "see no hope whatever that the weaker race would not be reduced to hopeless subjection, or utterly destroyed." By contrast, his plan for internal colonization and federal protection would both assist and protect blacks. In addition, it would have the positive political effect of blocking increased Southern representation in Congress because there would be fewer blacks counted as voters. He concluded that while he understood that military government could force a more democratic solution, "[n]either subject provinces nor military proconsulships can long co-exist with Republican Government."[18]

Cox was aware of the contradictory and inconsistent elements of his proposal, but he hoped that its publication would stimulate discussion and potentially lead to a more-refined plan. One of the contradictions involved his advocacy of the military as an essential player in the new "territory," despite his rejection of military government. Though he was a firm believer in limited government, Cox's plan would have required a wholesale increase in federal power in the new territories. Though he supported laissez-faire economics, Cox's plan would have guaranteed the basic needs of life to freedmen financed by the federal treasury. Finally, the plan ignored the possibility that a modus vivendi such as he had seen in North Carolina might ensue for a transition period in the South.

One other contradiction was that while Cox presented the "Oberlin Letter" in an academic tone, he opposed a multiracial society and amalgamation for other, more personal reasons. As he wrote later to his sister,

188   "I have given my opinions with what some will call more frankness than discretion; but my theory is that frankness is discretion if honesty is the best policy. . . . [T]he subject bristles with difficulties, but upon the principles underlying the whole subject, my mind is fixed. . . . The argument that if political interfusion did not lead to fighting, it would logically lead to amalgamation, is one which I did not desire to urge in the document I have referred to, because it would seem like appealing to an odium against the negro, and I wished to make the argument without saying a syllable to imply that he was not equal in manhood and intellect to any of us." He then repeated his arguments against amalgamation, emphasizing again that it would lead to conflict and race war, terrible consequences that could be avoided only by internal colonization.[19]

The "Oberlin Letter" and Politics

Cox sent copies of the "Oberlin Letter" to Ohio newspapers, and its publication on August 1 brought forth a storm of controversy. The Democrats were surprised and pleased. One Democratic organ declared that Cox had "turned tail on his party's pet project" and should have been a Democrat. Radical Republican organs denounced Cox's stand, and their support for him diminished. Cox's friend Murat Halstead, editor of the moderate Republican organ *Cincinnati Commercial,* wrote that Cox had shown that Radicals did not have unanimous support. Cox's political friends were worried that he had gone too far, with Garfield noting, "I cannot agree with all the positions you take." Nevertheless, they promised their continuing support. Cox told his sister that he found "in the partial opinion of friends the antidote for the abuse" he was receiving for his views and that this enabled him "to estimate truly the value of the attacks made" on him.[20]

    Dennison wrote him on August 5, "All [the] men I've talked to from Ohio favor it. I begin to doubt the wisdom of my 'doubts,' and do most sincerely hope I may have been a false prophet." The test of Dennison's analysis would be whether Cox could keep the Western Reserve in the party fold. Cox's speech at his first campaign event in Warren on August 15 typified his approach to achieving that objective. He intimated in his talk that he knew his "Oberlin Letter" proposal would not be adopted in its present form. Moreover, he implied that because as governor he would have no role in Reconstruction policy, the "Oberlin Letter" should be seen as an academic exercise designed primarily to enrich the public debate. Garfield spoke next, and he illustrated that he had sensed the shift in political winds. He praised Cox's war record but spoke against the plan and declared himself flatly for black suffrage. Having experienced the new Garfield in Washington, Cox could see that his friend was becoming what he could never be, a practical politician adapting to shifting public opinion to gain and keep office.[21]

An important test for his campaign would come at Oberlin, where Cox spoke at commencement exercises on August 21. He praised the war effort, the end of slavery, and his Oberlin training, which he said had given him the resolve to do his duty. Prophetically putting his finger on what would be a fundamental reason for the failure of Reconstruction, he said that political equality meant nothing if social and economic equality were not attained, and Southern whites would never allow or accept that. He alleged that the vote would be no protection for blacks if its holders dared not use it from fear of repression. That was why, he said, he had proposed that the freedman have a place of refuge where he could advance without fear. In response to a question, Cox said that he favored black suffrage in Ohio. When he finished, Cox received polite applause, and the expected storm of protest did not ensue; however, the city's and college's ultimate electoral support would not be as great as Cox would have hoped.[22]

State and national Republican leaders were unsure how to react to Cox's ideas. Those who opposed him were not so much disturbed by his advocacy of colonization and segregation, because the overwhelming majority of Northerners did not support multiracialism. Rather, they feared that the proposal could lead to backlash within the party and the resultant loss of votes. They also came to recognize that Cox was an independent-minded politician who would be disinclined to accept party discipline if it meant not being able to speak out. One Ohio politician told Chase, "Politics run wild in Ohio. Cox, your old friend, seems to have ignored all the former teachings of Oberlin. His course . . . must greatly reduce the Union majority and thus give an impulse to the Copperhead faction." Chase too was disappointed with Cox's stance, writing to Charles Sumner in late August that Cox had "pitched his pipe to the Executive tune" by taking a conservative stance in line with Johnson's.

Chase discussed these concepts and Cox's ideas with Johnson in early September. According to Chase's account, Johnson said that if blacks stayed intermingled in the South, they would elect other blacks to office at all levels. Presuming that this was something to be avoided, Johnson reportedly said, "Is it not a great deal better that the two races should be separated, & each control everything within their own limits?" Chase argued against this approach, and Johnson promised that they would discuss the issue again in the future. They did not do so, and Johnson continued to implement Reconstruction with no further reference to internal colonization or to Cox's ideas.[23]

Back in Ohio, Cox remained the favorite to win the gubernatorial election, in part because of his war record. The Democrats needed a candidate with a military record to oppose Cox, and they settled on General George W. Morgan. During the war he had opposed using black troops and had resigned after Sherman accused him of disobeying orders. The Democratic platform supported states' rights, immediate readmission into the Union for the South, and Johnson's Reconstruction policy. Morgan accepted the nomination with a scathing attack on the "Oberlin Letter," saying that never was there "a more obnoxious and odious idea."

Cox campaigned actively statewide, emphasizing that the Republican/Union Party would protect the gains of the war, while the Copperheads/Democrats would endanger them. He made few references to the "Oberlin Letter," stressing that he would have no role in national Reconstruction policy. Underscoring that he saw it as an academic exercise, Cox also made no effort to have his plan even considered by Congress. Furthermore, in Washington that fall the intensifying clash of the two radically different visions of Reconstruction put forward by Johnson and the Radical Republicans ensured that the political focus would be on those two extremes, not alternatives such as the "Oberlin Letter." Gradually, but inevitably, Cox's ideas would be forgotten. Having said when he proposed the plan that the only thing to fear was delay, Cox acknowledged later that "the time for it was 1865, and 1865 will never come again."[24]

While Cox campaigned, Ohioans gained their first impressions of their potential governor. In his speeches he took a tutelary approach, underscoring his view that political leaders should focus on intellectual concepts. He exhibited an unemotional, uninspiring speaking style; in an age when charisma on the stump was important to political success, Cox proved lacking. An article in a friendly paper accurately portrayed the new man in politics. It read, "General Cox disappointed everyone not acquainted with him. The popular idea is that he is rather old, grave, and somewhat stern, but on the contrary, he is quite young looking—is not over 35 and yet possesses a bland, quiet disposition, which seeks seclusion, yet renders him agreeable and pleasant upon acquaintance."[25]

Despite Cox's lackluster campaigning style and the fears of party leaders because of the "Oberlin Letter," the Union Party ticket swept the state, gaining large majorities in both the state senate (25–12) and the state house (70–35). Cox defeated Morgan by over thirty thousand votes, a substantial win, but by a margin much smaller than John Brough's one hundred thousand in 1863 over Vallandigham. The difference reflected the return of many War Democrats to their former party and the lack of participation of many Republicans, who likely stayed home in protest. Cox ran one thousand to two thousand behind the others on the state ticket and even further behind among Western Reserve voters. Oberlin gave him a large majority, though fewer votes than Brough in 1863. In a harbinger of electoral problems for Republicans, referenda in three other Northern states to give blacks the franchise were defeated, though the party won all eight gubernatorial elections.[26]

On January 8, 1866, a week after he resigned his military commission, Cox delivered his inaugural address as governor. He emphasized that the terms of peace should confirm the principles of human liberty in a prompt, moderate, and just Reconstruction policy. He added that the use of military power in the South to force concessions would be only a confession of the failure of Republicanism. Reflecting his firm belief in Anglo-Saxon ethnic leadership, he stated that "a nation is strong in proportion to the homogeneity of its people," though he also called for increased immigration to "fill up the uncultivated lands" of the state. He preferred German immigrants, many of whom had fought under him during the war. Finally, he advocated payments to Ohio's wounded soldiers and their families to supplement "meager" federal pensions.[27]

At the time, the governor of Ohio had no role in the legislative process, having neither the veto nor the requirement to sign laws for them to go into effect. What power his office did have in state politics was based on patronage and his prestige as titular leader of his party. As for patronage, Cox's first response to those making recommendations for office was noncommittal, and he began the policy he was to follow in later political offices, not to appoint anyone whose honesty and integrity he had not carefully checked. He also oversaw the sale of 630,000 acres granted to the state by the Morrill Act to build what would eventually be the Ohio State University. (One of the first decisions by the new school's board of directors was to offer Cox the opportunity to be the first president, but he declined.) In short order, Cox realized that being governor was a part-time job that did "not call for severe mental application usually." As a result, he had sufficient free time to devote to his favorite leisure activity, reading, as well as to get involved in national politics.[28]

Reconstruction Arbiter: Caught in the Middle

While Cox had been campaigning, one historian asserted, "an uneasy feeling that somehow the South had never really surrendered" began to permeate the North. As the new Southern governments refused to change their policies or their ways, Johnson remained adamant against changing his own policies. The 1865 state elections, including Cox's success as a moderate opposed to Radical Reconstruction, "emboldened Democrats and the white South, strengthened Johnson's hand, and weakened the Radicals." In response, the Radical Republicans began considering harsher measures toward the South, and Cox believed they were promoting "the conviction in North and South that they [were] acting on a bitterly hostile spirit toward the Southern States and want[ed] to treat them as subjugated provinces." When, in December 1865, Johnson implied that Reconstruction was substantially over, the lines of opposition hardened even more.[29]

After Cox was elected, some Ohio Republican Party leaders appealed to him to be an arbiter between Congress and Johnson. Garfield told him that he hoped the election results would modify Johnson's policies, and he said that Cox, one of Johnson's strongest supporters, could help that process with a visit to Washington. Dennison told Cox that because he was respected by both sides, he could provide both Johnson and Congress with disinterested advice. While Cox eventually agreed to make this effort, he decided not to travel before his inauguration because, he told Garfield, a Washington "full of cliques, passions, and prejudices" was no place to discern public opinion.[30]

In Congress in February 1866, some moderates in the party tried to find a middle ground by urging Johnson to renew the Freedman's Bureau and accept a modest Civil Rights Act. That month, Senator John Sherman and General W. T. Sherman joined in Dennison's and Garfield's pleas that Cox come to Washington to help bring Johnson around. General Sherman also said he hoped Cox would continue to work "for moderation and against Stevens and Sumner." Cox finally agreed to go in late February, but on February 20 Johnson vetoed the extension of the Freedmen's Bureau. Two days later, after Congress refused to permit newly elected representatives from the defeated states to take their seats, Johnson attacked the

Radicals and declared himself the defender of the Southern viewpoint, an action that historians called Johnson's "declaration of war." Cox now faced a more difficult mediation task, and he feared that Johnson's actions could split the party. But he was more concerned about the Radicals' push for "military rule and despotism," because "blacks should be content with freedom for now and wait for a time when they could show what they could do."[31]

During their February 24 meeting, Johnson artfully justified his policies to Cox, who later told Perry, "If you could meet his straightforward, honest look as I did," Perry would not be concerned that Johnson would not keep to the principles on which he and Lincoln had been elected. (Cox would realize eventually that the president was manipulating him.) After that meeting, Cox met with Ohio's Republican congressional representatives on February 26 to try to persuade them to trust Johnson. But most of them, as Garfield put it at the meeting, believed that Cox's intervention "only put a decent suit of clothes on Executive nakedness." Cox was startled by Garfield's statement, because two days before, he had told Cox exactly the opposite. Cox told Perry of his disappointment that his mission did not succeed, despite all his "suavity." Now, he said, he was "realizing the fate of meddlers in a family broil."[32]

Cox worried that one consequence of the intransigence on both sides would be the formation of a new party fusing Johnson's supporters and the War Democrats. That might happen, he feared, because "[t]he country won't consent to postpone the complete organization and restoration of the South much longer." He was determined to remain loyal to the Republican Party in the hope that it would ultimately support Johnson; as for the other party, he said, "I detest the Democrats so much that action with them or in a party they control is out of the question." But he was in a precarious position because the Radicals were beginning to transfer some of their wrath to men like Cox for trying to remove the pretext for a fight.[33]

The situation was so difficult that in March Cox began to believe Johnson would have to make at least some compromise, including support for the pending civil rights bill. Cox wrote to Johnson that he should understand that those who had fought in the war needed to see that the cause they had fought for was secured. He admitted there were potential constitutional problems with the bill but that it was better "to strain a point to meet the popular spirit." If Johnson signed the bill and it became law, Cox emphasized, he would be the "master of the situation" and regain party support. But above all, he warned, Johnson should not accept Democratic support.[34]

Meanwhile, Dennison told Cox that he was coming to the conclusion that Johnson's actions were "very near an abandonment of the Union party." A gloomy Cox responded prophetically on March 27 that a veto of the civil rights bill would be taken "as conclusive evidence that Johnson's purposes are what his enemies declare them to be." Johnson's veto that same day was the step that many historians see as the ultimate turning point in the imbroglio, and one historian opined, "Cox's position was decidedly exposed." John Sherman's colleague monitoring Ohio affairs wrote, "I do not doubt Mr. Cox's entire uprightness, but his superserviceable zeal in behalf of Johnson has fatally compromised his influence with the party." Cox plaintively told Garfield he found himself "agreeing with nobody and in accord with no system of measure."[35]

Splitting with Johnson and with the Radicals

The next crisis in both Washington and Ohio came when the Fourteenth Amendment was proposed on April 30, 1866. Cox was opposed at first because it was a further extension of federal power, and he believed it could ruin the party because it violated the Republican theory of limited government. Recognizing the evolution of politics and of his friend Garfield, he told Dennison, "It is fine for Garfield and others to be radical to save their seats, but when they see that this draws the lines of parties in 1868, they will see [that] their course is indefensible."[36]

That issue was still undecided when the Ohio Union Party convention met in Columbus on June 20. Faced with conflicting demands from the moderates and Radicals, Cox was able to put off a confrontation by convincing the Reserve delegates to postpone the black suffrage question for a year and persuading the moderates to endorse the Fourteenth Amendment. Cox had by then concluded that in the interest of party comity he would no longer oppose that amendment. The next day Cox wrote to Johnson in an almost desperate tone, urging him too to support the Fourteenth Amendment. He said that if the president did so, he foresaw that the "crisis of our [sic] struggle with extremism will have ended with the present session of Congress." This would prove to be his final appeal.

On June 25, 1866, Johnson announced that he would work for the defeat of his Republican opposition. While Cox was disappointed, he still refused to support the Radicals; in any case, he thought they would not want any assistance from conservatives like him unless it was "on the basis of full partisanship against the President." He told Dennison, who had just resigned from the cabinet in protest, that he could neither go over to the Radicals nor "eat his words." Instead, he would "stay in the old party ranks with such graces" as he could, putting his faith chiefly in time.[37]

Cox's patience with the president finally ran out after an August convention of moderates and Democrats declared its support for Johnson and his policies. Cox told a friend that he "could not hesitate to remain with the party which saved the nation during the war," and though it was "badly piloted," he felt "no temptation to coalesce with Copperheads on that account." Halstead's paper wrote that "Cox showed he had gone to the precipice with Johnson, but had come back to endorse the party and was somewhat apologetic."

Johnson's infamous "Swing around the Circle" tour pushed Cox over the edge. When Johnson arrived in Columbus on September 12, Cox was not there to greet him, using the excuse that he had to be out of town at a previously scheduled campaign meeting. Cox did arrive later, and he had a short chat with Johnson and also met with Grant, who was accompanying the president. Grant was uncomfortable doing so, telling his wife regarding the president's speeches, "I look upon them as a national disgrace." Johnson was angered by Cox's slight, which might have been deliberate, and the two never had friendly relations again.[38]

Cox made public his break with Johnson on September 25 at the anti-Johnson Pittsburgh Convention of Soldiers and Sailors. Cox was elected as presiding officer because, as one delegate put it, he had once been tainted by Johnsonism but now favored the Congressional platform. He gave what one historian called "a vigorous and (for him) fiery speech" emphasizing his break with Johnson. The gathering backed congressional control of Reconstruction and, likely at Cox's suggestion, passed a resolution advocating that effective service in the army be considered equal to an education at West Point.[39]

The 1866 national elections were a triumph for the Radical Republicans, who won a House majority of 173–47 and a Senate majority of 45–8. Johnson still refused to compromise, and in December the new Congress began working out the means to ensure its control of Reconstruction. That Congress also made the first movements toward modifying executive patronage powers, which Cox vainly hoped would "rid us of the abomination" that had been "endured under the maxim of 'to the victor belong the spoils.'" Among the bills passed was the Tenure of Office Act. Garfield, who was taking a lead in pushing this legislation, told Cox that "[a] formidable attempt" would "be made to impeach the President." The Tenure of Office Act would be the basis for the ultimate impeachment resolution.[40]

In a letter to Monroe on November 21, Cox wrote an incisive and introspective apologia about his relationship with Johnson. He admitted that for many months he had continued to hope Johnson would act correctly. In the end, he asserted, "Johnson has disappointed everybody: the Democrats who adopted him as well as the Republicans whom he abandoned." Calling Johnson a "failure" and a "cipher," an embittered Cox said he had stayed loyal as long as he did only to protect against the kind of Reconstruction that no one could accept. Cox wrote acerbically of Johnson, "He is obstinate without being firm, self-opinionated without being capable of systematic thinking, combative and pugnacious without being courageous." He concluded, "The Democracy played with him as an angler with a trout," and their Southern allies, who had "always looked down upon him as a 'mean white,' puffed him with the idea that he was to be the leader of the class of Southern gentlemen."[41]

These developments motivated Cox to begin thinking about a future out of politics, though with a strong sense of ambivalence. By January 1867 he admitted that his "influence in political affairs" was "almost purely negative," and his continuing concern about income and inability to reestablish his law practice weighed heavily on him. He told Perry that he was reasonably sure he could be renominated and reelected, though he feared that the Democrats might win the state legislature if the Radicals became more extreme at both the state and national levels. He also knew that his independent approach to politics, first evidenced by his "Oberlin Letter" and then by his lengthy support for Johnson, had dismayed party leaders. At a time when Radical influence was growing, Cox was increasingly unpopular within the party. He could have swallowed these differences, as most of his contemporaries would have done, but that would have been inconsistent with Cox's nature. Instead, those two steps would later prove to be the first two nails in his political coffin.

Later in January he told Perry that he had no great love for politics, especially in their then-divisive state. Nevertheless, he was fully aware that if he did not run again, he would be giving up "what would commonly be considered a flattering prospect for a political career." In the end, he decided that now that he had been reduced to silence on major political questions, he would make the break. On January 25 Cox officially notified the Central Committee that he would not be a candidate for reelection. Cox's decision, a disappointed Halstead wrote, was regrettable "when a most brilliant future in the political world was opening," and it came at a time when "strong personal friends" (Halstead among them) assured him that "he would be the second strongest" national presidential candidate in 1868. In sharp contrast, another Republican paper wrote that though he was "a good governor," he was "not in accord with the Union party on the great issues of the day."[42]

Financial reasons related to the state of politics also influenced Cox in his decision not to run. As he told a friend that April, he was fully aware of "the insecurity of public position and the necessity of laying a foundation for a modest independent income before committing further to politics." He wrote that if his views about Reconstruction and race were eventually accepted, then he could return to politics with increased power. Even if they were not, he would devote himself for ten years to accumulating enough wealth to be independent of office for a livelihood. If a taste for politics survived all that, he said, he would still be less than fifty years old and better prepared financially for a public career on his own terms.[43]

A Hard (Money) Campaign

In his annual message in 1867, Cox's only comment on national affairs was his regret that a final solution to Reconstruction had yet to be achieved. He also recommended passage of the Fourteenth Amendment as the best way to secure permanent peace in the South. Most of the attention of the state legislature for the next few months was given to the resolution to amend the state constitution to allow black suffrage in Ohio, which in April passed the state senate by 23–11 and the state house by 63–29, almost entirely along party lines. Cox was opposed at first because one clause in the resolution effectively disenfranchised deserters, and Ohio had many men who had "deserted" when the Confederate surrender was announced. The law was later amended to protect their civil rights.[44]

During this period, machinations between supporters of Grant and Chase as they vied for the presidential nomination led to an impasse in deciding on a successor to Cox. Ultimately the Republicans decided on Cox's former subordinate, Congressman Rutherford B. Hayes. As Cox campaigned for Hayes and the Republican ticket in the fall, a new issue emerged that would be a core subject of national debate for the rest of the century. Democratic representative George Pendleton's "Ohio Idea" favored the use of war greenbacks to pay off bank notes held against the government and thereby solve the problem of the war debt. Cox told his brother Allyn, a Wall Street financier, that soft money would be the ruin of the economy and that paying the debt in "inflated currency will be a national dishonor." As one historian put it, "Among the respectable political leaders of New England their views [on hard money] were economic gospel . . . and they cultivated such westerners as Garfield, Jacob Dolson Cox, and William Allison, whom they considered salvageable."[45]

But neither national finance nor the Republican appeal against Copperheadism proved effective in the state elections, and Cox's gloomy predictions about the results of the Republican Party's moving away from moderation were fulfilled. The Democrats reversed the Republican majorities in both houses; the suffrage amendment was roundly defeated by more than thirty-eight thousand votes; and Hayes eked out a victory by less than three thousand votes.

After the election, a dismayed Cox lamented in his letters not only the state of politics but also the kind of Reconstruction that he feared was about to ensue. Returning to the themes of the "Oberlin Letter," he made predictions that sadly proved to be accurate. He told his brother Allyn that while the Radicals would still dominate in the Congress, their harsh policies toward the South would not last. He said the people of the North would inevitably tire of military Reconstruction. Then, he added, "The whites [in the South] will seize all power and Congress will accept whatever they do." They would implement policies, the end result of which would be either genocide of the blacks or black subservience as a "low, servile caste." He said, "I had hoped our exodus from the barbarism of slavery wouldn't be as fatal to the negro as our civilization has been to the Indian," but he feared he was wrong. Eventually, he implied, the people and the party would see how wrong they had been and would return power to their rightful leaders, perhaps himself included. But for the moment, he noted, "I think myself much more likely to make them discard me than to modify their policy materially."[46]

In his annual report early in 1868, Cox implicitly scolded the Republican Party for its mistakes. After reporting on the defeat of the suffrage amendment, he justified his stand, saying, "The progress of events has only strengthened the convictions I have heretofore made public in regard to it." Further proving Cox's distancing from the party and underscoring that he would have some difficulty resurrecting his career, the *Cleveland Leader* wrote that Cox's message, in which "a Republican governor congratulated a Democratic legislature on the defeat of his own party on a vital issue[,] deserve[d] condemnation."[47]

Private Life: Return to Politics

Before leaving office, Dolson and Helen had decided to settle in Cincinnati, the state's largest city and "beyond all question the best point for business in Ohio." He hoped the governorship, as well as the contacts he had made when administering the military district, would be "part of the capital on which" he could "obtain business." After setting up his law office in January 1868 in the same building as Perry, Cox was disagreeably surprised when only a few minor civil cases came his way at first. He found that contrary to his earlier expectations, "a political reputation [was] in many respects hostile to" gaining business. His financial situation was such that he refused his younger brother's request to live with the family and attend the Cincinnati Law School. The birth of his and Helen's sixth child, a son named Dennison, on December 8, 1867, had added to the financial burden. It added to the psychological burden when the child died in April 1868. As a result, in the spring of that year Cox was both exhausted and discouraged, even as Helen's melancholy increased with another child's death.[48]

During this period, Cox learned both that he still had a positive public image and that most of the body politic presumed that he really wanted to stay in politics. He nearly became involved in national Reconstruction politics again when Sherman suggested to Grant that one way to resolve the standoff between Stanton and Johnson would be to nominate Cox for secretary of war. In late 1867 Sherman and Grant agreed to recommend this choice to Johnson; though Johnson told Sherman that Cox would be a good secretary, he refrained from nominating Cox because he believed doing so would look as if he were compromising with his enemies. On February 24, 1868, the House impeached Johnson, and a few days later his trial began in the Senate. After he escaped conviction, Johnson named Schofield as the new secretary of war.[49]

While in Cincinnati that summer, Cox fielded several other offers, including as a congressional candidate and as commissioner of internal revenue. He turned them all down because his business was finally showing signs of prospering. The end of August saw the new firm of Cox and (Henry) Burnett hang out its shingle for the first time. Cox also planted the seeds for his future role as an educator, in which he would find his greatest civilian professional success. In September he accepted an offer to conduct a course of lectures as a professor in the Law Department of the Cincinnati College (later the Cincinnati Law School). On October 27 he delivered the opening address to students, beginning an attachment with that school that would last until 1897.[50]

In mid-1868 Cox had been pleased to see Grant nominated for president, because he knew "Grant so well personally" that Cox believed he would "prove a truly conservative and sagacious President . . . backed by popularity like Lincoln's." Some of his friends thought that Grant might choose him for the new cabinet, but because Cox had had little contact with Grant, he had no expectations. His chances were improved when on December 15, representing the Army of the Ohio, Cox gave a speech to the "Army of the West" reunion to celebrate the anniversary of the Battle of Nashville. He gave a hearty tribute to Grant, who was in attendance, saying, "With the administration of the country in such hands . . . who will doubt we will have peace?" At the gathering, Sherman told him that Grant was going to offer him a cabinet position, and he strongly recommended that Cox accept.[51]

Cox got no word from the taciturn Grant, and he told one brother in late January 1869 that "just enough was said of the possibilities of his being called to Washington to prevent" his feeling entirely settled. The day before Grant's inauguration on March 4, Cox told another brother, "Ordinarily I'd regard it as sheer folly to think my name could possibly be in the list without my knowing it today. . . . [T]o go would only be an onerous though honorable duty." On March 5, having not informed any of his cabinet nominees of his decisions, Grant sent to the Senate and House the long-awaited list, which included Cox as the nominee as secretary of the interior. The surprise with which each name was greeted prompted Democratic Congressman Charles Eldredge to say wryly, "I move that the House take a recess of ten minutes, that the mourners may have an opportunity to condole each other."[52]

After the cabinet was ratified by the Senate later that day, Grant wrote Cox cryptically, "You have been nominated and confirmed as Secretary of the Interior. I hope you will inform me of your acceptance and meet me here as soon as possible." Cox received the news by messenger while he was teaching at the law school. He responded, characteristically, "Under the circumstances I can do no otherwise than respond to the call, which has been entirely unsolicited and is therefore a duty which cannot be avoided." In fact, he was thrilled. As Helen Cox wrote to her son William Cochran, "There was nothing which has happened to us since our marriage that has given Pa such satisfaction as this appointment. . . . [H]e is beamingly happy."[53]

Assessing the Postwar Politician

Despite facing a sunny political future in early 1865, by 1869 Cox's promising career had been clouded over because of several decisions and actions he took. His periods of service in elected political office were characterized by his lifelong commitment to honest and open discussion and by his abhorrence of manipulation and chicanery, traits that were not always to his political advantage. He also rejected the idea of professionalization of politics, underlining his view that politics should be an avocation wherein men would debate ideas and serve the public only when duty called.

His "Oberlin Letter," a typical example of Cox's devotion to thoughtful and open debate, was a creative, unique, and controversial proposal appropriate as a topic for discussion in a college classroom but not as the first public statement of an aspiring gubernatorial candidate. The problem for Cox was not that the proposal was radical. In many ways, it was in the mainstream of thinking in a North where few supported equal rights for blacks in a multiracial society. The problem was that it was seen as politically unwise and insufficiently "loyal" by both camps as the ideological and divisive war between Johnsonian and Congressional Reconstruction ground on. Furthermore, Cox showed that he was inclined to be intellectually independent and disinclined to accept party discipline or stay silent. Warned by practical politicians to sweep his thoughts under the rug, Cox both stubbornly plunged ahead and implied that that would be his modus vivendi in the future. That was the first step in ensuring his ultimate political demise in a political climate in which hewing to the party line would be required of aspirants to higher office.

The second step was his adamant support for Johnsonian Reconstruction, even as the president steadily lost popularity in both the party and the nation. Cox believed that this position was the essence of practical politics because it represented the views of both the majority of Northern whites and the returning soldiers. In the short term, he proved correct.

202   In the long term, however, as the Radicals gained prominence in both Washington and Ohio, public opinion reversed, and practical politicians like Garfield evolved to match the popular mood. Cox would not and could not bend if he were to remain true to himself and his ideals. When Johnson refused to compromise, Cox cut ties with the president and stayed in the party, but he waited too long to do so. Political memories are strong, and he had come to be seen as the proverbial man in the middle, especially when in his final message as governor he publicly criticized the party's support for the suffrage amendment.

The fact that during 1868 Cox was still being considered for a variety of offices underlined that despite his self-inflicted political wounds, he retained a reputation as an honest, deep-thinking man of integrity. Having him take any office would enhance the reputation both of the office and of the person getting it for him. Cox resisted all offers except for becoming a member of Grant's cabinet. Nevertheless, even though he was about to enter national politics for the first time, his chances to become a major political figure were already on the decline.

8

Citizen-Statesman

> The trouble was that Cox thought the Interior Department
> was the whole Government, and that Cox was the Interior
> Department. . . . A good and efficient man, but not
> indispensable. Where an officer imagines himself bigger than
> the Government, then there is going to be trouble.
>
> —Ulysses S. Grant, quoted in Poore, *Life of U.S. Grant*

A Unifying President and His Interior Secretary

The judgment of history about Grant as president is decidedly mixed, but there is no question that his most important achievement was helping the nation to reunite and move beyond the fissures of the midcentury. His early Indian policy, his support for the passage of the Fifteenth Amendment, and his efforts to rein in the Ku Klux Klan were other positive aspects of his tenure.[1] Grant's initial choice of cabinet officers was not one of his positive achievements, however; Cox was one of the few of them uniformly regarded positively.[2]

As he had when preparing for war, Cox quickly attacked the steep learning curve about issues with which he had never dealt when he became secretary of the interior. As ever, he would be independent in his thinking and action, and he took advantage of Grant's policy that cabinet members should be the autonomous heads of their departments. He saw this policy as an open invitation to put into practice his vision of a limited government led by well-educated, enlightened, and honest men focused on public service as an avocation, not a career. In a sense, Cox's bias in this office toward skilled self-made men like himself paralleled his view of volunteer officers like himself during the war. Those beliefs would bring him into conflict with a postwar political leadership focused on a radically different set of ideals at a time when the size of the government and the patronage system had undergone enormous growth and the professionalization of politics had grown apace.

The Interior Department had expanded considerably after the Mexican War led to the creation of new territories. It also administered the Patent, Land, Pensions, and Indian Affairs Offices, the Census, marshals and officials of federal courts, and all matters related to the transcontinental railroads. Cox's responsibilities were wide and varied: giving grants for the ongoing construction of those railroads; supervising the National Hospital for the Insane and the maintenance of all government buildings in Washington; functioning as mayor of Washington; supervising all territorial and federal penitentiaries; overseeing the Bureau of Education; and paying the salaries of all federal judges.[3]

By chance, in July 1867 Cox had had an experience that helped prepare him for the new responsibilities. He accepted an invitation from Jack Casement, chief builder of the Union Pacific Railroad, to take a trip west to observe the progress of the construction and to get his first real glimpse of the region. Along with General Sherman and a few other guests, Cox and Casement entrained to Chicago and then to Omaha, from where they took the Union Pacific to its terminus. There were bands of hostile Indians all around, and the visitors did not dare go more than fifty miles beyond the end of the track. On the trip, Cox gained his first impressions about Indian life. The trip also introduced him to the questionable practices related to the railroad business in that era. When he returned to Columbus with Casement, his stepson remembered, Cox was "tempted to take stock in Credit Mobilier, or some similar construction company, but he declined. General Casement said . . . 'I can't understand the General sometimes. Here he had the chance to make a hundred thousand dollars just as easy as turning his hand over, and he would not turn it. . . . All that was wanted was the use of his name as a stockholder.'"[4]

Reforming the Civil Service and Indian Policy

The significant growth of the federal government during wartime had been accompanied by a vast expansion of the spoils system. While Cox had at first naively believed that the Tenure of Office Act and related legislation would lead to the demise of that system, the opposite was true. As the quantity of jobs increased, so too did the number of candidates proposed by politicians, many of whom regarded government service as a career, not an avocation. For them patronage was essential to achieving reelection, their primary objective in office. Not surprisingly, Cox found that "the job-seekers in March and April infested the White House all day long and were frightful to behold." After only a week in office, Cox told his brother that he was "the center of attack for a swarm of office hunters a hundred times more numerous than the places at [his] disposal."[5]

Grant gave cabinet members discretion on employment decisions, requiring that all applications for office come through cabinet departments. Cox saw that as a golden opportunity to reform the department's personnel system, and he implemented the first extensive civil service reform of a federal government department. He saw his reforms as a way to limit the spoils system because employees would no longer be beholden to political ties to get and hold their positions. Further, Cox saw the changes he implemented as an additional check on expansion of the federal government's power and influence.

Having been warned by Dennison that every department had one-third more clerks than it needed, Cox discharged a great number of his clerks because of unsatisfactory service. He instituted examinations for most appointments in the Patent and Census Offices, and he "requested" clerks in the Pension Office to take examinations to prove their capabilities. Many declined to take the test and resigned instead. Further emphasizing his commitment to integrity, Cox told his brother Charles, who asked for a job, "I must be free from any possible charge of nepotism, so I can't do anything for you at present." Having told this same brother that a career in the army in peacetime was "semi-death," Cox echoed that sentiment in saying, "A clerkship in Washington is nine times out of ten a grave of all a young man's hopes." Even William Cochran got his job as a Trust Fund clerk only after passing the required examination.[6]

Indian affairs was another area in which Cox was actively involved in reform efforts. By mid-1869, at least in part because of the completion of the Union and Central Pacific railroads, the condition of the beleaguered Indians in the West was coming under new stresses from settlers and the army. General Sherman's cold-blooded and stark analysis of the situation in mid-1868 was prophetic: "The Indian War on the plains need simply amount to this. We have now selected and provided reservations for all. . . . All who cling to their old hunting grounds are hostile and will remain so till killed off. We will have a sort of predatory war for years." As a result, he opined, it was necessary to "clean out Indians as we encounter them. . . . [W]hen winter starves their ponies they will want a truce and shan't have it, unless the civil influence compels me. . . . If Grant is elected, that old Indian system will be broken up."[7]

In Grant's 1869 State of the Union message he announced his "Indian Peace Policy," a significant reform approach that reflected a policy direction reformers had advocated for years. It was based on the presumption, he said, that "no matter what ought to be the relations between the settlers and the aborigines, the fact is they do not harmonize well, and one or the other has to give way in the end." He lamented that all too many people advocated extermination of the Indians, which he dismissed as "too horrible." Instead, he averred, there was "no substitute for . . . placing all the Indians on large reservations, as rapidly as it can be done, and giving them absolute protection" from not only the army and settlers but also rapacious Indian agents. There, with federal help, they would have the opportunity to assimilate and become farmers.

Cox, whose department would implement this policy, had a paternalistic view of Indians that paralleled the one he had regarding the freedmen, including his advocacy of separate, federally protected areas for habitation: reservations. Soon after taking office, he wrote, "The question of immediate and thorough action looking to civilization is the only alternative or mode of escape from exterminating wars." The Indians, furnished with the "means of agriculture and clothes adapted to their new mode of life," would, he hoped, gradually become "civilized." In Cox's and Grant's views, survival for the Indians required that they abandon their beliefs and traditions, none of which, at least officially, were considered worth saving. As noted in the Interior Department's 1869 report, the government would fulfill its responsibilities honestly, because "the savages must feel that [the federal government's] promises are certain."[8]

The new policy included reform of aid distribution to the Indians. This approach was initiated after a delegation of philanthropists met with Grant and Cox and suggested the creation of a board of commissioners to oversee government expenditures and, most pointedly, eliminate corrupt Indian agents from the process. Grant, Cox, and the Congress agreed, and by mid-April 1869 appropriate legislation had been passed. The board of commissioners would serve as an intermediary between the department's Indian Office and the Indians and would, among other things, "inspect purchases and supplies to correct old abuses." Felix Brunot, the chairman of the board, wrote that the group's approach would be to educate the Indian nation "in the principles of Christian love toward an oppressed and heathen race." Additional reforms implemented by Grant included the appointment of his former staff member Ely S. Parker, a full-blooded Seneca Indian chief, to head the Indian Office and the appointment of Quakers as Indian agents. The second change came about, Cox wrote, "not because the 'Friends' had a monopoly on honesty, but because it would help cultivate peaceful relations between the tribes and agents who would not seek personal gain."[9]

By the middle of 1869, the Grant administration was receiving widespread acclaim for the success of its Indian policy. Cox reported that while the progress was "'imperfect,' it warrant[ed] confidence in the system adopted." Further, he could report by the end of 1869 that the "general condition of the tribes [was] more peaceful than [had been] expected, and there [had] been no hostilities." That December Episcopal Bishop H. B. Whipple optimistically told Cox, "[T]he success of your Indian commission and reform will save this poor race."[10]

Networking

During his first year in office, Cox became a rising figure in the leading social and political circles of Washington, and at first his family formed a close bond with the Grants. As Cox had learned during the war, the president was reticent with those he did not know well but could be just the opposite in the company of intimates. Cox's stepson, William Cochran, describing a social call by the Grants on the Coxes in September 1869, said he was surprised that the "fluency and ease of Grant's conversation and the enjoyable talk between the wives were pleasant aspects of the occasion." Grant also visited once to express his concern over the health of the Coxes' son Kenyon, who had two major operations in 1869.[11]

Cox's other acquaintances made him more of a national figure and reinforced his close ties to the Anglo-Saxon elite of the eastern establishment. He formed a close friendship with the diffident, austere Attorney General Ebenezer Hoar and through him befriended the young Henry Adams, who saw himself as the political and intellectual heir of his family. Adams had come to Washington in 1868 determined to assert himself as a leader of American society. Like Cox, Adams was unhappy at the growth of patronage-oriented political machines and their effect on government, including populating departments with political appointees. He believed that significant changes in the way government functioned, including civil service reform, were necessary for him and men of the elite to regain power in Washington. Noting Cox's efforts, Adams flattered him in late November 1869 that he was "the reserved force, the silent agency" that would enable civil service reform: "Give the country a lead! We are wallowing in the mire for want of a leader."[12]

Cox wrote of his relationships with the Washington intelligentsia: "I think of the pleasant tea-clinking in Henry Adams' parlors in Washington, when [E. L.] Godkin (editor of "The Nation" [magazine]), [Carl] Schurz, [David A.] Wells, and [Francis A.] Walker made a circle that seemed no small part of literary and scientific young America bound together in hearty friendship and general accord on questions affecting public welfare." One historian wrote that this group, many of whom were later active in the Liberal Republican Party, "wanted to recapture the liberal dream of individual responsibility and independence within the political strictures of the postwar era." They also wanted to refocus government on ideas and ideology and away from crass patronage practiced by the men who had professionalized politics. Though Cox was reticent about it, some in the group saw him as "the central figure." Halstead's *Cincinnati Commercial* referred to him as "the finest-looking man in Washington" and went on, "[H]is friends intimate he will be President someday."[13]

Another group with which Cox became close was the new breed of journalists who were making both Washington and political news a focus of their writing. His friends in the press, in addition to Halstead, included Donn Piatt, one of Halstead's reporters and later owner of his own paper, the *Sunday Capital;* H. V. Boynton, a reporter for the *Cincinnati Gazette;* and Charles Nordhoff, editor of the *New York Evening Post,* who was also a close friend of Cox's brothers Kenyon, Allyn, and Theodore, all Wall Street financiers. These journalists not only recounted political news but also made news through their involvement in politics and patronage. They tended to have a jaundiced view of Gilded Age politics and had helped create a negative image of Andrew Johnson as he engaged in his self-destruction. Ultimately they would do the same to Grant.[14]

The Coxes had some official social and representational duties, but Helen found it difficult to adapt to Washington manners and mores. An article written by a "lady correspondent" in 1870 opined that Helen was "more suited for domestic than social life" despite being "very well read and decidedly intelligent." Though she had come to Washington as "an utter stranger, . . . her evening receptions [were] densely crowded." However, she was criticized for having "some strict notions," among them that she "emphatically disapprove[d] of the round dances, never allowing her daughter [Helen, then twenty years old] to dance them." This caused a minor diplomatic incident when at a White House reception, visiting British Prince Alfred asked young Helen to dance a "round dance" with him. Helen declined because "her mother was religiously opposed to those performances." The prince then asked whether she would participate in a square dance with him, though the only opening on his dance card was at 2 a.m. Helen declined again, noting that her mother required that she be home by midnight. "So the young lady was obliged to decline any dance with H.R.H."[15]

Dabbling in Foreign Policy: Black Colonization?

In cabinet meetings Cox spoke occasionally when the rare foreign policy issue was discussed, but he usually deferred to Secretary of State Hamilton Fish, with whom he developed a good professional relationship. One issue with implications for both foreign and domestic policy, and Cox's future, was Grant's attempt to annex the "Republic of San Domingo" (Dominican Republic). During the Johnson administration, the Dominican government had requested annexation by the United States, which Johnson had endorsed. On April 6, 1869, after the Dominican government renewed the request, the subject was first raised in a cabinet meeting. Cox wrote that there seemed to be a consensus against the proposal, but no decisions were made. Later, Grant advised the cabinet that he would send his personal secretary, Oliver Babcock, to that country to discuss leasing the port of Samana as a coaling station. Soon after, an astonished Fish told Cox, Babcock returned with a draft treaty of cession.[16]

Grant had apparently concluded that annexation was not only an appropriate expansion of American power but also a means to help the freedman in the South, potentially by external colonization. In a handwritten memo, Grant wrote that an annexed Dominican Republic would attract white settlers from the North as well as Southern blacks who were fleeing the Ku Klux Klan, among other hardships. He believed annexation would also make slave labor unprofitable elsewhere in the Caribbean and hasten abolition there. He added that "if Providence designed that the two races should not live together, black Americans would find a home in the Antilles."[17]

Grant told a dumbfounded cabinet that he wanted to move forward with a treaty of annexation. The taciturn Grant had not bothered to explain his thinking on this matter, perhaps assuming, as he had in the military, that once he issued orders, they would be carried out. Fish did not comment. After an awkward interval, Cox, instinctively desiring to discuss this important issue in depth, said, "But Mr. President, has it been settled that we want to annex San Domingo?" Grant smoked hard on his cigar and looked at the other members to see whether they had anything to say. None did, and Grant moved on to other business. Cox told Perry later that he had done what he could, but "a Cabinet officer can't go and make speeches at the President on subjects not directly connected with his own department."[18]

Grant continued determinedly, and at another cabinet meeting, on October 19, 1869, he had Fish read the draft annexation treaty. Cox once again asked for clarification, but he did not pursue the matter when Grant seemed disinclined to discuss it in depth. Soon after, the president, becoming what Cox called "a thorough party man," began negotiating with the Senate to get the treaty passed by using patronage, a method that Cox believed "compromised the dignity of the Executive." Despite Cox's hopes that Grant would support civil service reform, the president believed he had to bargain with the tools he had available, including cabinet positions, to persuade a majority of the Senate to approve the treaty.[19]

Problems at Home and on the Reservation

The Interior Department's annual report for 1869 summarized Cox's first year in office. Other than a lengthy commentary on improvements in Indian affairs, the report noted that over seven million acres of public lands had been sold and that geological surveys of the territories were being carried out. It also summarized the completion of the Union Pacific and Central Pacific railroads and their deficiencies. Further, it reported that Cox had been the only cabinet member to institute civil service reform, and it advocated legislation for further reforms, which it said reflected strong public demand.[20]

Meanwhile, elements that would lead to Cox's eventual split with Grant were falling into place. Fish and Hoar were growing increasingly perplexed at Grant's unpredictable managerial style and decision making, but like Cox they seemed incapable of drawing Grant out. Grant's blind loyalty to his own friends and family was already getting him into trouble, most visibly when Jim Fisk tried to corner the gold market in September 1869. Cox's close ties to the increasingly anti-Grant intellectual elite and press reinforced his growing concerns about the administration's integrity. Finally, many leaders of Congress were growing angry at Cox's determination to restrict their patronage powers in his department and in appointments for Indian agents.[21]

In early 1870 another problem for the administration arose in Indian affairs. Sioux Indians in Wyoming Territory under the leadership of chiefs Red Cloud and Spotted Tail were angered that white settlers were moving into areas the Indians had been told would be closed to whites. Rumors of a new Sioux war began spreading, and the military stationed in the area began preparing for action. The war fears were assuaged when Red Cloud asked to come to Washington to make his case. In mid-May, Cox told a colleague that he looked forward to the visit of "Red Cloud and the other Sioux chiefs (especially Spotted Tail) who have been the terror of the frontier." He planned to show them "evidence of the nation's determination to keep faith in instead of repudiating solemn treaties" and to impress them with the power and grandeur of the nation "so that they would be fearful of ever again attacking it."[22]

One historian described the Indian leaders' visit to Washington as a mixture of "high carnival with serious purpose." The chiefs' several conversations with Cox, Ely Parker, and Grant would feature "much confusion, irrelevance, and misunderstanding, enlivened by much impatience and ill humor on both sides." On June 1 the chiefs were given a tour of Washington in the expectation that they would be awed into submission, a strategy that did not work. Spotted Tail began his June 2 meeting with Cox by scolding the secretary for not fully carrying out the treaty of 1868. In response, Cox began to lecture him about the positive results of the administration's new policies. He emphasized that Spotted Tail should face trouble in a manly way and not complain. Spotted Tail replied laughingly that if Cox had had as much trouble as he had had, he would have cut his throat long before.[23]

The next day Red Cloud took a similar tack with Cox, adding that he was intent on keeping the old ways to the extent possible. After asking for food and ammunition so his people could hunt and kill enough game to survive, Red Cloud railed against whites for breaking their treaties and forcing Indians into starvation and death. Cox put him off, emphasizing that the Indians would be able to discuss their problems directly with

Grant. On June 7 Cox again tried to placate the chiefs by emphasizing that the "Great White Father" acted not out of fear but out of a desire to do the right thing. At that meeting, Cox agreed to give them everything they had asked for, except guns, and he promised to see that treaties were kept to the letter. Cox also tried to put a good public face on the visit by giving Halstead interviews, which resulted in detailed reporting about the trip in the *Cincinnati Commercial*.[24]

The group eventually met Grant, who, though warm and welcoming, merely repeated Cox's sentiments, saying nothing new and providing no additional assets, though he later convinced Congress to release funds that had been blocked in the Indian Appropriations Act. Grant hosted the Indian leaders at a state dinner where the clash of cultures was evident. According to one historian, the Indians were unsure about eating some of the fine foods and wines, but they did enjoy the ice cream and strawberries. Spotted Tail reportedly wryly commented, "The white hosts evidently ate far more elaborate foods than they sent to the Indians as rations." At his final meeting Cox offered several more concessions, including permission for the Indians to provide the names of agents they would prefer as their interlocutors with the government. He took under advisement Red Cloud's request for seventeen horses. The only further "accomplishments" of the trip were Red Cloud's apology to Cox for his rudeness and Cox's promise to promote the Indians' interests.[25]

The chiefs then traveled to New York to speak at public meetings, and for a few days afterward eastern papers loudly demanded a more generous Sioux policy. Cox later sent Red Cloud the seventeen horses and arranged for a group of reformers to accompany the promised goods. The arrival of the aid package helped calm the situation and divert the possibility of war, though the Sioux were far too weak to cause problems in any case. In the end, one historian adjudged, the visit was somewhat of a success. He wrote that it brought about "peace with Red Cloud and the Oglala Sioux, [which] was a major achievement." From then on, another historian noted, the tempestuous relationship between Red Cloud and officialdom "was one of diplomacy and not war."[26]

Patronage Wars: Forcing the Issue of Reform

Not surprisingly, Cox's moralistic views on civil service reform inevitably clashed with Grant's practical approach as the president became increasingly convinced that the use of patronage and cooperation with political machines was necessary to the functioning of his office, as well as to his reelection. Cox summarized his opinions on patronage and Grant's policies in a letter to Perry, writing, "A man like Grant, who never pretended to political influence as such, can only make his personal opinions control Congress by the use of patronage. . . . My theory is that except for the use of patronage, which is in itself corruption, the Executive has little control of measures or influence in forming policy." Cox's idealistic reaction to this was to "set [his] face like a flint in the direction of Civil Service reform." He proclaimed, "I hold it necessary to our existence as a Republic to cut up patronage corruption by the roots. . . . I am committed to the utter destruction of patronage."[27]

By contrast, Grant later said of patronage: "You cannot call it corruption—it is a condition of our representative form of government." One biographer stated that Grant "believed deeply in reform, but he was not sanctimonious about it." Grant noted, "The most troublesome men in public life are those over-righteous people who see no motives in other people's actions but evil motives, who believe all public life is corrupt[:] . . . they are narrow-headed men."[28] Though he did not say so, when making that statement Grant may have been thinking of the strait-laced and crusading Cox setting his "face like a flint in the direction of Civil Service reform."

Cox's inevitable clashes with the political system and its patronage-focused leaders began in earnest in mid-May 1870. He received letters from the Ohio and congressional Republican campaign committees asking that his departmental employees be given "the opportunity" to contribute for the coming campaign. Challenging both these groups and the system as a whole, a crusading Cox responded in his typically well-reasoned, self-righteous, and ultimately futile manner. Advising men who believed that their political survival depended on patronage about the evils of that practice, he provocatively wrote, "In my efforts to bring about an improvement of the civil service in this Department, I hold it essential that it be understood by clerks and employees that they hold their places subject to removal for lack of efficiency or integrity, and that no subscriptions to political funds or show of political zeal will secure their retention if capacity and industry be lacking. . . . Any compulsory assessment would be a political immorality." He later told the Ohio Republican Executive Committee that he would not comply with a similar request "because it is not right to do so and therefore not to the advantage of the Republican

Party." He said that instead he would send the party a fifty-dollar contribution, and he offered his services as a speaker in the fall campaign.[29]

Cox was unhappy about another patronage-related custom in his department whereby clerks were allotted thirty days' vacation each year, in part so that they could go back to their states to campaign. Early in 1870 Cox told potential campaigners among his employees that they had to reserve time out of their allotted thirty days or else lose pay for additional days. Because of the intense heat of the 1870 summer, many clerks took extra days off, leaving them with few for the fall campaign. Several clerks advised party leaders that they could not campaign, and they blamed Cox for restricting their freedom.[30]

A patronage-related episode illustrated for Cox the depths to which the administration had fallen. On December 16, 1869, Grant nominated Hoar to the Supreme Court. Hoar had previously given Grant a letter of resignation to use when he found it appropriate to resolve the problem of having two cabinet members from Massachusetts, himself and Treasury Secretary George Boutwell. Like Cox, Hoar had resisted Senate "requests" regarding patronage appointments for circuit judgeships. He suffered the consequences when in February 1870 the Senate did not confirm him as a Supreme Court justice. Meanwhile, prospects for passage of the treaty to annex San Domingo were fading. As a final vote loomed in June 1870, a desperate Grant acquiesced to a request from Southern senators to replace Hoar with a Southerner in return for their votes. On June 15 the president sent a note to Hoar stating that he would accept Hoar's previously submitted resignation.

At Grant's request, Hoar promised to keep the resignation secret for a time, but the resignation letter was accidentally publicized. The news created an uproar, as did the fact that the new attorney general was to be Amos Akerman, an unknown Georgia lawyer and former Confederate. The tie vote in the Senate of 28–28 on the treaty on June 30 would put that issue aside for the moment, but Cox was becoming increasingly convinced that in Washington neither person nor principle was above political manipulation.[31]

By the middle of 1870 Cox knew that his policies and independent streak were irritating party leaders, some of whom began agitating with Grant to fire him. In response, Cox had begun seriously thinking about forcing a confrontation in the hope of persuading Grant to support him. If the president did not do so, he would resign to call public attention to the importance of reform. Cox had by then concluded that Grant could not (or would not) stand up to "the combined efforts of intriguing politicians" and that the only recourse for cabinet members was to continue their departmental work and hope that Grant would change course. As the situation showed no change that summer and the drumbeat of criticism against him within the party increased, however, Cox told Perry in late August that he had decided to force a decision on civil service reform.[32]

Meanwhile, some of Cox's friends in the press had taken it upon themselves to buttress his reform efforts and defend him against political attacks. This group saw Cox as a unique individual: an independent-oriented politician who diligently fulfilled his responsibilities, did not seek or use patronage, did not drink or smoke, and refused to bend any of his principles to political "realities." Donn Piatt's views were typical. That July he wrote, "There are indications Cox is to be replaced—this would be a great public loss.... [W]hile knocking about among lobbies and rings, the uniform comment when his name is mentioned is 'Oh, d___ it, nothing can be done with him.' Grant should listen to him and not the fast men and women at Long Branch."[33]

The series of events leading to Cox's resignation began on September 7 when the Pennsylvania Republican committee wrote Cox that it was seeking "voluntary" contributions from its state employees in his department. He agreed, but only on the "condition that that subscription should be really voluntary." Meanwhile, Boynton, who had inside information, told Cox that that group had denounced him for refusing to allow the assessments. A few days later Cox and Helen left Washington for a vacation and to visit his mother on Staten Island. He had no sooner departed than, he wrote later, "the attack opened in form. The so-called Pennsylvania association was only the cat's paw, used by [Senators Simon] Cameron, [Zach] Chandler, and that ilk to make a noise under cover of which they intended to make their attack." On September 24 the press reported that Cameron and Chandler were insisting to Grant that he change Cox's rules on employees' leave. Cameron reportedly said, "Damn Secretary Cox! We'll see the President about this fool business." Their pressure worked. On October 3 Grant instructed Cox's deputy, sitting in for him at a cabinet meeting, not to implement the rule.[34]

An Apparently Minor Land Claim

Looming in the background of this growing contretemps was a minor land claim that would have major consequences for Cox. Early in his tenure,

Cox had been advised by the House Judiciary Committee that it was considering a claim by a certain William McGarrahan for mining land in California whose ownership was also claimed by the New Idria Mining Company, represented by former Attorney General William Evarts. The committee requested that Cox wait for congressional action, and he agreed. The committee voted against McGarrahan's claim in late July 1870, but when no final congressional action took place, Evarts demanded that Cox determine the case in his client's favor. Cox instead sent the case to the Land Office and gave no opinion on the matter. McGarrahan fought back. On July 22 one of his attorneys wrote to Donn Piatt, "How would it do then, to make the proposition to pay $20,000 in stock, provided you can bring sufficient personal influence on the Secretary of the Interior?" Piatt refused and reported this to Cox. Piatt neglected to mention that he was on the payroll of the New Idria Company.[35]

On August 22 Cox received a letter from Grant telling him to act on neither the McGarrahan nor the New Idria claim, noting that "fraud is charged and believed to exist on both sides." Cox told Perry he was "astonished beyond measure" by Grant's letter because he had heard about the bribe offer to Piatt and saw McGarrahan as a fraudulent claimant. Having two days earlier told Perry that he would confront Grant on the issue of civil service reform, he now decided to make his confrontation on the McGarrahan issue. Cox replied to Grant that the president had probably been misinformed as to the *status* (he emphasized) of the case in Congress. He noted that the committee had deemed McGarrahan to be a fraudulent claimant, and he pointed to the bribe attempt as further proof of McGarrahan's "unblushing knavery." Cox concluded, dramatically, "For myself, as I am conscious of having only fought fraud with such vigor as I could, I can make no compromise, and if I fail to secure to the fullest extent your approval of my cause, I must beg you to relieve me at once from duties which without your support I shall utterly fail in."

But Cox got no reply. Later, he learned that his letter had "cut Grant to the quick" because the president interpreted it as an intimation that *he* wanted to protect fraud. Cox admitted, "If the President had answered the letter the day he received it, his reply would certainly have been a request for" Cox's immediate resignation. Eventually the president calmed down, but he never answered Cox's letter. When Cox met Grant several times afterward, the president's cordial manner led Cox to believe that Grant did not want to reopen the subject. Eventually, the Interior Department Land

Office declared the New Idria claim to be valid, but Cox did not finalize
the decision, leaving it to Congress as Grant had requested.[36]

Leaving the Cabinet: The Press Gang and Grant

In September the nation's press began to run articles implying that Cox
would soon resign. Cox believed that the stories were the product of attacks from party regulars vexed by his policies, and he later opined that he
was quite "blind not to recognize the fact the time had come" for him to
"bring matters to a focus." Everything came to a head when, on October
3, his chief deputy telegraphed Cox at Staten Island about Grant's decision to reverse his policy about clerks going home to campaign. Cox once
again decided to force an issue, and he resigned.[37]

In his letter he told the president, "When Congress adjourned in the
summer, I was credibly informed that a somewhat systematic effort would
be made before their reassembling to force a change in the policies we
have pursued in the Interior Department." He indicated that the removal
of the Indian service from political patronage had been distasteful to many
congressmen and that his views of the necessity of civil service reform had
brought him into "collision with the plans of some of our active political
managers." Cox said he was certain that eventually public sentiment would
sustain his reform efforts. But he admitted that for the present those efforts
brought opposition that it might not be in the interest of Grant's administration to provoke. So Cox had decided to resign rather than change
his policy. The resignation would take effect after he presented his annual
report, and he assured Grant that it would only be announced later so that
it would not affect the fall elections.[38]

This missive was, like the one before it, not really designed to be a
resignation. It was Cox's forlorn attempt to change Grant's mind—as he
had tried to do with Andrew Johnson. Cox wrote later, "If the President
was disposed to give me good backing, and had he said, 'You are mistaken
about my being embarrassed by your action, and I will guaranty your
freedom to carry out your ideas,' I should willingly have remained. . . . I
certainly thought he would at least have expressed some general approval
of civil service reform."[39]

But Grant was not about to change, an attitude that was reinforced at
an October 4 cabinet meeting, at which all were present except the vaca-
tioning Cox. During the meeting, Boutwell reportedly remarked that he
understood that Cox had issued the disputed patent to New Idria. "Grant

then said angrily, 'If the Secretary to sign patents has put my name to that patent I will have him out *instanter.*" Boutwell replied that his information must have been incorrect. Grant then pulled out of his desk Cox's August 23 letter on the McGarrahan case, remarking that he had been deeply hurt by it. While acknowledging that Cox had run his department well, Grant said he had almost asked for Cox's resignation then.[40]

At that point, Grant appears to have had enough of Cox's crusading spirit. So when he received Cox's resignation letter the next day, he responded immediately, though graciously, "Your letter is received. . . . In parting company permit me to say that I highly appreciate the zeal and ability which you have ever shown in the discharge of all your official duties." The letter was sent by regular mail to the Interior Department, where the chief clerk read it and circulated the news to other employees. Soon rumors about the resignation and its background began to fly around Washington, and a minor political crisis for the Grant administration gathered steam.[41]

The six weeks after Cox resigned were among the more politically turbulent periods of the president's first term. Grant attempted to minimize the potential damage from the resignation to Republican electoral chances and to his reputation by trying to manage the press, an effort that would boomerang. As one historian noted, "All too many people around the president knew just how the story ought to be managed and did just about everything wrong they possibly could. . . . It was one of the defining moments of Grant's administration in reformers' eyes."[42]

On October 6 Cox was startled to read in the New York papers that his resignation had been accepted and that he was being accused of making it public to influence the October state elections. Cox believed that to comment would only worsen the situation, so he remained silent, even as the press began to conjecture openly about the causes of the resignation. At first the White House told the press there was no resignation, which was technically correct. In mid-October, Cox wrote to Hoar, "The President, whilst withholding the correspondence," allowed "it to be given out as from 'the best authority'" that Cox had resigned for purely personal reasons and that there were no differences regarding civil service reform. Several New York papers published articles to this effect. Boynton told Cox that Grant had put out this story personally.[43]

In response, Cox initiated his own public relations campaign. He declared to his friends in the press that he would not tolerate being called a liar, and he asked his brother Charles to brief Nordhoff about the details of the case. The *Nation* wrote on October 20 that Cox had resigned "simply because of the President's failure to support him in maintenance and prosecution of reforms in the Interior Department." Two days later, Cox wrote to Hoar that, because of the renewed press attention, he might "be forced to allow the letters to be published in self-protection." Soon after, Nordhoff's paper wrote, "Print the letter—Cox is willing, and Grant should do so in order that the garbled or false accounts can be corrected." Garfield's advice to "get the truth out" hardened Cox's resolve. He wrote, "Whatever be the outcome I shall not fail to expose the whole matter."[44]

Cox supplied the correspondence to his press friends, and on October 31 it was published, along with press commentary extolling civil service reform and lambasting Grant and his cronies for lying. Nordhoff led the charge, his *New York Evening Post* calling the matter "General Grant's Unconditional Surrender" to politicians. In response, an angry Grant began a series of conferences with his journalistic and political allies about putting a positive spin on the issue. They realized that to discuss civil service reform would show that Grant did not favor it. So, Boynton told Cox, they settled upon the McGarrahan affair as an alternative, with a dash of character assassination. On November 5 a Grant ally issued an "authorized statement" that impugned Cox for being an apologist for Andrew Johnson and a "judge and jury" in the McGarrahan case. The statement asserted that every department of Grant's administration was open to all citizens, and it defended political assessments as necessary to the health of the party. Grant's allies alleged that Cox was trying to make himself a political martyr to affect the elections.[45]

A few days later Grant told the press that Cox's handling of the McGarrahan case was the true cause for his leaving the cabinet. In the ensuing article, he summarized his views of the issues and of Cox the independent man who always thought for himself: "The trouble was that Cox thought the Interior Department was the whole Government, and that Cox was the Interior Department." Grant said that Cox had allegedly attempted to subvert the will of Congress, and he stated, "I would not have it. Cox got miffed and resigned. A good and efficient man, but not indispensable. Where an officer imagines himself bigger than the Government, then there is going to be trouble."[46]

The reaction was immediate. With the correspondence in the public domain, the press ridiculed Grant. Henry Adams wrote Cox, "How the President, even were his mind twice as narrow as it is, could have made the

blunder of publishing that letter as an attack on you, I can't understand."
Nordhoff wrote in his paper, "Who is more capable of saving the Republican party from defeat two years hence—General Cox, who demands civil
service reform, or General Grant, the promoter of such abuses?"[47]

Meanwhile, Grant's supporters continued their character assassination
of Cox, including the assertion that his bureau heads had been the true
initiators of civil service reform. Some even charged that Donn Piatt had
lied about the twenty-thousand-dollar bribe and that a bureau chief, S. S.
Fisher, falsely identified as Cox's brother-in-law, had written articles criticizing Grant that Helen Cox had sent to Mrs. Grant.[48]

Cox remained silent for a time, believing it was "unworthy of an ex-
Cabinet officer to enter a personal controversy with a President." But
when congressman Ben Butler, a Grant ally, published an inflammatory
letter about the case, Cox had finally had enough. He "felt an indignant
disgust at the insincerity of the whole effort to avoid the civil service
discussion by the pretense that the real difference was in regard" to the
McGarrahan claim. He gave Charles Nordhoff a full statement on these
issues, which Nordhoff used in further attacks on Grant. Cox told Garfield,
"I knew not only that Grant had blundered in seeking an alliance with
tricksters and not the people's support, but that he was trying to cover his
blunder at the expense of his honor and friendship for me. What must
be my opinion of the man who can try to cover his stolid folly in that
manner[?] . . . [W]ithout some pretty full acknowledgment on his part, our
personal relations are of course entirely ended."[49]

The Grant forces made no further assaults on Cox's character, and the
issue of his resignation and its cause slowly disappeared from the public
forum. Interest in the elimination of patronage also faded away, in great
part because it was not a popular issue and only the elite cared about civil
service reform. As Nordhoff told Cox, "As far as I can see Reform of the
civil service is not a live subject. I do not believe we shall be able to make
it a popular question."[50]

A few days after Nordhoff wrote that letter, there was another example of the depths to which politics had fallen. It involved the McGarrahan matter, and once again that odd character Ben Butler played a role.
When the House discussed the McGarrahan case in February 1871, Butler advocated for a minority committee report favoring McGarrahan. He
noted that while he would not allow the patent himself because it was
probably fraudulent, he would vote for it because it had been granted

(though reversed) several years before. Defending Cox's interest, Garfield responded that this meant Butler believed the government should not "cheat him out of his fraud." Butler agreed and said, "Do not steal from a thief either." The minority report was adopted, but the bill was tabled in the Senate. This matter would linger undecided for many more years, and it was punctuated by other strange events, including a fistfight between McGarrahan and Piatt outside the Senate chamber in 1879.[51]

Cincinnati and the Liberal Republican Movement

While the hubbub over Cox's resignation proved to be a minor irritant for the Grant administration, the latter's growing number of scandals, coupled with dissatisfaction over military reconstruction, made 1870 an important year for opposition to Grant within the Republican Party. That sentiment first blossomed into official and formidable opposition that fall in Missouri, where a group of Republican dissidents styling themselves "Liberals" allied with the Democrats over the issues of military reconstruction and patronage. They swept the state elections by forty thousand votes, with Gratz Brown winning the governorship. This state party would become a foundation for creation of the Liberal Republican Party and the effort to unseat Grant.[52]

At first Cox opposed such divisions, believing "we must act for reform within the party." But because the Missouri victory coincided with the media focus on his resignation, Cox found himself the object of presidential speculation. Henry Adams, who had become editor of the *North American Review*, was then "under the effect of a rage of reform." Adams planned to use the influence of the magazine, one historian judged, to become "one of the powers of the land . . . passing critical judgment upon American society, manners, culture, and literature, as well as instructing his readers on the correct course to pursue in politics," just as Cox was inclined to try to do.[53]

As part of that process, Adams was actively considering forming a new anti-Grant party based on civil service and tariff reform, and he saw Cox as a potential leader. Adams arranged a New York meeting of reformers in late November, during which, exhibiting the political naïveté that would ultimately be an important factor in their downfall, the group decided to delay forming a new party to give Congress an opportunity to act on these issues. Another reason for delay was Cox's refusal to encourage speculation about a presidential bid. He had just begun to reestablish his Cincinnati law practice and had joined the board of directors of the University of Cincinnati. Further, he told Nordhoff, "I am jealous of my character for honesty, but I won't push the controversy further than keeping my reputation." He did agree to write an article advocating civil service reform for Adams's magazine. The article, which appeared in January 1871, decried the problems he had tried to correct, which were already reappearing under the new secretary, Columbus Delano. In the article, Cox said that executive departments had become "the asylum for the worthless and incompetent dependents of persons of influence."[54]

Cincinnati would later become a center of Liberal Republican Party activity. This inevitably meant that even though Cox refused to be a candidate for president, wide recognition of his character and integrity ensured that he would be actively involved in party deliberations. He would ultimately be recognized as an ideological and philosophical cornerstone of the movement. On March 11, 1871, a critical step toward the creation of the party took place at a "private meeting" of Cincinnati civic leaders who were sympathetic to the efforts of the Missouri Liberals. The group, which included Stanley Matthews, a Cincinnati lawyer and future Supreme Court justice, and Friedrich Hassaurek, a leader of Ohio's German population, formed the "Central Republican Association of Hamilton County." Cox, to emphasize his desire to stay on the sidelines, had not attended, but on March 18 the group's leaders got Cox's endorsement of a platform that tracked very closely with his political views. It called for amnesty and enfranchisement for Southern whites, revenue and tariff reform, an early return to specie payments, civil service reform, and an end to using government for party purposes.[55]

When the news of this "New Departure," as Halstead called it in the *Cincinnati Commercial,* was publicized, one of Cox's friends told him it "fell like a bombshell among the administration sycophants." One paper reported that the group openly favored Cox for president. Cox was reticent, still believing that there was "no dream of a new party organization." As for the presidency, Cox assured Perry that "the leading men in the movement would not be any special supporters" of his. He said he was "under no hallucination on *that* subject." Accurately appraising his own temperament, Cox told his brother, "My firm belief is that I shall not be supple or easily molded enough to make me any party's candidate."[56]

In Ohio that fall, Cox nearly became a candidate for the Senate instead. Some in the "New Departure" group opposed the reelection of the moderate Senator John Sherman and favored Cox in his place. Again he resisted, preferring that Garfield or Perry be chosen. His brother Charles, expressing a frustration over his reticence that many of his friends and other family members likely felt, told him frankly, "It is very seldom that a man had greatness thrust upon him as persistently as it was held out to you." Cox told a friend that he did not want to run, because of his "repugnance to the hand-to-mouth life of a public officer with no security of tenure of office." He also was likely worried about Helen's health, since she was pregnant again, at the age of forty-three. She gave birth to their last child, Charlotte Hope, on December 11, 1871. Cox did keep the door open for a return to office, stating, "It could only be under a sense of duty" that he would consent to "forego [sic] any private interest for public employment."[57]

Cox's Republican supporters, led by the ever-pugnacious Casement, now a party leader, told Cox that his reserve "was one of the many reasons why [he] should be compelled to accept" a senatorial candidacy. Casement told Cox that he would pursue the seat for him whether he wanted it or not, and Cox could "put that in [his] pipe and smoke it." The efforts by Casement's group, which included bargaining for Democratic support, did not succeed. Indicating that he probably regretted not running, Cox told James Monroe that the maneuvers Sherman's men had used to win the seat in the Ohio legislature were a "bare-faced wrong and a piece of dishonesty of the worst type." Nevertheless, Cox admitted that if he had won, he would have had to rely on the Democrats, whom he hated; moreover, to Republicans, he would have appeared to be an intriguer. He did admit that his election "might have hastened the day of more healthy political organizations."[58]

Ideologues and Pragmatists

On the national level, Missouri Senator Carl Schurz was leading the effort to create a third party, and he believed Cox's support would be critical to its success. He also believed Democratic support would be helpful, a prospect that he knew Cox would oppose. Schurz wrote to Cox twice in October 1871 to urge him to be open-minded about working with "progressive" Democrats. In November, Schurz began speaking around the country calling on "progressives" in both parties to unite to oust Grant and reform the government. In January 1872 one of Schurz's allies, *Missouri Democrat* editor William Grosvenor, asked Cox, "What would you think of the possibility of holding a mass consultation of reform Republicans from all parts of the country at Cincinnati?" The objective would be formal planning for creating what Cox began calling "the party of the future." Cox agreed. The Missouri Liberal Republican state convention of January 24, 1872, issued the formal call for a national convention at Cincinnati on May 1, 1872.[59]

Schurz negotiated with Democratic Party Chairman August Belmont to delay that party's 1872 presidential nominating convention until after the Liberal Republican meeting, presumably so the groups could unite on a candidate. Both men supported the candidacy of Henry Adams's father, Charles Francis Adams, as did Halstead in his paper. But Adams was almost as diffident as Cox, and no other candidate emerged from among the reformers. Garfield prophetically told Cox, "The great difficulty with the reform movement is that there seems to be no well-formed organization and no tendency to concentrate on a man."

Another problem for the party was that its leaders, drawn from the elite, lacked the common touch. Their causes tended to be both abstract and mostly irrelevant to the common man. They did not focus sufficiently on the fact that Grant the war hero could only be defeated for reasons that the common man could understand. Furthermore, the Liberal Republican leadership planned to use the mechanism of a party convention while curling their collective lips at the way party machines had used such mechanisms.[60]

In this vacuum of organization and leadership, the practical politicians moved in. Disappointed office-seekers and others seeing an opportunity for spoils joined a party ostensibly dedicated to destroying the spoils system. Among this group were supporters of *New York Tribune* editor Horace Greeley, who gained control of the New York element of the emerging party and began maneuvering for support. Greeley was a well-known public figure, but his pro-tariff views made him suspect in this group. Further, he had no political experience and, as E. L. Godkin put it, was a "conceited, half cracked, obstinate old creature" widely seen as an eccentric. Halstead wrote that his nomination would result in a campaign "of caricature and derision."[61]

Cox the purist was disturbed by the "practical" steps the leadership had taken by cooperating with the Democrats and accepting Greeley into the party. He told Garfield, "Our present danger arises from the disposition of Greeley and the protectionists to come and offer cooperation. To this I cannot assent. I am not anxious to be in a movement designed only to beat

Grant." Cox told Schurz, "To start with affiliating with our most natural opponent would be too great a load" to carry. Ambiguity and avoidance of issues, he wrote, "might be the life of decaying parties, but were surely the death of new ones." Reverting to his tutelary and impractical view of politics, Cox told another party leader, "We don't have to win, but must educate the public." That utopian attitude would be swept aside by one leader's realistic sentiment that "if [the party] is to win this year it will be obliged to" compromise its principles.[62]

In late April the platform committee, which Cox was chosen to chair, began its deliberations for the May 1 convention. Cox crafted a draft document reflecting the new party's belief that the Republican Party, having achieved its original objectives, had become stagnant. It was, in this view, focused solely on patronage and thievery of the public purse by professional politicians and thus had to be radically changed—or replaced. The platform focused on a return to republican principles, defined as good government, free trade, moral rejuvenation, civil service and tariff reform, amnesty for Southern whites, an end to military reconstruction, and laissez-faire economics. Despite his prestige and influence, however, Cox was unable to block the New York delegation's pushing through an amendment to the tariff plank. The changed plank, as Cox had feared, involved "ambiguity and avoidance of issues." Rather than advocating free trade, it merely said the issue of tariffs should be left to Congress to decide.[63]

On May 1 the convention's opening ceremonies were highlighted by Schurz's speech calling on the delegates to remove "that which is obnoxious to the American people and put something better in its place." That "something" could have been Cox, whose law partner Henry Burnett recalled that if Adams could not be nominated, "there was a distinct understanding that General Cox's name would be brought before the convention at the proper moment and opportunity . . . for the first place." Halstead and Schurz called on Cox the day before the convention to ask once more whether he would consider being nominated. Cox replied that it would be an honor, but he came up with another excuse. He said that because he had been born in Canada, there might be a constitutional question of his eligibility. Cox did not even attend the convention, and he instructed Burnett that if he were nominated, Burnett should refuse it for him.[64]

Late in the day, Gratz Brown, who had parted with his former ally Carl Schurz over patronage in Missouri, made a deal with the New York delegation to support Greeley in return for the vice-presidential nomination.

On May 3 the first ballot divided the votes among Adams, Greeley, Brown, and Senator Lyman Trumbull, though Adams had a plurality. Brown then withdrew and gave his support to Greeley, who took the lead on the sixth ballot and was eventually nominated. Burnett withdrew Cox's name after an Iowa delegate nominated him for vice president.

Rationalizing the results, a despondent Cox told his brother Allyn that the party's leaders "agreed that the manner in which the original reformers had been overwhelmed absolved them from any responsibility for supporting the convention's action." Ignoring that their inaction and lack of decisiveness and organization had helped lead to Greeley's nomination, the party leaders opposing Greeley unrealistically agreed to wait to see if the Democrats would nominate someone else or if Grant would retire.[65] Some in the group were still disappointed that Cox had not run. They believed he would have had a good chance of being nominated, though, given his dry and unemotional campaigning style and Grant's enduring strength, there was only the smallest chance he would have won.

An End to Politics? Garfield and Scandal

In mid-May, a disillusioned and unrealistic Cox and some others in the party leadership still hoped that the Democrats might split over a Greeley nomination. They called for a new convention to be held before July 9 (the date of the Democratic convention) to nominate another candidate. Grasping at straws, Cox and his friends also sent delegates to the Free Trade League conference on May 30 in the desperate hope that group would nominate an acceptable candidate. Instead, these men proved once again that they were better at talking than at acting. Having had enough of open conventions, the latter meeting called for a convention on June 20 "of well-known men especially invited" to consider whether to nominate a presidential candidate.[66]

Again playing a central ideological role, Cox presided over the June 20 "Fifth Avenue Conference." But instead of nominating another candidate, the meeting's focus was a lengthy debate primarily between Schurz and Cox over support for Greeley. Schurz gathered at least some support, and Cox departed the meeting with dismay, all hope for reform that year gone. Grant won the election handily and portrayed his overwhelming victory as a mandate for the kind of politics he had practiced. Greeley's death within days of the election prompted one of Cox's friends to say, "At last it seems a defeat has driven a Presidential candidate mad and killed him." He added a comment that could well apply to the Liberal Republican movement: "What a strange tragi-comedy it has turned out to be."[67]

A few weeks later a discouraged Cox saw further proof of the declining state of politics. In mid-January 1873 Garfield was accused of accepting payments in the Credit Mobilier scandal. Cox felt that this news "was shocking . . . and for such men as Colfax and Garfield to be involved [was] terrible." He blamed Garfield's involvement on "the general demoralization in Congress, when men who have stood highest in reputation and character are thus found to have yielded to temptation." In keeping with his idealistic and impractical temperament, he asserted that for the guilty "no favorable course is left but confession, square, plain, unreserved."[68]

Garfield admitted to Cox that he had had contact with Oakes Ames, the chief agent for Credit Mobilier, but he claimed that because he did not buy the stock, he was not guilty of any transgressions. He added that he now had a strong disgust for political life but could not leave it because he had to defend his good name. Cox, who understood that his friend had become part of the system, accepted Garfield's rationalization that "whatever negotiations were tendered, he had rejected them and not gotten a penny of profit." Nevertheless, as Cox said afterward in a speech, this episode further convinced him that "politics have fallen to such a low order that no decent man could feel right in it."[69]

The failure of the Liberal Republican movement, added to Cox's split with the Republican Party over the "Oberlin Letter" and support for Andrew Johnson, ensured that his national political career was over. The Republican Party's national leadership as then constituted, focused as it was on professionalization and patronage, would not want such an independent-oriented ideologue to be their candidate for any office. As Cox would write presciently in mid-1872, he found himself a "wholly independent looker-on" in politics because he supported neither party. The Republican Party, he said, had no future because "in the South it is the negro party . . . and as the champion of the negro race and social equality, it cannot succeed and its defeat will signal its dissolution." The Democrats were in his view even worse because of their support of the South in the war. Grant's reelection and the dissolution of the "party of the future" put the exclamation point on these views and ended any opportunity for Cox's national political leadership.[70]

A Side Track from Politics

After the 1872 election's disappointments, Cox planned to focus on private life as a lawyer, law school lecturer, and leader of Cincinnati society, and perhaps to begin writing his history of the Civil War. In late 1873, however, he unexpectedly took a new career direction, as he became a railroad president.

228 The Panic of 1873 caused serious problems for his brother Kenyon's New York investment firm, Kenyon Cox and Company, one of whose partners was Jack Casement. Kenyon Cox and Casement had been planning to take control of the Toledo, Wabash, and Western Railway at a stockholders' meeting on October 1, 1873. Just before the meeting, a desperate Casement told Cox that his efforts to control the company and protect the interests of the Cox family (including Cox's investments) were in trouble. As a solution, he proposed that if Cox could "be induced to accept the presidency of the road it would largely add to the public confidence in the concern and greatly enhance its value." At the meeting, Kenyon and Jacob Cox, as well as Casement, were named directors, and Cox reluctantly agreed to become president.[71]

Cox told Hayes, "I have not had time to collect my thoughts enough to be entirely sure whether I am pleased or not with the new position, but incline to the opinion that I shall like it very much." He told Monroe that the job was "very attractive in itself—it deals with very large interests, it represents an investment of over $40 million, and it is directly connected with the growth and prosperity of the country." He would have a decent salary, which further justified his having once again to move the family, this time to Toledo, Ohio.[72]

At first it was thought that Cox would hold the job for only a short time and only until the Panic's effects eased; but the economic situation proved too dire. Profits continued to decline, and Cox found that extensive repairs and new passenger and freight equipment were desperately needed. In 1874 he had to cut salaries across the board and fire six executives, requiring that he and two superintendents do the work previously assigned to nine officials.[73] Cox was not surprised when the creditors and some of the stockholders brought suit in early 1875 for the appointment of a receiver, and he was appointed to that position. When conditions still did not improve, some bondholders sought foreclosure of the company in mid-December 1875. On April 7, 1876, Cox's appointment as "Special Master Commissioner" to sell the railroad was announced. On January 1, 1877, Cox formally turned over to the buyers the renamed "Wabash Railway Company," which would eventually join other roads under the control of Jay Gould.[74] A few months later, he would begin yet another unexpected career, as a congressman.

Return to Politics: Advising Hayes

The events of 1876 proved to be a heartening political surprise for Cox. He was pleased when his Civil War subordinate and fellow Ohioan Rutherford

Hayes was nominated for president by the Republicans. Cox believed that Hayes had some genuine instincts toward reform; hoping he might be a key adviser, Cox began informally counseling Hayes on public policies. Most of his advice echoed the Liberal Republican platform. In one letter, he told Hayes to avoid political cliques and rings and to implement civil service reform. Hayes, who always had had a high opinion of Cox, told him, "I am inclined to say something that will hint at least in the direction you suggest. It is probably the only topic which I shall add to the platform."[75]

After a political meeting in Toledo that summer, at which Cox spoke for Hayes, a party paper, the *Toledo Blade,* began speculating that he might be a good candidate for the House of Representatives. However, because his railroad salary would soon be cut off, Cox told Monroe on August 14 that he preferred to return to Cincinnati and his law practice. That same day the *Toledo Blade* printed a headline that read, "General Jacob D. Cox for Congress." Cox reluctantly agreed to accept the nomination, hopeful that with Hayes in the White House, reforms he supported might be implemented.[76]

During his campaign, Cox announced that he was pleased that Hayes had vowed support for civil service reform, which Cox promised to push forward in the House. He also discussed the crucial issue of greenbacks, and for one of the few times in his political career, he changed a position. Drawing on his experiences running the Toledo, Wabash, and Western Railway, Cox once again took independent stances on two public policy issues. He announced that he supported a return to bimetallism, advocating the solution the British used in 1819 after the Napoleonic Wars to gradually retire greenbacks and bonds. In a speech in mid-1877, he advocated the creation of unions, noting, "To the poor and industrious working men, the condition of human society is apt to seem a 'muddle.' The distribution of gains seems strangely unequal." The capitalistic system, he said, was producing uncontrollable monopolies and losing all its elements of humanity and generosity. A counter force was needed, and he saw a good future for labor unions. Cox won his election easily, and all across Ohio the Republican Party did well. Once again the 1860 Ohio Senate's "Radical Triumvirate" of Cox, Garfield, and Monroe were going to represent contiguous districts, this time in Washington. They were joined in the Ohio delegation by a congressional newcomer, Cox's former commissary sergeant, William McKinley.[77]

At the national level, attention was focused on the lengthy electoral dispute between Hayes and Samuel B. Tilden. When he had first considered running for governor in 1865, Cox had told Perry that the party should be focused on "Principles, not men." Now in 1877, commenting on the presidential election issues, Cox again exhibited his rigid and genuine opposition to pragmatic politics. He told one correspondent that the "Republicans would rather be beaten than succeed by the assumption of a single doubtful fact." As the electoral dispute festered, Cox met with Hayes on January 17, 1877, and followed up with a lively correspondence. Cox advocated an early end to military reconstruction and a speedy return of power to "decent and respectable" Southerners. Having accepted the futility of the creation of a separate territory for former slaves, Cox advocated helping the freedmen to gradually gain social and political rights. He also advised Hayes to support moving toward specie resumption, and he endorsed Schurz for the cabinet. In each case, Hayes said he would follow Cox's advice, typically telling him, "Of the Southern question your views and mine are so nearly the same that if called on to write down a policy I could use your language." After he took office, Hayes continued for a time to seek Cox's counsel. In late June, Cox met with Hayes in Washington and told him he had to "shear his and our [congressional] offices of patronage as a power for political or personal purposes."[78]

As he prepared to go to Congress late in 1877, however, Cox was experiencing a familiar frustration with politics, reflecting his ideological rigidity. Contrary to his earlier assurances, Hayes was showing little indication of following Cox's advice, except on ending military reconstruction. Cox was especially disappointed about the lack of civil service reform. Garfield agreed, complaining that Hayes "has appointed friends and friends of friends, removing worthy men for no reason." Cox reasoned, "We can't campaign on the basis of his record, but we rather need a policy." Cox, Garfield, and Monroe visited Hayes in October to discuss these issues, but according to Garfield, "Hayes' six months administration partially blinded the President to the dangers of criticism of his course." In fact, it was the opposition of the spoilsmen in Congress, especially Senator Roscoe Conkling of New York, that forestalled any effort by Hayes to enact civil service reform. Cox, however, refused to accept any excuses.[79]

With one exception, Cox's tenure in Congress would be equally disappointing. Soon after Congress opened, Representative Richard Bland had offered a bill calling for the free coinage of silver and its use as legal tender. To the astonishment of Henry Adams and other of his friends from the eastern establishment, Cox took yet another independent step, reflecting his rethinking of financial issues. Believing that debts contracted on a silver basis should be paid back the same way, Cox joined the majority that passed the bill. The bill was amended in the Senate into the Bland–Allison Act, the first large-scale attempt to inflate the currency through silver coinage. Cox was disappointed when Hayes vetoed it, but he joined the large majority that overrode the veto in March 1878. Cox said he supported the bill as an alternative to more extreme measures being considered, thereby saving "the world from a financial revolution which would bring other revolutions in its train."[80]

The rest of this session was devoted to ordinary business, and Cox had little of importance to do. As dutiful as ever, he was present for every roll call, but he inevitably became bored and frustrated. Furthermore, disillusioned that he was not influencing his good friend Hayes, he complained that he merely drifted along with the party, "smitten with a paralyzing sense of the utter uselessness of trying to impose one's ideas upon men who wouldn't change." Soon afterward, Garfield wrote in his journal that Cox had grumbled to him that "the President had pursued no system that could be defended by any class of politicians. The impression is deepening that he is not large enough for the place he holds." Having reentered politics because of his hopes for a Hayes presidency, Cox had now come to believe that his optimism was unjustified.[81]

In December 1877 Cox returned to his district for a family visit and to think over his future. His frustration with Hayes, coupled with his genuine reluctance to serve in government again and his inability to live well on his three-thousand-dollar annual congressional salary, convinced him not to run for reelection in 1878. During the congressional recess of 1878, Cox moved his family back to Cincinnati to pave the way for a return to legal practice, with his stepson, William Cochran, as his partner. He also decided to return to lecturing at the Cincinnati Law School. When Hayes was forced to call an early session of the 46th Congress early in 1879 because of budgetary problems, Garfield the professional politician was there. Cox was not, for his active political career was finally over.[82]

An End to Politics

Early in 1879 the law firm of Cox and Cochran was in "the condition of waiting for clients and picking up the broken threads of business." Cox, however, found legal work as dull and boring as that of Congress and felt "a sense of more or less repugnance to entering again into professional management of other people's contests at law." He admitted that he did it

232 only "under the necessity of making a living." Still, he said he was satisfied that he "had done wisely in getting out of politics again." Moreover, these were happy times for the family, as four of the children—Helen, Jacob Dolson, William Cochran, and Charles—were married between August 1878 and October 1879.[83]

Cox's interest in politics peaked again in January 1880, when Garfield was elected to the Senate. Soon thereafter, he felt "no small satisfaction in seeing the Grant [presidential campaign] bubble collapse." When his good friend Garfield surprisingly got the presidential nomination, Cox was thrilled, saying, "The party and the country deserved to be congratulated." Having had much of his advice disregarded by Hayes, Cox hoped for better luck with Garfield. He repeated to Garfield similar advice: "[M]ake no pledges that are personal, stand on your record, and commit yourself to no one."[84]

Garfield won a victory that, as Cox told his friend, was made possible "by the thinking people of the country, honest in their purposes and wise in their broad common sense." Cox again had high hopes that he would be a trusted adviser of a new president, and Garfield called Cox to his Mentor, Ohio, home to discuss the cabinet choices and presidential policies. On January 29, 1881, they went over all relevant issues, with Cox giving Garfield his thoughts "from the viewpoint of an independent."[85]

Once again, however, Cox saw his advice ignored and his lofty principles unimplemented as his friend's practical political instincts came to the fore. In one ironic instance, showing that Cox was not above asking for favors, he advised Garfield to accept their friend James Monroe's request to be appointed as minister to Brazil. The president assured Cox that he would take care of it, but as the months went by and nothing was done, Cox told Monroe that he was feeling "disgusted and disappointed to the last degree." When June came and Garfield's promises remained unfulfilled, Cox felt that he would never do it.[86]

All ill feeling was put aside when Garfield was shot by an assassin in July. As Garfield's condition worsened, Cox became greatly concerned over "the terrible and prolonged uncertainty in Garfield's case." He wrote that he found the desperate hovering between life and death that the president went through for over two months "very hard to bear." After Garfield died, Cox told the attending physician that it had "been a sadly memorable time."[87] Garfield's death ended Cox's active involvement in politics. Despite his frustrations with Garfield over the years, Cox had continued to regard him as a very good friend and a man of honor. Once Garfield was gone, there were few men left who shared Cox's beliefs or were so close to him. Inevitably, Cox then faded from the public's political consciousness.

Assessing the Reluctant Politician

There were many reasons why this rising political star of 1865 failed to have a more successful political career, but the obvious causes related to his own decisions, made consciously without regard to political consequence. Most fundamentally, he was an independent-minded man of principle and an ideologue who insisted on thinking for himself at all times and who could be overly pious. He would not adapt to changing times or engage in the compromise, self-promotion, and wheeling-and-dealing so necessary to success in practical politics. He did not believe in the professionalization of politics. He refused to use patronage and denigrated a system wherein that element was central to electoral success. He was also not a charismatic public speaker, and he lacked the "common touch," often presenting the image of an aloof scholar trying to teach an unreceptive populace and political leadership, which did not prove to be apt "pupils." But unlike many politicians, Cox seemed to always be fully conscious of the effects of these elements of his personality and to be comfortable with his fate.

An introspective letter Cox wrote to a friend in 1885 is an incisive and perceptive encapsulation of why he did not have a more substantive national political career and why he and the evolving political system did not mesh: "I have rarely, if ever, felt the need of repudiating the aims of my youthful enthusiasm, but have generally stuck consciously to the principles while recognizing the limitation and incompleteness of the earlier application of it." He said that he was not especially enamored of public life, nor was he as susceptible as some of his friends, such as Garfield, "to the attractions and pleasures of place." He wrote, "I am so egotistic that I do not need this proof of my consequences." He repeated his constant refrain that the office should seek the man, and not vice versa, and that when that happened, it was a duty to accept. He admitted, "This is perhaps partly a matter of temperament" but he also argued that it reflected his experience with men in public life who had no idea what to do with themselves if they lost their public positions.

He complained that in contemporary politics, officeholders were the "mere register of the will of the party cliques and rings." He regretted that

234   "it is notorious that a man of ideas and of independence [like himself] is not 'available' for office," because the parties were focused not on ideology or principles, but only on reelection. He wrote that in 1876 Garfield had asked him about leaving politics, but Cox had told him that it was too late for his friend to do so because he had become integrated into the system and had no other real professional options. Cox did not want to end his own professional life that way.

    He concluded with a final and apt apologia: "My experience of public life had probably been about as great as may come unsought to one who has stubbornness of opinion. Enough, at best, to warrant me in thinking that I too could have cut a more prominent figure had I thought the game worth the candle . . . and so without disappointment or envy, regret or longing, I have been able to go my way thinking my own thoughts, advocating my own opinions, calling no mob master."[88]

9

Civil War Historian

> I have little reason to complain of my treatment as an author.
> The most competent judges have accepted the authority of
> my volumes, and the publication of the government records
> has practically quieted discussion.
>
> —Cox, *Battle of Franklin,* 1897

The early 1880s were a watershed period in Cox's life, when he would leave politics behind and shift his career focus from the law to several intellectual pursuits, all of which were in keeping with his academically oriented personality. Those years would see him become dean of the Cincinnati Law School, president of the University of Cincinnati, a world-renowned amateur scientist, and a civic leader in Cincinnati. But by far his most important intellectual activity was as a historian of the Civil War.

Modern historians of the Civil War acknowledge the importance of the memoirs of the leading actors in the war as vital primary sources and foundations of its memory. One historian posited that "most present controversies about the conduct of military operations during the American Civil War first appeared" in the earliest memoirs and first attempts to chronicle the war. However, most historians are justifiably dismissive of Civil War histories and biographies written during the nineteenth century because of deficiencies in scholarship and research. Few of those works were well researched or objective. Many were written as part of the post-war's political-military wars through which participants and their supporters engaged in the zero-sum game of "refighting the Civil War."

Furthermore, the books about Northern generals almost always gave only West Point graduates credit for victories, while "political generals" were ignored or mentioned only for their incompetence. As for books about Southern military leaders and their military activity, many Confederate histories were written with at least the implicit purpose of laying the groundwork for the "Lost Cause" myths. Given the above, it is easy to understand why two historians of the historiography of the war have commented that it was not until "about the time the veterans were hearing their final roll calls, [that] serious scholarly studies of the Civil War got under way."[1]

A Recognized Scholar

The scholarly studies written by Cox are, to a significant degree, an exception to that judgment. Given the continuous proliferation of Civil War–related literature, Cox's self-satisfied judgment (see the chapter epigraph) more than a hundred years ago about his historical writings is open to debate.[2] That his influence on the memory of the Civil War continues to be significant is nonetheless undeniable. A review of the literature on the war since the nineteenth century will show that in descriptions of the battles of South Mountain, Antietam, Atlanta, and Franklin, the West Virginia campaign, and the nature of military leadership and training, Cox's books, letters, book reviews, and official reports have been recognized by historians as both accurate analyses and essential sources. As Cox wrote to Garfield late in the war, "It is known here that rank and ability are often quite different in the field and that history will change many records." Cox's work helped "change many records."[3]

As early as 1861 Cox began thinking about writing a history of the war. In his letters home, his official diary and reports, and his commentaries to Garfield, Chase, Perry, and General Hitchcock, the evolving scholar included both in-depth descriptions of the realities of war and analyses of problems and possible solutions. That, plus his thorough scrutiny of topics ranging from the role of the press and the Congress to military education and organization, as well as his advocacy for self-made military men, would provide bases for much of his historical writing.

In the first years after the war, Cox was too busy to write, but he hoped to compose a full history of the rebellion and the war when he had sufficient time. In early 1867, after he decided not to run for reelection as governor, he began gathering materials and organizing his letters, while poring carefully over the emerging war-related literature. In an event that year that likely spurred his desire to set the record straight, he corresponded with Horace Greeley about the second volume of the latter's history of the war, *American Conflict*. Cox told his future political bête noire that he had made major mistakes in the book in his description of the battles of South Mountain and Antietam. In addition, he questioned the reliability of Confederate "official reports" of the strength of the armies upon which Greeley had based some of the work. Greeley accepted much of Cox's critique and promised he would change what he could in future editions.[4]

Cox's historian-related career was formally launched in 1874 when his friends E. L. Godkin and W. P. Garrison, editors of the *Nation,* the leading intellectual magazine in the country, asked him to be their anonymous reviewer of books about the war. They could see that Civil War books were flooding the marketplace, and they knew Cox not only had a significant war record but also was an able writer who shared their classical liberal philosophy. Cox accepted, but because of the severe time constraints of his position as railroad president, he reviewed only three books in the first three years. Ultimately, Cox would write 161 articles and reviews for the *Nation,* most related to Civil War books, and he came to be acknowledged as a leading military critic. As he read and wrote about the literature, Cox was well placed to assess and analyze the "battle of the books" involving leading generals' inflated egos and their and their supporters' zero-sum game efforts to secure credit and cast and deflect blame. Furthermore, as Cox saw his role and that of other citizen-generals being diminished or ignored in the literature, he became more and more convinced of the need to finally write his own works. His objectives would be both to set the record straight and to contribute to an accurate and more objective history.[5]

The "Battle of the Books": Thomas versus Sherman and Schofield

The first volley in the battle of the books in which Cox was involved was fired less than five years after the war. Jealousies, resentments, and ambitions that had collided during combat had continued to simmer and were erupting in a variety of ways. One frequently used method was the published article or book in which information was interpreted to favor the subject and cast others in a negative light. One of the earliest examples of such literary warfare occurred in early 1870 when H. V. Boynton wrote an article in the *Cincinnati Gazette* about George Thomas, under whom he had served in the Army of the Cumberland. During the war, Grant, Sherman, and Halleck all believed that Thomas was slow to act and ponderous when leading his troops. Thomas knew Grant and Sherman had doubts about his abilities. But he did not know the extent of their lack of confidence until he read Boynton's article, which quoted from Grant's orders relieving Thomas with Schofield, Logan, and Grant himself before the Battle of Nashville.

Schofield, whose acrimonious relations with Thomas had continued after the war, interpreted Boynton's article and related editorial commentary implying that replacing Thomas would have been disastrous as an attack on him. In response, using a tactic several military leaders followed in the "battle of the books," Schofield had an aide write an anonymous letter to the *New York Tribune,* which was published on March 12, 1870. The letter criticized Thomas's plan for the entire Franklin-Nashville campaign and implied that Schofield would have done as well as commander in Nashville as Thomas had. Thomas was apparently enraged. While writing an in-depth response, he suffered a stroke. He died March 28.

Thomas's death expanded this episode into a multidecade series of political-military skirmishes between Schofield and Thomas's supporters in the Society of the Army of the Cumberland. The latter rose to the defense of their fallen hero, and some even suggested that the anonymous letter had precipitated his death. Presuming accurately that Schofield was behind it, Thomas's partisans attacked Schofield viciously, first in the press and later in letters and memoirs. Cox, still close to Schofield, was on the receiving end of one of those attacks, which implied that he had written the letter. Eleven years later Schofield told Cox he "deeply regretted" having the letter written.[6]

Cox's second and third reviews for the *Nation,* in 1875, of Sherman's memoirs and of a book critical of them, directly involved him in another Thomas-related imbroglio. His first review in 1874 had been of a prototypical self-serving memoir by a general who blamed others for his defeats and was unwilling to admit error. Cox told his readers that Joseph Johnston's *Narrative of Military Operations* was "not an historic memoir, but a passionate defense of himself against the South's charges of having caused their defeat." Johnston's consistent theme was that John Bell Hood had undermined him with Jefferson Davis and had been an ineffective subordinate. Six years later Cox reviewed Hood's memoir, *Advance and Retreat,* which maligned Johnston and blamed others for his failures. Cox said of Hood, "He had a sense of personal wrong and unmerited blame." He concluded that this book was written primarily as a defense against Johnston's book.[7]

In his review of Sherman's memoirs, Cox was adulatory. He said he had found no errors of fact and few areas to criticize in the book. Even when Sherman defended his decisions to deny political generals senior commands, Cox mildly attributed this flaw to Sherman's mistaken assumption that all political generals were motivated by political ambition. Later that year Cox reviewed Boynton's book, *Sherman's Historical Raid: The Memoirs in the Light of the Record,* which was a hard-hitting attack on both Sherman's record and his memoirs. Once again taking on the role of Thomas's defender, Boynton used information provided to him surreptitiously by Grant's personal secretary, Orville Babcock, to put Sherman in a bad light. Sherman was enraged, telling Cox that Boynton had been paid to write the book by "jealous men" in Washington. Cox's review accepted none of Boynton's contentions, stating that the book "refutes the charges it was supposed to prove against Sherman." As modern scholarship has shown, Boynton's critique, though overblown and melodramatic at times, was close to the mark in several areas. His review would end the close friendship Cox had had with Boynton, who knew Cox was the anonymous reviewer.[8]

"Taking Up the Cudgels"

A few weeks after that review appeared, Cox began an intense correspondence in early 1876 with his friend Emerson Opdycke that would be an important impetus to his career as a historian. Opdycke had established during the war a well-founded reputation as an intense warrior with a hot temper and contempt for those he believed were not valiant in combat. He carried those tendencies over into civilian life, especially as an active member of the Society of the Army of the Cumberland. He followed the developments in the Schofield-Thomas dispute carefully.[9]

Opdycke wrote Cox that he was contemplating writing an article about the Battle of Franklin. Still believing that he deserved sole credit for "saving the day" at Franklin and fearing that he was being forgotten in the histories of the battle, he asked Cox for both editorial input and endorsement of his claim. Writing in a commiserative tone, an introspective Cox responded that he too was becoming increasingly anxious to correct the record of history and assert his own role in the Union's successes. He told Opdycke that, having read every book published about the war, he was displeased at being ignored for his actions at Antietam and seeing "narration after narration of . . . [the Battle of Franklin] printed without even a solitary mention of [his] part in them." Cox went on, "In the two most important pitched battles of my military career [Antietam and Franklin],

I am more frequently ignored than mentioned." He conjectured that this was the bad luck of men second in command.

Reflecting his self-effacement, Cox told Opdycke that he had not "felt it quite consistent with [his] sense of right to take up the cudgels" for himself. But more than ten years had elapsed since the war had ended, the memory of his role was fading, and many other generals were asserting their role in history. Moreover, he realized that unlike West Pointers, citizen-generals were being either dismissed or forgotten—except for those like Ben Butler who had performed poorly. As a result, he told Opdycke that he was edging toward "taking up the cudgels" on his own behalf in the history he had long planned to write.[10]

Soon after this correspondence, Cox wrote an unpublished essay both to elucidate his commitment to thorough and objective historical research and to act as a guideline for his eventual writing. In the manuscript entitled "Growth of the History of the Rebellion," Cox described the challenges for a historian of the war in his era. One was, unlike in previous wars, the abundant source material. Newspapers had published daily accounts of battle after battle, and many generals had even become correspondents for papers and journals. Individual soldiers had sent home thousands of letters, "nearly all of which had something valuable to offer" the historian, for whom they represented a "mine of precious metal for investigation." Hundreds of soldiers kept diaries in which they had recorded daily events of the war. Cox's military diary of the last eighteen months of the war not only proved useful when he wrote his histories but also was included in the Official Records of the war.

Asking the rhetorical question, "[H]ow shall sources be used?" Cox responded, "The formal or official reports are the most weighty evidence on which the historian must build. . . . [T]hey profess to be history itself." Most were reliable, he wrote, because they did not contain excessive praise or denigration of the men involved. He warned that they were subject to verification, however, and that the same was true of correspondence between general officers and their departments, which were "a picture of how they felt at the very moment of truth, without gloss." Personal memoirs should be highly valued, he believed, because they came from eyewitnesses. He warned, however, that the historian had to exercise meticulous judgment because letters, memoirs, and diaries were based on events taking place immediately around their authors and necessarily lacked perspective.

Given his problems with journalists during the war and the nature of journalism at the time, Cox believed that "using newspapers required great discrimination." While they were accurate as to dates and places, "everything else [was] opinionated." He noted that many journalists wrote only from rumors they had heard and in fact never even went to the battlefields. Cox recalled reading an account of one of his campaigns that was rife with errors. He added that the friendships between newspapermen and officers were patently obvious when those officers were excessively praised while others were downgraded or ignored. He concluded that to get the essence of what happened using newspaper accounts, a historian had to "tackle a mountain of material" and assess it carefully.

In conclusion, Cox said that no books had been written to that point utilizing all the available sources of information, painstaking research, and scrupulous attention to accuracy. He said of contemporary writers, "Many are the historians, but few are the ideal." He wrote that there were many books on the war, but *the* history of it had not yet been written. He predicted, "We will have a great historian of the war like Gibbon or Macauley some day, but not soon." He concluded that most historians would be content to write about only some part of the war, as he would in the end.[11]

Echoes of the Past: The Fitz-John Porter Case

Early in 1880, just before Cox began writing his first formal history of the war, he became involved in a controversy that sprang from his military criticism and from an event some seventeen years earlier. In 1863 Garfield had been a member of the military board that convicted Fitz-John Porter. After many years of pressure from Porter partisans, President Hayes had agreed in 1878 to create a new military board to review the conviction. That board, chaired by Schofield, announced on March 19, 1879, that it had exonerated Porter, and it even applauded some of his actions. The issue was referred to Congress for further action, but under the leadership of an adamantly opposed Senator "Black Jack" Logan, Congress refused to act.[12]

In February 1880 Garfield decided to make a statement about the case in the House of Representatives, and he asked Cox to review the new board's actions and give Garfield his legal opinion. In a "private letter," Cox responded that at first he had presumed the new board had acted correctly because he knew its members were men of integrity. However, after an in-depth analysis, he determined that the decision was eminently wrong and that the board had acted out of pity or kindness, becoming "apologists for poor strategy." He was especially taken aback at the board's praise for some of Porter's actions. Unfortunately for Cox, Garfield did not protect the privacy of the letter. Porter learned of the letter's contents and asked Cox for a copy and an explanation. Cox refused at first.[13]

Later in the year, presidential nominee Garfield was informed of Porter's intention to attack him in the press. At Garfield's request, Cox agreed to send the letter to Porter. During the next few months, these two engaged in a heated correspondence. Cox also discussed these issues with Schofield, who read in Cox's letter to Porter an implicit criticism of him and his judgment. Cox was then working with Schofield on his two books on Sherman's campaigns and did not want to harm their close relationship. At the same time, Cox the independent thinker would not compromise his views. Cox emphasized to his former commander that he had impartially judged that the board made the wrong decision, and that appeared to satisfy Schofield. However, Schofield's faint praise of Cox in his memoirs could have been a result of residual ill will over this episode.[14]

The president's death led Cox to prepare a paper, later published in book form, on the entire matter "as a solemn duty to Garfield" and so that "it would go into the materials on which a final historical judgment will be made up." On February 28, 1882, he gave the paper in a speech to a veterans group that focused on Porter's inaction at important times in the Second Battle of Bull Run and his disregard of significant information. As Cox explained to Schofield later, based on his own experiences in the war, he had a disposition "to bear down upon the tendency of commanders not to act unless they have orders," as Porter had done on August 29, 1862. As he would note in his memoirs, Cox had seen too many examples of regular officers refusing to act without orders when they should have thought for themselves, as he had. The fact that Porter's inaction reflected his distaste for Pope only made the situation worse, in Cox's view.[15]

While most modern historians believe that Cox was wrong about the Porter case, he remained firmly committed to his opinion. Cox's analysis of Porter in this paper, coupled with the release of the official records in the early 1880s, influenced his later writings about the Maryland campaign, in which he concluded that Porter was an éminence grise influencing McClellan against Burnside. This conclusion became even more likely when in 1886 President Cleveland and a Democratic Congress formally overturned Porter's conviction and restored him to his rank. While that process was ongoing, Cox would be preparing his first histories of the Antietam campaign.

Atlanta and Sherman; Undercutting the "Lost Cause"

Charles Scribner's Sons Publishing Company had decided in 1880 that public interest in the war had grown to such an extent as to merit a comprehensive multivolume history, *Great Campaigns of the Civil War.* The upcoming release of the first volumes of the Official Records enhanced interest in the project. One historian wrote that "there seemed to be a need for a type of narrative that would serve as a transition from the first generation of participant-prepared accounts to the subsequent work of scholars, military historians, popularizers, and buffs."[16]

That August, having just become dean of the Cincinnati Law School, a position that would finally give him sufficient leisure time to focus on writing history, Cox accepted Scribner's offer to write the volume about the Atlanta campaign. Lacking access to many official records, he relied on his letterpress copybooks and campaign diary, reports to Schofield, the histories and memoirs already written, and testimony from participants. Cox took a year to write his account, originally titled *Atlanta,* and it was published early in 1882, just before his book-length pamphlet on the Porter issue. It was the only complete study of the Atlanta campaign for over a hundred years, which is a tribute to its quality and objectivity.

All of the books in this series would be part of the "battle of the books," and like the other authors, Cox was compelled to deal with the personal foibles and biases of the still-living participants, including his own. Sherman, for example, wrote to Cox that he hoped the book could help calm his relations with Thomas's supporters. Sherman specifically asked Cox not to quote him about Thomas's shortcomings because, he said, "[T]he men of Cumberland are looking for problems and accusing me of being envious," as they had done in 1875. He also explained to Cox "the real story" behind his not choosing Logan to replace McPherson and his dismay that he had had to "stand the brunt of Logan's anger and hatred" ever since.[17]

Cox could not completely overcome the inherent difficulty of chronicling events in which he had participated. In the book he was too muted in his criticism of Sherman, and he provided strong evidence for the rightness of all of Sherman's actions. Even though in a letter to Helen he had implicitly criticized Sherman's ill-advised frontal attack at Kennesaw

Mountain, in this book he suggested that it might have succeeded because the Confederates would not have expected it. Cox did write that by then everyone in the army knew such attacks were unwise, but this one went ahead, "so hard it is to free ourselves from the trammels of old customs and a mistaken practice!"

Despite his occasional partiality, Cox's in-depth research and unemotional, restrained writing style produced in this book one of the best histories of the era. It was, for over a century, the definitive work on the campaign, as well as a foundation of the memory of Sherman's leadership. Furthermore, consistent with his self-effacing character, Cox rarely mentioned his own name or accomplishments, for he was determined that the work be neither an apologia nor a memoir. The author of the best modern history of that campaign wrote of Cox's book that it was the "one legitimate historical work which dealt with the campaign as such and as a whole" and was "broadly accurate and containing much of value." Another historian, discussing the Scribner's series, wrote that Cox's books "are particularly good."[18]

Cox's book on the Atlanta campaign also made an important contribution to the "battle of the books" by disputing Confederate descriptions, including Johnston's and Hood's memoirs, of the numbers of troops they had and their casualties. Those accounts were part of the growing "Lost Cause" myth of Confederate honor and resolution in the face of allegedly overwhelming Union numbers and resources. Cox carefully documented Confederate accounting of troop numbers, showing that it had been far less meticulous than that of the Union. He noted, for example, that while at the end of the war Johnston told Schofield he had sixteen thousand effectives, twice that number were paroled by the Union forces. Judging that the Union army on the Atlanta campaign likely outnumbered the Confederates by a ratio of 10 to 7, he said that Johnston's defensive tactics made for a de facto balance of forces. He added that the balance could even have been tilted toward the Confederates if Sherman had continued to use frontal attacks as at Kennesaw.[19]

Franklin and Nashville: Renewed Political-Military Wars

In the midst of his work on *Atlanta*, Cox was asked by Scribner's to write a companion volume about three campaigns: Sherman's March to the Sea, Franklin-Nashville, and North Carolina. Working on it from October 1881 to July 1882, Cox used his same careful methods of research and analysis.

He also had access to more of the Official Records, and in one appendix he included several official messages relating to the Battle of Franklin. He corresponded with other participants to seek their input, and in a letter that would prove important during a later controversy, David Stanley confirmed the accuracy of Cox's information.[20]

Cox's second book, *Sherman's March to the Sea: Hood's Tennessee Campaign and the Carolina Campaigns of 1865,* was published in October 1882. Because he was writing about three separate campaigns, Cox was not able to write with the depth he would have preferred. As he noted later in his book about the Battle of Franklin, "it was an altogether natural result that I should find some of my statements and conclusions challenged. The brevity of my narrative made it impossible to give the evidence which supported it." Two conclusions that he undoubtedly knew would be challenged were his commentary on a myth of the "Lost Cause" school and his analysis of Thomas's actions at Franklin.

One of the major tenets of the "Lost Cause" involves the barbarity of the Northerners as contrasted to the chivalry of Southern soldiers. In this book, Cox wrote that while Sherman forbade excessive actions by his men on his march to the sea, in an army of sixty thousand there were "men enough who are willing to become robbers, and officers enough who are willing to wink at irregularities or to share the loot." Cox wrote that since the war, the South had claimed repeatedly that only Northerners had committed this kind of act. To refute this claim, Cox included an appendix section entitled "Confederate Stragglers." In it he quoted from several Southern newspapers during the war lamenting contemporaneous depredations committed by Confederate forces that matched those by Sherman's men.[21]

Given the sensitivities he had seen between Schofield and Thomas's supporters since 1870, Cox knew he would be criticized for his exhaustive analysis of Thomas's failure to provide sufficient support to Schofield's forces leading up to the Battle of Franklin. This segment of the book was a case study of the difficulties faced by a participant-historian. When writing about the Atlanta campaign, where he played a relatively minor role, it was easier to be objective and above the fray. By contrast, in these campaigns, especially Franklin, he had been a major actor, and so his reputation and his historical memory were at stake. He did his best to write an objective account of Thomas's actions, resulting in what one modern historian called a "rather balanced assessment." Further, he again rarely mentioned his own name, not even to characterize himself as "commandant on the line" at Franklin, the title that he most wanted. But in the end, Thomas's partisans paid careful attention to every word written about their former leader.[22]

Another difficult situation with which Cox had to deal as he wrote this book was Opdycke's relentless campaign to gain recognition for having "saved the day" alone at Franklin. Cox became increasingly exasperated with Opdycke, writing him in December 1881, "I am sorry that you have been angry at me for 17 years about Franklin and credit for that battle, your role in it, and under whose command you were operating." Cox wrote that Opdycke was not, as he claimed, operating independently but was under Cox's command. Most important, Cox added, "We all agree that your act saved the day; your error is assuming little or nothing was done by others. You must give others their roles." Critiquing the zero-sum nature of the postwar "battle of the books," Cox said he had found that all too often "all are jealous of each other, all tried to magnify their successes and diminish their misfortunes." By contrast, Cox emphasized, while he had finally "taken up the cudgels" on his own behalf, he had done so very carefully. As a result, in his books he spread both credit and blame widely, including to himself.[23]

Early in 1882 Opdycke sent Cox for review his article about the Nashville campaign. Cox told him that it was accurate only insofar as what Opdycke had seen himself that day. Characteristically diffident, Cox said Opdycke praised him and his contributions too highly. Cox added, "I differ with your feeling on Schofield, and your zeal for Thomas has led you astray." Opdycke refused to back down, and Cox became indignant. The following June he wrote Opdycke, "[Y]ou have had a false idea of the general scope of Franklin for many years." He also noted with disdain Opdycke's "feeling that to debate things about which you've given your memory is an 'outrage.'"

In what would be his final letter to Opdycke, written the same day he submitted his manuscript on *Sherman's March to the Sea,* Cox explained in depth his approach to the writing of history. He emphasized, "I treat you as well as I treat myself," noting that he rarely mentioned his own name, saying only that at Franklin the unnamed "commandant upon the line" gave orders to both the 23rd and 4th AC, including Opdycke. Cox ended his correspondence and his relationship with Opdycke by emphasizing the changing role of history and the historian. He wrote that he would "let nobody's assertion be the 'end all' of any point of fact." He stated, "I have done my best to get the true history—that is all. No man can do more than approximate it, and my errors will be corrected by someone else who may again err in a different way." An unconvinced Opdycke responded, "I wish to be justly dealt with. . . . [I]t is a monstrous injustice to refuse us [him and his men] full credit."[24]

Because Cox's book was going to be published in October 1882 and the Army of the Cumberland would be having its annual reunion in September, Opdycke moved to preempt public attention from Cox's book by arranging for his article to be published in the *New York Times* on September 10, 1882. It was a well-documented essay, but it slanted every event to show Schofield in a negative light and Thomas in a positive one. Cox told Schofield that Opdycke's article had been the focus of a "painful and long controversy" between them, adding that he had ended his relationship with Opdycke "with a tartness" that he "was sorry to use." Cox conjectured that Opdycke's actions were intended as "an opening attack" for the upcoming reunion, where Cox was scheduled to give a eulogy of Garfield. He added, "I suppose I will have to prepare for reckless assaults on my little book." That did not happen at the reunion, partly because Schofield was the focus of their attacks and partly because his book had not yet been published.[25]

Ultimately, Cox had to face criticism from Thomas's partisans, though it was not as vitriolic as the criticism Schofield faced. General James Wilson, whom Cox criticized mildly in the book for what in fact were major blunders when he was Schofield's cavalry commander, said in his review that the book was "neither truthful nor sound history." Wilson nevertheless admitted that Cox was "a gentleman and a scholar and one of the best of the volunteer generals," as well as a good writer. Wilson said Cox seemed to be biased against Thomas and the Army of the Cumberland while shutting "his eyes to the blunders of Schofield." By contrast, Sherman told Cox, "There is no page or paragraph which I could amend or alter." Schofield also praised the book, noting that Cox dealt "liberally with all who had a responsible part in it."[26]

Commenting on Commanders

On July 30, 1885, the *Nation* contained Cox's obituary of Ulysses S. Grant. Despite the disillusionment Cox still harbored about the former president, he wrote a balanced and objective analysis of the man, including his achievements in the war and his failings and successes as chief executive. Cox recognized that most of the public saw Grant only as a pure and patriotic hero, noting that although "President Grant [had] disappointed many, the memory of the war years were so strong that this was excused." A year later Cox exhibited his objectivity again when he reviewed Grant's military memoirs. He said most critics had expected that Grant would produce a mediocre, self-serving tome like those which others had written since the war. Instead, Cox acknowledged, Grant had written an excellent autobiography. While he did not mention it in the review, Cox undoubtedly believed that Grant was still angry over their political split. The fact that Grant did not mention his name once, while giving Stanley significant credit for Union success at the Battle of Franklin, drove home that point.[27]

Cox was not as kind early in 1887 in his review of the autobiography of his first commander, George McClellan's *Own Story*. This book clearly startled and shocked Cox, who to that point still felt positively inclined toward McClellan and thought of him as a friend. While he identified many distortions in the book, Cox was primarily displeased that McClellan scapegoated Burnside for the army's failure to achieve a complete victory at Antietam because of "the very pernicious effects of Burnside's inexcusable delay in attacking the bridge and the heights in rear" after the alleged 8 a.m. order to attack. McClellan also implied that Burnside lacked courage, stating erroneously that he had never crossed the bridge during the fighting. Furthermore, McClellan said he had refused Burnside's request for reinforcements to renew the battle on September 18 because Burnside allegedly said the 9th AC was "demoralized" and his men were "badly beaten." McClellan claimed that on September 18 Burnside retreated over the Antietam because "he could not trust his men on the other side." Finally, McClellan noted that Burnside had claimed during his testimony before the Joint Committee on the Conduct of the War that his men were in "superb condition" on September 18 and that McClellan had erred by not ordering an attack. McClellan snidely riposted that he would not say that Burnside would "deliberately lie" in such testimony but that perhaps "his weak mind was turned" and he was "talked by his staff into any belief they chose."

While preparing his review, Cox made multiple notes to himself, many in the margins of his copy of the text. Because he was the key Burnside staff member being implicitly accused, and because he and Burnside had acted in full concert before and after the battle, he felt deeply insulted, and his marginal notes reflected that state of mind. Among his outraged comments were "I don't believe a word of it"; "Quintessence of nonsense!"; "What Stuff"; and "Always a lion in the way!" He added, firmly, "There was no intimation from anyone that the 9th AC except part of Rodman's division was not in good condition and heart on the evening of the 17th. McC as I believe exaggerates what B. said to him, and the other hearsay is not worthy of notice."

His review, though stated in more formal terms, was no less negative. His ultimate conclusion in the review was that this book was full of "blinding self-esteem," in which "everyone is a rogue and incapable except McClellan." He cited several examples of McClellan's errors of commission and one critical error of omission. McClellan's failure to make any comment at all about the critical issue of troop numbers on both sides during the Maryland campaign was in Cox's view an "admittance of being wrong" in his overinflated estimates at the time. Cox now realized that McClellan had been dishonest and two-faced throughout; this would have an impact on Cox's future writings about his first commander and former friend.[28]

Battles and Leaders: A Warrior Again

In 1883 the editors of the *Century* magazine began to plan a series of articles and memoirs about specific aspects and battles of the war. Unlike Scribner's, this group invited both Union and Confederate commanders to write articles, which would give the reader a view of the war in its entirety. Not unexpectedly, Cox was one of those asked to contribute, and between 1884 and 1887 he wrote five articles of varying lengths. The articles were compiled into the four-volume *Battles and Leaders of the Civil War*. This collection of expert testimony, firsthand accounts, maps, source material, and narration achieved its objective of covering the entire war and broadening the opinions expressed, while providing significant primary source material.[29]

Cox's five articles, which stretched over seventy-five pages in the first two volumes, focused on the early years of the war, and he wrote with access to more of the Official Records. Cox's contributions, unlike most of the other articles in this series, were descriptive of both political issues and military activity. Another difference was that Cox wrote in a style very different from that of his first two books. In 1864 the intensity of the Battle of Franklin had turned him, for a short time, into a fervent warrior. In the mid-1880s, the intensity of the "battle of the books" was slowly transforming him into a more combative historian, which was first exhibited in these articles.

In his early histories he had made every effort to distance himself from the events in which he played a role. He had approached his subject as a classical historian, the word "I" rarely appeared, and he consciously spread the credit and the blame equitably. Moreover, Cox had always emphasized that because he did not have access to all of the records, his opinions and judgments were conditional. By contrast, Cox's tone in the *Battles and Leaders* series was more judgmental and assertive and less restrained, though no less scholarly. His experiences from refighting the war through his reviews; his involvement in the controversies over Thomas, Schofield, Sherman, and Fitz-John Porter; his knowledge of all the literature written about the war; and his access to the Official Records motivated him to become more personal in his judgments. Though he was still uncomfortable writing about his own role, his concern for his place in history made him less self-effacing and reserved. While he would always fundamentally be a serious scholar devoted to research and evidence, the nature of his writings began to shift slowly away from pure history to memoir-oriented history. He clearly had come to realize that no one else was better placed to prevent his slide into historical irrelevancy than he was, and he now began to "take up the cudgels" on his own behalf.

The first three articles—on war preparations in the North, McClellan in West Virginia, and West Virginia operations under Fremont—provided a foundation for the memory of those aspects of the war. (All five articles would be included, in expanded form, in Cox's memoir, *Military Reminiscences of the Civil War*.) The article on war preparations was straightforward history, including Cox's experiences at Camp Dennison. The short article about Fremont's campaign gave cursory treatment to what he saw as a hopeless endeavor from the start, made even more negative for the Union because of the poor generalship of Fremont, Banks, and McDowell.

He was more thorough and analytical in his article entitled "McClellan in West Virginia." Cox emphasized the importance of this early campaign in pushing the Confederacy away from the borders of the North and protecting the pro-Union residents as they created the new state of West Virginia. His treatment of McClellan underlined Cox's willingness to take a more balanced position toward his first commander. He noted that at first he had had full trust and confidence in McClellan, but he came to see, in retrospect, that McClellan's flaws were apparent during this period.

His description of McClellan's actions during and after the Battle of Rich Mountain and their implications is a foundation of historical memory both of that part of the war and of McClellan as an evolving leader.[30]

McClellan's actions during the Maryland campaign too have been the subject of considerable debate among historians since that time, with Cox's historical writing an important element of those discussions. Cox's other two articles in the *Battles and Leaders* series, "Forcing Fox's and Turner's Gaps" and "The Battle of Antietam" (both on the Maryland campaign), were the most serious studies of this campaign up to that time. Francis Palfrey's book in the Scribner series, *The Antietam and Fredericksburg*, was only a solid summary. Though Cox's articles were well documented, he was clearly writing with the secondary purpose of setting the record straight in the "battle of the books." He was especially resolute in his examination of McClellan's and his partisans' efforts to blame Burnside and, by extension, Cox for any lack of success at Antietam. He wrote not only as a respected historian but also as a primary source with a point of view.[31]

These articles, and Cox's expansion on them in his memoirs, reflected Cox's disillusionment with his former commander's motives and thoughts as revealed in his autobiography. Cox wrote of McClellan as an indecisive, overly cautious leader more fearful of failure than willing to commit to success. The image of McClellan in these articles is of a commander who did not understand the value of time, issued uncoordinated orders, did not guard his flanks, overestimated his enemy's strength, distorted the truth, blamed others for his own mistakes, and was possessed of both internal and external chimera.

Cox's specific criticisms in his memoirs on these issues focused on his own belief that he and Burnside could have won the day at Antietam if the cavalry had protected his left flank, if Couch or Porter had been ordered to reinforce the left wing, or if a parallel attack had been made in the center to accompany Cox's and Burnside's offensive. He was especially critical of McClellan's decision to withhold Porter's assistance, concluding, "As troops are put in reserve, not to diminish the army, but to be used in a pinch," the sole reasons for their inaction were McClellan's "rooted belief" in the chimera of vast Confederate reserves and his desire to keep "something in hand to fill a gap or cover a retreat." He also acerbically noted McClellan's claim in his memoirs that because he led the Maryland campaign without written orders, the administration could have charged him with usurpation of command. Cox commented, "The suggestion of

McClellan twenty years afterward that it had all been a pitfall prepared for him, would be revolting if, in view of the records, the absurdity of it did not prove that its origin was in a morbid imagination." Finally, underscoring that throughout his campaigns McClellan's army "greatly outnumbered" the enemy and his equipment and supplies were far better, Cox commented that "McClellan's persistent outcry that he was sacrificed by his government destroys even that character for dignity and that reputation for military intelligence which we fondly attributed to him."[32]

Cox's analysis of McClellan's personality and motivations in these two articles and in his memoirs, as well as his analysis in his memoirs about the Iago-like behavior of Fitz-John Porter, set firmly in historical memory an interpretation of McClellan and his leadership that has been echoed by most historians. The first and perhaps most important historian to agree with Cox's theses was Ezra Carman, a veteran of the war who was the head of the Antietam Battlefield Board for many years. Over a period of many years, Carman meticulously researched every aspect of the Maryland campaign. His methods included gathering information from participants, including Cox, who wrote him extensively and also met with him. Carman respected Cox's judgment completely, believing him to be not only an accomplished historian but also a man of unquestioned integrity. Carman made careful notes from Cox's book reviews in the *Nation* and referred frequently in his text to Cox's articles on South Mountain and Antietam, as well as his *Military Reminiscences of the Civil War.* Carman's 1,800-page unpublished manuscript has been accepted by modern historians as the most comprehensive account of the Maryland campaign.

The editor of the most recently published version of Carman's book noted that Carman's "rather severe judgment" of McClellan "seems more rooted in 1890's historiography than fact." While that analysis is open to debate, the mention of "1890's historiography" refers significantly to Cox's writings, letters, and reviews. The above-mentioned editor has acknowledged that Cox was one of the most important and influential sources for Carman. Furthermore, as one major historian who disagreed with Cox's analysis of McClellan's actions in the Maryland campaign has acknowledged, Carman's study casts a shadow over any work on the Maryland campaign. "This in turn," he wrote, "is a reflection of the influence of Cox's writings, as Carman's account of the Ninth Corps's operations during the Maryland campaign draws heavily upon them, as do all modern studies of the campaign."[33]

Even though Cox did not write about the western theater in the *Battles and Leaders* series, he became embroiled in another "refighting the war" controversy related to the article in that series about the Battles of Franklin and Nashville written by Colonel Henry Stone of Thomas's staff. The article, though relatively objective, included melodramatic praise for Thomas. Stone wrote that the Northwest "was saved by the steadfast labors, the untiring energy, the rapid combinations, the skillful evolutions, the heroic courage and the tremendous force of one man, whose name will yet rank among the great captains of all time."

Cox was undoubtedly pleased at Stone's comments in the article that at Franklin "all the troops in the works were ordered to report to General Cox, to whom was assigned the command of the defenses," and that at the critical moment, "General Cox was everywhere present, encouraging and cheering on his men." In a footnote to the article in the book version, however, the editors noted that David Stanley had taken exception to Stone's description of Cox as in command on the line and had written a dissenting letter to the magazine in January 1888. Stanley, who had clear paranoid tendencies, had been adjudged by his superiors in the war as a mediocre leader who tended to get into disputes with other generals and who despised political generals. Cox was his favorite target and personal bête noire. Stanley even resigned from an Ohio veterans group when Cox was named its commander because, he said, "I could not stand him." In his letter, Stanley claimed that because he was on the field, he and not Cox commanded the 4th AC troops on the line. He added that because he could not have been under the authority of the lower-ranking Cox, he himself was the commander on the line.[34]

Cox's modesty unwittingly laid the groundwork for this controversy. In his final report about Franklin, he had written that every soldier on the line was under his command. He had, however, only implied that he was "commandant on the line." Not even in his diary, which is included in the Official Records, or in a letter to Helen just after the battle did he explicitly state that he was "commandant on the line." In his report, Schofield only noted that Cox had temporary command of the 23rd AC, and that most of the troops had reported to him as he set up the line and the entrenchments. Furthermore, in his preliminary report Cox had said that for a short period before he left the field, the wounded Stanley "assumed command of the troops of the Fourth Corps." Cox told Opdycke and

Schofield later that he regretted his generosity in giving Stanley what he knew was undeserved credit.[35]

Instead of responding to Stanley's letter directly, Cox sent a letter to Schofield that included a copy of Stanley's 1881 letter to him in which he had confirmed Cox's description of the battle. That letter was forwarded to the editors of the *Century*. Not realizing that his false version had been exposed, Stanley added a new lie, that he had never left the field at all. An editor asked Cox for proof that Stanley was wrong, and when he did so, pointing to the relevant reports, the *Century* refused to print Stanley's reply in later editions. The editors closed the controversy in Cox's favor by writing in a footnote to Stone's article, "General Schofield said in his report of December 31, 1864, 'The troops were placed in position and intrenched under his [Cox's] immediate direction, and the greater portion of the line engaged was under his command during the battle.'" The hapless Stanley then further exhibited his lack of mental stability when he wrote an article for the *New York Sun* that called Cox "the notorious one-term man, a native Canadian, a military tramp, a miserable filcher of reputation." He provided no new evidence for his assertions, and the controversy died down, for a time.[36]

Defending Citizen-Generals; "Leavening the Lump" of History

In the late 1880s, Cox was considering writing two more books: a monograph on the Battle of Franklin to more forcefully push the case for his importance there and his comprehensive military reminiscences. As he worked on them, he confined most of his other historical writing to reviewing and commenting on works such as the *Personal Memoirs of P. H. Sheridan* (1889) and John G. Nicolay and John Hay's *Abraham Lincoln* (1891). He also wrote obituaries of leading military and political figures such as Sheridan, Jefferson Davis, W. T. Sherman, and Johnston and showed in them his growing appreciation and awareness that his generation was dying out. Once again emphasizing his admiration for Sherman, in that obituary he stated, "We would follow him anywhere."[37]

In his 1888 review of Comte de Paris's *History of the Civil War in America*, Cox rose to the defense of citizen-generals, using themes he had first enunciated in his 1863 letters to Chase and the military board. Cox wrote, "It is time that it should be distinctly recognized that three years of actual experience with a great war and in responsible command was, for a man of intelligence and of courage, a school in military art in comparison to which any academic preparation is insignificant." He emphasized that by contrast, a military education did not guarantee success. He concluded that "no one can be called a general until he has stood the test of responsible command."

Cox's strong reaction to this book reflected a dominant theme in the contemporary military literature, which held that only professionals were proven capable during the war and that "political generals" should be recognized only for their incompetence. As one historian noted, "The struggle for Civil War history began immediately after the guns fell silent, as the two strands of the American military tradition reemerged to present two conflicting portraits of the army that won the war. Was the Union army an army of trained soldiers led by professionals ... or was it an enthusiastic mass of volunteers inspired by amateur generals?" Cox recognized that the first interpretation was far more prevalent in the war's literature, and he dedicated himself to leading the cause of the second interpretation. His *Military Reminiscences* was arguably the best effort to that time to achieve that objective.[38]

Around this period, two well-known citizen-generals attempted through their writings to counter the tide of credit claimed by professional soldiers and to establish in memory the valuable contributions made by political generals. Neither book had any long-term impact on the historiography of the war or recognition of the role of political generals. The first, "Black Jack" Logan's 1887 book, *The Volunteer Soldier in America,* was a comprehensive study of volunteers' role as the core of every American army. Logan disparaged West Pointers and wrote that if so many of them had not joined the Confederacy, the "sacrifices of life" and the war itself would not have been necessary, and "the limits of the Rebellion would scarcely have exceeded the proportions of a huge but badly organized mob." The book was poorly written and took a zero-sum game approach, heaping unvarnished praise on every political general but little on West Point graduates. Logan's death soon after the book's publication further diminished its impact.[39]

In 1892 Cox reviewed another work by a political general trying to combat the reputation of West Point. *Butler's Book* was written by one of the more bizarre characters in American political history, Ben Butler. That author had a well-established reputation as an eccentric, and this book only enhanced that status. Butler succeeded at none of the military responsibilities he was given, but in the book he blamed a "West Point clique" for his failures. In his review, Cox said that as Butler saw the world, "Butler did everything perfectly—everyone else was always wrong." Cox subtly derided the book, noting that it contained "hitherto unknown facts in history." Like Logan's book, it had little influence and is viewed today as a character study of an oddball.[40]

During this period, Cox made other valuable contributions to the historiography of the war. He sent the editors of the Official Records copies of his letterpress copybooks and other official correspondence, including his campaign diaries, which were of inestimable value as primary sources. His diaries were included in the Official Records in full text. Furthermore, Cox and James Ford Rhodes, the industrialist-historian whose highly regarded multivolume history of the United States was the standard text of its type for many years, had extensive discussions about the war's history. Rhodes used Cox's letters, books, and reviews in the *Nation* as source material for the later volumes of his *History* about the Civil War and Reconstruction.[41]

In his fourth volume, Rhodes quoted freely from Cox's manuscripts, praised Cox's actions at Antietam, and noted that the correct number of Confederate and Union troops at Antietam had been determined (by Rhodes) from the "fair and accurate collation and analysis of Confederate field returns by General Cox in his reviews." Not surprisingly, Rhodes gave Cox credit for being "commandant on the line" at Franklin and credited his discussion of the Civil War army's lack of knowledge in the arts of war and their lack of equipment and weapons to his many meetings with Cox. As Cox wrote to James Monroe, "Rhodes's volumes already show he was aided in his judgment of men by some of my papers in the *Nation*. . . . There is nothing I take more comfort in than in putting a bit of leaven into the lump of history."[42]

Cox did some behind-the-scenes writing when in the mid-1890s he completed a book about Sherman for General Manning F. Force, a Cincinnati friend who had taken ill. Cox devoted part of every day to this task, with his authorship of the section on Atlanta and everything subsequent noted only in the preface. Otherwise, Cox was still reviewing for the *Nation* and occasionally the *American Historical Review*. In fact, he was reviewing more books than he had ever done before: from 1897 to 1900 he reviewed over twenty-five. He also wrote the article on Sherman for the 1900 edition of the *Encyclopedia Britannica* and compiled the list of entries for the Civil War period for *The Literature of American History: A Bibliography*.[43]

Cox's reviews over his last years touched not only on the Civil War but also on other contemporary events. These works included Richard M. Bache's *Life of General George C. Meade* (1898), G. F. R. Henderson's *Stonewall Jackson and the American Civil War* (1898), Rhodes's volume 4 of his *History of the United States* (1899), and John Fiske's *The Mississippi Valley in the Civil War* (1900). His final review was of a book concerning the Boer War, *London to Ladysmith via Pretoria,* by a young British correspondent named Winston Churchill.[44]

In his reviews, he did his best to be fair and to follow the guidelines he had formulated over twenty-six years in this position, though he would always have a blind eye for Sherman's faults. He showed an appreciation of good writing and research and a critical eye for the failings of authors. He had a solid knowledge not only of military and Civil War history but of all history, and he put this to use by comparing the events of one era with comparable ones in others. He had a full understanding of the military arts, and he often could spot errors in the treatments of these. He had a fine, easy style, at times a biting wit, a sense for objectivity, and a great concern for morality and dislike for corruption. Finally, and perhaps most important, he had an appreciation for the realities of war.

Final Works

During the 1890s, Cox completed his monograph about the Battle of Franklin and an in-depth, multivolume reminiscence of his entire military career. In these he finalized the transition in his approach to the writing of history: a pure history (*Atlanta*); a memoir-history (*Sherman's March*); history-oriented memoirs (the *Battles and Leaders* series); an apologia with a historical basis (*Battle of Franklin*); and a research-based memoir (*Military Reminiscences of the Civil War*). These writings also completed a separate transition in which each subsequent work became more of a primary source as the level of personal testimony steadily increased.

While Cox's monograph on the Battle of Franklin, published in 1897, was well-documented history, it was also his attempt to set the record straight on every aspect of that battle, especially his role. While this book was an apologia, Cox supported his conclusions with solid research and documentation. In the introduction, Cox described the "battle of the books" over the Franklin-Nashville campaign, noting that this battle had not been given an appropriate role in the history of the war, and that the final publication of the Official Records allowed for a more in-depth and

258   objective history and analysis. In that regard, Cox was apparently unaware that in 1893 Stanley was awarded the Congressional Medal of Honor for his actions at Franklin.[45]

This monograph is a thorough and well-researched account that is still cited in modern histories as a fundamentally sound treatment. It inevitably led Cox into controversy, however, as he attempted to clarify his treatment of Wagner and firmly set in "historiographical stone" his role as "commandant on the line." Regarding his own position, he wrote a full chapter in the style of a lawyer's brief, giving himself full credit for commanding the defensive line, including Kimball's division and Opdycke's brigade from the 4th AC. He noted that in his first book on the campaign he had almost totally avoided "the repetition of [his] own name in a narrative written by [him]self." Now he acknowledged his realization that his reticence had caused some of his problems. As regards Wagner, he explained in depth why, because he lacked information and tended to be generous, he had at first described Wagner's men's retreat as "leisurely," while later coming to realize that it had been made in a desperate panic.[46]

Cox's comment in this book that "the most competent judges have accepted the authority of [his] volumes, and the publication of the government records has practically quieted discussion" is valid for the most part, though subject to considerable debate. However, its appearance in this book gave the impression of defensiveness. In his review, Boynton alleged, with some justification, that Cox's extensive emphasis on proving his role as "commandant on the line" was his real purpose in writing the book. At the same time, Cox's former friend acknowledged that the book "undoubtedly presents the best account of the movements in the Battle of Franklin yet published." He praised how Cox, "a scholar, practiced writer, and excellent officer," had assessed the strategy, tactics, and fighting of the battle. Not surprisingly, he rejected Cox's appraisal of how Thomas had mismanaged his troops before Franklin.[47]

Schofield's memoirs were published the same year as Cox's monograph on the Battle of Franklin, and Schofield's resentment over the Porter case, as well as his vanity, may have led him to damn Cox with faint praise in that work. Schofield clearly wanted full credit for the success at Franklin, which he saw as his greatest achievement. In his preface he wrote that he and Cox had not coordinated or consulted about their two books, implying that each would be presenting a different version of events. In one example of his faint praise, Schofield subtly diminished Cox's contribution by stating, "Our intrenchments were of the slightest kind, and without any considerable obstructions in front to interfere seriously with the assault." In his review of the book, Cox did not betray feelings of disappointment. He did observe that the book was not a complete autobiography but rather "a collection of notes and comments."[48]

In 1897 Cox settled down in Oberlin to complete his greatest contribution to the history of the war, his *Military Reminiscences of the Civil War*, which he hoped to finish in two years. By late 1899 he had completed most of the text, which stretched over 1,300 pages. Included in that were revised versions of his *Battles and Leaders* articles and several historical papers he had delivered to veterans group meetings. By now totally over his diffidence but also cognizant that he was writing both a memoir and serious history, he told the publishers, "I wrote from my personal point of view with sufficient broader criticism of the campaigns and battles in which I had a personal part to make it a permanent authority in its field." The book's continued citation by scholars is proof of the validity of Cox's statement. Cox died before completing his editing of the text, and his stepson, William Cochran, finalized the manuscript for publication. The book was published in two volumes late in 1900.[49]

Cox wrote in the introduction that his objective was to reproduce his "own experience in our Civil War and to help the reader to understand just how the duties and problems presented themselves" to him as a self-made military man and citizen-general. In his earlier books, he did not have the space to include many events that illustrated the extracurricular character of war. Now that he had carte blanche to do so, he gave the reader a well-written, sprightly account of how one citizen adapted to unique and surprising turns of events in his life.

The book is replete with well-documented descriptions not only of battles and troop movements but also of the leaders, conditions, army organization, attitudes of the men, topography, and strategy. Cox's relations with other officers, personal and human interest anecdotes, a discussion of the best and worst features of army life, and many other facets of the war were all presented in his easy literary style. As Boynton wrote in his review, "Few if any volumes pertaining to the Civil War equal these in interest. . . . No part of the book should be overlooked by any student of our war history." He added that, just as Cox's narrative of Franklin was the best written to that point, "his narrative of McClellan's West Virginia campaign is the best ever given to the public." While also praising "the scholarly and agreeable style of which General Cox was the master," Boynton justifiably criticized Cox's continued tendency to downplay Sherman's mistakes.[50]

Determining the Makeup of a Successful General

Cox's *Military Reminiscences* has been cited throughout this text both because it reflected Cox's thinking and because much of it has been recognized as authoritative. One section of the book deserves additional attention. Like Cox's work on Antietam and Atlanta, it broke new interpretative ground and has been cited by many historians as a foundation for memory about military organization and political generals, military education, the role of the citizen-soldier, and military leadership. In particular, in those rare works in which "political generals" are discussed collectively, Cox's interpretations are cited as the first in-depth attempt to seriously compare that group to its West Point confreres.[51]

Cox's analysis was an expansion of his thoughts first elucidated in 1863 in his letters to Chase and the military board reconsidering army organization. Most fundamentally, he emphasized both that war was an art and not a science and that therefore self-made men could achieve success in it through hard work and/or "natural genius." He criticized sharply Scott's decision to create the dual army system and advocated creation of a unified system in which civilian-generals would have equal status with regulars. He stated, "Our army as a whole would have been improved if the distinction between regular and volunteer had been abolished and, after the first beginnings, a freer competition for even the highest commands had been open to all." Furthermore, showing his unhappiness with the focus on "political generals," he wrote, "[T]he whole organization of the volunteer force might be said to be political, though we heard more of 'political generals" than we did of political captains or lieutenants."

He stressed that at all levels, the volunteers had proven every bit as capable as the regulars. He claimed that in many ways they were better because they were unlike many regular personnel, for whom army life was "a last desperate resource when every other door to a livelihood was shut." By contrast, he stated, "The volunteer regiment was, in my judgment, unquestionably superior" because it was fighting for a cause it believed in. Realizing that this analysis could be seen as self-serving, Cox added defensively, "It is not the offspring of partiality toward the volunteer army on the part of one himself a volunteer. It was shared by most active officers in the field who came from the regular service."[52]

He underscored the importance of political generals because they reflected the popular will and were able to attract the huge numbers of volunteers needed: "They called the meetings, addressed the people to rouse their enthusiasm, urged enlistments, and often set the example by enrolling their names first. . . . They were the necessity of the time." Nevertheless, he admitted the weakness of the approach taken by the administration, because some political leaders used political influence to gain rank and advancement. He acknowledged that this was necessary to keep the political peace and "avoid antagonisms when the fate of the nation trembled in the balance," so it had to be endured "in spite of its well-known tendency to weaken the military service."

With an eye to proving that self-made generals equaled those with professional training at West Point, Cox analyzed the course of study at the latter institution. He emphasized that other than military engineering, the cadets learned little of the military arts. "At the close of the war there was no instruction in strategy or grand tactics, in military history, or in what is called the Art of War. . . . It did not pretend to include the military art." As a result, he concluded, "For field work with an army, therefore, the mental furnishing of the West Point man was not superior to that of any other liberally-educated man." He added that while he had read Jomini in the original French and a wide variety of relevant history and analyses, few of his West Point colleagues had read widely in military history in any language. The inference was clear: even though it was a "professional school," West Point produced military officers with a weak intellectual basis for leadership in the Civil War. The corollary was that citizen-generals like himself who were widely read were just as well prepared.

Cox acknowledged that there was value in the discipline the regulars learned and practiced in garrison duty, but regular army officers had formed habits of command wherein "the rule was arbitrary, despotic, often tyrannical." This in turn "institutionalized a rigid spirit unwilling to try new approaches." He gave several examples. Several times he had argued with regular army officers who insisted that muzzle loaders were the only acceptable rifle. As a result, "the utmost any commander could do was to secure repeating rifles for two or three infantry regiments in a whole army." A similar example came when he was ordered to use Napoleon guns on one campaign. When he argued with his commander that the lighter three-inch rifled ordnance guns could be moved more quickly and be more effective, his commander refused to change. As a result, he

262   observed, "[w]e were ordered to throw away our advantage . . . upon the
obstinate prejudice of a worthy man who had had all flexibility drilled out
of him by routine."

Cox concluded this section with a discussion of the elements of success for a military leader at the subordinate and command levels. His
conclusion, not surprisingly, was that while professional training was important, only on the field of battle would it become clear who should have
leadership responsibility. There the well-educated man like himself who
had innate and intuitive talent could emerge as a capable leader, at least at
the level of the subordinate. Cox clearly wanted the reader to understand
that he had possessed this level of command capability

At the subordinate level, he wrote, a general had to have a grasp of
"military art," which he defined as

> a set of qualities which intelligent people easily understand. . . . Self-
> command is proverbially one of the chief. Courage and presence
> of mind are indispensable. Ability to decide and firmness to stick
> to a decision are necessary. Intelligence enough to understand
> the duties demanded of him and to instruct his subordinates in
> theirs is another requisite. But beyond all these, there is a consti-
> tution of body and mind for which we can find no better name
> than 'military aptitude.' . . . [A] bold heart, a cool head, and practi-
> cal common sense were of much more importance than anything
> taught at school. With these, a brief experience would enable an
> intelligent man to fill nearly any subordinate position with fair
> success; without them any responsibility of a warlike nature
> would prove too heavy for him.

By contrast, Cox emphasized, much more was required of a commander of an entire army. He wrote, "The supreme quality of a 'general-
in-chief' is the power to estimate truly and grasp clearly the situation on
a field of operations too large to be seen by the physical eye at once, and
the undaunted temper of will which enables him to execute with persistent vigor the plan which his intellect approves." He added that to "act
upon uncertainties as if they were sure and to do it in the midst of carnage
and death when immeasurable results hang on it" were elements of "the
supreme presence of mind which marks a great commander." That quality, he averred, was innate: "[I]t is born in a man, not communicated." He
clearly did not think that he had these qualities, and in the book he did not

name anyone he thought fulfilled these requirements. It is likely, however, that he would have thought that for the Union, only Grant and Sherman could be considered to be "great commanders."[53]

A Call for Historical Preservation

In the last paragraph of the reminiscences, Cox made an appeal to preserve the memory and reality of the war as he had fought it. While military governor of North Carolina in 1865, he and his staff visited the Revolutionary War battlefield of "Guilford-Old-Court-House" near Greensboro. With an official report in his hand, he and his staff "could trace with complete accuracy every movement of the advancing enemy and his own dispositions to receive the attack." Cox recalled, "We could see the reasons for the movements on both sides." He found himself critiquing the movements "as if they had occurred on one of our own [Civil War] recent battlefields." That in turn, he noted, "made us realize, as perhaps nothing else could have done, how the future visitor will trace the movements in which we have had a part; and when we have been dust for centuries, will follow the path of our battalions from hill to hill, from stream to stream, from the border of a wood to the open ground where the bloody conflict was hand to hand, and will comment upon the history we have made."

He concluded that future historians would assess "what is accurate in our reports and narratives." Further, they will come to understand that "the face of the country itself will be an unalterable record which will go far to expose the true reason of things . . . to show what statements are consistent with the physical conditions under which a battle was fought, and what, if any, are warped to hide a repulse or to claim a false success. Nature herself will thus prove the strongest ally of truth."[54]

Cox could not have anticipated the degree to which his nineteenth-century vision has been fulfilled in our time. Every year millions of visitors walk on the ground where he and other Civil War soldiers fought, fell, and died, studying the strategy, tactics, and movements of two great armies, the memory of which Cox helped to make an indelible part of our nation's history.

10 Renaissance Man in the Gilded Age

> I have become used to being surprised at my own
> fate, and take it rather quietly, feeling a kind of third
> person's curiosity at looking on to see what is to
> become of me.
>
> —Cox, letter to Monroe, October 23, 1873

The Intellectual Life

While his historical writing was Cox's primary focus during the last twenty years of his life, during this period he became even more of a Renaissance man as he pursued additional vocations oriented to the life of the mind, where he felt most comfortable. In mid-1880, his careers in politics, the military, and railroading behind him,[1] and tired of mundane legal work, Cox happily accepted an offer to become dean of the Cincinnati Law School. At a time when it was the only law school in Ohio, it offered a two-year program (one year if the student had studied for a year under a competent attorney) and emphasized the works of Blackstone through the lecture system. When Cox became dean, the school was nearing its peak in popularity and reputation. His duties included teaching Junior Class courses and some lecturing for the Senior Class, and he also managed most of the school's official correspondence. He clearly enjoyed teaching; he told Hayes in 1885 that he was "living very quietly and plainly as a College Professor should."[2]

In 1879 Cox had turned down an offer to become president of the University of Cincinnati, primarily because he had just returned to the city and was not prepared to take on such a large task at that time. He did agree to serve on its board of directors. By 1884 that institution was in considerable trouble because of declining enrollment and a poor reputation. The board of directors decided that they needed a new executive officer of stature and integrity, so they again offered the position to one of the board's members, Cox. He agreed this time, but only after he got permission from the law school trustees to hold both positions simultaneously. Cox said he hoped to "prove that Cincinnati was worthy of such a University, one which had the complete confidence of all friends of higher education, a high moral tone, and an elevating influence on all its students."[3]

Cox's duties as president were mostly administrative. One of his major achievements was overseeing a long-planned consolidation of the city's higher educational institutions under the aegis of the university. Of the eleven schools sought out, six agreed to the proposal during Cox's tenure. His only academic responsibility was a series of ten lectures, "The Outlines of History," which he gave to the Junior and Senior Classes in 1886. During his tenure he sanctioned a new student newspaper and library society, the university's first college fraternities, and its first yearbook. He also oversaw the growth of student athletics.[4]

During the 1880s, Cox engaged in his spare time in a scientific avocation, microscopy, which he had begun practicing while living in Toledo. Over time he would become an internationally renowned amateur scientist. In the years after the Civil War, the use of microscopes in laboratories and universities had expanded, and one historian noted that "many laymen took up microscopy as an avocation, and most cities had a microscope society." A historian of this scientific endeavor wrote that Cox "first adopted it as a recreation. . . . [I]n 1874 he took up the subject of microphotography and in 1875 began a series of photomicrographs which were to make him famous throughout microscope circles around the world." His first article, "Multiplication by Fission in Stentor Nuclei," appeared in the May 1876 issue of the *American Naturalist*. Even though he modestly claimed that he was only an "amateur dabbler," Cox wrote thirty-two articles in microscopy journals from 1876 to 1893. His fellow microscopists twice elected him president of the American Microscopical Society and, in 1891, gave him the gold Medal of Honor at the Antwerp Exposition of Microscope Work.[5]

In 1889, after four years as president of the university, Cox decided to leave that office, advising the trustees that he had achieved the major objective for his hiring, reestablishing the reputation of the school. There was also another reason. As he wrote to Monroe, "The University gets money from public taxes and so everyone can lecture the Board as to its expenditure. Some questions of the propriety of paying a President's salary while his time is partly left to other work made me think such criticism well enough founded to be likely to return and become an annoyance." So, as in several other situations in his life, Cox decided to resign rather than risk having his integrity, independence, or actions questioned.[6]

To offset his loss of income, Cox asked the Cincinnati Law School trustees for a raise. His request was granted, putting his yearly income at five thousand dollars, a good-sized sum for those days but not sufficient to provide future financial security for the sixty-year-old dean. However, timely investments and the small sums he received for his book reviews and book royalties allowed him to avoid having to return to what he had called the "dry straw" of legal work. This comfortable situation was jarred, however, when in May 1896 the University of Cincinnati established its own law department, with future president of the United States William Howard Taft as its first dean. The Cincinnati Law School was in no position to compete, and its board, with Cox's support, agreed to a merger. In May 1897 the two schools formed an affiliation through which both would present degrees under the name of the Cincinnati Law School. Taft would be dean and Cox only an instructor. Sixty-nine years old and desiring time to complete his *Reminiscences,* Cox decided to retire. During his tenure as dean, 1,254 law students received the degree of LL.B.[7]

Family Man and Public Citizen

After his departure from the national political scene, Cox demonstrated his civic spirit in public affairs, serving as a trustee not only for the Law School and the University of Cincinnati but also for the College of Music of Cincinnati and Oberlin College. He was active in veterans' organizations, serving as president of both the Military Order of the Loyal Legion and the Society of Ex-Army and Navy Officers in Cincinnati. In early 1884 he played an important role in helping to clean up Cincinnati, which had become a wide-open town of gambling, prostitution, bars, and flourishing crime. After a series of riots that year because of public anger with the lawlessness, Cox chaired a citizens committee to advise the mayor on resolving the situation. In that capacity, he called on Governor George Hoadly to send 300 state troopers to maintain peace. When calm was restored, Cox requested the mayor to appoint 103 special policemen after the troopers had to leave, and tranquility returned to the city.[8]

Later in 1884, repelled by the violence and financially better off because of his increased income from becoming university president, Cox moved his family from the city center to a home in the upper-class Mount Auburn section. There, one historian wrote, "[t]he top echelons of Cincinnati's social and economic register lived ... in havens for the economically successful." On warm days, Cox would sit on the house's porch engaged in his favorite pastime, reading, with a tam-o'-shanter perched on his head. He and Helen would host the William Cochran family, which lived next door, for Sunday dinners.[9]

The 1880s and 1890s saw the Coxes' surviving children established in their chosen endeavors. Their eldest daughter, Helen Finney, married John Black, a mathematics professor at Wooster College. Cox's eldest son and namesake, Jacob Dolson Cox III, created a successful business, the Cleveland Twist Drill Company. Their son Kenyon trained as an artist in Paris and later became one of the best-known muralists in the United States. Some of his paintings are exhibited today at the National Museum of American Art in Washington, DC. Charles Norton Cox, the youngest son, after several short-lived careers, settled in Colorado to ranch.[10] Their daughter Charlotte Hope married a son of General John Pope in 1897. Cox's stepson, William Cochran, became a lawyer in Cincinnati and the author of legal textbooks. Helen Cox presided over the family until her death in 1912.

In the 1890s, health concerns forced Cox to think seriously about retirement. He was suffering from rheumatism, which had bothered him off and on since the war, and from a heart condition. In 1896, while on the way to Franklin, Tennessee, in preparation for his book about the battle, Cox caught a cold that kept him from all but necessary work for a month. The shakier handwriting in his letters after the mid-1890s indicates that he was weakening physically.[11]

He prepared financially for retirement by looking for secure and well-paying investments. Beginning in the late 1880s, he invested a considerable sum in a real estate venture in Lincoln, Nebraska, promoted enthusiastically by his former law student and future vice president of the United States, Charles G. Dawes. By 1893 Dawes had invested sixty thousand dollars of Cox's money, and he gave Cox a guided tour of the holdings that year. The effects of the Panic of 1893 dimmed their early optimism by 1895, but eventually the investments provided sufficient funds to support the Coxes' retirement.[12]

In 1897 the sixty-nine-year-old Cox, reduced to an instructorship at the law school, decided that it was time to "accept a retiracy a few years sooner than expected, go to some quiet college town, like Oberlin, put books in the College library, and settle down to 'writing history' in a quiet eddy of the stream." As part of his planning, he wrote a long letter to Dawes, then chairman of the Republican National Committee and an adviser to the new president, William McKinley, asking his advice about the Nebraska investments.[13]

To Cox's great surprise, Dawes saw in the letter a solution to McKinley's protracted search for an appointee to be the minister to Spain as the nation was on the verge of what would become the Spanish-American War. Dawes telephoned Cox and offered him the position, but Cox declined, citing poor health and lack of Spanish-language skills. He did not tell Dawes how the growth of American imperialism and the related nationalist spirit dismayed him. He had hoped that McKinley would reverse that trend, but once again, as with Grant, Hayes, and Garfield, Cox was distressed to see another presidential friend adopting policies he did not support. Dawes told McKinley, "You know his character—unless convinced it is best for all, his personal interests won't influence him." Ultimately, Dawes told McKinley that Cox would not accept. A few weeks later Cox told his son Kenyon why he really had refused to take the job, explaining, "To become the official mouthpiece of current jingoism in regard to Cuba was repellent."[14]

After rejecting this final chance to return to national political life, the Coxes traveled to Oberlin to judge its suitability for retirement. Cox had served as a trustee of Oberlin College since 1876, and from his many visits he had concluded that if Helen agreed, it would be the right choice. Hesitant at first because of her vivid memories of the rundown and primitive condition of the village, Helen now agreed that it had become quite charming and neat. They made arrangements to live in a local boardinghouse, the best in Oberlin, and in August 1897 began their "retiracy," as Cox called it. Soon after, he gave the Oberlin College Library his personal collection of over two thousand books, among them the many military works he had reviewed for the *Nation*. These represented a rich source of literature about the war, not least because of the insightful comments Cox had written in the margins of several books. The library opened its facilities to Cox to write his *Reminiscences* about the war in the rooms where he had spent his student days learning the ways of peace.[15]

On November 30, 1899, Helen and Jacob Cox celebrated their golden wedding anniversary at a family gathering at their son Dolson's home in Cleveland. It was their last anniversary together. On June 3, 1900, Cox telegraphed his son Kenyon, "Shall be off for the coast on Monday. . . . [E]xpect me for week September 3–10 as near as may be, wind and weather and the perils of the sea permitting." For a month, he and Dolson sailed off the coast of Massachusetts and Maine on the son's yacht, as they had every summer in the 1890s. They likely stopped in "the pretty little harbor in Folly Cove, near Halibut, [seeing] the house with the woods behind—the big dolphins for mooring."[16]

While sailing near Rockland, Maine, on July 25, Cox took ill, and on July 28 he began to sink rapidly. He died on August 4, 1900, the victim of a weakened heart and an attack of angina pectoris.[17] Four days later he was buried in Spring Grove Cemetery in Cincinnati, where his grave and those of most of his family lie under a stone obelisk on which is inscribed, "Jacob Dolson Cox, 1828–1900; Soldier, Statesman, Scholar, Patriot."

Creating a Memory of Jacob D. Cox—The "Game Worth the Candle"

The memory of Jacob D. Cox the Civil War historian and primary source is indelibly etched in countless and continuing references, footnotes, and bibliographies of Civil War–related books. The memory of Cox the multi-talented Renaissance man, statesman, and one of the Union's best citizen-generals is, by contrast, very limited. Cox attributed this, in part, to the result of "the bad luck of being a second in command." His disinclination for self-promotion and his lack of sufficient high-level supporters were also major factors. Furthermore, in the postwar "battle of the books," his contributions and those of his "political colleagues" were ignored or subordinated to those of "professional" generals. As one historian put it, "The degree of historical attention the regulars enjoy compared to their amateur peers reflects the triumph of the regulars' standard of what was required for successful generalship, and these criteria tend to base each general's historical standing on his record of tactical victories and operational success."[18]

In his later years, Cox effectively advocated for himself and other citizen-generals. It was a case, however, of "too little, too late," and Cox was and still is often folded into the historical judgment that "political generals" were marginal or mediocre at best. Moreover, the use in Civil War litera-ture of the term *political general,* rather than *citizen-general,* reinforces the view that these men were not, like Cincinnatus, disinterested patriots but rather politicians using their military positions for postwar advancement. Sherman's enunciation of that view, likely to Cox's chagrin, was one of the most influential elements creating that image and memory.

Given his earliest aspirations, it is ironic that military service and the writing of military history were the professions that brought Cox his greatest professional success and deserve the greatest historical attention. Few could have foreseen that the reserved, proper, introverted divinity student of 1849, at ease primarily in a library or in a classroom debating theological topics, would become a successful military leader. In his writings Cox would imply that the reason was that, like many other self-made men, he had an innate ability for leadership that first manifested itself on the battlefield. There he would prove both that citizen-generals could do well in the military arts and that he was one of the best of the group.

His transition from a life of contemplation and scholarship to one of practicing the military arts began when, as a state senator, he helped to bring Ohio's legislature and people to accept a more radical stand to better prepare them to meet the challenge of war. His role in training many of Ohio's large volunteer force and leading those troops in the early days of the war provided evidence that citizen-soldiers could be effective military leaders. His lengthy tenure in West Virginia was critical to taking and holding that new state militarily while ensuring its political allegiance for the Union. His unexpectedly critical roles at South Mountain and Antietam, his significant contributions to the Atlanta campaign, and his herculean efforts at Franklin were the major highlights of a rewarding military career. Cox proved throughout that he had a "military aptitude" as he earned the reputation of a capable general officer and a quintessential subordinate commander. His postwar role as military governor of western North Carolina illustrated how a citizen-general's political aptitude would be useful in calming tensions and seeking a new modus vivendi.

Moving from a political-military leadership position into a political-civilian leadership role seemed a natural transition for Cox, and in 1865 a future as a major actor on the national political scene seemed inevitable. Cox, however, did not have a political aptitude to match his military aptitude. In war he was comfortable with dutifully taking orders, but even then his independent spirit led him to think for himself, occasionally take an initiative without orders, and recommend alternative approaches to his commanders. That independent spirit would not be constrained in the peacetime political world as Cox insisted on being his own man and refused to sublimate his views.

His rigid adherence to his principles, a product of his upbringing, character, and experience, was the key factor in his failure to achieve national political prominence. As he once wrote to Monroe, "It is no new thing for me to be blinded by absorption in the view I may take at the moment," a blindness that often caused him to disregard practical considerations. His brother Charles once wrote to him expressing his frustration that Cox had had greatness thrust upon him so often yet had rebuffed it an equal number of times. Cox knew that he could have become a major political figure, but he also understood himself well enough to know why he hadn't. As he wrote to a colleague in 1885, "I could have cut a more prominent figure had I thought the game worth the candle." But he did not believe that the political game was worth compromising or abandoning his personal beliefs, his independent spirit, and his uncompromising intellect. At the same time, other political leaders recognized that Cox's aloof and stiff mien and lack of a "common touch" would be obstacles to his political popularity. In the end, in great part because of conscious actions he took, and fully aware of the consequences, Cox faded from the national political scene and its memory.[19]

Jacob Dolson Cox was a true Renaissance man in the Gilded Age, one whose intellect, hard work, and intuitive talents allowed him to take on and succeed in many vocations and avocations. While his political career did not fulfill his potential, in the others, ranging from military officer to Civil War historian, and including dean of the Cincinnati Law School, president of the University of Cincinnati, president of the Toledo, Wabash, and Western Railway, and amateur scientist, he achieved varying degrees of success and renown. If he had been asked, he most assuredly would have said that for him each of those professional vocations was, unlike politics, a "game worth the candle."

Notes

Preface

1. Mark M. Boatner III, *The Civil War Dictionary*, rev. ed. (New York: Vintage Books, 1991), xv.

Introduction

1. Jacob D. Cox, *The Battle of Franklin, Tennessee, November 30, 1864: A Monograph* (New York: Charles Scribner's Sons, 1897), 92.

2. Jacob Dolson Cox, *Military Reminiscences of the Civil War* (New York: Charles Scribner's Sons, 1900), 1:168.

3. William Marvel, *Burnside* (Chapel Hill: University of North Carolina Press, 1991), 112. For a discussion of the historiography of the war, see James M. McPherson and William J. Cooper Jr., *Writing the Civil War: The Quest to Understand* (Columbia: University of South Carolina Press, 2000).

4. Cox to Emerson Opdycke, January 24, 1876, Jacob Dolson Cox Papers, Oberlin College Archives (hereinafter referred to as "Cox Papers"); Thomas Goss, *The War within the Union High Command: Politics and Generalship during the Civil War* (Lawrence: University Press of Kansas, 2003), xiii.

Chapter 1: Citizen of the Western Reserve

1. Jacob D. Cox, *Dedicatory Speech of the Garfield Memorial, May 10, 1890* (Cleveland: Garfield Memorial Association, 1890), 1–2.

2. Andrew Cayton, *Ohio: The History of a People* (Columbus: Ohio State University Press, 2002), 3–5; Robert A. Wheeler, *Visions of the Western Reserve, Public and Private Documents of Northeast Ohio, 1750–1860* (Columbus: Ohio State University Press, 2000), 1–7.

3. William Cox Cochran, "Political Experiences of Major General Jacob Dolson Cox," unpublished ms. in 2 vols., Cincinnati, 1940, Oberlin College Archives, 1:1–5 (the sources on Cox's early life are scarce, and this work by Cox's stepson

274   is the basic source); Jacob Dolson Cox, "Why the Men of '61 Fought for the Union," *Atlantic Monthly,* March 1892, 25–26.

4. Cochran, "Political Experiences," 1:5–6; James Rees Ewing, "Public Services of Jacob Dolson Cox," Ph.D. diss., Johns Hopkins University, 1902, 8; Jacob Dolson Cox, "The Youth and Early Manhood of General James A. Garfield," oration, Reunion of the Army of the Cumberland, Milwaukee, 1882, 9, copy in Cox Papers.

5. Allan Guelzo, "Charles Grandison Finney," in *The Human Tradition in the Civil War and Reconstruction,* ed. Steven E. Woodworth (Wilmington, Del.: Scholarly Resources, 2000), 156; George W. Knepper, *Ohio and Its Peoples* (Kent: Kent State University Press, 1989), 201; Cochran, "Political Experiences," 1:6–7.

6. James B. Stewart, *Holy Warriors: The Abolitionists and American Slavery* (New York: Hill and Wang, 1997), 59–60; Robert S. Fletcher, *A History of Oberlin College* (Oberlin: Oberlin College, 1943), 236–70.

7. Fletcher, *History of Oberlin College,* 537, 538, 542; Cochran, "Political Experiences," 1:7; Cox to Charles F. Cox, December 13, 1864, Cox Papers.

8. Treasurer's Office Papers, Oberlin College, Oberlin College Archives; Cox to J. D. Cox I, September 1846, in William Cox Cochran, "General Jacob Dolson Cox: Early Life and Military Service," *Bibliotheca Sacra* (October 1901): 443; M. A. Broadner to Julia Clark, October 4, 1846, in Fletcher, *History of Oberlin College,* 821; Cox to J. D. Cox I, in Cochran, "Early Life," 443.

9. Cochran, "Early Life," 444–45.

10. William Cox Cochran, "Helen Finney Cox," *Oberlin Alumni Magazine* (October 1911): 9; *Oberlin Evangelist,* September 30, 1859; Cochran, "Political Experiences," 1:11. Finney and his wife had left on September 26, 1859, and did not attend the wedding.

11. Charles E. Hambrick-Stowe, *Charles G. Finney and the Spirit of American Evangelism* (Grand Rapids, Mich.: Wm. E. Eerdsman, 1996), 271; Jacob Dolson Cox III, *Building an American Industry: The Story of the Cleveland Twist Drill Co. and Its Founder; An Autobiography* (Cleveland: Cleveland Twist Drill Co., 1951), 34–35.

12. Cochran, "Political Experiences," 1:13–14; Hambrick-Stowe, *Finney,* 271. Cox made no mention of the incident in his extant papers. However, in letters to friends soon afterward he said he would have become a minister had he not been judged on the honesty of his theological conclusions instead of his means of coming to those conclusions. See letters of December 21, 1854, and June 26, 1853, to Thomas Robinson and J. A. R. Rogers, respectively, Cox Papers.

13. Harriet Taylor Upton, *History of the Western Reserve* (Chicago: Lewis Publishing, 1910), 1:87–88; Cox to Allyn Cox, May 25, 1852, Cox Papers; Cox to J. A. R. Rogers, December 21, 1854, Cox Papers.

14. Certificate signed by Jonathan Ingersoll, Clerk of District Court of County of Trumbull, Cox Papers; J. D. Cox to J. A. R. Rogers, July 19, 1852 and April 11, 1853, Cox Papers; Cochran, "Political Experiences," 1:16.

15. Cox to Charles Finney Cox, April 10, 1852, Cox Papers; Cox to J. A. R. Rogers, July 22, 1857, Cox Papers. The bylaws of the club as they were drawn up by Cox are in the Cox Papers.

16. Cox, *Dedicatory Speech,* 7; Theodore Clark Smith, *The Life and Letters of James Abram Garfield* (New Haven, Conn.: Yale University Press, 1925), 2:905.

17. Mary Rudd Cochran letter to the author, in the author's possession.

18. Helen Cox to William Cochran, January 13 and June 18, 1862, Cox Papers; Helen Cox to Lucy Garfield, July 19, 1863, Lucy Garfield Papers, Library of Congress (hereinafter referred to as "LC"); H. Wayne Morgan, *Kenyon Cox, 1856–1919: A Life in American Art* (Kent: Kent State University Press, 1994), 3.

19. J. D. Cox III, *Building an American Industry,* 15, 23; Morgan, *Kenyon Cox,* 175.

20. Among the best treatments of this era are James M. McPherson, *Battle Cry of Freedom: The Civil War Era* (New York: Oxford University Press), 41; John C. Waugh, *On the Brink of Civil War* (New York: Rowman and Littlefield, 2003); and Michael F. Holt, *The Political Crisis of the 1850s* (New York: W. W. Norton, 1983).

21. Knepper, *Ohio and Its Peoples,* 119, 203–7. See also Stephen Maizlish, *The Triumph of Sectionalism: The Transformation of Ohio Politics, 1844–1856* (Kent: Kent State University Press, 1983); and Cox, "Why the Men of '61," 27.

22. Cox to Redelia Cox, June 28, 1852, Cox Papers; Philip W. Magness and Sebastian N. Page, *Colonization after Emancipation: Lincoln and the Movement for Black Resettlement* (Columbia: University of Missouri Press, 2011), 3; Cox to J. A. R. Rogers, August 1, 1855, Cox Papers. Eric Foner posits that Lincoln eventually came to accept a permanent black presence in America; see Foner, *The Fiery Trial: Abraham Lincoln and American Slavery* (New York: W. W. Norton, 2010).

23. *Western Reserve Transcript and Whig,* June 30, 1853; *Western Reserve Chronicle,* September 15, 1853; *Western Reserve Transcript,* October 13, 1853. The definitive study of the Whig Party is Michael F. Holt, *The Rise and Fall of the American Whig Party: Jacksonian Politics and the Onset of the Civil War* (New York: Oxford University Press, 1999).

24. *Western Reserve Transcript and Whig,* February 23, 1854 (this was this paper's final issue, because it was merged with the Free-Soil organ to become the Republican organ); Cayton, *Ohio,* 125–26. For an analysis of the national political trends from 1840 to 1861, see Michael F. Holt, *Political Parties and American Political Development: From the Age of Jackson to the Age of Lincoln* (Baton Rouge: Louisiana State University Press, 1992). For discussions of Republican ideology, see Eric Foner, *Free Soil, Free Labor, Free Men* (New York: Oxford University Press, 1995); and Heather Cox Richardson, *The Death of Reconstruction: Race, Labor, and Politics in the Post–Civil War North, 1865–1901* (Cambridge, Mass.: Harvard University Press, 2004).

25. Nicholas Guyatt, "A Vast Negro Reservation: Black Colonization in the Postbellum United States, 1863–1871," unpublished ms., 2012, 6, 16. For background on this movement, see Eric Burin, *Slavery and the Peculiar Solution: A History of the American Colonization Society* (Gainesville: University Press of Florida, 2005); Magness and Page, *Colonization after Emancipation;* and James T. Campbell, *Middle Passages: African American Journeys to Africa, 1787–2005* (New York: Penguin, 2007).

26. *Western Reserve Chronicle and Transcript,* October 18, 1854, and June 13, 1855.

27. Eugene H. Roseboom, *The Civil War Era, 1850–1873,* vol. 4 of *The History of the State of Ohio,* ed. Carl Wittke (Columbus: Ohio Archeological and Historical

276

Society, 1944), 349; Frederick Blue, *No Taint of Compromise: Crusaders in Antislavery Politics* (Baton Rouge: Louisiana State University Press, 2006), 79–85; Knepper, *Ohio and Its People,* 213–14; Cochran, "Political Experiences," 1:326, 396–98.

28. *Western Reserve Chronicle,* August 24, 1859; Garfield to Cox, August 30, 1859, James A. Garfield Papers, LC (hereinafter cited as "Garfield Papers"); Cox to Thomas Robinson, November 8, 1859, Cox Papers.

29. James A. Garfield to Lucy Garfield, December 31, 1859, as quoted in Smith, *Life and Letters,* 1:144; Cox, "The Youth and Early Manhood of General James A. Garfield," Oration, Reunion of the Army of the Cumberland, 1882, 14, Cox Papers; Smith, *Life and Letters,* 2:148, 905; Cox to Garfield, April 4, 1860, Garfield Papers, LC. Bascom's son Gustavus would become Cox's aide during the war.

30. Clement Eaton, *A History of the Southern Confederacy* (New York: Simon and Schuster, 1965), 12–14; George B. Porter, *Ohio Politics during the Civil War Period* (New York: Columbia University Press, 1911), 28–29; *Ohio Senate Journal,* 54th General Assembly, First Session, 1860, 5; *Western Reserve Chronicle,* January 18 and February 8, 1860.

31. Cox, "Why the Men of '61," 31. The books were an edition of U.S. Army Regulations, *Mueller's Field Engineer* (1760), and Forbes's *Manual for Patriotic Volunteers* (1855). Cochran (in "Political Experiences," 1:483–85) noted that Cox bought two more books: W. J. Hardee, *Rifle and Light Infantry Tactics;* and Baron Henri Jomini, *Treatise on Grand Military Operations.*

32. Cox to Garfield, April 25, 1860, Garfield Papers, LC; Cox to Monroe, April 27, 1860, James Monroe Papers (hereinafter referred to as "Monroe Papers"), Oberlin College Archives; Joseph P. Smith, *History of the Republican Party in Ohio* (Chicago: Lewis Publishing, 1898), 1:124; Cox to Garfield, June 16, 1860, Garfield Papers, LC.

33. Cox to Garfield, July 13, 1860, Garfield Papers, LC; *Western Reserve Chronicle,* August 29, 1860, 2; Cox to J. A. R. Rogers, November 29, 1860, Cox Papers; Porter, *Ohio Politics,* 56; Henry H. Simms, *Ohio Politics on the Eve of Conflict* (Columbus: Ohio State University Press, 1961), 14; *Ohio Senate Journal,* 54th General Assembly, Second Session, 1861, 16; James A. Garfield to Lucy Garfield, January 13, 1861, as quoted in Smith, *Life and Letters,* 1:152; Cox to Helen Cox, February 4, 1861, Kenyon Cox Papers, Avery Library, Columbia University.

34. Clipping from an unnamed newspaper in Helen Cox's scrapbook no. 1, Cox Papers. The speech was made on January 30, 1861, in the Ohio Senate.

35. *Western Reserve Chronicle,* April 10, 1861; Cox, *Military Reminiscences,* 1:1–2.

36. Mary Rudd Cochran, Cox's step-granddaughter, related this story in a conversation with the author; Cox to Helen Cox, April 19 and 28 and November 15, 1861, Kenyon Cox Papers; Helen Cox to Lucy Garfield, April 6, 1862, Lucy Garfield Papers, LC.

37. Cox, *Military Reminiscences,* 1:6–7; Cox, "War Preparations in the North," in *Battles and Leaders of the Civil War,* ed. Robert Underwood Johnson and Clarence Clough Buel (New York: Charles Scribner's Sons, 1887), 1:89 (hereinafter cited as *Battles and Leaders*).

38. McPherson, *Battle Cry of Freedom,* 312–13. Among the many works that deal with this aspect of the era, the following, other than Cox's writings and McPherson's book, are of particular value: Kenneth P. Williams, *Lincoln Finds a General,* 4 vols. (New York: MacMillan, 1957); T. Harry Williams, *Lincoln and His Generals* (New York: Alfred A. Knopf, 1952) and *The History of American Wars from 1745 to 1918* (New York: Alfred A. Knopf, 1981); Russell Weigley, *The American Way of War: A History of United States Military Strategy and Policy* (New York: Macmillan, 1977); Wiley Sword, *Courage Under Fire: Profiles in Bravery from the Battlefields of the Civil War* (New York: St. Martin's Press, 2007); Goss, *War within the Union;* David Work, *Lincoln's Political Generals* (Urbana: University of Illinois Press, 2009); Grady McWhiney and Perry Jamison, *Attack and Die: Civil War Military Tactics and the Southern Heritage* (Tuscaloosa: University of Alabama Press, 1984); and Allen C. Guelzo, *Fateful Lightning: A New History of the Civil War and Reconstruction* (New York: Oxford University Press, 2012).

39. Cox to Chase, January 1, 1863, Cox Papers; Wayne Wei-siang Hsieh, *West Pointers and the Civil War: The Old Army in War and Peace* (Chapel Hill: University of North Carolina Press, 2009), 145; Stephen Ambrose, *Duty, Honor, Country: A History of West Point* (Baltimore, Md.: Johns Hopkins University Press, 1966), 174; John Eisenhower, *Agent of Destiny: The Life and Times of General Winfield Scott* (Norman: University of Oklahoma Press, 1999), 381–83; E. D. Townsend, *Anecdotes of the Civil War in the United States* (New York: D. Appleton, 1884), 56–57.

40. Work, *Lincoln's Political Generals,* 7; Ambrose, *Duty, Honor, Country,* 172; Goss, *War within the Union,* xi; Hsieh, *West Pointers,* 145.

41. Lori A. Lisowski, "The Future of West Point: Senate Debates on the Military Academy during the Civil War," *Civil War History* 34, no. 1 (1988), 5–21; Bruce Tap, *Over Lincoln's Shoulder: The Committee on the Conduct of the War* (Lawrence: University Press of Kansas, 1998).

42. Cox, *Military Reminiscences,* 1:171. Guelzo discusses these issues in *Fateful Lightning,* 146–51, and notes the analysis from Cox's *Military Reminiscences.* See note 38 for a selection of books that use Cox as a source.

43. Cox, *Military Reminiscences,* 1:182–84.

44. Official Records (hereinafter referred to as "OR"), published as *The War of the Rebellion: A Compilation of the Official Records of the Union and Confederate Armies* (Washington, D.C.: Government Printing Office, 1880–97), vol. 51, part 1, 369–70; Cox, *Military Reminiscences,* 1:33–34.

45. W. T. Sherman, "The Grand Strategy of the Last Year of the War," in *Battles and Leaders,* 4:255. The following, among others, are relevant to understanding Jomini, his influence, and the evolution of strategy: Herman Hattaway and Archer Jones, *How the North Won: A Military History of the Civil War* (Urbana: University of Illinois Press, 1991); Edward Hageman, *The American Civil War and the Origins of Modern Warfare* (Bloomington: Indiana University Press, 1992); Richard Beringer, Herman Hattaway, Archer Jones, and William N. Still Jr., *Why the South Lost the Civil War* (Athens: University of Georgia Press, 1986); Paddy Griffith, *Battle Tactics of the Civil War* (New Haven, Conn.: Yale University Press, 2001); Ethan Rafuse, *McClellan's War: The Failure of Modernization in the Struggle for the Union* (Bloomington:

278   Indiana University Press, 2005); Sword, *Courage Under Fire;* W. J. Wood, *Civil War Generalship: The Art of Command* (New York: DaCapo Press, 2000); Donald Stoker, *The Grand Design: Strategy and the U.S. Civil War* (New York: Oxford University Press, 2010); Archer Jones, *Civil War Command and Strategy* (New York: Free Press, 1992); Brian Reid, *America's Civil War: The Operational Battlefield, 1861–63* (Amherst, N.Y.: Prometheus Books, 2008); Carol Reardon, *With a Sword in One Hand and Jomini in the Other* (Chapel Hill: University of North Carolina Press, 2012); and B. H. Liddell Hart, *Strategy,* 2nd rev. ed. (New York: Penguin Group, 1967).

46. Sword, *Courage under Fire,* 14, 39, 42; Cox, *Atlanta* (New York: Charles Scribner's Sons, 1882), 129.

47. Tap, *Over Lincoln's Shoulder,* 14–15, 44–45.

48. *Ohio Senate Journal,* 54th General Assembly, Second Session, April 15–18, 1861, 209–302; Porter, *Ohio Politics,* 75–77; Cox, *Military Reminiscences,* 1:8; Cox, "War Preparations," 89–94; Roseboom, *Civil War Era,* 381.

49. Aaron F. Perry, "A Chapter in Interstate Diplomacy," in *Sketches of War History, 1861–1865,* ed. Robert Hunter (Cincinnati: R. Clarke, 1890), 3:346; Perry described Cox as "a young gentleman of agreeable presence, slender figure, and apparently nervous organization"; Knepper, *Ohio and Its Peoples,* 222; Cox, *Military Reminiscences,* 1:3, 355.

50. Cox, *Military Reminiscences,* 1:9–10.

51. Cox, "War Preparations," 89–90; Thomas W. Cutrer, ed., *The Mexican War Diary of George B. McClellan* (Baton Rouge: Louisiana State University Press, 2009), 67; Stephen Sears, *George B. McClellan: The Young Napoleon* (New York: Ticknor and Fields, 1988), 112–13; Stephen Sears, ed., *The Civil War Papers of George B. McClellan* (New York: DaCapo Press, 1992), 44, 67.

52. Cox, "War Preparations," 96; Matthew Oyos, "Ohio Militia in the Civil War," *Ohio History* 98 (Summer–Autumn 1989): 147–74.

53. Cox, *Military Reminiscences,* 1:31; OR, vol. 51, part 1, 388; Frank J. Jones, "Personal Recollections and Experience of a Soldier during the War of the Rebellion," in Hunter, *Sketches of War History,* 6:116; Gustavus Bascom to W. T. Bascom, May 18, 1861, William Bascom-Hiram Little Family Papers (hereinafter cited as "Bascom-Little Papers"), Western Reserve Historical Society, Cleveland, Ohio.

54. J. H. Horton and Solomon Teverbaugh, *A History of the Eleventh Regiment, Ohio Volunteer Infantry* (Dayton, Ohio: W. J. Shuey, 1866), 276–77; Cox to Helen Cox, April 30, 1861, Cox Papers.

55. Cox, "Public Life of James Monroe," Memorial of the Honorable James Monroe, October 30, 1898, Cox Papers, 5; Cox to Helen Cox, June 27, 1861, Cox Papers; Sears, *Young Napoleon,* 71.

56. Cox, *Military Reminiscences,* 1:14; Cox to Helen Cox, May 7 and June 14, 1861, Cox Papers. See Steven Woodworth, ed., *The Loyal, True, and Brave: America's Civil War Soldiers* (Wilmington, Del.: Scholarly Resources, 2002), 1–22; Cox to Helen Cox, June 19 and 27, 1861, Cox Papers.

57. Cox, *Military Reminiscences,* 1:21–25, 35; OR, vol. 51, part 1, 388.

58. Cox, *Military Reminiscences,* 1:23; Cox to Helen Cox, May 5, 1861, Cox Papers.

59. Cox to Helen Cox, June 27, 1861, Cox Papers.

1. Cox, *Military Reminiscences,* 1:144–45.

2. For overviews of these campaigns, see W. Hunter Lesser, *Rebels at the Gate: Lee and McClellan on the Front Line of a Nation Divided* (Naperville, Ill.: Sourcebooks, 2005); and Clayton R. Newell, *Lee vs. McClellan: The First Campaign* (Washington, D.C.: Regnery Publishing, 2010).

3. For a discussion of the role of railroads and the B&O, see Festus Summers, *The Baltimore and Ohio in the Civil War* (New York: G. P. Putnam's Sons, 1939); Thomas Weber, *The Northern Railroads in the Civil War, 1861–1865* (Bloomington: Indiana University Press, 1952); John E. Clark, *Railroads in the Civil War* (Baton Rouge: Louisiana State University Press, 2004); and Robert Hodges, *American Civil War Railroad Tactics* (Oxford, U.K.: Osprey Publishing, 2008). For information about McClellan and the Ohio militia, see Cox, "McClellan in West Virginia," in *Battles and Leaders,* 1:127–28; OR, 2:46–49; Richard Curry, "McClellan's Western Virginia Campaign of 1861," *Ohio History* 71 (July 1962): 83–96; Whitelaw Reid, *Ohio in the War* (Columbus: Eclectic Publishing, 1867), 1:48–49; Matthew Oyos, "Ohio Militia," 167; Sears, *Young Napoleon,* 79–80; Stephen Sears, "Building the Army," *Military History Quarterly* 20 (Winter 2008): 80–81.

4. OR, 2:64–69, 236–38; Sears, *Young Napoleon,* 83; Cox, *Military Reminiscences,* 1:57.

5. OR, 2:239–41; OR, vol. 51, part 1, 338–39, 369–70; Cox, *Military Reminiscences,* 1:47; Perry, "Chapter in Interstate Diplomacy," 345–46; Sears, *Young Napoleon,* 74–76; Ethan Rafuse, "Impractical? Unforgiveable?: Another Look at George B. McClellan's First Strategic Plan," *Ohio History* 110 (Summer–Autumn 2001): 153–64.

6. OR, 2:197.

7. Salmon P. Chase to Cox, June 17, 1861, Cox Papers; Cox to Helen Cox, July 7 and 10, 1861, Cox Papers; OR, vol. 51, part 1, 417.

8. Cox, *Military Reminiscences,* 1:63; Cox to Helen Cox, July 3, 1861, Cox Papers; OR, 2:200.

9. Cox, "McClellan in West Virginia," 1:138–39; Cox to Helen Cox, July 12, 1861, Cox Papers; Jones, "Personal Recollections," in *Sketches of War History,* 6:115.

10. Cox, *Military Reminiscences,* 1:65–66; Cox to Helen Cox, July 12, 1861, Cox Papers.

11. OR, 2:199, 203–8. For descriptions of this affair, see McPherson, *Battle Cry of Freedom,* 300–301; Sears, *Young Napoleon,* 86–92; Lesser, *Rebels at the Gate,* 102–5; and Rafuse, *McClellan's War,* 113–15. See also Rosecrans's testimony before the committee in U.S. Congress, *Report of the Joint Committee on the Conduct of the War, 2nd Session, 38th Congress* (Washington, D.C.: Government Printing Office, 1865).

12. OR, 2:202–4, 236, 743, 753; William Lamers, *The Edge of Glory: A Biography of General William S. Rosecrans, U.S.A.* (Baton Rouge: Louisiana State University Press, 1999), 36; Lesser, *Rebels at the Gate,* 122–26.

13. Cox, "McClellan in West Virginia," 135, 137; McPherson, *Battle Cry of Freedom,* 300.

14. OR, 2:208, 210–11; McClellan to Cox, July 14, 1861, in Sears, *Civil War Papers of McClellan,* 55–56.

280   15. Gustavus Bascom to W. T. Bascom, July 17, 1861, Bascom-Little Papers; Cox to Helen Cox, July 16, 1861, Cox Papers; OR, vol. 51, part 1, 421.

16. Cox to Helen Cox, July 20, 1861, Cox Papers; OR, 2:288, 291–92, 746; Cox, *Military Reminiscences,* 1:46–48; McClellan to his wife, as quoted in Lesser, *Rebels at the Gate,* 128; Sears, *Young Napoleon,* 92.

17. McClellan to Cox, July 19, 1861, as quoted in Sears, *Civil War Papers of McClellan,* 62.

18. Cox to Helen Cox, July 22, 1861, Cox Papers.

19. McClellan to Cox, July 22, 1861, as quoted in Sears, *Civil War Papers of McClellan,* 67.

20. Cox, *Military Reminiscences,* 1:72; Gavin Mortimer, *Double Death: The True Story of Pryce Lewis, the Civil War's Most Daring Spy* (New York: Walker Publishing, 2010), 46–50, 80–84; Gary Gallagher, ed., *The Shenandoah Valley Campaign of 1864* (Chapel Hill: University of North Carolina Press, 2006), 356–57. Cox also wrote, "I confess to a contempt for all organizations of spies and detectives" (*Military Reminiscences,* 1:250). Patton's grandson and namesake became a major U.S. general in the twentieth century.

21. Cox, "Message to the People of Charleston," July 25, 1861, Roy Bird Cook Papers, West Virginia University Collection, West Virginia University Library; OR, vol. 51, part 1, 425–26.

22. Cox to Helen Cox, July 25, 1861, Cox Papers.

23. Cox, *Military Reminiscences,* 1:73–79. In his memoirs, Cox noted these messages from McClellan and Rosecrans, but they are not in the Official Records. Cox kept copies of the original documents, which he said he had sent to the editors of the Official Records, but they were apparently lost; Newell, *Lee vs. McClellan,* 178–79.

24. OR, 2:292, 1011–12; OR, vol. 51, part 1, 440; Cox to Helen Cox, July 28 and 30, 1861, Cox Papers; Newell, *Lee vs. McClellan,* 267.

25. Cox, *Military Reminiscences,* 1:74–76. Charles Whittlesey, the quoted aide, was Cox's chief engineer, and the quotation is from his book, *War Memoranda: Cheat River to the Tennessee 1861–1862* (Cleveland: William W. Williams, 1884), 78.

26. William D. Sloan and Lisa M. Purcell, *American Journalism: History, Principles, Practices* (Jefferson, N.C.: Macfarland, 2002), 231; Mark W. Summers, *The Press Gang: Newspapers and Politics, 1865–1878* (Chapel Hill: University of North Carolina Press, 1994), 21–22. See also J. Cutler Andrews, *The North Reports the Civil War* (Pittsburgh: University of Pittsburgh Press, 1985); and David Bulla and Gregory A. Borchard, *Journalism in the Civil War* (New York: Peter Lang Publishing, 2010).

27. Cox, *Military Reminiscences,* 1:76–78; Andrews, *North Reports the Civil War,* 108–9; *New York Times,* August 2, 1861.

28. Cox to Helen Cox, August 11, 16, and 18, 1861, Cox Papers.

29. OR, 2:762; Lesser, *Rebels at the Gate,* 205; Cox, "McClellan in West Virginia," 142–43; Cox to Helen Cox, July 28, 1861, Kenyon Cox Papers; Mrs. Ellen Tompkins to Sarah Cooper, August [ ], September 10, and September 13, 1861, as quoted in Ellen Wilkins Tompkins, "The Colonel's Lady: Some Letters of Ellen

Wilkins Tompkins, July–December, 1861," *Virginia Magazine of History and Biography* 69, no. 4 (October 1961): 392–94. This is the first time Cox's command is called "Kanawha," a title it would carry for the remainder of the war. It was the only Union command that did not receive a specific number.

30. OR, vol. 51, part 2, 220, 225; Clarice Lorene Bailes, "Jacob Dolson Cox in West Virginia," *West Virginia History: A Quarterly Magazine* 6 (October 1944): 51. Cox noted in his memoirs that he was "gratified" in retrospect to learn about Lee's and Floyd's views at the time; see Cox, *Military Reminiscences,* 1:164.

31. Cox, *Military Reminiscences,* 1:91, 98–99; Cox to Helen Cox, August 16, 1861, Cox Papers; OR, vol. 51, part 1, 456–57; J. H. Horton and Solomon Teverbaugh, *A History of the Eleventh Regiment, Ohio Volunteer Infantry* (Dayton, Ohio: W. J. Shuey, 1866), 259–60. The regimental historians noted that many critics thought Cox moved too slowly, and "he was frequently bitterly denounced and ridiculed," but in the Antietam campaign both Cox and his men proved their mettle and, they wrote, "our favorite General" was recognized for his contributions.

32. OR, 5:118; OR, vol. 51, part 1, 459–64; Cox to Helen Cox, August 29, 1861, Cox Papers; Cox, *Military Reminiscences,* 1:93–97. In that text Cox noted that he allowed Tyler to issue a second report, and "the unfortunate affair was treated as a lesson. . . . It made trouble in the regiment, however, where the line officers did not conceal their opinion that he had failed in his duty as commander, and he was never afterward comfortable among them." Tyler did not appreciate Cox's help, perhaps because he knew that Cox had favored Garfield. The latter told Cox later that he had heard that Tyler blamed Cox and that some of his men "made no hesitation openly to threaten [Cox's] life . . . under cover of battle"; see Garfield to Cox, October 30, 1861, Cox Papers. In letters to Helen (September 4 and 25, 1861, Cox Papers), Cox noted that someone, probably Tyler, was leaking documents to the press that were being distorted to blame Cox for this incident.

33. OR, 5:809; Cox to Helen Cox, August 29, 1861, Cox Papers; Cox, *Military Reminiscences,* 1:93–96; Cox, "McClellan in West Virginia," 145.

34. Newell, *Lee vs. McClellan,* 204; Cox, "McClellan in West Virginia," 146; OR, 5:149; OR, vol. 51, part 1, 482; see also Cox to Helen Cox, September 10, 1861, Cox Papers.

35. Cox, *Military Reminiscences,* 1:113; Cox to Helen Cox, September 17, 1861, Cox Papers.

36. Drew Faust's *This Republic of Suffering: Death and the American Civil War* (New York: Alfred A. Knopf, 2008) is a study of how the war significantly altered how Americans dealt with death; Cox to Helen Cox, September 10 and 17, 1861, Cox Papers; Cox, *Military Reminiscences,* 1:103.

37. See Mark S. Schantz, *Awaiting the Heavenly Country: The Civil War and America's Culture of Death* (Ithaca, N.Y.: Cornell University Press, 2008).

38. Cox, *Military Reminiscences,* 1:72, 116; OR, 5:148–49, 487; OR, vol. 51, part 1, 487; Cox to Helen Cox, October 8 and 17, 1861, Cox Papers; Bascom to W. T. Bascom, October 15, 1861, Bascom-Little Papers.

39. McPherson, *Battle Cry of Freedom,* 302–3; Cox, *Military Reminiscences,* 1:131–34.

40. Cox to Helen Cox, November 15 and 24 and December 2, 1861, Cox Papers. Benham was not convicted, but he was arrested again in mid-1862 for disobedience of orders, and his commission was revoked; see Boatner, *Civil War Dictionary,* 58–59; OR, vol. 51, part 1, 251; OR, 5:286–88, 657, 669.

41. OR, 5:691; Cox, "McClellan in West Virginia," 148.

42. Cox, *Military Reminiscences,* 1:163–65; Cox to Helen Cox, November 24 and December 30, 1861, Cox Papers; Cox to Garfield, January 9 and February 2 and 26, 1862, Garfield Papers, LC; Dennison to Cox, November 25, 1861, Cox Papers.

43. Cox to Garfield, February 26, 1862, Garfield Papers, LC; Cox, *Military Reminiscences,* 1:151–52; Cox to Helen Cox, December 11, 1861, Cox Papers.

44. McPherson, *Battle Cry of Freedom,* 354–57; Cox, *Military Reminiscences,* 1:158–63. None of Cox's messages to Rosecrans about this matter have been preserved.

45. Cox to Garfield, September 9 and November 8, 1861, Garfield Papers, LC; Hayes letter to Lucy Hayes, September 29, 1861, and notation in his personal diary, February 2, 1862, both in Charles Richard Williams, ed., *Diary and Letters of Rutherford Birchard Hayes* (Columbus: Ohio Archeological and Historical Society, 1922–26), 2:104, 198; Glenn V. Longacre and John E. Haas, eds., *To Battle for God and the Right: The Civil War Letterbooks of Emerson Opdycke* (Urbana: University of Illinois Press, 2003), 8.

46. Cox to Helen Cox, February 25 and March 16, 1863, Cox Papers; OR, 5:54; John C. Fremont, "In Command in Missouri," in *Battles and Leaders,* 1:276–88; Tap, *Over Lincoln's Shoulder,* 81–98.

47. Cox, "West Virginia Operations under Fremont," in *Battles and Leaders,* 2:278–79; Cox to Helen Cox, March 16 and April 20, 1862, Cox Papers; Cox, *Military Reminiscences,* 1:195–201; OR, vol. 12, part 1, 7. For an overview of this campaign, see Peter Cozzens, *Shenandoah 1862: Stonewall Jackson's Valley Campaign* (Chapel Hill: University of North Carolina Press, 2008).

48. Williams, *Diary and Letters,* 225, 271, 277; Cox, *Military Reminiscences,* 1:207–16; Cox to Helen Cox, May 9, 15, and 20 and June 15, 1862, Cox Papers; William H. Armstrong, *Major McKinley: William McKinley and the Civil War* (Kent: Kent State University Press, 2000), 32.

49. OR, vol. 12, part 3, 203–4, 209; Cox's report is in OR, vol. 12, part 1, 505–8; Cox to Helen Cox, May 20 and 24, 1862, Cox Papers (in the second letter, Cox noted rumors in Charleston that he had been captured and his forces cut to pieces, which he called "war alarms"); Cox, *Military Reminiscences,* 1:202–22; Joseph Harsh, *Confederate Tide Rising: Robert E. Lee and the Making of Southern Strategy* (Kent: Kent State University Press, 1998), 106–7. T. Harry Williams opined that while Cox was too cautious, lacked dash, did not speak the common tongue, and did not know how to fire the hearts of his men, he always had their respect and their morale was high; see Williams, *Hayes of the 23rd, the Civil War Volunteer Officer* (New York: Alfred A. Knopf, 1965), 120–21.

50. Cox to Helen Cox, June 8, 1862, and July 7, 1864, Cox Papers; McPherson, *Battle Cry of Freedom,* 504; Sears, *Young Napoleon,* 227–28; Mark Grimsley, *The*

Hard Hand of War: Union Military Policy toward Southern Civilians, 1861–1865 (Cambridge, Mass.: Harvard University Press, 1995), 2–3, 94–95.

51. OR, vol. 12, part 3, 435, 440–41, 451; Cox to Helen Cox, June 19 and 28 and July 17 and 20, 1862, Cox Papers. In the July 17 letter, Cox complained that he was being blamed in the newspapers for inaction, and clearly Helen was worried about this harming his reputation. He responded, "Take it coolly Helen."

52. OR, vol. 12, part 3, 473–74; Cox, *Military Reminiscences,* 1:223–27; Charles Francis Adams Jr. to Charles Francis Adams Sr., August 27, 1862, as quoted in Brooks Simpson, "Command Relationships at Gettysburg," in *Civil War Generals in Defeat,* ed. Steven Woodworth (Lawrence: University Press of Kansas, 1999), 182. Cox and Pope became friends after the war, and Pope's son married Cox's youngest daughter, Charlotte.

53. Cox to Helen Cox, August 4, 1862, Cox Papers; OR, vol. 12, part 3, 560–61; Cox, *Military Reminiscences,* 1:220, 223–24.

54. OR, vol. 12, part 3, 567; Cox to Helen Cox, August 11 and 16, 1862, Cox Papers.

55. OR, vol. 12, part 3, 941–46; OR, vol. 19, part 1, 142–43; Cox, *Military Reminiscences,* 1:392–99.

56. K. Williams, *Lincoln Finds a General,* 1:281; Cox to Helen Cox, August 20 and 22, 1862, Cox Papers; Cox, *Military Reminiscences,* 1:227.

57. Cox to Helen Cox, August 24, 1862, Cox Papers.

Chapter 3: Citizen-General on the National Stage

1. Cox, *Military Reminiscences,* 1:245.

2. OR, vol. 11, part 1, 98; Sears, *Civil War Papers of McClellan,* 403–5, 416.

3. OR, vol. 12, part 3, 732–33. The best history of this campaign and battle is John J. Hennessy, *Return to Bull Run: The Campaign and Battle of Second Manassas* (New York: Simon and Schuster, 1993).

4. Cochran, "Political Experiences," 1:403; Cox to Helen Cox, August 30, 1862, Cox Papers; Herman Haupt, *Reminiscences of General Herman Haupt* (Milwaukee, Wis.: Wright and Joys, 1901), 98–99; OR, vol. 12, part 3, 709.

5. Cox to Helen Cox, August 30 and September 2, 1862, Cox Papers. In the second letter Cox noted that the debate about "who's responsible" would begin soon, adding that he thought Pope's selection had been "unfortunate"; Cox, *Military Reminiscences,* 1: 241–44, 253, 236.

6. Cox to Schofield, December 23, 1880, Cox Papers; OR, vol. 12, part 3, 805.

7. Cox, *Military Reminiscences,* 1:229–46.

8. Joseph Harsh, *Taken at the Flood: Robert E. Lee and Confederate Strategy in the Maryland Campaign of 1862* (Kent: Kent State University Press, 1999), 21; OR, vol. 19, part 2, 601–2; William Blair, "Maryland, My Maryland; or, How Lincoln and His Army Helped Define the Confederacy," in *The Antietam Campaign: Military Campaigns of the Civil War,* ed. Gary W. Gallagher (Chapel Hill: University of North Carolina Press, 1999), 74. On the issue of Union army views of Lee and the Confederates, see Michael Adams, *Our Masters the Rebels: A Speculation on Union Military Failure in the East, 1861–1865* (Cambridge, Mass.: Harvard University Press,

284   1978). For a discussion of foreign consideration of Confederate recognition, see Stephen Sears, *Landscape Turned Red: The Battle of Antietam* (New York: Ticknor and Fields, 1983), 166–67.

9. Jacob D. Cox, *The Second Battle of Bull Run, as Connected with the Fitz-John Porter Case* (Cincinnati: Peter G. Thompson, 1882); Cox to Helen Cox, September 4, 1862, Cox Papers; Sears, *Young Napoleon*, 263–65; Cox, *Military Reminiscences*, 1:259. The fact that the order to McClellan to take command was verbal and not documented in the Official Records would cause some problems later, although he had retained the command of the Army of the Potomac in any case.

10. OR, vol. 19, part 2, 226–27, 254–55; in the latter, McClellan wrote that even if the rebels took Washington, that was less important than if the army were defeated; Cox to Helen Cox, September 4, 1862, Cox Papers; D. Scott Hartwig, "Who Would Not Be a Soldier: The Volunteers of '62 in the Maryland Campaign," in Gallagher, *Antietam Campaign*, 147, 162; McClellan, "From the Peninsula to Antietam," 554.

11. Sears, *Civil War Papers of McClellan*, 357; Cox, *Military Reminiscences*, 1:264, 453; Marvel, *Burnside*.

12. Cox, *Military Reminiscences*, 1:265; Cox to Helen Cox, September 6, 1862, Cox Papers; Hayes to S. Birchard Hayes, September 7, 1862, in Williams, *Diary and Letters*, 2:347.

13. Cox to Helen Cox, September 10, 1862, Cox Papers; Cox, *Military Reminiscences*, 1:267–68. Sears notes Jeb Stuart's successful screening of the rebel forces against Union cavalry; see Sears, *Landscape Turned Red*, 103.

14. Marvel, *Burnside*, 112–30; Cox, *Military Reminiscences*, 1:268; Bascom to W.T. Bascom, September 10, 1862, Bascom-Little Papers; Diary of Sgt. John T. Booth, 36th Ohio, John T. Booth Papers, Ohio Historical Society, Columbus.

15. Cox, "Forcing Fox's Gap," in *Battles and Leaders*, 2:584; Willliams, *Diary and Letters*, 2:346–47; Diary of Hugh Ewing, September 7, 1862, in Hugh Boyle Ewing Papers (hereinafter cited as "H. B. Ewing Papers"), Ohio Historical Society, Columbus; Hayes to S. Birchard, September 8, 1862, in Williams, *Diary and Letters*, 2:348; Cox, *Military Reminiscences*, 1:269–70, 547–48. On September 4, 1882, Cox told Hayes that a history of the 21st Massachusetts regiment accused Hayes of pillaging and justified Reno's anger against him. Cox also wrote that someone had written a letter to the editor of the Boston "Journal" that a member of the 23rd regiment had killed Reno at South Mountain to prevent him from court-martialing Hayes. Hayes was appropriately angered, and he confirmed Cox's account of these incidents in a letter to Cox a few days later. Both letters are in the Cox Papers.

16. James Longstreet, "The Invasion of Maryland," in *Battles and Leaders*, 2:663–65; George B. McClellan, "From the Peninsula to Antietam," in *Battles and Leaders*, 2:552; OR, vol. 19, part 2, 189, 603–4; OR, vol. 19, part 1, 523, 757. Documents from the military inquiry into the failure to hold Harpers Ferry, which concluded that Miles, Wool, and McClellan (but not Halleck) were at fault, are in OR, vol. 19, part 1, 794–800.

17. OR, vol. 19, part 2, 219, 254–55; OR, vol. 19, part 1, 758; Sears, *Landscape Turned Red*, 106–10.

18. Cox, *Military Reminiscences,* 1:250–53. In his review of *McClellan's Own Story* in the *Nation* magazine (January 20, 1887, 57–58), Cox wrote that the fact that McClellan did not even address the issue of the numbers of forces on both sides was "an admittance of being wrong." Edwin C. Fishel used these quotations from Cox and came to the same conclusion, namely, "Someone did deceive General McClellan about enemy numbers, it was McClellan himself." See Fishel, "Pinkerton and McClellan: Who Deceived Whom?" *Civil War History* 34, no. 2 (September 1988): 118, 137, 142.

19. OR, vol. 19, part 2, 270–71; Sears, *Civil War Papers of McClellan,* 449–50.

20. Diary of Martin Sheets, Company A, 11th Reg., Ohio Volunteers, U.S. Army Historical Center, Carlisle, Pa.; Cox, "Forcing Fox's Gap," in *Battles and Leaders,* 2:583–84; Papers of Edwin E. Schweitzer, Captain, 30th Ohio Volunteer Regiment, in the U.S. Army Historical Center, Carlisle, Pa. See also John T. Booth's diary, Ohio Historical Society, Columbus; and Sears, *Civil War Papers of McClellan,* 450–52.

21. Cox, "Forcing Fox's Gap," 585.

22. OR, vol. 19, part 2, 270, 281–82, 603–4; Sears, *Civil War Papers of McClellan,* 456–57. It is unclear whether by "tomorrow" McClellan meant the fourteenth or the fifteenth. This message was sent at 11 p.m. on the thirteenth, but McClellan seems to have meant the battle would be on the fifteenth, because he made no preparations for it on the fourteenth.

23. John Gibbon, *Personal Recollections of the Civil War* (New York: G. P. Putnam's Sons, 1928), 73.

24. Cox, *Military Reminiscences,* 1:276–77, 302.

25. D. H. Hill, "The Battle of South Mountain, or Boonsboro," in *Battles and Leaders,* 2:565. Hill's comments were designed both to criticize Lee's plans and, implicitly, to add to the "Lost Cause" myth of Confederate steadfastness despite overwhelming odds.

26. Hill, "Battle of South Mountain," 559, 564–65; Cox, "Forcing Fox's Gap," 585. Hill spent much of the postwar years denying responsibility for losing the "Lost Order" and writing that it made little difference in any case; see Hal Bridges, *Lee's Maverick General: Daniel Harvey Hill* (Lincoln: University of Nebraska Press, 1991), 270–76.

27. Cox, "Forcing Fox's Gap," 586; Cox to Ezra Carman, January 22, 1897, Carman Papers, New York Public Library, copy provided by Thomas Clemens. In that letter, Cox told Carman, "I made the assault in the morning without any orders"; Sears, *Young Napoleon,* 288.

28. Cox, *Military Reminiscences,* 1:282–83; Cox to Helen Cox, September 16, 1862, Cox Papers; Bascom to W. T. Bascom, September 24, 1862, Bascom-Little Papers; OR, vol. 19, part 1, 458–61.

29. Cox, *Military Reminiscences,* 1:285; Cox to Ezra Carman, May 11, 1897, copy supplied by Thomas Clemens.

30. Hill, "Battle of South Mountain," 566–67; OR, vol. 19, part 1, 458–61 (Cox's report presumed that the imaginary force was real, stating, "The enemy withdrew their battery to a new position"); Cox, "Forcing Fox's Gap," 589–90; Cox, *Military Reminiscences,* 1:285.

31. Cox, *Military Reminiscences*, 1:291–92. Cox did not learn about Hooker's report until the Official Records were published in 1887. He wrote this section of the memoirs not only to defend his own honor against Hooker but also because it set the tone for events the next day when, he believed, Hooker conspired to be separated from Burnside's authority. Burnside's report, including his decision to send Hooker and Meade into action at South Mountain and his reaction to Hooker's lies, follows Hooker's report in OR, vol. 19, part 1, 213–16, 416–23. See also Diary of Hugh Ewing, September 14, 1862, in H. B. Ewing Papers; Cox to Helen Cox, September 22, 1862, Cox Papers; Cox, "Forcing Fox's Gap," 559; David S. Hartwig, *To Antietam Creek: The Maryland Campaign of 1862* (Baltimore, Md.: Johns Hopkins University Press, 2012), 430–31.

32. OR, vol. 19, part 1, 47–53; OR, vol. 19, part 2, 289, 294–95. For discussions of this series of events, see Sears, *Landscape Turned Red*, 150–58; Harsh, *Taken at the Flood*, 244–45; and Ezra A. Carman, *The Maryland Campaign of September 1862*, 2 vols., ed. Thomas G. Clemens (El Dorado Hills, Calif.: Savas Beatie, 2010, 2012), 1:368.

33. Cox to Helen Cox, September 16, 1862, Cox Papers.

34. Rafuse, *McClellan's War*, 301–4; OR, vol. 51, part 1, 834–37. Carman agrees that McClellan may have been satisfied by Lee's retreating back to Virginia; see Carman, *Maryland Campaign*, 1:423.

35. OR, vol. 19, part 2, 290 (the original order), states that Burnside was to command the right wing with two corps, "his own and Hooker's"; OR, vol. 19, part 2, 297, states that the previous order was to be temporarily suspended "owing to the necessary separation of the Third [First] corps" and that "General Hooker [would] report directly to these [McClellan's] headquarters."

36. Cox, *Military Reminiscences*, 1:380–83, 386–89. The latest author to echo Cox's interpretation of Porter's malice is Hartwig, who notes that McClellan "never offered a satisfactory explanation for his decision. Burnside's performance on the 14th certainly did not warrant it" (*To Antietam Creek*, 491–92). Hartwig adds that "it seems utterly fantastic . . . that McClellan might allow personal feelings to influence army operations at a critical point in the campaign . . . but this possibility must be considered, for from the morning of the 15th on, McClellan's once-warm relations with Burnside grew markedly cooler. One of the precepts of warfare is unity of command, but McClellan set about undoing that in the morning. The seeds he had sown would bear their unfortunate fruit over the next two days." He also notes, "Perhaps Fitz-John Porter influenced McClellan's actions. . . . By Porter's lights, Burnside could not be trusted and his loyalty to McClellan was questionable." For a discussion of the disruption to Sumner of the change to the wing structure, see Marion V. Armstrong, *Unfurl Those Colors: McClellan, Sumner, and the Second Army Corps in the Antietam Campaign* (Tuscaloosa: University of Alabama Press, 2008), 161–64. For plausible reasons for most of McClellan's and Porter's actions other than malice toward Burnside, see Ethan Rafuse, *McClellan's War*, and " 'Poor Burn?' The Antietam Conspiracy That Wasn't," *Civil War History* 54, no. 2 (June 2008): 146–75.

37. William Franklin, "Notes on Crampton's Gap and Antietam," *Battles and Leaders*, 2:596; OR, vol. 19, part 2, 296; OR, vol. 19, part 1, 47.

38. OR, vol. 19, part 2, 295; Cox, *Military Reminiscences*, 1:297, 383–84; George B. McClellan, *McClellan's Own Story* (New York: Charles L. Webster, 1887), 586.

39. OR, vol. 19, part 2, 296; Cox, *Military Reminiscences*, 1:297, 384, 388. Sears comments that Cox implied that Porter, "in the manner of an Iago, took his revenge by poisoning McClellan's mind against his old friend" (*Landscape Turned Red*, 259).

40. Cox, "The Battle of Antietam," in *Battles and Leaders*, 2:630–31; Cox, *Military Reminiscences*, 1:298; Hartwig, *To Antietam Creek*, 515. Lincoln's commentary about McClellan's "pets" Porter and Franklin is in OR, vol. 11, part 3, 154–55. Marvel writes that this was likely a very painful moment for Burnside; see Marvel, *Burnside*, 128.

41. Cox, *Military Reminiscences*, 1:354–55. Carmen commented that Key reportedly told a correspondent that McClellan's staff had discussed on September 13 marching to Washington to intimidate Lincoln to change his policies. Key took credit for stopping that initiative; see Carmen, *Maryland Campaign*, 1:422.

42. Cox, *Military Reminiscences*, 1:304; Sears, *Landscape Turned Red*, 259–60. An article in *Harper's Magazine* by one of McClellan's aides includes the following prescient analysis from his diary about the inaction of September 16: "I don't like the delay. We should have attacked on sight, Monday evening, or this morning at all risks. We might then have got Lee at a disadvantage. But while we take time to concentrate he will do the same or escape. If he is here tomorrow it will be because he feels quite confident of his game"; see David Strother, "Personal Recollections of the War by a Virginian, Tenth Paper," *Harper's Magazine* 23, no. 213 (February 1868): 281.

43. OR, vol. 19, part 2, 308. Cox describes these events in his memoirs (*Military Reminiscences*, 1:350, 384, 386–89); Porter's report can be found in OR, vol. 19, part 1, 338–41.

44. Cox, *Military Reminiscences*, 1:303–4.

45. Cox, *Military Reminiscences*, 1:303–4; Cox, "Battle of Antietam," 630–31; Cox to Helen, September 27, 1862, Cox Papers.

46. Cox, *Military Reminiscences*, 306–7. Rafuse defends McClellan's lack of holding councils of war, writing, "McClellan has been criticized for not issuing written orders or providing explicit verbal guidance to his subordinates laying out his intentions prior to the battle. This was a consequence of McClellan's desire—a commendable one given the unknowns he faced—to maintain maximum flexibility as the fighting developed and avoid committing himself to a course of action that circumstances might prove unwise" (*McClellan's War*, 310). See Hartwig's comment (note 36) that McClellan's actions harmed the "unity of command."

47. OR, vol. 19, part 1, 30, 55.

48. Cox, *Military Reminiscences*, 1:302, 350–53; Cox, "Battle of Antietam," 656–59; OR, vol. 19, part 2, 307–8; OR, vol. 51, part 1, 840; Sears, *Landscape Turned Red*, 175. Carmen notes that the cavalry "was not used" (*Maryland Campaign*, 2:21).

49. Harsh, *Taken at the Flood*, 571.

50. Cox, *Military Reminiscences*, 1:323–24; OR, vol. 19, part 1, 275.

51. Cox, *Military Reminiscences,* 1:331, 334. Douglas S. Freeman wrote, "Mercifully for the Confederates, the mismanagement of the battle by the Federals was such that" on several occasions it could have succeeded with just one more push; see Freeman, *Lee's Lieutenants* (New York: Simon and Schuster, 1998), 368.

52. OR, vol. 19, part 2, 314.

53. OR, vol. 51, part 1, 844. Cox's report of the battle is in OR, vol. 19, part 1, 423–27. For his descriptions of the battle, see Cox, "Battle of Antietam," 647–48, and *Military Reminiscences,* 1:334–39.

54. George B. McClellan, *Report on the Organization and Campaigns of the Army of the Potomac* (New York: G. Putnam's Sons, 1864), 634; Cox, *Military Reminiscences,* 335–37; *McClellan's Own Story,* 603. Maurice D'Aoust conjectured that the order was in fact sent at 8 a.m. and that Cox distorted the record. He cited only one source (and McClellan's second report, written to "correct the record" and also help his political career), while acknowledging that every other source places the timing at between 9 and 10. See D'Aoust, "Unraveling the Myth of Burnside Bridge," *Civil War Times Illustrated* 46, no. 7 (September 2007): 50–57.

55. Cox, "Battle of Antietam," 649–50. Most historians have agreed with Cox's assessment, e.g., Harsh, *Taken at the Flood,* 571.

56. Martin Schmidt, ed., *General George Crook: His Autobiography* (Norman: University of Oklahoma Press, 1946), 97. In the definitive biography of Crook, Paul Magid notes that Crook may have been "deliberately misrepresenting the facts to mitigate his subsequent failure to take the bridge"; see Magid, *George Crook: From the Redwoods to Appomattox* (Norman: University of Oklahoma Press, 2011), 145–46.

57. Letter from Sackett to McClellan, February 20, 1876, included in *McClellan's Own Story,* 609; Sears, *Landscape Turned Red,* 268.

58. David Strother, *Virginia Yankee in the Civil War: The Diaries of David Hunter Strother* (Chapel Hill: University of North Carolina Press, 1998), 110.

59. Cox, *Military Reminiscences,* 1:338–44.

60. Franklin, "Notes on Crampton's Gap and Antietam," in *Battles and Leaders,* 2:597. For a description of these events, see *McClellan's Own Story,* 600–604, and for McClellan's decision to stand fast, see his final report (OR, vol. 19, part 1, 62).

61. OR, vol. 19, part 2, 312 (the wording in this document talks about both flank movements being developed, even though the right flank had become dormant); Cox, "Battle of Antietam," 652–55. Sgt. (and future president) William McKinley was involved in getting rations to the men; see Armstrong, *Major McKinley,* 40–41.

62. Hartwig, "Who Would Not Be a Soldier," 162; Harsh, *Taken at the Flood,* 416–18; Cox, *Military Reminiscences,* 1:351; Sears, *Landscape Turned Red,* 286; OR, vol. 19, part 1, 138, 463; Personal Diary of Hugh Ewing, September 17, 1862, H. B. Ewing Papers; Cox to Helen Cox, September 22, 1862, Cox Papers.

63. OR, vol. 19, part 1, 426; Marvel, *Burnside,* 143.

64. Cox, "Battle of Antietam," 655–56; Cox to Helen Cox, September 22, 1862, Cox Papers.

65. Harsh, *Taken at the Flood,* 410–11; *Battles and Leaders,* 2:656n. The footnote was placed by the editors as part of the text of Cox's article, specifically referencing

his comment that "the conduct of the battle on the left has given rise to several criticisms, among which the most prominent has been that Porter's corps, which lay in reserve, was not put in at the same time with the Ninth Corps"; McPherson states that Porter's "testimony is suspect" (*Battle Cry of Freedom,* 544n).

66. Sears, *Civil War Papers of McClellan,* 467; Sears, *Landscape Turned Red,* 172; OR, vol. 51, part 1, 840, 845; OR, vol. 19, part 1, 212, 339; Carman, *Maryland Campaign,* 2:492. For a discussion of the ineffectiveness of cavalry charges in the "modern era," see Beringer et al., *Why the South Lost,* 14.

67. George Smalley, *New York Tribune,* September 19, 1862, as quoted in Sears, *Landscape Turned Red,* 291–92 (McClellan knew that Smalley would quote him and that likely was why he spoke histrionically); OR, vol. 51, part 1, 844. Rafuse agreed that McClellan had a chance to destroy Lee at this time, but Rafuse emphasized that McClellan's decisions not to use his reserves and cavalry were reasonable based on what he knew about his men and the Confederates; see Rafuse, *McClellan's War,* 326.

68. Cox to Helen Cox, September 22 and 27, 1862, Cox Papers. In the latter, Cox complained that he was in an anomalous position, because the published reports stated that Burnside commanded the 9th AC and Scammon his old division. He added, "As I am a modest man, this statement makes little difference to me and will not long endure." He presumably meant that the historical record would reflect reality.

69. OR, vol. 19, part 2, 322; Cox, *Military Reminiscences,* 1:349; Sears, *Landscape Turned Red,* 300, 302; Sears, *Civil War Papers of McClellan,* 468–69; Franklin, "Notes on Crampton's Gap," 597; Strother, "Personal Recollections," 285, 7. Strother notes that after he had left McClellan's staff, he wrote in his diary, "McClellan is the most capable man we have in military affairs [but] he wants force of character and is swayed by those around him. Fitz-John Porter with his elegant address and insinuating plausibility, technical power, and total want of judgment has been the evil genius, and has ruined him" (*Virginia Yankee,* 129).

70. OR, vol. 19, part 2, 330. For a discussion of this thesis, see Rafuse, *McClellan's War;* and Ethan Rafuse, "Toward a Better Understanding of George McClellan," *Civil War Times* 48, no. 3 (June 2009): 28–33.

71. Sears, *Civil War Papers of McClellan,* 375; Sears, *Landscape Turned Red,* 38; *McClellan's Own Story,* 85. For an assessment of whether McClellan and some of his supporters actively considered such a plot, see Richard Slotkin, *The Long Road to Antietam: How the Civil War Became a Revolution* (New York: Liveright Publishing, 2012). See also Michael Burlingame, ed., *Abraham Lincoln: The Observations of John G. Nicolay and John Hay* (Carbondale: Southern Illinois University Press, 2007), 114–15, which notes that Col. Key's brother was cashiered from the army by Lincoln after having allegedly said that McClellan purposely did not try to win at Antietam, in order to help ensure a draw with the Confederates as a way to stem the push to end slavery.

72. Cox to Helen Cox, September 27, 1862, Cox Papers; Cox, *Military Reminiscences,* 1:356–59. Cox told Ezra Carman that at the same service, "McClellan introduced [Cox] to the clergyman and some civilians as the officer to whom the

290   South Mountain success [was] officially due" (Cox to Carman, January 22, 1897, letter provided to the author by Thomas Clemens).

73. Cox, *Military Reminiscences,* 1:354–64; *McClellan's Own Story,* 652; OR, vol. 19, part 2, 395–96. Clemens wrote that "no evidence of McClellan's disloyalty has been presented. . . . Cox's political affiliations often color his memoirs, and this quotation [about McClellan's views] is an example of it" (*Maryland Campaign,* 2:421). That comment ignores the fact that Cox never said McClellan was disloyal, just weak for not ordering a stop to such talk. William B. Styple focuses on Key's role as McClellan's "evil genius" in *McClellan's Other Story* (Kearny, N.J.: Belle Grove Publishing, 2012).

74. OR, vol. 19, part 2, 627; Sears, *Civil War Papers of McClellan,* 477.

75. Cox to Helen Cox, October 9, 1862, Cox Papers; Cox, "President Lincoln at Antietam," May 2, 1894, speech to the Military Order of the Loyal Legion of the U.S., Cincinnati, 1894, copy in Cox Papers; Cox, *Military Reminiscences,* 1:365.

76. Cox to Helen Cox, September 27, 1862, Cox Papers; OR, vol. 19, part 2, 383–84; Salmon P. Chase, *Diary and Correspondence of Salmon P. Chase* (Washington, D.C.: Government Printing Office, 1903), 96.

77. OR, vol. 19, part 2, 380; Cox, *Military Reminiscences,* 1:391–92; Cox to Helen Cox, October 5 and 9, 1862, Cox Papers.

78. OR, vol. 19, part 2, 387, 394–95, 545–46. Cox described McClellan's approach to Lincoln's and Halleck's pushing him as "obstinacy of a feminine sort" (*Military Reminiscences,* 1:367). What he meant was that in the social mores of the times, women would never say "no" to a request but would always find ways to ensure that they did not have to ever say "yes" to a request they did not intend to accept.

79. Thomas Ewing to William T. Sherman, February 15, 1866, Thomas Ewing Papers, Ohio Historical Society, Columbus. Stanley Hirschon, in *The White Tecumseh: A Biography of General William T. Sherman* (New York: Wiley, 1998), 31, 150, notes Hugh Ewing's psychological problems and how they were an ongoing concern of his family. See also Kenneth Heinemann, *Civil War Dynasty: The Ewing Family of Ohio* (New York: New York University Press, 2012).

80. Schmidt, *General George Crook,* 100–101; Hugh Ewing to Thomas Ewing, October 1 and 7, 1862, Ewing Family Papers, LC. Cox recommended Hugh for a promotion to brigadier general, which he ultimately received.

81. Thomas Ewing to Hugh Ewing, October 9 and 12, 1862, H. B. Ewing Papers; for Ewing's orders, see OR, vol. 17, part 2, 550. See Hugh Ewing to Thomas Ewing, October 16 and 18, 1862, Ewing Family Papers, LC; Hugh Boyle Ewing Journal, entry for October 9, 1862, H. B. Ewing Papers (Hugh's journal said it was a barrel of "Old Rye"); Captain Edwin A. Schweitzer, diary entry for December 25, 1862, Schweitzer Papers, Carlisle, Pa., U.S. Army Historical Center.

82. Hugh Boyle Ewing Journal, entry for September 22, 1862, H. B. Ewing Papers; Schweitzer, diary entry for October 5, 1862, Schweitzer Papers, Carlisle, Pa., U.S. Army Historical Center (USAHC); Martin Sheets, 11th Ohio, diary entry for October 3[?], 1862, Martin Sheets Papers, USAHC. Schweitzer was in the 30th, Sheets in the 11th.

Chapter 4: Citizen/Political General

1. James A. Garfield to Lucy Garfield, October 7, 1862, in Smith, *Life and Letters*, 247.

2. Cox, *Military Reminiscences*, 1:400–401. Cox left behind a letter to Lincoln, dated October 7, 1862, in which he thanked Lincoln for his support; see OR, vol. 19, part 2, 311–12. For a description of the Confederate success in West Virginia in Cox's absence, see John Vance, "The Retreat of the Union Forces from the Kanawha Valley in 1862," in *Sketches of War History, 1861–1865,* ed. W. H. Chamberlain (Cincinnati: Robert Clarke, 1896), 4:118–32.

3. OR, vol. 16, part 2, 580; OR, vol. 19, part 2, 381, 422; Cox said Milroy was someone "in whose judgment [Cox] had less confidence than in that of any other of [his] subordinates" (*Military Reminiscences*, 1:445).

4. OR, vol. 19, part 2, 449, 529–37, 666–71, 684–91; Cox to Helen Cox, October 9, 14, 18, and 24 and November 1, 1862, Cox Papers; Harsh, *Taken at the Flood*, 479.

5. Cox to Helen Cox, November 24, 1862, Cox Papers; OR, vol. 19, part 2, 556; OR, 21:768, 778, 849, 855, 857, 943–44; Cox, *Military Reminiscences*, 1:426. West Virginia formally joined the Union on July 4, 1863.

6. Cox to Helen Cox, October 24, 1862, Cox Papers.

7. Cox to Perry, November 17 and December 18, 1862, Cox Papers.

8. Cox to Perry, February 9, 1863, Cox Papers.

9. Cox to Chase, April 24, 1863, Salmon P. Chase Papers, Historical Society of Pennsylvania. See also James McPherson, *The Negro's Civil War* (New York: Vintage Books, 1965), 161–92.

10. Cox to Charles F. Cox, July 2, 1862, Cox Papers.

11. Ethan Allen Hitchcock, *Fifty Years in Camp and Field: Diary of Major General Ethan Allen Hitchcock* (New York: G. P. Putnam's Sons, 1909), 445.

12. Cox to Chase, January 1, 1863, Cox Papers. For Cox's extended thoughts on these issues, see Cox, *Military Reminiscences*, 1:165–91.

13. Cox to E. A. Hitchcock, January 24, 1863, Cox Papers. See also Cox, *Military Reminiscences*, 1:438–41.

14. Cox, *Military Reminiscences*, 1:427–35; Cox to Chase, March 25, 1863, Salmon P. Chase Papers, Historical Society of Pennsylvania.

15. Hugh Boyle Ewing Journal, entry for October 9, 1862, H. B. Ewing Papers; Thomas Ewing to Hugh Ewing, March 12, 1863, Thomas Ewing Papers, Columbus; Garfield to Cox, December 14, 1864, Cox Papers; Frederick Williams, ed., *The Wild Life of the Army: Civil War Letters of James A. Garfield* (East Lansing: Michigan State University Press, 1964), 264–65; Cox, *Military Reminiscences*, 2:44.

16. Cox to Helen Cox, April 5, 1863, Cox Papers. This letter is evidence that he did not know of the Ewing family's actions and the resultant likelihood that Stanton was not going to help him.

17. Cox, *Military Reminiscences*, 1:443–45; OR, vol. 25, part 2, 175; Cox to Helen Cox, March 25, 1863, Cox Papers.

18. Cox, *Military Reminiscences*, 1:446, 449, 450–53; Summers, *Press Gang*, 65–67. Helen noted that she had visited Dolson in Cincinnati, "which . . . was enough in

292   itself to insure complete happiness" (Helen Cox to Lucy Garfield, July 19, 1863, Lucy Garfield Papers, LC).

19. Cox to Helen Cox, April 21 and 26, 1863, Cox Papers; OR, vol. 23, part 2, 237; Cox, *Military Reminiscences,* 1:454–57.

20. OR, Ser. 2, 5:633–46; OR, 23:316; Cox to Helen Cox, May 11 and June 7, 1863, Cox Papers; Cox, *Military Reminiscences,* 1:458–72.

21. Cox, *Military Reminiscences,* 1:495–509; Louis L. Tucker, *Cincinnati during the Civil War* (Columbus: Ohio State University Press, 1962); Cox to Helen Cox, August 12, 1863, Cox Papers; Allen Keller, *Morgan's Raid* (New York: Bobbs-Merrill, 1961).

22. Cox to Helen Cox, October 15, 1863, Cox Papers; OR, Ser. 3, 3:1023–25.

23. Cox, *Military Reminiscences,* 2:55; Cox to Helen Cox, October 24, 27 and 31 and November 5, 1863, Cox Papers.

24. OR, vol. 31, part 3, 314, 457; Cox to Garfield, December 6, 1863, Garfield Papers, LC; Cox to Helen Cox, December 4, 19, 1863, Cox Papers; Cox, *Military Reminiscences,* 2:67–83.

25. Cox, *Military Reminiscences,* 2:99; Longacre and Haas, *To Battle for God,* 149; Cox to Helen Cox, December 23 and 26, 1863. For a comprehensive study of this campaign, see Earl J. Hess, *The Knoxville Campaign: Burnside and Longstreet in East Tennessee* (Knoxville: University of Tennessee Press, 2012).

26. Cox to Helen Cox, February 2 and 26, 1864, Cox Papers; Special Order no. 41, HDQTRS, Dept. of Ohio, February 10, 1864, Cox Papers.

27. Cox to Helen Cox, February 11 and March 16, 1864, Cox Papers; Bascom to W. T. Bascom, April 8, 1864, Bascom-Little Papers.

28. Cox, *Military Reminiscences,* 2:140, 151–53; Cox to Helen Cox, February 11, 1864, Cox Papers; Cox to Perry, March 10, 1864, Cox Papers; OR, vol. 32, part 3, 105–6. In the letter to Perry, Cox described an example of Schofield's appreciation of his ideas. Cox wrote that he had suggested that the Army of the Ohio be ordered to Virginia to be a new right wing of Meade's forces. Schofield liked the idea and sent it on to Grant, but the latter was already committed to his own plan; see Donald B. Connelly, *John M. Schofield and the Politics of Generalship* (Chapel Hill: University of North Carolina Press, 2006), 86–87.

29. OR, vol. 32, part 3, 245–46, 312–14, 409; Cox to Helen Cox, April 6 and 16, 1864, Cox Papers.

Chapter 5: Division and Army Commander

1. Cox, *Atlanta,* 129, 210.

2. Cox, *Atlanta,* 50; OR, vol. 32, part 3: 245–46. Albert Castel's *Decision in the West: The Atlanta Campaign of 1864* (Lawrence: University Press of Kansas, 1992) has been recognized as the successor to Cox's book. While tilted against Sherman, this book's research is superb, and its analyses are well supported by documentation. Castel was critical of the "indirect method" and Liddell Hart (see B. H. Liddell Hart, *Strategy,* 131–34, in which he discusses his theories of warfare).

3. Cox, *Military Reminiscences,* 2:101–4, 203–6.

4. Joseph Johnston, *Narrative of Military Operations Directed during the Late War Between the States* (New York: D. Appleton, 1874), 298; OR, vol. 32, part 3, 666; Cox, *Atlanta,* 24.

5. Cox, *Military Reminiscences,* 2:200, 107; Cox to Helen Cox, April 24 and 26 and May 5, 1864, Cox Papers; Longacre and Haas, *To Battle for God,* 169–70.

6. Cox to Helen Cox, May 11 and 29, 1864, Cox Papers. Cox told Helen that Opdycke's brigade had suffered casualties, and he waited to finish the first letter until he could report that Opdycke was safe.

7. Cox, Diary, May 14–16, 1864, Cox Papers; Cox, *Military Reminiscences,* 2:222–23; Joseph Johnston, "Opposing Sherman's Advance to Atlanta," in *Battles and Leaders,* 4:267–68; Cox to Helen Cox, May 17, 1864, Cox Papers. In the latter Cox told Helen that he saw a wounded Opdycke being carried to the rear. The wound was not serious.

8. Cox, *Military Reminiscences,* 2:214; OR, vol. 38, part 4, 122.

9. Cox, *Military Reminiscences,* 2:235; OR, vol. 38, part 4, 243, 511; OR, vol. 38, part 2, 581, 610, 611; Cox to Helen Cox, May 17, 1864, Cox Papers; Longacre and Haas, *To Battle for God,* 161. Opdycke wrote to his wife, "Gen. Hascall spoke very appreciatively of Gen. Cox: 'I like Gen. Cox very much, he was so thorough, that he was never at fault. . . . Genl. Cox pleased us in all respects.'" Opdycke added, "I was very glad to hear a 'regular' officer speak thus of one we esteem so highly."

10. Cox, *Military Reminiscences,* 2:249–50. See also OR, vol. 38, part 4, 433, 439, 443, 448; Castel, *Decision in the West,* 265–66.

11. Cox, *Military Reminiscences,* 2:230–31. See also Johnston, "Opposing Sherman's Advance," 267–69; Castel, *Decision in the West,* 197–200; Cox, *Atlanta,* 55–56; OR, vol. 38, part 4, 242.

12. W. T. Sherman, *Personal Memoirs* (New York: Literary Classics of the United States, 1990), 2:511–13; Cox, *Military Reminiscences,* 2:237; OR, vol. 38, part 4, 273; Cox, *Atlanta,* 82–83. For a discussion of the evolution of defensive tactics and trench warfare, which presaged the fighting in World War I, see Hagerman, *American Civil War,* 175–210.

13. Cox, *Military Reminiscences,* 2:238, 242, 247, 249; Sherman, *Personal Memoirs,* 2:515; OR, vol. 38, part 4, 219, 408; Cox, *Atlanta,* 81–83; Cox to Helen Cox, June 3 and 5, 1864, Cox Papers; Castel, *Decision in the West,* 242; Johnston, "Opposing Sherman's Advance," 270.

14. Cox to Helen Cox, June 24, 1864, Cox Papers. See also Castel, *Decision in the West,* 264; Sherman, *Personal Memoirs,* 2:520, 523; OR, vol. 38, part 4, 408, 582; Cox, *Military Reminiscences,* 2:256–59; Sherman, *Personal Memoirs,* 2:524–25; Johnston, "Opposing Sherman's Advance," 270–72.

15. Cox, *Military Reminiscences,* 2:260; Cox, *Atlanta,* 117–18; Sherman, *Personal Memoirs,* 2:530–31; John M. Schofield, *Forty-Six Years in the Army* (New York: Century Company, 1897), 143–44; Castel, *Decision in the West,* 598; Cox to Helen Cox, June 29 and July 3, 1864, Cox Papers; OR, vol. 38, part 4, 607, 617–21; Connelly, *John M. Schofield,* 183; Johnston, "Opposing Sherman's Advance," 273; Earl J. Hess, *Kennesaw Mountain: Sherman, Johnston, and the Atlanta Campaign* (Chapel Hill: University of North Carolina Press, 2013), 138–44.

16. Sherman, *Personal Memoirs,* 2:539, 543–44; OR, vol. 38, part 5, 66, 85–90, 193; Cox to Helen Cox, July 10, 1864, Cox Papers; Cox, *Military Reminiscences,* 2:270.

17. OR, vol. 38, part 5, 885; Wiley Sword, *Embrace an Angry Wind: The Confederacy's Last Hurrah; Spring Hill, Franklin and Nashville* (New York: Harper Collins, 1992), 33 (for Howard's comments); Castel, *Decision in the West,* 344–58; Johnston, "Opposing Sherman's Advance," 274–77.

18. Cox, *Military Reminiscences,* 2:277; Cox, *Atlanta,* 149; Castel, *Decision in the West,* 364–65; John B. Hood, *Advance and Retreat* (New Orleans: G. T. Beauregard, 1880), 199.

19. Hood, "The Defense of Atlanta," in *Battles and Leaders,* 4:337–41; Cox, *Atlanta,* 150–58; OR, vol. 38, part 5, 208, 219, 900; Cox to Helen Cox, July 21, 1864, Cox Papers; Cox, *Military Reminiscences,* 2:280.

20. OR, vol. 38, part 5, 909. For an assessment of Hood's shortcomings as a general in chief, see Richard M. McMurry, *John Bell Hood and the War for Southern Independence* (Lincoln: University of Nebraska Press, 1962).

21. OR, vol. 38, part 5, 247, 289; Sherman, *Personal Memoirs,* 2:561; Cox to Helen Cox, July 27, 1864, Cox Papers; Hood, "Defense of Atlanta," 341; Cox, *Atlanta,* 183–87; Cox, *Military Reminiscences,* 2:280.

22. Cox, Diary, July 13 and 29, 1864, Cox Papers; Cox to Helen Cox, July 13, 1864, Cox Papers; Sherman, *Personal Memoirs,* 2:567–69; OR, vol. 38, part 5, 247, 259, 271.

23. Sherman, *Personal Memoirs,* 2:86; OR, vol. 38, part 5, 240, 272–73; OR, vol. 47, part 3, 532; Mrs. John A. Logan, *Reminiscences of a Soldier's Wife* (New York: Charles Scribner's Sons, 1913), 170–74; Castel, *Decision in the West,* 419. After the war, Logan would use his position as a senator to rail against West Point and Sherman.

24. Cox, *Atlanta,* 177–78; Cox, *Military Reminiscences,* 2:308; *Nation,* June 17, 1875, 411–12. A letter Sherman wrote to Cox (May 21, 1882, Cox Papers) illustrated that both Sherman and Cox "pulled their punches" in the Logan controversy. Sherman wrote, "I was disposed to leave Logan in command of the Army of the Tennessee and called Thomas and Schofield for consultation, . . . Thomas was unusually emphatic that he never could or would act in UNISON with Logan, in fact that he would not stay if he was to be brought in contact with him as an equal. . . . His army was so large that I could not risk his displeasure . . . and I had to stand the brunt of Logan's anger and hatred." Sherman added, not surprisingly, "On this point I am still satisfied with your text."

25. OR, vol. 38, part 5, 354–59, 364–66, 368–72, 378–85, 391–94, 438; Cox, *Atlanta,* 189–94; Cox, Diary, August 4–7, Cox Papers; Cox to Helen Cox, August 7, 1864, Cox Papers. Palmer's dereliction of duty did not harm his political career— he was later elected both governor of and U.S. senator from Illinois.

26. Cox to Helen Cox, August 7, 1864, Cox Papers; OR, vol. 38, part 5, 940–43, 946; Hood, "Defense of Atlanta," 342; Cox, *Atlanta,* 196.

27. Sherman, *Personal Memoirs,* 2:576–77; Cox, *Atlanta,* 196–98; Cox, *Military Reminiscences,* 2:299; OR, vol. 38, part 5, 642, 649; Cox, Diary, August 26, Cox Papers.

28. OR, vol. 38, part 5, 990–93; OR, vol. 38, part 3, 691–93; Cox, *Atlanta,* 197–98; Castel, *Decision in the West,* 486–87 (Castel dismissed the idea that Hood

was deluded about Sherman's possible retreat, but for almost two days Hood took few steps to find out where Sherman was going); Hood, "Defense of Atlanta," 343; Cox, *Military Reminiscences*, 2:526–27.

29. Cox, *Atlanta*, 198–203; Cox, *Military Reminiscences*, 2:282; Hood, "Defense of Atlanta," 343; OR, vol. 38, part 3, 703, 717–21, 733–35, 764–65; Nathaniel Gorgas to his father, September 10, 1864, Nathaniel Gorgas Papers, Ohio Historical Society, Columbus.

30. OR, vol. 38, part 3, 732–35; OR, vol. 38, part 5, 1021–23; Hood, "Defense of Atlanta," 343; Cox to Helen Cox, September 8, 1864, Cox Papers.

31. McPherson, *Battle Cry of Freedom*, 760–73.

32. OR, vol. 38, part 5, 717–21, 771, 791, 801, 1023; Hood, "Defense of Atlanta," 344; Castel, *Decision in the West*, 506–7; Cox, *Atlanta*, 208–9; Cox to Helen Cox, September 8, 1864, Cox Papers; Sherman, "The Grand Strategy of the Last Year of the War," in *Battles and Leaders*, 4:254.

33. Cox to Helen Cox, September 8, 1864; OR, vol. 39, part 2, 355–58, 370–71, 414–22; OR, vol. 38, part 5, 822; OR, Ser. 2, 7:791; Sherman, *Personal Memoirs*, 2:591–602, 612; Cox, *Atlanta*, 220–21.

34. Hood, *Advance and Retreat*, 254; OR, vol. 39, part 2, 846–47, 862, 880.

35. Hood, *Advance and Retreat*, 206, 252–53; Sherman, *Personal Memoirs*, 2:615–17; OR, vol. 39, part 2, 501, 880; OR, vol. 38, part 5, 1023–24; Castel, *Decision in the West*, 551; Arthur Manigault, *A Carolinian Goes to War: The Civil War Narrative of Arthur Middleton Manigault, Brigadier General, CSA* (Columbia: University of South Carolina Press, 1983), 276–77; J. A. W. Wright, "Hood's Nashville Campaign," in *New Annals of the Civil War*, ed. Peter Cozzens (New York: Stackpole Books, 2004), 472–73.

36. OR, vol. 39, part 2, 366, 540; OR, vol. 39, part 3, 6, 10, 413; Cox, *Atlanta*, 223–24; Cox to Helen Cox, October 17, 1864, Cox Papers; Cox, *Military Reminiscences*, 2:320–22.

37. Cox, *Atlanta*, 225–39; Sherman, "Grand Strategy," 255; Castel, *Decision in the West*, 552–53; Hood, *Advance and Retreat*, 263–64.

38. Cox, *Military Reminiscences*, 2:330–31.

39. OR, vol. 39, part 3, 11, 13; Sherman, "Grand Strategy," 254; Cox, *Military Reminiscences*, 2:312–20.

40. OR, vol. 38, part 5, 793; Cox to Helen Cox, October 17 and 22, 1864, Cox Papers; Cox, *Military Reminiscences*, 3:320–22. Connelly discusses the reasons for Schofield's absence. Connelly opined that "the forward looking" Sherman interpreted Schofield's "rearward orientation" as troubling; see Connelly, *John M. Schofield*, 116–20.

41. Cox to Helen Cox, October 27, 1864, Cox Papers; OR, vol. 39, part 3, 357–58, 377–78, 511, 534, 535, 537, 594–95; Cox, Diary, October 30, 1864, Cox Papers.

Chapter 6: Citizen-Warrior

1. Levi Scofield, *The Retreat from Pulaski to Nashville, Tenn.: Battle of Franklin, Tennessee, Nov. 30, 1864* (Cleveland: Press of the Caxton Co., 1909), 38. Other reports of an emotional Cox at this critical moment at the Battle of Franklin

296   include the following. Henry Stone wrote, "General Cox was everywhere present, encouraging and cheering on his men" ("Repelling Hood's Invasion of Tennessee," in *Battles and Leaders*, 4:452). Opdycke told his wife, "I saw Genl. Cox during the battle with his hat off, rallying the stragglers under a terrific fire" (quoted in Longacre and Haas, *To Battle for God*, 250). By contrast, typically Cox made no mention of this event in his first book about Franklin, *Sherman's March to the Sea: Hood's Tennessee Campaign and the Carolina Campaigns of 1865* (New York: Charles Scribner's Sons, 1882). In his *Battle of Franklin, Tennessee, November 30, 1864: A Monograph* (New York: Charles Scribner's Sons, 1897), Cox only stated, "Changing my direction toward Opdycke's brigade, I passed the flank of his advancing line, and on the turnpike, urging his brave men to redoubled exertion, I joined Colonel Opdycke himself" (98).

   2. OR, vol. 39, part 3, 64–65, 638, 666, 684, 703; Schofield, *Forty-Six Years*, 160.

   3. Sherman to Cox, May 27, 1882, Cox Papers; Cox, *Military Reminiscences*, 2:328; Cox to Helen Cox, November 3 and 17, 1864, Cox Papers.

   4. Cox, *Sherman's March*, 11–19; Cox, *Battle of Franklin*, 4–6; Stone, "Repelling Hood's Invasion," 441; Hood, *Advance and Retreat*, 276–78; Cox, *Military Reminiscences*, 2:338; OR, vol. 45, part 1, 1215, 1220, 1225, 1226, 1236.

   5. OR, vol. 45, part 1 contains Thomas's report of his forces (52), Hood's report of his forces (678–79), and Thomas's report of the campaign, with his estimates of the forces and a summary of his strategy (32–46).

   6. OR, vol. 39, part 3, 535, 768; OR, vol. 45, part 1, 32, 1159; Cox, *Sherman's March*, 64.

   7. Sherman to Cox, May 27, 1882, Cox Papers; Cox, *Military Reminiscences*, 2:343, 346; Cox, *Sherman's March*, 131–36; OR, vol. 45, part 1, 33. Schofield made a similar assessment in his memoirs (*Forty-Six Years*, 195–96). These sentiments by Schofield and Cox were part of a postwar conflict between advocates of Thomas and his Army of the Cumberland on one side and Schofield, Sherman, Cox, and others on the other. Historian Brooks Simpson, in his introduction to Cox's book *Sherman's March*, wrote of Cox's analysis, "[T]o the modern reader it seems a rather balanced assessment." (xvii). Even Henry Stone, one of Thomas's aides, implicitly admits in his "Repelling Hood's Invasion" that Thomas's uncertainty led to Schofield having far fewer troops than Hood did.

   8. Cox, *Military Reminiscences*, 2:334; OR, vol. 45, part 1, 955–58; Hood, *Advance and Retreat*, 328; Schofield, *Forty-Six Years*, 166–67; Cox, Diary, November 17, 1864, Cox Papers. Longacre notes that on November 17 Cox and Opdycke had "a quiet chat over public affairs and personal prospects," and Opdycke wrote to his wife, "It seems to me that Mr. Lincoln will not fail to do justice to Gen Cox' claims to promotion very soon"; see Longacre and Haas, *To Battle for God*, 246.

   9. OR, vol. 45, part 1, 339–45 is the relevant section of Schofield's report.

   10. OR, vol. 45, part 1, 958, 989, 998; Schofield, *Forty-Six Years*, 167–68; Cox, *Military Reminiscences*, 2:340; Cox, *Sherman's March*, 65.

   11. Cox to Helen Cox, November 27, 1864, Cox Papers; OR, vol. 45, part 1, 1015–17, 1019–21; Hood, *Advance and Retreat*, 282; Schofield, *Forty-Six Years*, 168. In his memoirs, Schofield dismissed Cox's actions as a "brush with the enemy's

cavalry," though he had reported officially to Thomas, "Cox arrived just in time to beat it back, and punished it pretty severely." In *John M. Schofield,* Connelly posits that Schofield wrote his memoirs in ways that enhanced his own actions and diminished those of others. James H. Wilson does not mention his own mistakes; see Wilson, "The Union Cavalry in the Hood Campaign," in *Battles and Leaders,* 4:465–71. See also Boatner, *Civil War Dictionary,* 930–31.

12. OR, vol. 45, part 1, 358, 1017, 1039, 1086–91; Cox, *Military Reminiscences,* 2:344; Cox, Diary, November 27, 1864, Cox Papers; Schofield, *Forty-Six Years,* 175; Hood, *Advance and Retreat,* 282.

13. OR, vol. 45, part 2, 289–90; OR, vol. 45, part 1, 1107–8, 1138; Schofield, *Forty-Six Years,* 175–76; Connelly, *John M. Schofield,* 125. It seems clear that Schofield should have stated definitively that he had destroyed his pontoons.

14. OR, vol. 45, part 1, 1109–16; Hood, *Advance and Retreat,* 283–84.

15. Hood, *Advance and Retreat,* 283; OR, vol. 45, part 1, 1106–8, 1137, 1144–45; Cox, *Battle of Franklin,* 24–26; Schofield, *Forty-Six Years,* 217; Cox, *Sherman's March,* 69; Cox, *Military Reminiscences,* 2:350. Wilson's biographer, Edward Longacre, agrees that Wilson was befuddled and made just about every possible misstep; see Longacre, *Grant's Cavalryman: The Life and Wars of General James H. Wilson* (Mechanicsburg, Pa.: Stackpole Books, 1972), 168–74.

16. OR, vol. 45, part 1, 1111–16, 1137, 1143–44; Cox, *Military Reminiscences,* 2:348; Hood, *Advance and Retreat,* 284; Cox, Diary, November 28, 1864, Cox Papers; Cox to Helen Cox, December 2, 1864, Cox Papers.

17. OR, vol. 45, part 1, 1138–42; Cox to Helen Cox, December 2, 1864, Cox Papers.

18. Cox, *Sherman's March,* 73–76; Stone, "Repelling Hood's Invasion," 444–45; Cox, *Battle of Franklin,* 31–32; Longacre and Haas, *To Battle for God,* 249–50; B. F. Cheatham, "General Cheatham at Spring Hill," in *Battles and Leaders,* 4:438.

19. Hood, *Advance and Retreat,* 286; OR, vol. 45, part 1, 713; Cheatham, "General Cheatham," 438; Sam D. Elliott, *Soldier of Tennessee: General Alexander P. Stewart and the Civil War in the West* (Baton Rouge: Louisiana State University Press, 2004), 228–34. Connelly writes that Schofield was very lucky on November 28–29, "but his vanity refused to accept it" (i.e., in his memoirs Schofield was dismissive of the threat Hood had presented); see Connelly, *John M. Schofield,* 132. See also Sword, *Confederacy's Last Hurrah,* 136; and Brian Craig Miller, *John Bell Hood and the Fight for Civil War Memory* (Knoxville: University of Tennessee Press, 2010), 153.

20. Cox, *Battle of Franklin,* 34; OR, vol. 45, part 1, 342, 1138; Stone, "Repelling Hood's Invasion," 448; Schofield, *Forty-Six Years,* 174; Cox, *Sherman's March,* 79.

21. Hood, *Advance and Retreat,* 287; Cheatham, "General Cheatham," 439; Cox, *Sherman's March,* 79; Schofield, *Forty-Six Years,* 173; Scofield, *Retreat from Pulaski,* 21; Cox to Helen Cox, December 2, 1864, Cox Papers. Cox's copy of Hood's memoirs is in the Cox Papers.

22. Schofield, *Forty-Six Years,* 175; Cox, *Battle of Franklin,* 38. November 29 was the Coxes' fifteenth wedding anniversary.

23. Cox, *Battle of Franklin,* 39; OR, vol. 45, part 1, 1172; Cox to Helen Cox, December 2, 1864, Cox Papers.

24. Richard M. McMurry, *John Bell Hood and the War for Southern Independence* (Lincoln: University of Nebraska Press, 1962), 167, 174; James Lee McDonough, *Nashville: The Western Confederacy's Final Gamble* (Knoxville: University of Tennessee Press, 2004), 93–98; Elliott, *Soldier of Tennessee*, 228–34; Hood, *Advance and Retreat*, 289–91.

25. Miller, *John Bell Hood*, 152–54; Hood, *Advance and Retreat*, 291; OR, vol. 45, part 1, 657–68, 743; Castel argued that "even the stupidest frontal assault of the war, Burnside's at Fredericksburg and Hood's at Franklin, took place *after* (and in large part because) these generals had tried in vain to outflank the opposing army. . . . [N]o matter how foolish these attacks seem in retrospect, the general who ordered them believed they were the best, if not the only way to achieve the sort of tactical success he wanted" (Castel, "Mars and the Reverend Longstreet, or Attacking and Dying in the Civil War," in *Winning and Losing in the Civil War*, ed. Albert Castel [Columbia: University of South Carolina Press, 1996], 128–29). In fact, both Forrest and Schofield deduced that a renewed flank attack was the best option for the Confederates, and Cox noted that an attack to his right wing would have been a far better approach.

26. Cox, *Battle of Franklin*, 50; OR, vol. 45, part 1, 1168–71.

27. Cox, *Battle of Franklin*, 48–49, 59–60.

28. Cox, *Sherman's March*, 84–85, 88; Cox, *Battle of Franklin*, 53, 60; Hood, *Advance and Retreat*, 293. OR, vol. 45, part 1 contains the reports: Cox's report of the battle (349–56) goes into detail about forming the line; the part of Lee's report about Cox's work is on page 688; and Hood's report is on pages 652–56. This is only one of the many attempts by Hood to distort history, and it implicitly underlines his poor planning and impulsiveness. For a description of the topography and the barriers that had previously been formed on the battlefield, see James Lee McDonough, *Five Tragic Hours: The Battle of Franklin* (Knoxville: University of Tennessee Press, 1983), 79–80.

29. OR, vol. 45, part 1, 342–44, 352; Cox, *Sherman's March*, 87; Connelly, *John M. Schofield*, 133; Sword, *Confederacy's Last Hurrah*, 198.

30. Cox describes the background and orders regarding the imbroglio between Wagner and Opdycke in *Battle of Franklin*, 64–82. Cox's orders and report are in OR, vol. 45, part 1, 352, 1174; Opdycke's report is in OR, vol. 45, part 1, 239–41. Connelly notes that Cox's account is the best summary of these events; see Connelly, *John M. Schofield*, 138–39. Sword (in *Confederacy's Last Hurrah*, 170–75) says that "from the evidence," Cox likely told Wagner that the gathering rebel forces were probably just a sham and a deception, implying that that was one of the reasons Wagner was willing to hold the line. Sword cites no evidence for this statement. While Cox did not think Hood would make a frontal attack, he was prepared for one (note Wagner's comment about the strong defenses). Thus, "from the evidence," Sword's interpretation seems unsubstantiated.

31. OR, vol. 45, part 1, 352. Theodore Cox's statement, dated June 16, 1881, is in Cox, *Battle of Franklin*, 336; Cox's comment is on page 79 of that book. For a discussion of Wagner's drinking, see Connelly, *John M. Schofield*, 138; and Sword, *Confederacy's Last Hurrah*, 190.

32. Cox, *Battle of Franklin*, 87–92; Hood, *Advance and Retreat*, 293; OR, vol. 45, part 1, 653.

33. Cox, *Battle of Franklin*, 92; Cox, *Sherman's March*, 88; OR, vol. 45, part 1, 653–64, 269–70; Schofield, *Forty-Six Years*, 178; Cox to Helen Cox, December 2, 1864, Cox Papers. Hood wrote in both his report and his memoirs that he had decided not to use artillery because of the danger of hitting women and children in the town—something which Sherman had done when he bombarded Atlanta. Cox wrote in the margins of his copy of Hood's memoirs that this was "not true"; Cox noted, "I saw them fire & the Confed. records show they did." Also, Hood said in his report that he intended to use all of his artillery the next day if there were a battle.

34. Cox to Helen Cox, December 2, 1864, Cox Papers; OR, vol. 45, part 1, 358; Hood, *Advance and Retreat*, 293–94; Cox, *Sherman's March*, 89–91; Cox, *Battle of Franklin*, 96. Cox's preliminary report is in OR, vol. 45, part 1, 348–49, and his final report follows immediately thereafter to 356. The latest, and among the best, works to look at this battle in depth are Eric Jacobsson and Richard A. Rupp's *For Cause and Country: A Study of the Affair at Spring Hill and the Battle of Franklin* (Franklin, Tenn.: O'More Publishing, 2008) and, by the same authors, *Baptism of Fire: The 44th Missouri, 175th Ohio and 183rd Ohio at the Battle of Franklin* (Franklin, Tenn.: O'More Publishing, 2011).

35. OR, vol. 45, part 1, 353; Cox, *Sherman's March*, 89.

36. Thomas Speed, "The Battle of Franklin," in *Sketches of War History* (Columbus, 1890), 3:78. For an in-depth analysis of the movement of Union forces to meet this challenge, see Jacobson, *Baptism of Fire*, 151–81.

37. Cox, *Battle of Franklin*, 96–97.

38. Cox to Helen Cox, December 2, 1864, Cox Papers; Longacre and Haas, *To Battle for God*, 249–50; Cox, *Battle of Franklin*, 96–97; OR, vol. 45, part 1, 240; Charles Clark, *Opdycke Tigers, 125th O.V.I., A History of the Regiment* (Columbus: Spahr and Glenn, 1895), 327–45.

39. Cox, *Sherman's March*, 95; OR, vol. 45, part 1, 354; Cox to Helen Cox, December 2, 1864, Cox Papers.

40. Cox noted that several of his men had repeater rifles, which made their ability to keep up a constant "sheet of fire" that much easier. However, he also said that the men using muskets were almost able to keep up with the repeaters because the ranks were three to four deep and those in the rear kept reloading and passing ready-to-shoot muskets to the front; see Cox, *Battle of Franklin*, 218. See also Cox, *Sherman's March*, 91–94; OR, vol. 45, part 1, 343–55; Samuel Rush Watkins, *Company Aytch; or, A Side Show of the Big Show, and Other Sketches* (Nashville: Cumberland Presbyterian Publishing House, 1882), 202; McDonough, *Five Tragic Hours*, 158.

41. Cox, *Battle of Franklin*, 11, 167.

42. OR, vol. 45, part 1, 1171–74; Cox, *Battle of Franklin*, 169, 192, 338; Schofield, *Forty-Six Years*, 187–88; Cox to Helen Cox, December 2, 1864, Cox Papers. In *Battle of Franklin*, 195–96, Cox made the case again for staying in Franklin.

43. OR, vol. 45, part 2, 628, 643–44; OR, vol. 45, part 1, 653–54; Hood, *Advance and Retreat*, 298–99.

44. Watkins, *Company Aytch,* 218; Wright, "Hood's Nashville Campaign," 472–73.

45. Union reports of casualties on both sides are in OR, vol. 45, part 1, 35, 343–47, and 356. On page 650 of that volume is a statement from Confederate General Beauregard noting that Hood did not supply an official report of the campaign.

46. Hood, *Advance and Retreat,* 299; OR, vol. 45, part 1, 654; OR, vol. 45, part 2, 640; Cox to Helen Cox, December 2 and 5, 1864, Cox Papers; Cox, *Sherman's March,* 102.

47. OR, vol. 45, part 1, 348–49; Cox to Helen Cox, December 2, 1864, Cox Papers; Cox to Opdycke, December 2, 1881, Cox Papers.

48. Longacre and Haas, *To Battle for God,* 254, 256–57, 261, 270, 272, 275; OR, vol. 45, part 1, 240.

49. Cox, *Battle of Franklin,* 222–32; OR, vol. 45, part 1, 229–33, 269–72, 343, 409. The latter is Cox's commendation of Opdycke's actions at Franklin, addressed directly from Cox to Thomas. Later, Cox could point to this communication as evidence of his status as commandant on the line. The most vehement critic of Cox was John K. Shellenberger, whose *The Battle of Franklin, Tennessee* (Cleveland: Arthur H. Clarke, 1916) blamed Schofield, Stanley, and Cox for putting him and his men in that difficult position. Schofield was not as understanding as Cox, stating in his memoirs that Wagner and his subordinates should have been court-martialed; see Schofield, *Forty-Six Years,* 180–82. Connelly believed that if Schofield had brought charges, he, along with Cox and Stanley, could have been adjudged guilty of complacency; see Connelly, *John M. Schofield,* 139.

50. OR, vol. 45, part 2, 117; OR, vol. 45, part 1, 349–56; Cox, *Battle of Franklin,* 230–32. Stanley's report is in OR, vol. 45, part 1, 112–18.

51. OR, vol. 45, part 2, 58, 72, 86, 104; Cox, *Military Reminiscences,* 2:357–58.

52. Hood, *Advance and Retreat,* 298–99; OR, vol. 45, part 2, 15–20, 84. Stone describes some of the problems Thomas was facing; see Stone, "Repelling Hood's Invasion of Tennessee," 454–56. See also Sword, *Confederacy's Last Hurrah,* 290–93, 318.

53. Connelly, *John M. Schofield,* 139–40; Schofield, *Forty-Six Years,* 226–27, 238; OR, vol. 45, part 2, 18, 114. For a discussion of the allegations against Schofield and the dispute, see Sword, *Confederacy's Last Hurrah,* 311–12; and Connelly, *John M. Schofield,* 149–54. There are no records of Schofield trying to undermine Thomas.

54. OR, vol. 45, part 2, 194, 202; OR, vol. 45, part 1, 405–7, 699; Cox, *Sherman's March,* 115, 122–23; Watkins, *Company Aytch,* 213–16; Sword, *Confederacy's Last Hurrah,* 313–17; Hood, *Advance and Retreat,* 303; Cox to Helen Cox, December 21, 1864, Cox Papers.

55. Cox, *Military Reminiscences,* 2:367–68, 371–72; OR, vol. 45, part 1, 360; Cox to Helen Cox, December 21, 1864, Cox Papers. During this movement Cox passed through Franklin and, as described in his memoirs, mused about the desperation of Hood's men as they charged his defensive line.

56. Watkins, *Company Aytch,* 216, 218; Cox, *Sherman's March,* 126; OR, vol. 45, part 1, 361, 402–3; Cox to Helen Cox, January 2 and 13, 1865, Cox Papers; Cox, *Military Reminiscences,* 2:385; OR, vol. 45, part 2, 295, 419–20, 441–42, 481, 529, 781. The latter document contains Hood's resignation from command, dated January 13.

57. OR, vol. 45, part 2, 377–78, 519, 540, 560, 568, 586; Schofield, *Forty-Six Years*, 254–55; Cox, *Military Reminiscences*, 2:379; J. D. Cox III, *Building an American Industry*, 33. In an example of the pettiness of such disputes, Schofield's request to leave the West would be seen by Thomas's partisans as yet another attack on their commander, because Schofield was "abandoning" him.

58. OR, vol. 47, part 2, 131, 154–56; Cox, *Diary*, January 30–February 2, 1865, Cox Papers; Cox, *Military Reminiscences*, 2:390–91.

59. Perry to Cox, May 13, 1865, Cox Papers; Cox, *Military Reminiscences*, 2:395–99.

60. Cox to Helen Cox, February 2, 1865, Cox Papers; Cox, *Military Reminiscences*, 2:396; McPherson, *Battle Cry of Freedom*, 838–40.

61. Cox to Helen Cox, February 3, 8, and 11, 1865; Special order no. 7, Hdqtrs., Department of North Carolina, February 17, 1865, Cox Papers; OR, vol. 47, part 1, 910–11, 927–31; Cox, *Sherman's March*, 147–54; Cox, *Military Reminiscences*, 2:42, 417. Terry was a political general who, unlike Cox, decided to stay in the army after the war once he was given a commission as a brigadier general in the regular army.

62. Cox, *Military Reminiscences*, 2:420; OR, vol. 47, part 2, 1247–48, 1256–57, 1271.

63. Cox to Helen Cox, February 25 and March 2 and 12, 1865, Cox Papers; Cox, *Military Reminiscences*, 2:427, 430–44; Cox, *Sherman's March*, 155, 161; Cox, *Diary*, March 8–10, 1865, Cox Papers; OR, vol. 47, part 2, 559, 579–80, 772, 803, 1359, 1361, 1364, 1366; OR, vol. 47, part 1, 973–80.

64. Cox, *Military Reminiscences*, 2:445, 451–53; Cox to Helen Cox, March 17, 1865, Cox Papers; OR, vol. 47, part 1, 44, 1055; OR, vol. 47, part 2, 948–49, 960–61; OR, vol. 47, part 3, 18, 20, 34, 68.

65. OR, vol. 47, part 3, 129, 140; A. J. Ricks, "Carrying the News of Lee's Surrender to the Army of the Ohio," in *Sketches of War History* (Cincinnati, 1890), 2:235; Cox, *Diary*, April 12, 1865, Cox Papers.

66. OR, vol. 47, part 3, 151, 177, 206–7, 221; Cox, *Diary*, April 18, 1865, Cox Papers; Cox, *Military Reminiscences*, 2:485–86.

67. OR, vol. 47, part 3, 323, 672; Cox, *Diary*, May 1–5, 1865, Cox Papers. It was during this period that W. J. Hardee told Schofield and Cox the story about Cox's alleged cursing at Atlanta. See Cox, *Military Reminiscences*, 2:526–27.

68. Cox, *Diary*, May 8, 1865, Cox Papers; Cox, *Military Reminiscences*, 2:540–41.

69. Cox, *Military Reminiscences*, 2:540, 542–48; OR, vol. 47, part 3, 535. See also Mark L. Bradley, *Bluecoats and Tarheels: Soldiers and Civilians in Reconstruction North Carolina* (Lexington: University Press of Kentucky, 2007).

70. For the recommendations, see OR, vol. 45, part 2, 273–74. Cox wrote to Garfield to advise him about Franklin and ask "Did Sherman's recommendation get to Lincoln and can I get promoted?" Garfield responded a few days later that Stanton told him Cox's name would be put on the promotion list; Cox to Garfield, December 6, 1864, Cox Papers; Garfield to Cox, December 14, 1864, Garfield Papers, LC.

71. Cochran, "Political Experiences," 2:881.

72. Cox to Schofield, July 12, 1866, Schofield Papers, LC.

Chapter 7: From Citizen-General to State and National Political Leader

1. Knepper, *Ohio and Its Peoples*, 246; Roseboom, *Civil War Era*, 444–45.

2. Jacob D. Cox, *Reconstruction and the Relations of the Races in the United States* (Columbus: Ohio State Journal Press, 1865), 10 (hereinafter referred to as the "Oberlin Letter").

3. Porter, *Ohio Politics*, 204–7; *Cincinnati Commercial*, May 1, 1865; Cox to Garfield, June 1, 1865, Garfield Papers, LC; Perry to Cox, May 13, 1865, Cox Papers; *Cleveland Leader*, June 19, 1865.

4. Sherman, *Personal Memoirs*, 2:723–30; Joseph Glatthaar, *The March to the Sea and Beyond* (New York: New York University Press, 1985), 52–65; McPherson, *Battle Cry of Freedom*, 841–42; OR, vol. 47, part 2, 60–62; Cox, *Military Reminiscences*, 2:470–71. Some in Washington were also upset when they heard that Sherman's troops were complaining that blacks were receiving favorable treatment from the federal government as part of the Port Royal Experiment, a public-private partnership in South Carolina that had created a fully functional black community on land abandoned by its white owners. This project is discussed in Willie Lee Rose, *Rehearsal for Reconstruction: The Port Royal Experiment* (Indianapolis: Bobbs-Merrill, 1964).

5. OR, vol. 47, part 3, 405, 427–30.

6. OR, vol. 47, part 3, 410–12, 440, 461–63; Sherman, *Personal Memoirs*, 2:373–74.

7. Nicholas Guyatt, "A Vast Negro Reservation: Black Colonization in the Postbellum United States, 1863–1871," unpublished ms., 2012, 6, 16; a copy of Goodloe's pamphlet is in the Cox papers. For an analysis of how the ideological bases of men such as Cox guided the formation of national policy after the war, see Richardson, *Death of Reconstruction* and, by the same author, *West from Appomattox: The Reconstruction of America after the Civil War* (New Haven, Conn.: Yale University Press, 2007). Nicholas Guyatt posits that internal colonization had been discussed in some circles for many decades before the war, and so Cox's advocacy of it was not as extreme as might seem at first; see Guyatt, "'An Impossible Idea?' The Curious Case of Internal Colonization," to be published in 2014.

8. Cox to Perry, December 18, 1862, and February 9, 1863, Cox Papers.

9. Cox, Diary, May 12, 1865, Cox Papers.

10. Cox to Perry, May 25, 1865, Cox Papers.

11. Judge W. M. Dickson to Cox, June 17, 1865, Cox Papers; Perry to Cox, June 4, 1865, Cox Papers; Cox to Perry, June 12, 1865, Cox Papers. For a description of Johnson's Reconstruction policy, see Eric McKitrick, *Andrew Johnson and Reconstruction* (Chicago: University of Chicago Press, 1960), 19–20, 48–51; and Kenneth Stampp, *The Era of Reconstruction, 1865–1877* (New York: Alfred A. Knopf, 1966), 62–63. On Reconstruction, see also Eric Foner, *Reconstruction: America's Unfinished Revolution, 1863–1877* (New York: Harper and Row, 1988) and *The Fiery Trial;* Richardson, *Death of Reconstruction* and *West from Appomattox;* John Cox and Lawanda Cox, *Politics, Principle, and Prejudice, 1865–1866: The Dilemma of Reconstruction America* (New York: Free Press of Glencoe, 1963); and Andrew L. Slap, *The Doom of Reconstruction: The Liberal Republicans in the Civil War Era* (New York: Fordham University Press, 2006).

12. Porter, *Ohio Politics,* 307; Schofield to Cox, June 26, 1865, Cox Papers; OR, vol. 47, part 3, 672; *Ohio State Journal,* July 14, 1865.

13. *Cincinnati Enquirer,* June 22, 1865; *Ohio Statesman,* July 11, 1865; *Portage Democrat,* July 5, 1865.

14. Cox to Dennison, July 9, 1865, Cox Papers; Cox to Charles F. Cox, July 26, 1865, Cox Papers.

15. Dennison to Cox, July 19, 1865, Cox Papers; Cox to Dennison, July 30, 1865, Cox Papers.

16. Cox to Garfield, July 21, 1865, Garfield Papers, LC; Garfield to Cox, July 26, 1865, Cox Papers.

17. Cox to John M. Ellis, July 22, 1865, Cox Papers; E. H. Fairchild and Samuel Plumb, "Committee" to Cox, July 24, 1865, Cox Papers.

18. Cox to Plumb and Fairchild, July 25, 1865, Cox Papers. Among the historians who commented on Cox's plan are the following: McKitrick, *Andrew Johnson,* 311; Foner, *Reconstruction,* 221–22; Slap, *Doom of Reconstruction,* 80; Robert Sawrey, *Dubious Victory: The Reconstruction Debate in Ohio* (Lexington: University of Kentucky Press, 1992), 35–40; and Roseboom, *Civil War Era,* 450. The most extensive discussions of the plan are in Eugene Schmiel, "The Oberlin Letter: The Post–Civil War Northern Voter and the Freedman," *Northwest Ohio Quarterly* (Fall 1971): 75–86; and Wilbert Ahern, "The Cox Plan of Reconstruction: A Case Study in Ideology and Race Relations," *Civil War History* 16 (1970): 293–308.

19. Cox to Redelia Cox, August 2, 1865, Cox Papers. Three years later, after a heated exchange of letters on these issues, one of Cox's Oberlin classmates, Reverend C. C. Starbuck, acerbically wrote to Cox, "I must say that the conclusion I have come to is that you do not care one cent for the negroes, and that if it were brought about by some means not derogatory to humanity, you would willingly see all of the American blacks at the bottom of the Atlantic" (Starbuck to Cox, August 30, 1868, Cox Papers).

20. The newspaper responses noted were from the *Cincinnati Enquirer,* August 2, 1865; *Bellefontaine Republic,* August 14, 1865; *Elyria Democrat,* August 11, 1865; *Cincinnati Commercial,* August 2, 1865. Perhaps not surprisingly, one Southern paper was postitive about the plan. The *Richmond Courier-Bulletin* said, "Cox has done well and has originality of mind and independence of character. A man of commanding intellect and force of character" (August 12, 1865). See also Perry to Cox, August 1, 1865, Cox Papers; Garfield to Cox, August 5, 1865, Cox Papers; and Cox to Redelia Cox, August 2, 1865, Cox Papers. A letter from W. T. Sherman to his brother states, "Cox's letter on the subject of negro suffrage is a new bombshell in your camp. . . . [H]e is as near right as he can get"; see Rachel Sherman Thorndike, ed., *The Sherman Letters* (New York: Charles Scribner's Sons, 1894), 252.

21. Dennison to Cox, August 5, 1865, Cox Papers; *Cincinnati Commercial,* August 16, 1865; *Western Reserve Chronicle,* August 16, 1865; Robert G. Caldwell, *James A. Garfield, Party Chieftain* (New York: Dodd, Mead, 1931), 161; Smith, *Life and Letters,* 386.

22. The account of this meeting is taken from William Cochran's note to an account of it in the *Cincinnati Commercial,* August 22, 1865, in the Cox Papers.

23. Flamen Ball, U.S. Attorney, to Chase, August 22, 1865, as quoted in Porter, *Ohio Politics,* 355; Brooks D. Simpson, LeRoy P. Graf, and John Muldowny, eds., *Advice after Appomattox: Letters to Andrew Johnson, 1865–1866* (Knoxville: University of Tennessee Press, 1987), 3–16; Chase to William Sprague, September 6, 1865, in John Niven, *The Salmon P. Chase Papers* (Kent, Ohio: Kent State University Press, 1998), 5:64–68.

24. Cox to Charles Anderson, November 29, 1867, Cox Papers.

25. Cox's Pocket Diary, 1865–66, Cox Papers; Boatner, *Civil War Dictionary,* 565–66; *Cincinnati Enquirer,* August 26, 1865; Porter, *Ohio Politics,* 353–54; *Cincinnati Commercial,* August 28, 1865.

26. Vote in Western Reserve counties (from *Annual Report of the Secretary of State of Ohio, 1865–6* [Columbus, 1866]):

County	Cox	Brough	Morgan	Vallandigham
Ashtabula	4,069	6,237	961	886
Cuyahoga	7,472	10,963	5,809	5,864
Lorain	3,474	4,887	1,674	1,379
Trumbull	3,989	5,331	1,851	1,668

Oberlin (Lorain County) voted Cox—469, Morgan—81.

27. J. C. Kelton, Assistant Adj. Gen., to Cox, December 20, 1865, Cox Papers; "Inaugural Address of Jacob D. Cox, Governor of Ohio," delivered before the Ohio Senate and House of Representatives, January 8, 1866 (Columbus: Richard Nevins, State Printer, 1866).

28. Governor of Ohio's Papers, 1866–68, Manuscript Department, Ohio Historical Society, Columbus; Cox to John Ellis, November 2, 1866, Cox Papers; James E. Pollard, *History of the Ohio State University* (Columbus: Ohio State University Press, 1952), 1–19; Cox to Albert Watson, February 19, 1866, Cox Papers.

29. McKitrick, *Andrew Johnson,* 21, 35–40; Foner, *Reconstruction,* 223–25; Cox to Dennison, December 12, 1865, Cox Papers; Cox to Perry, December 20, 1865, Cox Papers; Cox and Cox, *Politics, Principle, and Prejudice,* 169–72.

30. Garfield to Cox, November 28, 1865, Cox Papers; Dennison to Cox, November 29, 1865, Cox Papers; Cox to Garfield, December 13, 1865, Cox Papers; Cox to Perry, November 17 and December 20, 1865, Cox Papers; Perry to Cox, November 13 and 22 and December 22, 1865, Cox Papers.

31. Cox to John Sherman, January 27, 1866, Cox Papers; John Sherman to Cox, February 10 and 18, 1866, Cox Papers; W. T. Sherman to Cox, February 13, 1866, Cox Papers; McKitrick, *Andrew Johnson,* 292–93; Cox and Cox, *Politics, Principle, and Prejudice,* 172–73; Cox to Perry, February 21, 1866, Cox Papers.

32. Cox to Perry, March 10, 1866, Cox Papers; McKitrick, *Andrew Johnson,* 311. Cox's statement was printed in the *New York Herald,* February 27, 1866.

33. Cox to Lewis D. Campbell, March 12, 1866, Cox Papers; Cox to Murat Halstead, March 16, 1866, Cox Papers.

34. Cox to Andrew Johnson, March 22, 1866, Cox Papers.

35. Dennison to Cox, March 24, 1866, Cox Papers; Cox to Dennison, March 27, 1866, Cox Papers; McKitrick, *Andrew Johnson,* 311–14; Warner Bateman to

John Sherman, March 30, 1866, John Sherman Papers, LC; Cox to Garfield, April 10, 1866, Cox Papers.

36. Cox to Garfield, May 4, 1866, Cox Papers; Cox to Dennison, May 19, 1866, Cox Papers.

37. Cox to Andrew Johnson, June 21, 1866, Cox Papers; Dennison to Cox, July 16, 1866, Cox Papers; Cox to Dennison, August 3, 1866, Cox Papers; Cox to Charles Anderson, August 7, 1866, Cox Papers.

38. Cox to Willard Warner, August 27, 1866, Cox Papers; *Cincinnati Commercial,* August 22, 1866; Cochran, "Political Experiences," 2:923; Grant is quoted in William McFeeley, *Grant* (New York: W.W. Norton, 1981), 252; *Cincinnati Commercial,* September 13, 1866.

39. *Cincinnati Commercial,* September 26, 1866; McKitrick, *Andrew Johnson,* 446–47; clipping, "Resolutions of the Great Convention of Soldiers at Pittsburgh, September 26, 1866," in Cox's Pocket Diary, Cox Papers.

40. Albert Castel, *The Presidency of Andrew Johnson* (Lawrence: University Press of Kansas, 1979), 96–97; Roseboom, *Civil War Era,* 456–57; McFeeley, *Grant,* 252–57; Cox to William T. Coggeshall, December 5, 1866, Cox Papers. Cox would later learn, to his regret, that this legislation had the opposite effect; Garfield to Cox, December 25, 1866, Cox Papers.

41. Cox to James Monroe, November 21, 1866, Cox Papers.

42. Cox to Perry, January 14, 17, and 25, 1867, Cox Papers; Cox to Benjamin Cowen, January 25, 1867, Cox Papers; *Cincinnati Commercial,* January 25 and 29, 1867; *Cleveland Leader,* January 28, 1867.

43. Cox to William Coggeshall, April 8, 1867, Cox Papers.

44. State of Ohio, "Governor's Report," *Executive Document 1866* (Columbus: L. D. Myers and Bro., 1867), 261–83; Cox to William T. Coggeshall, April 8, 1867, Cox Papers; Roseboom, *Civil War Era,* 457–58.

45. Irwin Unger, *The Greenback Era: A Social and Political History of American Finance, 1865–1879* (Princeton: Princeton University Press, 1964), 80–84; Cox to Allyn Cox, September 13, 1867, Cox Papers; "The Currency," speech by Governor Cox, September 24, 1867, pamphlet in the Cox Papers.

46. *Cincinnati Enquirer,* October 24, 1867; *Cincinnati Commercial,* October 31, 1867; Cox to Garfield, November 22, 1867, Cox Papers; Cox to Allyn Cox, November 21, 1867, Cox Papers; Cox to Charles Anderson, December 6, 1867, Cox Papers; Cox to A. J. Ricks, October 18, 1867, Cox Papers.

47. *Cleveland Leader,* January 16, 1868.

48. Cox to Aaron Perry, November 21, 1867, Cox Papers; Cox, Manifold Letterbook #3, Cox Papers; Cox to Charles F. Cox, September 13, 1867, Cox Papers; personal interview with Miss Mary Rudd Cochran by the author.

49. William T. Sherman, *Personal Memoirs,* 2:421–22; Benjamin P. Thomas and Harold M. Hyman, *Stanton: The Life and Times of Lincoln's Secretary of War* (New York: Alfred A. Knopf, 1962), 568–70; Castel, *Presidency of Andrew Johnson,* 165; Michael Les Benedict, *The Impeachment and Trial of Andrew Johnson* (New York: W.W. Norton, 1999), 98–104; Connelly, *John M. Schofield,* 205–7. Cox opposed impeachment since it was not based on serious crimes; see Cox to Kenyon Cox, May 19, 1868, Cox Papers.

306 50. *Cincinnati Commercial,* August 2 and October 22, 1868; William Cochran, "The Scholar in Action," *Oberlin Alumni Magazine* 11, no. 6 (March 1915): 230; Alexander H. McGuffey to Cox, September 5, 1868, Cox Papers.

51. Cox to General I. N. Stiles, September 8, 1868, Cox Papers; Cox to W. T. Bascom, October 25, 1868, Cox Papers; Schofield to Cox, April 15, 1868, Cox Papers; Cox to Schofield, May 18, 1868, Schofield Papers, LC; *Chicago Tribune,* December 16, 1868; Cochran, "Political Experiences," 2:1026. The speech also included commentary on the importance of the defensive and the volunteer soldier.

52. Cox to Theodore Cox, January 27, 1869, Cox Papers; Cox to Charles F. Cox, March 3, 1869, Cox Papers; *Congressional Globe,* 45th Cong., 1st Sess., March 5, 1869, 15.

53. U. S. Grant to Cox, March 5, 1869, Cox Papers; Cox to G. B. Wright, March 6, 1869, Jacob D. Cox Papers, LC; Helen Cox to William Cochran, March 8, 1869, William Cochran Papers, Oberlin College Archives.

Chapter 8: Citizen-Statesman

1. Works about Grant include Jean Edward Smith, *Grant* (New York: Simon and Schuster, 2001); McFeeley, *Grant;* Geoffrey Perret, *Ulysses S. Grant, Soldier and President* (New York: Random House, 1998); William B. Hesseltine, *Ulysses S. Grant, Politician* (New York: Dodd, Mead, 1935); and Brooks Simpson, *Ulysses S Grant: Triumph over Adversity, 1822–1865* (New York: Houghton Mifflin, 2000).

2. For the dynamics of the administration, see Allan Nevins, *Hamilton Fish: The Inner History of the Grant Administration* (New York: Dodd, Mead, 1936). The *New York Times* said of Cox on March 6, 1869, "He is a man of singularly studious habits, absolute integrity, and wide and varied attainments. . . . He has a methodical, crisp way of doing business." Nevins said of the cabinet, "[T]he alarming fact was that it suddenly betrayed Grant as uninformed and groping. It was the Cabinet of an amateur, without . . . a plan"; see Nevins, *Hamilton Fish,* 108.

3. Hesseltine, *Ulysses S. Grant, Politician,* 159; W. B. Archer, *Memorandum History of the Department of the Interior* (Washington, D.C.: Government Printing Office, 1913), 2.

4. Cox to Charles F. Cox, August 6, 1867, Cox Papers; Cox to Allyn Cox, July 19, 1867, Cox Papers; William Cochran, "Political Correspondence of Jacob Dolson Cox," 3:63. Cox's review in the *Nation* on August 1, 1895, of explorer Henry Stanley's book on travels to the United States discussed his trip with Casement. For discussions of the building of the railroads and the related scandals, see Leslie E. Decker, "The Railroads and the Land Office: Administrative Policy and the Land Patent Controversy, 1864–1896," *Mississippi Valley Historical Review* 46, no. 4 (March 1960): 687–89; David Bain, *Empire Express: Building the First Transcontinental Railroad* (New York: Viking Press, 1999); and Stephen Ambrose, *Nothing Like It in the World: The Men Who Built the Transcontinental Railroad, 1863–1869* (New York: Simon and Schuster, 2000).

5. *Cincinnati Commercial,* March 14, 1869; Cox to Charles F. Cox, March 14, 1869, Cox Papers. The best account of the politics of patronage is Ari Hoogenboom,

Outlawing the Spoils: A History of the Civil Service Reform Movement, 1865–1883 (Urbana: University of Illinois Press, 1961).

6. Dennison to Cox, March 7, 1869, Cox Papers; Hoogenboom, *Outlawing the Spoils,* 79; Cox to E. L. Godkin, December 5, 1870, Cox Papers; Interior Department Appointments Division Letterbook, Records of the Department of the Interior, National Archives; Cox to Charles F. Cox, March 14, 1869, Cox Papers. Because of political pressures to keep some jobs open for patronage, especially in the Land Office, Cox was not able to make his examination system cover the entire department. On that issue see Cox to E. L. Godkin, December 5, 1870, Cox Papers.

7. W. T. Sherman to John Sherman, September 23, 1868, in Thorndike, *Sherman Letters,* 321–22.

8. Francis Paul Prucha, *The Great Father: The United States Government and the American Indian* (Lincoln: University of Nebraska Press, 1995), 479–83, 501–33 discusses the Grant administration's policy; Cox to Eli Price, et al., March 25, 1869, Cox Papers. See Grant's State of the Union message, December 6, 1869, 14–15; and U.S. Department of the Interior, *Report of the Secretary of the Interior,* 41st Cong., 2nd Sess., House Executive Document 3 (Washington, D.C.: Government Printing Office, 1869), given November 15, 1869. For further background on Indian affairs, see Stephen J. Rockwell, *Indian Affairs and the Administrative State in the Nineteenth Century* (Cambridge, Mass.: Harvard University Press, 2010); Elsie M. Rushmore, *The Indian Policy during Grant's Administration* (Jamaica, N.Y.: Marion Press, 1914); and Henry Fritz, *The Movement for Indian Assimilation* (New York: Greenwood Press, 1981).

9. Cox to John Farwell, April 15, 1869, Cox Papers; Cox, "The Indian Question," *International Review* 6 (June 1879): 617–34; Charles Lewis Slattery, *Felix Reville Brunot, 1820–1898: A Civilian in the War for the Union, President of the First Board of Indian Commissioners* (New York: Longman, Green, 1901), 141–43; William Armstrong, *Warrior in Two Camps: Ely S. Parker, Union General and Seneca Chief* (Syracuse: Syracuse University Press, 1990), 136–39.

10. Report of the Secretary of the Interior, Washington, 1869; *Annual Report of the Board of Indian Commissioners* (Washington: Government Printing Office, 1870); Bishop H. B. Whipple to Cox, December 3, 1869, Cox Papers. Cox's article, "The Indian Question," noted that the early optimism about the policy and the reforms he and Grant had put in place eventually withered away and that conditions for the Indians worsened even more.

11. Cochran, "Political Experiences," 2:1045, and "Why General Cox Left Grant's Cabinet," 13n, Cox Papers; Morgan, *Kenyon Cox,* 6–7.

12. Henry Adams, *The Education of Henry Adams* (New York: Book League of America, 1928), 266–67; Henry Adams, "Civil Service Reform," *North American Review* 109, no. 225 (October 1869): 443–76; Henry Adams to Cox, November 8, 1869, Cox Papers; Brooks Simpson, *The Political Education of Henry Adams* (Columbia: University of South Carolina Press, 1996), 42–57.

13. Cox to James Ford Rhodes, March 3, 1897, Cox Papers; Richardson, *West from Appomattox,* 123–24; *Cincinnati Commercial,* June 2, 1869.

14. The best treatment of this new breed of journalists is Summers, *Press Gang.*

308   15. *Lorain County News,* March 24, 1870, reprint of an undated article in the *New York World.*

16. Smith, *Grant,* 499–502; Cox, "How Judge Hoar Ceased to Be Attorney General," *Atlantic Monthly,* August 1895, 165–67.

17. Nicholas Guyatt, "America's Conservatory: Race, Reconstruction, and the Santo Domingo Debate," *Journal of American History* (March 2011): 978.

18. Cox, "How Judge Hoar," 163–66; Cox to Aaron Perry, July 29, 1870, Cox Papers.

19. Nevins, *Fish,* 271; Cox, "How Judge Hoar," 167.

20. U.S. Department of the Interior, *Report of the Secretary of the Interior,* 41st Cong., 2nd Sess., House Executive Document 3 (Washington, D.C.: Government Printing Office, 1869); Hoogenboom, *Outlawing the Spoils,* 68. Grant's first annual message ignored the topic.

21. Smith, *Grant,* 481–90; Cox to Theodore Cox, November 24, 1869, Cox Papers.

22. George E. Hyde, *Red Cloud's Folk: A History of the Oglala Sioux Indian* (Norman: University of Oklahoma Press, 1937 [reprint, 1975]), 172–73; Smith, *Grant,* 530; Cox to Edward Cromwell, May 14, 1870, Cox Papers.

23. Robert M. Utley, *The Indian Frontier, 1846–1890* (Albuquerque: University of New Mexico Press, 1984), 145–48; Smith, *Grant,* 530; Hyde, *Red Cloud's Folks,* 175; George E. Hyde, *Spotted Tail's Folks: A History of the Brulé Sioux* (Norman: University of Oklahoma Press, 1961), 170–80.

24. Robert Larson, *Red Cloud: Warrior-Statesman of the Lakota Sioux* (Norman: University of Oklahoma Press, 1999), 130–34; *Cincinnati Commercial,* June 8, 1870.

25. Larson, *Red Cloud,* 131, 133–34; Hyde, *Red Cloud's Folks,* 177; *Cincinnati Commercial,* June 12, 1870.

26. Hyde, *Red Cloud's Folks,* 180–81; Smith, *Grant,* 531–32; Utley, *Indian Frontier,* 148–52.

27. Cox to Aaron Perry, August 20, 1870, Cox Papers.

28. Smith, *Grant,* 587–90. The quotations of Grant are from John Russell Young, *Around the World with General Grant* (New York: American News Company, 1879), 265, 365.

29. Rodney Foos to Cox, May 14, 1870, Cox Papers; Cox to J. W. Clendening, Secretary, Congressional Republican Committee, July 28, 1870, Cox Papers; Cox to R. D. Harrison, August 10, 1870, Cox Papers Also see Matthew Josephson, *The Politicos* (New York: Harcourt, Brace, 1938), and Mark W. Summers, *Era of Good Stealings* and *Press Gang,* as well as the biographies of Grant. Evidence that Garfield was a practitioner of the new politics is discussed in James D. Norris and Arthur Shaffer, eds., *Politics and Patronage in the Gilded Age: The Correspondence of James A. Garfield and Charles E. Henry* (Madison: State Historical Society of Wisconsin, 1970).

30. Cochran, "Political Experiences," 2:1055.

31. Cox, "Why Judge Hoar," 166–71.

32. Cox to Aaron F. Perry, July 29 and August 20, 1870, Cox Papers; Cox to Hoar, October 18, 1869, Cox Papers.

33. *Cincinnati Commercial,* July 26, 1870; Summers, *Press Gang,* 123–42. See also Peter Bridges, *Donn Piatt: Gadfly of the Gilded Age* (Kent: Kent State University Press, 2012).

34. W. A. Short to Cox, September 7, 1870, Cox Papers; Cox to W. A. Short, September 8, 1870, Cox Papers; *Cincinnati Commercial,* September 6, 1870; Cochran, "Why General Cox," 25; Cox to Hoar, October 18, 1870, Cox Papers.

35. William Evarts to Cox, June 12, 1869, Cox Papers; John Bingham to Cox, March 23, 1869, Cox Papers. This account comes primarily from Cox's letter to Charles Nordhoff, editor of the *New York Evening Post,* December 3, 1870, Cox Papers. See also Clinton Rice to Donn Piatt, July 21, 1870, in an unnamed newspaper, Scrapbook #3, Cox Papers; Summers, *Press Gang,* 135, 123–24.

36. Cox to Judge Hoar, October 22, 1870, Cox Papers; Cox to U. S. Grant, August 23, 1870, Cox Papers; Hamilton Fish to Cox, September 5, 1870, Cox Papers. The *McGarrahan Memorial* (San Francisco, 1870), archived in the Cox Papers, includes the text of Grant's and Cox's letters and related materials.

37. Cox to Nordhoff, December 3, 1870, Cox Papers; Cochran, "Political Experiences," 2:1060. The *New York Times* reported the change in policy on October 4, 1862.

38. Cox to President Grant, October 3, 1870, Cox Papers.

39. Cox to Judge Hoar, October 18, 1870, Cox Papers.

40. Cox to Judge Hoar, October 22, 1870, Cox Papers.

41. Grant to Cox, October 5, 1870, Cox Papers. Grant replaced Cox with Columbus Delano, who reversed Cox's reforms, and under whom "corruption in the Indian Service reached new heights," according to a National Parks Service history of the Interior Department, http://cr.nps.gov/history/online_books /utleuy-mackintosh/interior5.htm.

42. Summers, *Press Gang,* 183.

43. Cochran, "Political Correspondence," 2:53; Cox to Hoar, October 22, 1870, Cox Papers; "Memoir of a conversation of J. R. Young with President Grant," October 1870, Cox Papers; Boynton to Cox, November 1, 1870, Cox Papers; Cochran, "Political Correspondence," 2:72; *New York Standard,* October 19, 1870; *New York Times,* October 21, 1870.

44. *Nation,* October 20, 1870; Cox to Hoar, October 22, 1870, Cox Papers; *New York Evening Post,* October 24, 1870; Garfield to Cox, October 26, 1870, Cox Papers; Hesseltine, *Ulysses S. Grant, Politician,* 317–18; Hoogenboom, *Outlawing the Spoils,* 79.

45. H. V. Boynton to Cox, November 2 and 3, 1870, Cox Papers; *Washington Daily Morning Chronicle,* November 5, 1870; *New York Standard,* November 7, 1870. The *Philadelphia Evening Telegraph* (October 31), the *Springfield Republican* (October 31), and the *Chicago Republican* (November 3) backed Cox, and the latter reported that "Grant's blinding imbecility" was leading him into trouble.

46. *New York Evening Post,* November 10, 1870; Benjamin Perley Poore, *Life of U. S. Grant* (New York: Edgewood Publishing, 1885), 157.

47. *Hartford (Connecticut) Evening Post,* November 12, 1870; *New York Evening Post,* November 4, 1870; Henry Adams to Cox, November 11, 1870, Cox Papers.

310 For other indications of reformers' interest in Cox as a presidential candidate, see Hoogenboom, *Outlawing the Spoils,* 80.

48. *Springfield Republican,* November 12, 1870. Cox told E. L. Godkin, "[S]o the work is done, in Heaven's name let anybody have the credit"; Cox to Godkin, December 6, 1870, Cox Papers.

49. Cox to Charles Nordhoff, December 3, 1870, Cox Papers; Cox to Charles F. Cox, November 25, 1870, Cox Papers; Cox to Garfield, December 9, 1870, Cox Papers.

50. Charles Nordoff to Cox, January 16, 1871, Cox Papers.

51. *Congressional Globe,* 41st Cong., 3rd Sess., appendix, 136–37; Garfield to Cox, February 27, 1871, Cox Papers; *Congressional Globe,* 41st Cong., 3rd Sess., February 18–20, 1871, 1402–57; *Cincinnati Commercial,* March 2, 1871; Summers, *Press Gang,* 135, 123–24. Another event in 1871 made Cox angry about Washington. Parker was accused of irregularities in purchasing goods for Indians. Parker claimed Cox had authorized the purchases, but Cox testified to the committee that this was not true. While ultimately Parker was not found guilty, he resigned from office; see Armstrong, *Warrior in Two Camps,* 152–60.

52. Earle Dudley Ross, *The Liberal Republican Movement* (New York: Henry Holt, 1919), 28–31.

53. Simpson, *Political Education of Henry Adams,* 74–75; Henry Adams to Cox, October 31 and November 11, 1870, Cox Papers; E. L. Godkin to Cox, December 3, 1870, Cox Papers.

54. Cox to Charles Nordhoff, December 3, 1870, Cox Papers; Henry Adams to Cox, November 17 and 28, 1870, Cox Papers; Simpson, *Political Education of Henry Adams,* 75–76; Cox to Garfield, December 9, 1870, Cox Papers; Cox to John Lynch, March 7, 1871, Cox Papers; J. D. Cox, "The Civil Service Reform," *North American Review,* January 1871, 81–113.

55. Cox to Aaron F. Perry, March 27, 1871, Cox Papers; *Cincinnati Commercial,* March 22, 1871; Carl Wittke, "Friederich Hassaurek: Cincinnati's Leading Forty-Eighter," *Ohio History* 67 (January 1959): 1–18; Slap, *Doom of Reconstruction,* 128–31.

56. Roeliff Brinkenhoff to Cox, March 24, 1871, Cox Papers; Donald W. Curl, "Murat Halstead, Editor and Politician," Ph.D. diss., Ohio State University, 1964; *New York World,* March 23, 1871; Cox to Garfield, March 20, 1871, Cox Papers; Cox to Perry, March 27, 1871, Cox Papers; Cox to Kenyon Cox, March 2, 1871, Cox Papers.

57. Cox to Garfield, August 9 and October 17, 1871, James A. Garfield Papers, LC; Charles F. Cox to Cox, November 1, 1871, Cox Papers; Cox to James Monroe, December 11, 1871, Cox Papers; Cox to W. T. Bascom, November 20, 1871, Cox Papers; Charles F. Cox to Cox, September 25, 1871, Cox Papers.

58. John Casement to Cox, November 23, 1871, Cox Papers; Cox to James Monroe, January 12, 1872, Cox Papers; Cox to W. P. Garrison, January 12, 1872, Cox Papers.

59. Ross, *Liberal Republican,* 48, 51–52; Schurz to Cox, October 14 and 22, 1871, Cox Papers; William Grosvenor to Cox, January 10, 1872, Cox Papers.

60. Slap, *Doom of Reconstruction,* 138–39; Garfield to Cox, March 3, 1872, Cox Papers.

61. Ross, *Liberal Republicans,* 65–66; Smith, *Grant,* 548; Armstrong, *Gilded Age Letters,* 187; *Cincinnati Commercial,* June 18, 1871. A leader of the New York party was John Cochrane, the political general whom Cox had met at the dinner with McClellan after the Battle of Antietam. Cochrane was a power in Tammany Hall.

62. Cox to Garfield, March 22, 1872, Garfield Papers, LC; Cox to William Grosvenor, March 23, 1872, Cox Papers; Cox to Carl Schurz, April 5, 1872, Cox Papers; Cox to David A. Wells, April 4, 1872, Cox Papers; Samuel Bowles to David A. Wells, March 23, 1872, Cox Papers.

63. Roseboom, *Civil War Years,* 471; Eric A. Goldman, *Rendezvous with Destiny* (New York: Alfred A. Knopf, 1952), 11; John G. Sproat, *"The Best Men": Liberal Reformers in the Gilded Age* (New York: Oxford University Press, 1968), 4, 280; Richardson, *West from Appomattox,* 122–26; Matthew T. Downey, "Horace Greeley and the Politicians: The Liberal Republican Convention in 1872," *Journal of American History* 53, no. 3 (December 1966): 737; Slap, *Doom of Reconstruction,* 144–45, 152–53; *New York Tribune,* April 30, 1872. Summers (in *Press Gang,* 240–46) notes that Greeley's ascendancy reflected the growing power of the press in American politics.

64. *Proceedings of the Liberal Republican Convention* (New York: Baker and Goodwin Printers, 1872), 3–5; Henry L. Burnett to William Cochran, November 20, 1901, Cox Papers; Roseboom, *Civil War Era,* 480–81; Cochran, "Political Experiences," 2:1136. Cox was eligible, having been a natural-born citizen of two American parents, so this was yet another example of his self-effacing and rigid approach to office-seeking.

65. For discussions of these conferences, see Cox to Allyn Cox, May 6, 1872, Cox Papers; and Downey, "Horace Greeley," 741–42. See also *Proceedings,* 29.

66. Cox to Oran Follett, May 23, 1872, Oran Follett Papers, Cincinnati Historical Society, Cincinnati, Ohio; Cox to Mahlon Sands, May 28, 1872, Cox Papers; Ross, *Liberal Republican Movement,* 110–12; Mahlon Sands to Cox, May 31, 1872, Cox Papers.

67. Armstrong, *Gilded Age Letters,* 188; Ross, *Liberal Republican Movement,* 119; C. C. Starbuck to Cox, December 30, 1872, Cox Papers. A few days after this meeting, George McClellan wrote Cox that he was equally discouraged by Greeley's candidacy and what it meant for American politics; McClellan to Cox, July 3, 1872, Cox Papers.

68. Cox to John Hutchins, January 28, 1873, Cox Papers.

69. Garfield to Cox, May 7, 1873, Cox Papers; Cox to Garfield, June 23, 1873, Cox Papers; J. D. Cox, "Our Country's New Era," an address to the Society of Alumni of Wittenberg College, June 25, 1873, ms. in Cox Papers.

70. Cox to John Lynch, July 11, 1872, Cox Papers; Cox to J. Q. Smith, August 6, 1872, Cox Papers; Cox to Garfield, August 14, 1872, Cox Papers.

71. Ellis Oberholtzer, *Jay Cooke, Financier of the Civil War* (Philadelphia: George W. Jacobs, 1907), 2:400–403; Bouck White, *The Book of Daniel Drew* (New York: George H. Doran, 1910), 403–7; Cochran, "Political Experiences," 2:1141–44; Casement to Cox, September 26, 1873, Cox Papers. The *Toledo Blade* on October

2, 1873, said of the new president, "He has filled many exalted positions in our state and has won a reputation for financial executive ability."

72. Cox to Hayes, October 6, 1873, Cox Papers; Hayes to Cox, October 3, 1873, Cox Papers; Cox to Monroe, October 23, 1873, Monroe Papers.

73. Julius Grodinsky, *Jay Gould: His Business Career, 1867–1892* (Philadelphia: University of Pennsylvania Press, 1957), 190; See also Edward J. Renehan Jr., *Dark Genius of Wall Street: The Misunderstood Life of Jay Gould, King of the Robber Barons* (New York: Basic Books, 2006); Henry V. Poor, *Manual of the Railroads of the United States for 1873–4* (New York, 1874), 498–500; Cochran, "Political Experiences," 2:1147; Cox to Monroe, April 8, 1875, Monroe Papers; and *Railroad Gazette*, August 22, 1874, 32–33.

74. *Railroad Gazette*, November 7, 1874, January 23, 1875, March 6, 1875, October 16, 1875, and April 7, 1876; Cox to James Monroe, April 8, 1875, Monroe Papers; circular issued by Cox as general manager, as quoted in *Railroad Gazette*, January 12, 1877, 20; Renehan, *Dark Genius*, 243.

75. Cox to R. B. Hayes, June 20, 1876, Cox Papers; Hayes to Cox, June 23, 1876, Cox Papers.

76. *Toledo Blade*, June 24 and August 14, 1876; Cox to James Monroe, August 14, 1876, Monroe Papers.

77. Cox, Campaign Speech, Toledo Opera House, August 28, 1876, ms. in Cox Papers; Cox, "The Relation of Educated Men to the Problem of Capital and Labor," Cincinnati, Lane Seminary, 1877, ms. in Cox Papers; Smith, *Ohio Republicans*, 1:365. For a discussion of the sociopolitical trends of the era, see Robert Weibe, *The Search for Order, 1877–1920* (New York: Hill and Wang, 1967).

78. Cox to L. A. Sheldon, November 13, 1876, Cox Papers; Cox to Hayes, November 14, 1876, January 31, 1877, and February 24, 1877, R. B. Hayes Papers, Hayes Memorial Library, Fremont, Ohio; Williams, *Diary and Letters*, 3:402; Carl Schurz to Cox, January 30, 1877, Bancroft, Schurz Papers, 3:380; Cox to Hayes, February 19 and 20, 1877, Cox Papers; Hayes to Cox, February 20, 1877, Cox Papers; Cox to Garfield, July 23, 1877, Garfield Papers, LC; Cox to Hayes, June 5, 1877, Hayes Papers; Hayes to Cox, June 4, 1877, Cox Papers.

79. Garfield to Cox, July 30, 1877, Garfield Papers, LC; Cox to Garfield, September 16, 1877, Garfield Papers, LC; Smith, *Garfield, Life and Letters*, 2:657.

80. Ernest Samuels, *Henry Adams: The Middle Years* (Cambridge, Mass.: Harvard University Press, 1958), 17; Irwin Unger, *The Greenback Era: A Social and Political History of American Finance, 1865–1879* (Princeton: Princeton University Press, 1964), 364; Cox to David A. Wells, February 28, 1878, Cox Papers.

81. *Congressional Record*, 45th Cong., 2nd Sess., May 14, 1878, 3410–11; Cox to Monroe, September 5, 1877, Cox Papers; Cox, "The House of Representatives," *Nation*, no. 666, April 4, 1878, 223–27; Smith, *Garfield, Life and Letters*, 2:664.

82. Cox to Monroe, December 31, 1877, Monroe Papers; Smith, *Garfield, Life and Letters*, 2:666, 674.

83. Cox to Garfield, March 18, 1879, Garfield Papers, LC; Cox to Francis A. Walker, May 28, 1879, Cox Papers; Cox to Charles F. Cox, March 31, 1879, Cox Papers; letter from Mary Rudd Cochran to the author, April 6, 1869.

84. Cox to Dr. C. S. Frink, January 12, 1880, Cox Papers; Cox to Monroe, January 31, 1880, Monroe Papers; Cox to Garfield, June 9, 1880, Garfield Papers, LC.

85. Cox to Garfield, November 3, 1880, Garfield Papers, LC; Smith, *Garfield, Life and Letters,* 2:1077.

86. Cox to Monroe, May 21, 1881, Monroe Papers; Garfield to Cox, May 22, 1881, Garfield Papers, LC; Cox to Monroe, June 8, 1881, Monroe Papers.

87. Cox to Monroe, August 30, 1881, Monroe Papers; Cox to Dr. James J. Woodward, December 24, 1881, Cox Papers.

88. Cox to William H. Smith, July 14, 1885, William H. Smith Papers, Manuscript Division, Ohio Historical Society, Columbus.

Chapter 9: Civil War Historian

1. Simpson, introduction to Cox, *Atlanta,* vi; James McPherson and William J. Cooper Jr., *Writing the Civil War: The Quest to Understand* (Columbia: University of South Carolina Press, 2000), 2. On the "Lost Cause," see, among others, Thomas Connelly, *The Marble Man: Robert E. Lee and His Image in American Society* (Baton Rouge: Louisiana State University Press, 1977); Gaines M. Foster, *Ghosts of the Confederacy: Defeat, the Lost Cause, and the Emergence of the New South* (New York: Oxford University Press, 1987); William Davis, *The Cause Lost: Myths and Realities of the Confederacy* (Lawrence: University Press of Kansas, 2003); and Gary Gallagher, *The Myth of the Lost Cause and Civil War History* (Bloomington: Indiana University Press, 2010). On political generals, see Work, *Lincoln's Political Generals;* and Goss, *War within the Union.*

2. Cox, *Battle of Franklin,* 221.

3. Cox to Garfield, December 31, 1864, Garfield Papers, LC.

4. Cox to Greeley, April 22, 1867, Cox Papers; Greeley to Cox, May 28, 1867, Cox Papers; Horace Greeley, *The American Conflict: A History of the Great Rebellion,* 2 vols. (Chicago: Geo. and C. W. Sherwood, 1864, 1867).

5. Brooks Simpson, in his introduction to Cox's *Atlanta,* calls that book "a model narrative" (ix–x).

6. Donn Piatt and H. V. Boynton, *General George H. Thomas: A Critical Biography* (Cincinnati: Robert Clarke, 1893), 649–50; Schofield to Cox, October 18, 1881, Schofield Papers, LC. Connelly's *John M. Schofield* has an in-depth discussion of these "battles" between Schofield and Thomas and their supporters on pages 149–54. One of Thomas's supporters accusing Cox of writing the letter was General David Stanley, who would become one of the strongest critics of Cox's books about Franklin and Nashville.

7. Review of *Narrative of Military Operations,* by Joseph E. Johnson, *Nation,* May 21, 1874, 333–34; review of *Advance and Retreat,* by John Bell Hood, *Nation,* March 25, 1880, 236–37 and April 1, 1880, 254.

8. Review of *Sherman's Memoirs, Nation,* June 10 and 17, 1875, 397–99, 411–12; Review of *Sherman's Historical Raid, Nation,* November 25 and December 2, 1875, 342–43, 358–59; Michael Feltman, *Citizen Sherman: A Life of William Tecumseh Sherman* (Lawrence: University Press of Kansas, 1997), 324–26; Sherman to Cox, November 29, 1875, Cox Papers; Cox to Monroe, January 6, 1876, Cox Papers.

314   Castel, in his *Decision in the West,* makes many of the same criticisms of Sherman
that Boynton did but does not cite Boynton's book in his bibliography or notes.

9. Longacre and Haas, *To Battle for God,* xxvii–xxx.

10. Cox to Emerson Opdycke, January 24, 1876, Cox Papers.

11. Cox, "Growth of the History of the Rebellion," undated, unpublished ms.,
Cox Papers.

12. On the Porter case, see Otto Eisenschiml, *The Celebrated Case of Fitz-John
Porter, An American Dreyfus Affair* (Indianapolis: Bobbs-Merrill, 1950), which is an
overdrawn treatment; Henry Gabler, "The Fitz-John Porter Case, Politics, and
Military Justice," Ph.D. diss., City University of New York, 1979, which is a balanced review; Donald Jermann, *Fitz-John Porter, Scapegoat of Second Manassas* (New
York: McFarland, 2008), which is defensive of Porter; and Curt Anders, *Injustice
on Trial: Second Bull Run, General Fitz-John Porter's Court Martial, and the Schofield Board Investigation that Restored His Good Name* (Zionsville, Ind.: Guild Press,
2002), which is also defensive of Porter. Hennessy, in *Return to Bull Run,* 465, assessed that Porter was an average officer of limited energy but that he should not
have been court-martialed.

13. Cox to Garfield, February 14, 1880, Cox Papers; Cox to Fitz-John Porter,
June 8, 1880, Cox Papers.

14. These letters are in the Cox Papers. Cox's letter to Schofield of November 20, 1880, was the key one in that correspondence, and it was followed by
several more that year in which Cox explained his position in detail. Cox wrote
to Porter on June 8, June 29, July 19, and November 22. See also Connelly,
John M. Schofield, 249–56.

15. Cox to General I. T. Wood, May 2, 1882, Cox Papers; Cox to Lucretia Garfield, March 11, 1882, Lucretia Garfield Papers, LC; Cox, *Second Battle of Bull Run;*
Cox to Schofield, December 23, 1880, Cox Papers; Cox, *Military Reminiscences,*
1:182–84.

16. Brooks Simpson, introduction to Cox, *Atlanta,* vi.

17. Cox to Charles Scribner's Sons, August 20, 1880, Cox Papers; Cox, *Atlanta;*
Sherman to Cox, November 7, 1880, May 21 and 27, 1882, and October 11, 1882,
Cox Papers; Cox to O. O. Howard, November 5, 1881, Cox Papers.

18. Cox, *Atlanta,* 129; Castel, *Decision in the West,* xii; Steven E. Woodworth, *The
American Civil War: A Handbook of Literature and Research* (New York: Greenwood
Press, 1996), 274.

19. Cox, *Atlanta,* 211–17. The reviews of the book were generally positive. For
example, the *New York Times's* anonymous reviewer called it "comprehensive and
fair-minded," though adding that Cox "at no point in his volume discovers where
anything could have been done more perfectly by General Sherman." The review
appeared on June 19, 1882.

20. For his correspondence with Stanley, see Cox, *Battle of Franklin,* 260–63;
Cox to Stanley, August 24 and October 31, 1881, Cox Papers.

21. Cox, *Battle of Franklin,* 220–21; Cox, *Sherman's March,* 39–41, 230–31.

22. Cox, *Sherman's March,* 134–36. The comment by Brooks Simpson is on page
xvii of that book's 1994 edition. For a discussion of the renewed tensions between

Schofield and Thomas's partisans after Schofield wrote a paper for the Society of the Army of the Cumberland in which he maintained that Grant had greater confidence in him than in Thomas, see Connelly, *John M. Schofield,* 150–52.

23. Opdycke to Cox, August 17, 1881, Cox Papers; Cox to Opdycke, December 2, 1881, Cox Papers.

24. Cox to Opdycke, January 18 and 27, June 28, and July 25, 1882, Cox Papers; Opdycke to Cox, December 9, 1882, Cox Papers.

25. Cox to Schofield, September 11, 1882, Cox Papers; Cox to Monroe, October 14, 1882, Cox Papers.

26. Wilson's review was in the *New York Sun,* October 22, 1882; Sherman to Cox, October 6, 1882, Cox Papers. The quotation from Schofield is from Cox, *Battle of Franklin,* 265.

27. *Nation,* July 30, 1885, 87–89; *Nation,* February 25, 1886, 172–74; *Nation,* July 1, 1886, 12–13.

28. *Nation,* January 20, 1887, 57–58 and January 27, 1887, 79–80; *McClellan's Own Story,* 604–11. For an analysis of McClellan's postwar writings, see Stephen W. Sears, "The Curious Case of General McClellan's Memoirs," *Civil War History* 34, no. 2 (September 1988): 102–3. In that article Sears notes Cox's "penetrating analysis" in his review. Cox's annotated copy of *McClellan's Own Story* is in the Cox Papers.

29. Richard V. Johnson and Clarence C. Buel, eds., *Battles and Leaders of the Civil War,* 4 vols. (New York: Charles Scribner's Sons, 1887–88).

30. Cox, "War Preparations in the North," in *Battles and Leaders,* 1:84–98; Cox, "McClellan in West Virginia," in *Battles and Leaders,* 1:126–48; Cox, "West Virginia Operations under Fremont," in *Battles and Leaders,* 2:270–81.

31. Cox, "Forcing Fox's Gap and Turner's Gap," in *Battles and Leaders,* 2:583–90; Cox, "The Battle of Antietam," in *Battles and Leaders,* 2:630–59.

32. Cox, *Military Reminiscences,* 1:261, 350–51. For McClellan's sentiments, see both *McClellan's Own Story* and his article, "From the Peninsula to Antietam," in *Battles and Leaders,* 1:552.

33. For the comment about the historiography of the 1890s, see Carman, *Maryland Campaign,* 1:172n. Clemens, the editor of Carman's manuscript, made these comments to the author on September 16, 2012, during the celebrations of the Sesquicentennial of the Battle of Antietam. The quotation about Cox's influence is from Rafuse, "Poor Burn?" 175. The latest examples of the enduring influence of Cox's writings are John David Hoptak, *The Battle of South Mountain* (Charleston, S.C.: History Press, 2011); Brian Jordan, *Unholy Sabbath: The Battle of South Mountain in History and Memory, September 14, 1862* (New York: Savas Beatie, 2012), and Hartwig, *To Antietam Creek.*

34. Stone, "Repelling Hood's Invasion," 450, 452; Smith, *Garfield, Life and Letters,* 1:358. Stanley's letter to the editors was sent on January 20, 1888, and appeared in the October 1888 edition, along with Cox's responses. Stanley's autobiography, *Personal Memoirs of General David S. Stanley* (Cambridge, Mass.: Harvard University Press, 1917), is a paranoiac screed replete with charges against a variety of people, including Cox, for allegedly lying and undermining Stanley;

316 e.g., he said Opdycke "proved an ingrate and turned against [him]" and "was a very false man" who "wrote letters to Cox full of lies" (138). Stanley also wrote that Schofield's "fear of politicians had made him play a very low, mean part in many things" (213–14). Cox was Stanley's favorite target, however, as noted by the quotations, which are on 213–14. For Grant's criticism of Stanley's abilities, see OR, vol. 39, part 3, 684.

35. OR, vol. 45, part 1, 349–56; Cox to Opdycke, January 24 and February 2, 1876, Cox Papers; Cox, Battle of Franklin, 265. Stanley's report is in OR, vol. 45, part 1, 112–18. Cox told Schofield, "I was so anxious to give him a share in the honors that in my official report I said I gave no orders to the 4th Corps after Stanley came on the field"; Cox to Schofield, November 15, 1880, Cox Papers.

36. Cox to Schofield, July 9, 1888, Schofield Papers, LC; New York Sun, September 22, 1889. The following are a few of the letters Cox received from staff members who had been at Franklin and verified his version: R. W. Johnson to Cox, March 2, 1889, Cox Papers; Oliver W. Case to Cox, December 10, 1889, Cox Papers; John Fuller to Cox, December 14, 1889, Cox Papers.

37. Nation, February 26, 1891, 7. As of 1893 Cox was one of the highest-ranking officers from the Civil War still living.

38. Review of History of the Civil War in America, by Comte de Paris, Nation, November 8, 1888, 379–80; Goss, War within the Union, 192–95.

39. John Logan, The Volunteer Soldier in America (Chicago: R. S. Peale, 1887), 336.

40. Review of Butler's Book, by Ben Butler, Nation, March 10, 1892, 195–97.

41. Cox to James F. Rhodes, September 22, 1896, Cox Papers; Thomas J. Pressly, Americans Interpret Their Civil War (New York: Free Press, 1966), 179–81.

42. James F. Rhodes, History of the United States from the Compromise of 1850 (New York: Harper and Row, 1899–1906), 4:133, 152, 153; Rhodes, History, 5:36, 242; Cox to Monroe, January 15, 1894, Monroe Papers.

43. Manning F. Force, General Sherman (New York: D. Appleton, 1899); Cox to Force, January 18, 1898, Cox Papers; Cox to H. W. Coates, February 2, 1899, Cox Papers; J. N. Larned, ed., The Literature of American History: A Bibliographical Guide (Boston: American Library Association, 1902), 213.

44. Review of London to Ladysmith, by Winston Churchill, Nation, June 28, 1900, 501.

45. Cox, Battle of Franklin, 1–20. The website listing Congressional Medal of Honor winners is www.history.army.mil/html/moh/civwarmz.html. Cox asked the owner of the Carter house at Franklin, whom Cox had "met" before the battle, when the sun set and darkness came over the area on November 30 that year, information he needed for his book; Cox to M. B. Carter, November 20, 1895, Cox Papers.

46. Cox, Battle of Franklin, 220–32.

47. Cox, Battle of Franklin, 221; H. V. Boynton, Review of Battle of Franklin, by Jacob D. Cox, American Historical Review 3, no. 3 (April 1898): 578–80.

48. Schofield, Forty-Six Years, viii, 175, 180; Review of Forty-Six Years, by John M. Schofield, Nation, April 28, 1898, 327–28; Connelly, John M. Schofield, 131–32.

49. Cox to Charles Scribner's Sons, September 16, 1899, Cox Papers. Cochran later wrote a political companion to the reminiscences, and his two-volume

unpublished manuscript, "Political Experiences of Major General Jacob Dolson Cox," is in the Cox Papers.

50. H.V. Boynton, Review of *Military Reminiscences,* by Jacob D. Cox, *American Historical Review* 6 (April 1901): 602–6.

51. Goss, *War within the Union,* 194–99. A selection of other relevant books includes K. Williams, *Lincoln Finds a General;* Ambrose, *Duty, Honor, Country;* T. H. Williams, *Lincoln and His Generals* and *History of American Wars;* Weigley, *American Way of War;* Sword, *Courage Under Fire;* Work, *Lincoln's Political Generals;* Mc-Whiney, *Attack and Die;* and Hsieh, *West Pointers.*

52. Cox, *Military Reminiscences,* 1:171–74, 191. Cox cited Grant's and Sherman's memoirs, both of which noted the value of the volunteer soldier.

53. Cox, *Military Reminiscences,* 1:165–91. Bruce Catton agreed with Cox's analysis and also assessed the issue of West Point versus civilian generals, concluding that there were good and bad on both sides, making the generalizations about poor political generals inappropriate; Catton, *Mr. Lincoln's Army* (New York: Doubleday, 1951), 208–16. Guelzo quotes Cox's writings extensively, including on these issues, and cites his *Reminiscences* as "a particularly useful officer memoir" (*Fateful Lightning,* 146, 148, 545).

54. Cox, *Military Reminiscences,* 2:548–49.

Chapter 10: Renaissance Man in the Gilded Age

1. The letter to Monroe quoted in the chapter epigraph was written as Cox was about to become a railroad president, the first of his several unexpected careers.

2. Minutes of the Board of Trustees of the Cincinnati College, June 27, 1880, College of Law Library, University of Cincinnati; Alexander McGuffey to Cox, June 23, 1880, Cox Papers; Cox to Alexander McGuffey, June 23, 1880, Cox Papers; Reginald G. McGrane, *The University of Cincinnati: A Success Story in Urban Higher Education* (New York: Harper and Row, 1963), 5–50; Cox, Letterpress Copybook no. 5, Cox Papers; Cox to R. B. Hayes, December 14, 1885, Hayes Papers.

3. McGrane, *University of Cincinnati,* 97–109; "Minutes of Cincinnati College Trustees," April 4 and 8, 1885; J. D. Cox, "Circular Address to the Citizens of Cincinnati," 1886, ms. in Cincinnati Historical Society, Cincinnati, Ohio.

4. McGrane, *University of Cincinnati,* 113–14, 117–20; Cox, "Outline of a Course of Ten Lectures on the Outlines of History," ms. in Cox Papers; Zane L. Miller, *Boss Cox's Cincinnati* (New York: Oxford University Press, 1968), 98–99.

5. Russell L. Haden, "The Early Use of the Microscope in Ohio," *Ohio History* 51 (October–December 1942): 271–78; C. M. Vorce, "Memoir of Jacob Dolson Cox," *Transactions of the American Microscope Society* 22 (1900): 197–98.

6. Special report of J. D. Cox, president, December 17, 1888, in "Records of the Minutes of Board of Directors, University of Cincinnati," 1885–89, in possession of Legal Adviser's Office, University of Cincinnati; Cox to Monroe, January 19, 1889, Monroe Papers; "Minutes of University of Cincinnati Trustees," January 21 and June 17, 1889; McGrane, *University of Cincinnati,* 114.

318   7. Cox to Law Faculty, October 24, 1888, Cox Papers; Cox to Monroe, January
19, 1889, Monroe Papers; McGrane, *University of Cincinnati,* 129–30; Cox to Kenyon Cox, July 20, 1897, Kenyon Cox Papers. Two of Cox's more famous students,
both of whom also studied in Cox's law office, were future vice president of the
United States Charles G. Dawes and Byron Bancroft ("Ban") Johnson, who later
became the commissioner of major league baseball.

8. McGrane, *University of Cincinnati,* 109; J. S. Tunison, *The Cincinnati Riot:
Its Causes and Results* (Cincinnati: Keating, 1888), 8, 19; Miller, *Boss Cox,* 57–61;
Charles F. Goss, *Cincinnati, the Queen City, 1788–1912* (Chicago: S. J. Clarke Publish-
ing, 1912), 1:253–54; *Cincinnati Enquirer,* March 31, 1884; Cox to George Hoadly,
April 2, 1884, Cox Papers.

9. Cox to Monroe, March 27, 1883, Monroe Papers; letter from Miss Mary
Rudd Cochran to the author; Miller, *Boss Cox,* 41, 48, 51, 55. See the picture in
the gallery of Cox and Helen on their porch with the Cochran children, including Mary Rudd Cochran.

10. This son's letters from 1890 to 1897 from Colorado, which are in the Cox
Papers, trace the ups and downs of life in the territory. They are also interesting
for some insight into the one child of Cox's who did not make out nearly as well
as the others.

11. Cox to Thomas Speed, February 5, 1896, Cox Papers. According to Miss
Mary Rudd Cochran, Cox kept his illnesses from Helen, who herself was sickly
all through these years.

12. Bascom N. Timmins, *Portrait of an American: Charles G. Dawes* (New York:
Henry Holt, 1953), 22; Bascom N. Timmins, ed., *Charles G. Dawes: A Journal of
the McKinley Years* (Chicago: Lakeland Company, 1950), 38–39; Cox to Dawes,
December 3, 1895, Cox Papers.

13. Cox to Alexander McDonald, May 29, 1897, Cox Papers; Cox to Charles G.
Dawes, May 29, 1897, Cox Papers.

14. Cox to Monroe, December 23, 1895, Cox Papers; Cox to W. R. Dawes,
November 17, 1896, Cox Papers; Timmins, ed., *Dawes Journal,* 120–22; Cox to Kenyon Cox, July 20, 1897, Kenyon Cox Papers. Miss Mary Rudd Cochran told the
author that she and the other neighborhood children followed Cox to the corner
drugstore where he received the call from Dawes (the Coxes had no phone),
thinking it all a great sport.

15. Cox to Alexander McDonald, May 29, 1897, Cox Papers; "Minutes of
the Meetings of the Trustees of Oberlin College," 1876–1901, Oberlin College
Treasurer's Office, Oberlin, Ohio. The boardinghouse may have been the best in
Oberlin, but according to Miss Mary Rudd Cochran, it was fairly shoddy. She was
a student at Oberlin College from 1899 to 1903 and visited the Coxes at home
quite often. The contract for Cox's exchange of his books for access to the library
is in the Cox Papers, dated January 1, 1898.

16. Cox to Charles Cox, December 2, 1899, Cox Papers (describing the festivi-
ties); Cox to Kenyon Cox, June 30, 1900, Kenyon Cox Papers; Cox to J. D. Cox
III, March 30, 1895, Cox Papers.

17. *Cincinnati Commercial Tribune,* August 6, 1900.

18. Cox to Opdycke, January 24, 1876, Cox Papers; Goss, *War within the Union,* 319 xiii.

19. Cox to William H. Smith, July 14, 1885, William H. Smith Papers, Ohio Historical Society; Cox to Monroe, October 23, 1873, Monroe Papers.

Selected Bibliography

I list here only the writings and source materials that have been of the greatest importance in the making of this book. The notes include the full range of sources used, and I consulted many others to which I do not make reference either here or in the notes. A full listing of all the relevant elements of the extensive and ever-growing literature on the Civil War would require a multivolume study of its own.

Primary Sources

PERSONAL INTERVIEWS, LETTERS

Personal interview by the author with Miss Mary Rudd Cochran, March 25, 1969, Monroe, Ohio

Personal letters from Miss Mary Rudd Cochran to the author, December 14, 1968, to April 6, 1969, in possession of the author

MANUSCRIPTS

Library of Congress, Washington, D.C.
    Jacob Dolson Cox Papers
    James A. Garfield Papers
    John M. Schofield Papers
    Thomas Ewing Family Papers
National Archives, Washington, D.C.
    Department of the Interior Records, 1869–70
Oberlin College Archives, Oberlin, Ohio
    William Cochran Papers
    Jacob Dolson Cox Papers
    James Monroe Papers

322   Ohio Historical Society, Columbus, Ohio
            Hugh Boyle Ewing Papers
            Thomas Ewing Family Papers
            Ohio Governors Papers, 1866–68
        Western Reserve Historical Society, Cleveland, Ohio
            Jacob Dolson Cox Papers
            William Bascom-Hiram Little Family Papers

DOCUMENTS

Official Records: published as *The War of the Rebellion: A Compilation of the Official Records of the Union and Confederate Armies.* 70 vols. Washington, D.C.: Government Printing Office, 1880–97.

Ohio, State of. *Executive Document, 1866.* Columbus: L. D. Myers and Bro., State Printers, 1867.

Ohio, State of. *Executive Document, 1867.* Columbus: L. D. Myers and Bro., State Printers, 1868.

Ohio Senate. *Journal of the Senate of the State of Ohio of the 14th General Assembly,* vol. 56. Columbus: Richard Nevins, State Printer, 1860 and 1861.

U.S. Congress. *Report of the Joint Committee on the Conduct of the War.* 3 vols. Washington, D.C.: Government Printing Office, 1863–65.

U.S. Department of the Interior. *Report of the Secretary of the Interior.* 41st Cong., 2nd Sess., House Executive Document 3. Washington, D.C.: Government Printing Office, 1869.

U.S. Department of the Interior. *Report of the Secretary of the Interior.* 41st Cong., 3rd Sess., House Executive Document 4. Washington, D.C.: Government Printing Office, 1870.

LETTERS, DIARIES, AND MEMOIRS

Adams, Henry. *The Education of Henry Adams.* New York: Book League of America, 1928.

Bates, David Homer. *Lincoln in the Telegraph Office.* New York: Century Co., 1907.

Brown, Harry James, and Fred B. William, eds. *The Diary of James A. Garfield.* 2 vols. East Lansing: Michigan State University Press, 1967.

Cochran, William Cox. "Political Experiences of Major General Jacob Dolson Cox." Unpublished manuscript in 2 vols. Cincinnati, 1940. Oberlin College Archives.

Cox, Jacob Dolson, III. *Building an American Industry: The Story of the Cleveland Twist Drill Co. and Its Founder; An Autobiography.* Cleveland: Cleveland Twist Drill Co., 1951.

Hood, J. B. *Advance and Retreat.* New Orleans: G. T. Beauregard, 1880.

Horton, J. H., and Solomon Teverbaugh. *A History of the Eleventh Regiment, Ohio Volunteer Infantry.* Dayton, Ohio: W. J. Shuey, 1866.

Johnson, Robert Underwood, and Clarence Clough Buel, eds. *Battles and Leaders of the Civil War.* 4 vols. New York: Charles Scribner's Sons, 1887–88.

Johnston, Joseph. *Narrative of Military Operations Directed during the Late War Between the States.* New York: D. Appleton, 1874.

McClellan, George B. *McClellan's Own Story.* New York: Charles L. Webster, 1887.

Reid, Whitelaw. *Ohio in the War.* Columbus: Eclectic Publishing, 1867, 1893 (rev. ed.).

Sherman, William T. *Personal Memoirs.* 2 vols. New York: Charles L. Webster, 1891.

Strother, David H. "Personal Recollections of the War by a Virginian, Tenth Paper." *Harper's Magazine* 23, no. 213 (February 1868): 273–91.

———. *A Virginia Yankee in the Civil War: The Diaries of David Hunt Strother.* Chapel Hill: University of North Carolina Press, 1998.

Townsend, E. D. *Anecdotes of the Civil War in the United States.* New York: D. Appleton, 1884.

Watkins, Samuel Rush. *Company Aytch; or, A Side Show of the Big Show, and Other Sketches.* Nashville: Cumberland Presbyterian Publishing House, 1882.

HISTORICAL WRITINGS OF JACOB D. COX

Atlanta. New York: Charles Scribner's Sons, 1882.

"The Battle of Antietam." In *Battles and Leaders of the Civil War,* edited by Robert Underwood Johnson and Clarence Clough Buel, 2:630–59. New York: Charles Scribner's Sons, 1887–88.

The Battle of Franklin, Tennessee, November 30, 1864: A Monograph. New York: Charles Scribner's Sons, 1897.

"Forcing Fox's Gap and Turner's Gap." In *Battles and Leaders of the Civil War,* edited by Robert Underwood Johnson and Clarence Clough Buel, 2:583–90. New York: Charles Scribner's Sons, 1887–88.

"McClellan in West Virginia." In *Battles and Leaders of the Civil War,* edited by Robert Underwood Johnson and Clarence Clough Buel, 1:126–48. New York: Charles Scribner's Sons, 1887–88.

Military Reminiscences of the Civil War. 2 vols. New York: Charles Scribner's Sons, 1900.

Nation. 161 articles, 1874–1900.

The Second Battle of Bull Run as Connected with the Fitz-John Porter Case. A paper read before the Society of Ex-Army and Navy Officers of Cincinnati, February 28, 1882. Cincinnati: Peter G. Thompson, 1882.

Sherman's March to the Sea: Hood's Tennessee Campaign and the Carolina Campaigns of 1865. New York: Charles Scribner's Sons, 1882.

"War Preparations in the North." In *Battles and Leaders of the Civil War,* edited by Robert Underwood Johnson and Clarence Clough Buel, 1:84–98. New York: Charles Scribner's Sons, 1887–88.

"West Virginia Operations under Fremont." In *Battles and Leaders of the Civil War,* edited by Robert Underwood Johnson and Clarence Clough Buel, 2:270–81. New York: Charles Scribner's Sons, 1887–88.

Secondary Sources

BOOKS AND ARTICLES

Ahern, Wilbert H. "The Cox Plan of Reconstruction: A Case Study in Ideology and Race Relations." *Civil War History* 16 (1970): 293–308.

324   Ambrose, Stephen. *Duty, Honor, Country: A History of West Point.* Baltimore, Md.: Johns Hopkins University Press, 1966, 1996 (rev. ed.).

Archer, W. B. *Memorandum History of the Department of the Interior.* Washington, D.C.: Government Printing Office, 1913.

Bailes, Clarice Lorene. "Jacob Dolson Cox in West Virginia." *West Virginia History: A Quarterly Magazine* 6 (October 1944): 5–58.

Beringer, Richard E., Herman Hattaway, Archer Jones, and William N. Still Jr. *Why the South Lost the Civil War.* Athens: University of Georgia Press, 1986.

Blue, Frederick. *No Taint of Compromise: Crusaders in Antislavery Politics.* Baton Rouge: Louisiana State University Press, 2006.

Boatner, Mark M., III. *The Civil War Dictionary.* Rev. ed. New York: Vintage Books, 1991.

Carman, Ezra. *The Maryland Campaign of 1862.* 2 vols. Edited by Thomas Clemens. El Dorado Hills, Calif.: Savas Beatie, 2010, 2012.

Castel, Albert. *Decision in the West: The Atlanta Campaign of 1864.* Lawrence: University Press of Kansas, 1992.

Connelly, Donald B. *John M. Schofield and the Politics of Generalship.* Chapel Hill: University of North Carolina Press, 2006.

Cox, John, and Lawanda Cox. *Politics, Principle, and Prejudice, 1865–6: The Dilemma of Reconstruction America.* New York: Free Press of Glencoe, 1963.

Donald, David, ed. *Why the North Won the Civil War.* Baton Rouge: Louisiana State University Press, 1960.

Elliott, Sam D. *Soldier of Tennessee: General Alexander P. Stewart and the Civil War in the West.,* Baton Rouge, Louisiana State University Press, 2004.

Feltman, Michael. *Citizen Sherman: A Life of William Tecumseh Sherman.* Lawrence: University Press of Kansas, 1997.

Fishel, Edwin C. "Pinkerton and McClellan: Who Deceived Whom?" *Civil War History* 34, no. 2 (September 1988): 116–42.

———. *The Secret War for the Union: The Untold Story of Military Intelligence in the Civil War.* New York: Houghton Mifflin, 1996.

Foner, Eric. *The Fiery Trial: Abraham Lincoln and American Slavery.* New York: Norton, 2010.

———. *Free Soil, Free Labor, Free Men.* New York, Oxford University Press, 1995.

———. *Reconstruction: America's Unfinished Revolution, 1863–1877.* New York: Harper and Row, 1988.

Glatthaar, Joseph. *The March to the Sea and Beyond.* New York: New York University Press, 1985.

Goss, Thomas J. *The War within the Union High Command: Politics and Generalship during the Civil War.* Lawrence: University Press of Kansas, 2003.

Griffith, Paddy. *Battle Tactics of the Civil War.* New Haven, Conn.: Yale University Press, 2001.

Grimsley, Mark. *The Hard Hand of War: Union Military Policy toward Southern Civilians, 1861–1865.* Cambridge: Cambridge University Press, 1995.

Guelzo, Allen C. *Fateful Lightning: A New History of the Civil War and Reconstruction.* New York: Oxford University Press, 2012.

Guyatt, Nicholas. "America's Conservatory: Race, Reconstruction, and the Santo Domingo Debate." *Journal of American History* (March 2011): 974–1000.

Hageman, Edward. *The American Civil War and the Origins of Modern Warfare.* Bloomington: Indiana University Press, 1992.

Harsh, Joseph. *Confederate Tide Rising.* Kent: Kent State University Press, 1998.

———. *Taken at the Flood: Robert E. Lee and Confederate Strategy in the Maryland Campaign of 1862.* Kent: Kent State University Press, 1999.

Hartwig, David S. *To Antietam Creek: The Maryland Campaign of 1862.* Baltimore, Md.: Johns Hopkins University Press, 2012.

Hattaway, Herman, and Archer Jones. *How the North Won: A Military History of the Civil War.* Urbana: University of Illinois Press, 1991.

Hennessy, John J. *Return to Bull Run: The Campaign and Battle of Second Manassas.* New York: Simon and Schuster, 1993.

Holt, Michael F. *The Rise and Fall of the American Whig Party: Jacksonian Politics and the Onset of the Civil War.* New York: Oxford University Press, 1999.

Hoogenboom, Ari, *Outlawing the Spoils: A History of the Civil Service Movement, 1865–1883.* Urbana: University of Illinois Press, 1961.

Hoptak, John David. *The Battle of South Mountain.* Charleston, S.C.: History Press, 2011.

Hsieh, Wayne Wei-siang. *West Pointers and the Civil War: The Old Army in War and Peace.* Chapel Hill: University of North Carolina Press, 2009.

Hyde, George E. *Red Cloud's Folk: A History of the Oglala Sioux Indians.* Norman: University of Oklahoma Press, 1937.

———. *Spotted Tail's Folk: A History of the Brulé Sioux.* Norman: University of Oklahoma Press, 1961.

Jordan, Brian. *Unholy Sabbath: The Battle of South Mountain in History and Memory, September 14, 1862.* New York: Savas Beatie, 2012.

Lesser, W. Hunter. *Rebels at the Gate: Lee and McClellan on the Front Line of a Nation Divided.* Naperville, Ill.: Sourcebooks, 2005.

Liddell Hart, B. H. *Strategy.* 2nd rev. ed. New York: Penguin Group, 1967.

Longacre, Glenn V., and John E. Haas, eds. *To Battle for God and the Right: The Civil War Letterbooks of Emerson Opdycke.* Urbana: University of Illinois Press, 2003.

Magness, Phillip W., and Sebastian N. Page. *Colonization after Emancipation: Lincoln and the Movement for Black Resettlement.* Columbia: University of Missouri Press, 2011.

Marvel, William. *Burnside.* Chapel Hill: University of North Carolina Press, 1981.

McKitrick, Eric. *Andrew Johnson and Reconstruction.* Chicago: University of Chicago Press, 1960.

McPherson, James M., ed. *The Atlas of the Civil War.* Philadelphia: Running Press Book Publishers, 2005.

———. *Battle Cry of Freedom: The Civil War Era.* New York: Oxford University Press, 1988.

———. *The Negro's Civil War.* New York: Vintage Books, 1965.

McPherson, James M., and William J. Cooper Jr., eds. *Writing the Civil War: The Quest to Understand.* Columbia: University of South Carolina Press, 2000.

326   Miller, Brian Craig. *John Bell Hood and the Fight for Civil War Memory*. Knoxville: University of Tennessee Press, 2010.

Morgan, H. Wayne. *Kenyon Cox, 1856–1915: A Life in American Art*. Kent: Kent State University Press, 1994.

Newell, Clayton R. *Lee vs. McClellan: The First Campaign*. Washington, D.C.: Regnery Publishing, 2010.

Prucha, Paul. *The Great Father: The United States Government and the American Indian*. Lincoln: University of Nebraska Press, 1995.

Rafuse, Ethan, "Impractical? Unforgiveable? Another Look at George B. McClellan's First Strategic Plan," *Ohio History* 110 (Summer–Autumn 2001): 153–64.

———. *McClellan's War: The Failure of Modernization in the Struggle for the Union*. Bloomington: Indiana University Press, 2005.

———. "'Poor Burn'? The Antietam Conspiracy That Wasn't." *Civil War History* 54, no. 2 (June 2008): 146–75.

———. "Toward a Better Understanding of George McClellan." *Civil War Times* (June 2009): 28–33.

Richardson, Heather Cox. *The Death of Reconstruction: Race, Labor, and Politics in the Post–Civil War North, 1865–1901*. Cambridge, Mass.: Harvard University Press, 2004.

———. *West from Appomattox: The Reconstruction of America after the Civil War*. New Haven, Conn.: Yale University Press, 2007.

Roseboom, Eugene H. *The Civil War Era, 1850–1873*. Columbus: Ohio Archeological and Historical Society, 1944.

Schmiel, Eugene D. "The 'Oberlin Letter': The Post–Civil War Northern Voter and the Freedman." *Northwest Ohio Quarterly* (Fall 1971): 75–86.

Sears, Stephen W., ed. *The Civil War Papers of George B. McClellan*. New York: DaCapo Press, 1989.

———. "The Curious Case of General McClellan's Memoirs." *Civil War History* 34, no. 2 (September 1988): 100–115.

———. *George B. McClellan: The Young Napoleon*. New York: Ticknor and Fields, 1988.

———. *Landscape Turned Red: The Battle of Antietam*. New York: Ticknor and Fields, 1983.

Simpson, Brooks D. *The Political Education of Henry Adams*. Columbia: University of South Carolina Press, 1996.

Slap, Andrew L. *The Doom of Reconstruction: The Liberal Republicans in the Civil War Era*. New York: Fordham University Press, 2006.

Smith, Jean Edward. *Grant*. New York: Simon and Schuster, 2001.

Summers, Mark W. *The Press Gang: Newspapers and Politics, 1865–1878*. Chapel Hill: University of North Carolina Press, 1994.

Sword, Wiley. *Embrace an Angry Wind: The Confederacy's Last Hurrah; Spring Hill, Franklin and Nashville*. New York: Harper Collins, 1992.

Tap, Bruce. *Over Lincoln's Shoulder: The Committee on the Conduct of the War*. Lawrence: University Press of Kansas, 1998.

Weigley, Russell F. *The American Way of War: A History of United States Military Strategy and Policy.* New York: Macmillan Publishing, 1977.

Williams, Kenneth P. *Lincoln Finds a General.* 4 vols. New York: Macmillan, 1957.

Williams, T. Harry. *Hayes of the 23rd, the Civil War Volunteer Officer.* New York: Alfred A. Knopf, 1965.

———. *Lincoln and His Generals.* New York: Alfred A. Knopf, 1952.

Work, David. *Lincoln's Political Generals.* Urbana: University of Illinois Press, 2009.

THESES AND DISSERTATIONS

Bower, Jerry. "The Civil War Career of Jacob Dolson Cox." Ph.D. diss., Michigan State University, 1971.

Losson, Christopher. "Jacob Dolson Cox: A Military Biography." Ph.D. diss., University of Mississippi, 1993.

Schmiel, Eugene D. "The Career of Jacob Dolson Cox, 1828–1900: Soldier, Scholar, Statesman." Ph.D. diss., Ohio State University, 1969.

Index